Endorsements

Accidental Diplomats is a highly successful contribution to American diplomatic history, to the history of Protestant missions, and to the global history of the Christian project. The roles evangelical missionaries played in Cold War Ethiopia, Kenya, and Congo have never been explored with the range of archival sources and personal interviews that Philip Dow brings to the task. Wonderfully sensitive to the dynamic relationship between missionaries, government officials, and local populations, Dow has given us one of this generation's most professionally rigorous and deeply enlightening studies of missionaries.

DAVID A. HOLLINGER, PHD
Professor Emeritus, University of California, Berkeley
Author, *Protestants Abroad*

Spanning a century of neglected history, three pivotal African countries, the vital yet oft-misunderstood work of American missionaries, and the crucible of the Cold War, Philip Dow has delivered a masterpiece of historical scholarship. He combines compelling characters, vivid stories, and subtle analysis to craft a persuasive and readable book.

WILLIAM INBODEN, PHD
Professor and Director, Hamilton Center for Classical and Civic Education, University of Florida

After World War II, America's political and diplomatic engagement with Africa grew dramatically in response to decolonization and the Cold War competition with the Soviet Union. American missionaries were instrumental in building ties and deepening relations between important communities on the African continent and the grassroots evangelical community in United States. *Accidental Diplomats* tells the captivating story of how ordinary Americans played an extraordinary role in enhancing the nation's diplomatic and political presence throughout Africa. Thoroughly researched and clearly written, there is much that students of American foreign policy can learn from Dow's engaging new book.

WALTER RUSSELL MEAD
Global View Columnist, *The Wall Street Journal*
Distinguished Fellow in Strategy and Statesmanship, Hudson Institute
Professor of Foreign Affairs and Humanities, Bard College

ACCIDENTAL DIPLOMATS

American Missionaries and the Cold War in Africa

PHILIP DOW

visit us at missionbooks.org

Accidental Diplomats: American Missionaries and the Cold War in Africa
© 2024 by Philip Dow. All Rights Reserved.

No part of this book may be reproduced, stored in a retrieval system, or transmitted in any form or by any means—electronic, mechanical, photocopy, recording, or otherwise—without prior written permission from the publisher, except brief quotations used in connection with reviews. This manuscript may not be entered into AI, even for AI training. For permission, email permissions@wclbooks.com. For corrections, email editor@wclbooks.com.

William Carey Publishing (WCP) publishes resources to shape and advance the missiological conversation in the world. We publish a broad range of thought-provoking books and do not necessarily endorse all opinions set forth here or in works referenced within this book.

The URLs included in this workbook are provided for personal use only and are current as of the date of publication, but the publisher disclaims any obligation to update them after publication.

Scriptures taken from the Holy Bible, New International Version®, NIV®. Copyright © 1973, 1978, 1984, 2011 by Biblica, Inc.™ Used by permission of Zondervan. All rights reserved worldwide. www.zondervan.com. The "NIV" and "New International Version" are trademarks registered in the United States Patent and Trademark Office by Biblica, Inc.™

Published by William Carey Publishing
10 W. Dry Creek Cir
Littleton, CO 80120 | www.missionbooks.org

William Carey Publishing is a ministry of Frontier Ventures
Pasadena, CA | www.frontierventures.org

Cover and Interior Designer: Mike Riester

ISBNs: 978-1-64508-567-6 (paperback)
       978-1-64508-569-0 (epub)

Printed Worldwide
28 27 26 25 24   1 2 3 4 5   IN

Library of Congress Control Number: 2024935192

To Catherine

"We shall never save civilization,
as long as civilization is our main object.
We must learn to want something else
even more."
—C. S. Lewis, *Mere Christianity*, 104.

Contents

Foreword by Dr. Melani McAlister   xi
Preface   xv
Introduction   xix
    Cold War American Evangelicals in Historical Context   xx
    American Evangelicalism and the Religious Cold War   xxvi
    The Evangelical Missionary Movement During the Cold War   xxix
    A Preview and the Parameters   xxxi

Part 1: Influence of American Evangelical Missionaries on US-Ethiopian Cold War Relations

Chapter 1: Romance in a Marriage of Convenience: The Missionary Factor in Early Cold War US-Ethiopian Relations, 1918–1960   3
    "Dating," 1918–1941   4
    The Proposal, 1941–1945   11
    The Long Engagement, 1945–1952—Part One: Growing Intimacy between Selassie and the American Missionary Community   15
    The Long Engagement, 1945–1952—Part Two: Winning over the Extended Family   21
    The Long Engagement, 1945–1952—Part Three: Evangelical Religion and "Enchanted Internationalism" in Black America   25
    The Wedding, 1953–1954   28
    The Honeymoon, 1955–1960   32

Chapter 2: The Great Reversal: The Missionary Factor in US-Ethiopian Cold War Relations, 1960–1991   37
    US-Ethiopian Relations, 1960–1974: A Decline in the Influence of Missionaries?   37
    The First Crisis: The 1960 Coup Attempt and Aftermath   40
    The Media and Evangelical Elites, 1960–1974   43
    A Second Crisis: The Famine of 1973–1974   47
    Missionaries and an Initially Ambiguous Ethiopia Revolution, 1974–1976   49
    The Turn Towards the Soviet Union, 1976–1978   53
    The American Response to the Ethiopian Revolution, 1974–1978   54
    Evangelical Missionary Activism in Revolutionary-Era Ethiopia, 1974–1991   56
    Conclusion   68

Part 2: Influence of American Evangelical Missionaries on US-Congo Cold War Relations

Chapter 3: Accidental Diplomats: The Missionary Factor in US-Congo Relations, 1959–1963   73

The Context of Independence-Era Congo   74

Religion and Anti-American Sentiment in the Congo   77

Ethnicity, Propaganda, and Anti-West Sentiment   81

The Missionary Factor in the Battle for Congolese Hearts and Minds   83

Missionaries and Pro-American Sentiment in Independence-Era Congo   91

The Influence of American Missionaries on US Public Opinion on the Congo, 1959–1963   95

Missionary Activism in Katanga, 1959–1963   96

The Influence of American Missionaries on the Perceptions of US Policymakers, 1959–1963   100

Missionaries and Formal Diplomacy, 1959–1963   104

Conclusion   109

Chapter 4: "Red and Yellow, Black and White": American Evangelical Missionaries and the Rise and Fall of the Simba Rebellion, 1963–1967   111

Continuity—American Missionaries and the Simba Rebellion   112

Change—American Missionaries and the Simba Rebellion   114

American Missionaries and the Simba Rebellion in Full Flower   120

American Missionaries and Congolese Elites During the Simba Rebellion   125

Simba Treatment of American Missionaries and Their Congolese Converts   127

Dr. Paul Carlson and American Public and Political Opinion   131

Mobutu's Rise and the Decline of American Missionary Influence   138

Dr. William Close—The Exceptional Exception to the Rule   139

Conclusion   145

Part 3: Influence of American Evangelical Missionaries on US-Kenyan Cold War Relations

Chapter 5: Constructing a Pro-Western Kenya, 1895–1963 — 149

- The Early Years of the American Missionary Enterprise in Kenya, 1895–1930 — 149
- Early American Missionaries and the Politicization of Kenya — 152
- Early American Missions and Education — 154
- The American Gospel Missionary Society and Harry Thuku — 155
- Early American Missionaries and the Politics of Culture: Bible Translation — 159
- Early American Missionaries and the Politics of Culture: Female Circumcision — 162
- Education, Health Care, and Conversions: The American Missionary Advance, 1930–1963 — 166
- The Growth of the Independent Church and School Movement — 170
- American Missionaries, Chief Waruhiu and the War over Kenya's Political Soul — 172
- American Missionaries and the Crucible of Mau Mau — 174
- American Missionaries, African Evangelicals, and Moderate Pro-Government Politics — 178
- Conclusion — 184

Chapter 6: "A Broad Popular Consensus," 1963–1991 — 187

- American Missionaries, Moi's Promotion, and US-Kenyan Relations, 1967–1978 — 193
- American Missionaries and US-Kenyan Relations in the Early Moi Years, 1978–1982 — 200
- American Missionaries and US-Kenyan Relations, 1982–1991 — 212
- Conclusion — 217

Conclusion — 219
Acknowledgments — 227
Bibliography — 229
Index — 259

Foreword

By Melani McAlister, PhD

Philip Dow has written a remarkable and compelling history of the relationship between American evangelical missionaries in Africa and the US state during the Cold War. Other fine scholars have written about missionaries, of course, but few have so carefully parsed the role of missionaries as non-state actors, with their own agendas and loyalties, as they navigated their relations with the US state at the height of its Cold War reach into Africa.

This is a serious and often riveting book, but also a lively history of a distinctly tumultuous period in Africa. The missionaries that Dow describes are complex human beings, who operate in a shifting political terrain. They are invited and sometimes pressured into symbiotic relationship with American diplomats and policymakers, who are anxious to expand US power and influence in decolonizing Africa. But missionaries were first and foremost evangelists, and the story of decolonization also unfolds in their intimate relationships with the local people in each of the countries studied here—Ethiopia, Congo, and Kenya. During the "global Cold War," in Arne Odd Westad's apt phrase, Africans had their own perilous paths to navigate, as they reconsidered their relationship to missionaries, to the United States, and to their own goals for independence.[1]

Dow's book is fully in line with recent developments in the historiography of both missionaries and the Cold War. Early studies of missionaries in the field of US history had often been hagiographic; then, in the 1960s and beyond, missionaries were rightfully subject to profound skepticism as harbingers of empire. Dow's research is part of a more recent body of work, which does not in any way deny the ways in which missionaries enabled forms of US (or European) state power, but which recognizes the deep ambivalence and complexity of their role. In Cold War history, too, the move has been away from a focus on state actors and the centering of Europe toward a broader look at the role of non-state actors, operating across the globe. The Cold War now looks more centered in Africa and Asia, with a

---

1 Westad, *The Global Cold War*.

broader range of complex actors—missionaries are joined by businessmen, artists and writers, travelers, and students as key players in the muddied transnational terrain of the Cold war.

This is a deeply researched book, drawing on extensive work in the US and Kenyan National Archives, presidential libraries, the archives of numerous Christian denominations and schools, as well as missionary organizations, and scores of personal interviews and correspondence. As a result, the book is filled with richly documented stories of evangelical influence in Ethiopia, Congo, and Kenya. In Kenya, for example, Dow shows convincingly that evangelical missionary schools had a deep impact on both the first and second generations of the postcolonial Kenyan elite. His discussion of President Moi's visit to the United States in 1981 describes how a sense of shared religiosity led Reagan to embrace Kenyan President Daniel arap Moi, and how Moi's foreign policy team was stocked with graduates from various evangelical schools. The missionary influence in Kenya was direct and undeniable. In other places, it was no less significant, perhaps, but more nuanced and complex. As visible and prominent Americans living in revolutionary times in Africa, missionaries sometimes served, in effect, as agents of the US state; but they also sometimes struggled against the will of America's diplomats, and almost always had to negotiate the changing realities of the people they lived among.

Dow also makes the case that evangelical missionaries to Africa in the Cold War era were "ordinary" people—not wealthy, not titled, not always even particularly credentialed—who did the extraordinary thing of moving their lives and often their families to Africa. Missionaries for Dow are important not just because of their role in the Cold War, or even their work of proselytism, but also because they represented a certain kind of American abroad. Missionaries were the leading edge of what he calls "populist transnationalism." Decades before students regularly descended on Europe for summer travel or joined in humanitarian missions over spring break, before "short-term missions" and eco-adventurism, evangelical missionaries were part of the long and transformative wave of twentieth-century globalization. As with American military abroad, they were a visible symbol of the United States to a world riveted (and often angered) by the country's wealth and power. But, unlike most military personnel, missionaries in the middle of the Cold War era generally made lifetime or at least long-term commitments. They learned languages and built families. And their children, in particular, became part of a distinctive group of transnational people, whose lives and worldviews were shaped by living abroad. Perhaps that story is for another book: the history of missionary kids has yet to be fully written. What we do know is that missionaries' relation to the US state was neither uniform nor static, as they had to negotiate their commitments as Americans and anti-communists with equally passionate commitments to the people they worked with and had often converted.

For me, what makes this a particularly important book is the fact that Dow brings together the advantages of an insider's perspective—he engages deeply with the issues of conversion, community norms, and morality that were important to missionaries—with the rigor and critique of a first-class scholar. He shows how missionaries in all three countries, but especially Congo, were often deeply compromised by racism and even segregationist ideologies. Most crucially, however, Dow argues that it was the relatively democratic and open structure of evangelical churches that provided spaces and practices for thinking about democracy and power in nations that were learning how to govern themselves. He recounts in detail the ways in which American missionaries could be culturally arrogant and presumptuous, even greedy, across all three countries. But he also shows how other missionaries lived simply among local people, sharing in their way of life, loving, and becoming loved in return. This reality is not always easy to talk about; scholarship on emotions has yet to do justice to the feelings that attend connection across great difference. But the feelings that missionaries had for their calling and the people they worked with were, in the end, not separate from the decisions they made about when and how to try to influence US policy.

This is, in the end, a book about the often-inadvertent work that American missionaries did for the US state during the Cold War. But it is also about the relationships within the mission community and their converts, how trust or the lack of it, racism, or its refusal, could and did create a network of believers, African and American, who struggled with what they owed their church, their states, and each other.

Preface

I was born in Ethiopia to pioneering American educator parents in the final years of the reign of Emperor Haile Selassie. By the age of ten I had lived in four countries and travelled with my deeply religious parents to many more. International life was exotic to my parents and their generation, but it was all I knew.

By the end of the Cold War stories like mine were not uncommon. My own first child was born to her British mother and me in the Princess Zahra Pavilion of the Aga Khan hospital in Nairobi, surrounded by children from a multitude of nations. And in her young life, she has lived and been educated in three different countries, none of which is the nation of my citizenship, reflecting the global experience of her parents that has taken them to over sixty countries on six continents.

When I first wrote these words it was 2020. I was sitting on the balcony of a once isolated colonial coffee plantation house that is now home to a school of 700 students from over fifty nations, representing the diplomatic, missionary, and international business communities who help make up the bustling cosmopolitan city that is twenty-first century Nairobi. If I had strained my eyes, I could have seen through the fifty-three flags representing the students' nationalities to the sports fields where another "Third Culture Kid," President Barack Obama, landed in Marine One during the American leader's historic state visit to Kenya in 2016.[1] In March of 2020, however, the typically vibrant campus was eerily still. The only sounds were the occasional flapping of flags in an empty courtyard symbolizing the ninety-one percent of the world's students whose schools would close in response to an astonishingly global pandemic.[2]

It is a truism that cross-cultural exchanges between peoples are as old as humanity. But it is still important to remember that the profoundly interconnected and transnational world we inhabit—that we now take for granted—is a very recent development. Eminent historians like C. A. Bayly have argued that the roots of contemporary globalism can be traced to the end of the eighteenth century. But what we have seen after World

---

1 Pollock & Van Reken, *Third Culture Kids*.
2 UNESCO, "Education: From COVID-19 School Closures to Recovery."

War II represents an increase in global interconnectedness by orders of magnitude.³ It used to be that what happened in a proverbial Vegas, stayed in Vegas—not because of any pact of fraternal secrecy, but because the ways, means, and incentives for cultural, political, and economic diffusion were limited. Today, what happens in Wuhan will not stay in Wuhan.

As we have tried to understand the origins of our interconnected and transnational world, historians have followed a number of promising paths including studies on cross-cultural commerce, technology, tourism, diplomacy, and other related fields.⁴ Together, these studies are helping us understand the story of our rapidly shrinking twenty-first century world—a world that, up through the end of World War II at least, was dominated by global elites. Outside of largely unidirectional immigration to the United States, and to a much lesser extent colonies like Australia, in the eighteenth and nineteenth centuries, transnationalism was almost entirely driven by the wealth and power of a few governments and corporations. And when it wasn't, the only other people with the time and capacity to engage in the developing transnational world freely and meaningfully were the most wealthy and powerful individuals of the most wealthy and powerful nations.⁵

Accidental Diplomats tells a new and important story emerging after World War II. To an extent unprecedented in world history, common people, acting by and large independent of the political and economic elite, had the capacity to voluntarily spread out across the globe in large numbers—not as immigrants (leaving one nation to become members of another) but as the globally-engaged vanguards of a new populist transnationalism.

In one sense, the fact that Christian missionaries were pioneers of populist transnationalism is not surprising. From its very beginning, Christianity has been a missionary faith, as the history of the faith's slow

---

3 Bayly, *The Birth of the Modern World*, 1–3. See also among many others, Bender, ed. *Rethinking American History in a Global Age*, Akira Iriye, *Global and Transnational History* and Ian Tyrrell, *Transnational Nation*.

4 See previous footnote and, among others, Zuelow, *Touring Beyond the Nation*. Boon, "Towards a Transnational Business History," 511–25. Vleuten, "Towards a Transnational History of Technology," *Technology and Culture*, 974–94.

5 Immigration and slavery represent the only other areas in which large numbers of non-elite people moved globally, but in the case of slavery this was, of course, not voluntary (and so the nature of the influence was distinct) and in the case of immigration the movement was distinctly international—leaving one nation state to become members of another.

spread across the globe demonstrates.⁶ But the phrase "slow spread" is instructive here. Before the twentieth century, Christianity's expansion was, relatively speaking, modest and largely limited to European borderlands. After World War II, that changed, and Christianity's spread became rapid and truly global. Africa, for instance, which had been less than 10 percent Christian in 1910, exploded to just under 50 percent of a rapidly growing population by the year 2000.⁷ While local converts were the driving force behind this astonishing growth, expatriate missionaries were almost always the spark that ignited this spiritual and cultural revolution. So the question is, why then? If Christianity has always had a strong missionary impulse, what is special about the post-World War II world? And why did American evangelical missionaries, in particular, play such a critical part?

There are at least three reasons. First, the Cold War period, and the decades preceding it, witnessed significant breakthroughs in communications and travel technology, allowing more people access to more places, more quickly, and more affordably. Second, the American economy was growing at an unprecedented rate, giving Americans in the 1950s and 1960s, the highest per capita income in the world—a place they would hold (more or less) for much of the Cold War.⁸ Combined, technological advances and rapidly increasing disposable income gave the average American the ability to travel globally in a way that had never, in the history of the world, been possible.⁹

But these things did not guarantee that Americans would use this newfound capacity to engage in global missionary outreach. Indeed, technological and economic capacity grew impressively throughout the "Christian" West during the Cold War and nothing comparable to the

---

6 According to the New Testament book of Matthew, Jesus's last words were what is known as the Great Commission, the command for his followers to "make disciples of all nations" (Matt 28:19), something that the history of Christianity demonstrates his followers have, to varying degrees, sought to follow.

7 *World Christian Encyclopedia.*

8 Patterson, *Grand Expectations.*

9 For instance, the number of Americans who travelled outside of the country throughout the nineteenth century varied from one-hundredth of a percent of the American population in 1830 (less than 1000 people) to four-tenths of a percent (76,000) in 1900; but then jumped to 1 percent (565,000) in 1960, and six percent (15 million) in 1990. Dupont, Gandhi, and Weiss, *The American Invasion of Europe.*

American missionary effort developed elsewhere.[10] The missing third piece was, of course, religious enthusiasm. While Christian belief and practice was in retreat in many parts of "Christendom" as the Cold War began, the United States was experiencing what William McLoughlin called a "religious awakening"—and one that had a distinctly evangelical tenor.[11] In short, unprecedented prosperity and rapid advances in transportation and communications technologies, combined with an evangelical re-awakening in America to unleash the largest outpouring of Christian missionary activity in history.

Unlike earlier versions of the modern missionary movement, the post-World War II iteration did not hail from the halls of respectability and power. The missionaries who made up this movement were not people of means, from prominent families within the established mainline denominations, and they could not boast of degrees from Harvard, Princeton, or Yale. Instead, they typically came from small churches in places like Blairsville, Pennsylvania or Macon, Georgia, and had been educated at relatively unknown schools like Houghton or Toccoa Falls. They did not represent the economic, cultural, or political center. Theirs was a movement of the margins, funded by the grassroots, fuelled by salt-of-the-earth spiritual fervour, and largely made up of average Americans.

Accidental Diplomats is about how the cultural margins shaped the political center. It describes how the vanguard of a new populist transnationalism—ordinary American evangelical missionaries, working towards distinctly religious aims in places like Ethiopia, Congo, and Kenya—ended up playing a decisive role in their nation's Cold War engagement in Africa.[12]

---

10 The only parallels to evangelical American missionary fervour during the Cold War are the missionary movements that have developed in Korea and Brazil as those economies have grown during the last decades of the twentieth century and the first decades of the twenty-first.

11 McLoughlin, *Revivals*, 1–2.

12 While she did not use the term populist transnationalism, and may question the term itself, the most powerful description of global evangelicalism as a transnational phenomenon is McAlister's, *The Kingdom of God Has No Borders*.

Introduction

Near the desolate and sand swept Ethiopian border with Somalia sits the nondescript and largely forgotten grave of Don McClure. The son of a rural Pennsylvanian pastor and his wife, McClure had first come to Africa as a spiritually zealous and adventuresome twenty-two-year-old missionary in 1928. For the next forty-nine years McClure and his wife Lyda, pioneered work in education, tropical medicine, and agricultural development, while sharing their Christian faith with the people of the Ethiopian periphery. During one fourteen-year period among the Anuak people, for instance, Don and Lyda developed a clinic that cared for thousands each week, started several schools, and communicated the gospel message to every person in every Anuak village. By the time that they handed this work over to indigenous leadership in the early 1960s, approximately 25,000 of the roughly 40,000 previously animist ethnic group identified themselves as Christians; and on any given Sunday, could be found in one of the many small churches now dotting the rural landscape.[1]

The couple's pioneering work attracted the attention of Ethiopian Emperor, Haile Selassie, with whom Don was to develop a friendship lasting almost thirty years. This relationship, and Don's leadership role among the American missionary community in Ethiopia, led to regular interaction with both Ethiopian and American government officials where, at the peak of the Cold War, he sometimes acted as a diplomatic bridge between the two policymaking communities. Rubbing shoulders with the political and social elite did not rank high on the missionary couple's priority list; and it never threatened their primary calling to preach and live out the Christian message in Africa. Nevertheless, by the time of his death at the hands of Somali rebels in 1977, McClure's list of contacts betrayed influence that extended well beyond the communities of rural Ethiopia. In addition to thousands of regular Ethiopians, the McClure's friends and acquaintances included: Emperor Haile Selassie, most of the Ethiopian royal family, multiple American Ambassadors, Cabinet Secretaries, Senators, and Congressmen, and even one President.[2]

---

[1] McClure and Fairman, *Red-headed, Rash, and Religious*; Partee, *Adventure in Africa*. See also, Pittsburg Theological Seminary, "Ministry of Don McClure," YouTube.

[2] "Attachment III: ... the Prayer Breakfast with H.I.M. ..." BGC/CN459/210/9. Partee, *Adventure in Africa*. It should be noted that Selassie and a few others on the list had already passed away prior to McClure's death in 1977.

Simultaneously, approximately one thousand miles to the southwest in Congo, and a thousand miles directly south in Kenya, other stories of American missionary influence were unfolding. Many of these stories were less impressive than that of Don and Lyda McClure. Few, for instance, were directly responsible for the conversion of thousands. And most did not hob knob with royalty or act as intermediaries for diplomats. Laboring at the neglected margins, their work reflected priorities and aims that were worlds away from the geopolitical concerns that consumed policymakers during the Cold War. Yet, despite this, when the spotlight of the Cold War shifted from the European center to the African periphery, evangelical missionaries like these ended up playing an important, and at times critical, role in their nation's Cold War relationship with the quickly changing region. This is the story of these "accidental diplomats."

Accidental Diplomats tells the story of the influence of American evangelical missionaries on US relations with East and Central Africa during the Cold War. On the surface it is concerned primarily with the influence of the actions of evangelical missionaries, not who they were. And yet, who they were mattered a great deal. To understand why they did what they did, and how they had the sort of impact they had, we need to know something of their lives, their stories, and in particular, the beliefs, motivations, and values that inspired them to exchange the comforts of home for the risks and challenges of the mission field. To do that we need to first place them within the larger story of twentieth century American Protestantism—a story whose outline began to emerge during the final decades of the nineteenth century.

Cold War American Evangelicals in Historical Context

Thanks to the symbolic end of the American frontier in the 1880s, a thriving and outward-looking American economy, and a culture still largely infused with an evangelical spirit, the period between 1880 and the First World War witnessed a significant expansion of American missionary activity abroad.[3] While the majority of American missionaries during this period came from the wealthy and influential Presbyterian, Methodist, and Congregationalist denominations, the theological and cultural ethos inspiring the movement was substantially evangelical.[4]

---

3 Turner, "Significance of the Frontier"; Fairbank, "Assignment for the 70s," 877–78.
4 Noll, *Scandal of the Evangelical*, 152; Sweet, "Nineteenth Century Evangelicalism," 896; Hanely, "Revolution at Home," 44–58.

Introduction

The short life of William Borden is, in some ways, an appropriate metaphor for this era of American missionaries. Born in 1887 into the family of a wealthy silver magnate and his evangelical wife, Borden was raised in both affluence and the religious spirit of the age. Even as a boy William demonstrated a deep connection to his mother's faith, making a public declaration of faith as a seven-year-old in D. L. Moody's Chicago church, and then acting as the president of the Missions club at the prestigious Hill School as a teenager. Borden's interest in missions continued throughout a gap year during which he visited missionaries in Japan, China, India, Syria, and Egypt.[5]

When he started university at Yale in 1904 it seemed like Borden was everywhere, active in several of the university's sports teams and excelling in his studies. But even here, Borden's Christian faith was the dominant force in his life. As a freshman he started Bible studies that quickly divided and expanded to include 150 students by the end of the year, and one thousand of Yale's thirteen hundred undergraduates by the time he graduated three years later. In his second year Borden founded, funded, and helped run the Yale Hope Mission, an outreach to New Haven's growing population of men struggling with alcoholism, gambling, and extreme poverty. This quiet outreach, nevertheless, acted as an inspiration to many. When asked what had impressed him most during his visit to America, one British theologian replied immediately, "The sight of that young millionaire kneeling in prayer beside a bum at Yale Hope Mission."[6]

Throughout this period, Borden's commitment to foreign missions was fueled by the Student Volunteer Movement (SVM) and their ambitious goal of "evangelizing the world in this generation." Feeling called to work amongst the three million Chinese Muslims who had never heard the Christian gospel, he applied twice to the non-denominational China Inland Mission (CIM). And twice was told to wait. Finally, after completing his degree at Yale, and then his theological training at Princeton, Borden was ordained in his home church in Chicago and accepted into missionary service by CIM. Six months later, on 17 December 1912 Borden finally boarded the steamer to Cairo where he planned to study Arabic and Islam in preparation for China. But it wasn't to be. After three energetic months in Egypt, the young missionary contracted spinal meningitis. By 9 April 1913 he was dead. His mother, who was on her way to visit her son received word of his death just hours before arriving in Cairo. News of Borden's

---

5 Casper, "Forgotten Final Resting Place"; Taylor, *Borden of Yale*.
6 Casper, "Forgotten Resting Place."

death spread quickly with memorial services being held in Chicago, New Haven, Cairo, China, and notably, at a small Black AME congregation near Princeton where he had quietly worked while in Seminary.[7]

Not every missionary of this era came from the type of privilege Borden enjoyed, and few if any could boast of his energy and charisma, and yet Borden was typical of his era in several important ways. First, it is clear that prior to World War I, Borden and his evangelical brand of Christianity continued to be welcomed within the halls of establishment respectability. This would not remain the case for much longer. Borden's life also demonstrates the absence of a dichotomy between evangelical Christianity and the concerns of social justice. While later generations would often associate social causes with liberal mainline Protestant and post-Protestant activism, Borden and his peers, like generations of evangelicals before them, assumed that compassion, justice and evangelism were inseparable and complementary pieces of the Christian gospel and lived accordingly.[8] Finally, even if Borden's life seemed to exemplify the existence of an influential Christian consensus in which establishment Protestantism and evangelicalism were intimately intertwined, it also provides clear harbingers of cracks in that consensus. Borden's choice to seek missionary service with the conservative CIM and not the mission boards associated with his alma maters; as well as his choice to study under the future standard-bearer of fundamentalism, J. Gresham Machen, both highlight evangelical concern over the liberal theological trends prevalent in the first decades of the twentieth century that would lead to a divorce between theologically liberal and conservative Protestants in America.[9]

Yet throughout Borden's life, and up to at least World War I, evangelically minded mainline missionaries inspired by the SVM, D. L. Moody, and other popular preachers of the time, continued to spread out across the globe, going to places like China, Japan, India, and the Middle East. Wherever they went, their work reflected their establishment heritage. While many would have expressed the same concern for lost souls that had driven Borden, this earlier wave of American missionaries was ultimately much more successful in building lasting and influential cultural institutions. American University of Beirut in Lebanon, Yonsei

---

7 Casper, "Forgotten Resting Place."

8 Evangelical Christianity was, of course, intimately linked to the abolitionist movement in the nineteenth century, the prohibitionist movement in the early twentieth century, and many other causes.

9 Casper, "Forgotten Resting Place."

University in Korea, and Peking Union Medical College Hospital in Beijing are just a few of the numerous world leading schools, universities, and hospitals started by American missionaries between the end of the American Civil War and the start of World War I.[10]

Even before the time of Borden's death on the eve of World War I, however, things were clearly changing; and by the end of the 1920s, the once influential evangelical strain in mainline Protestantism, and the vibrant missionary movement it had produced, were in serious trouble. Several factors contributed to the crumbling influence of evangelicalism within the still dominant mainline denominations in America. At the top of the list was the ascendency of a new set of ideas. Foremost among these was an approach to the study of the Bible called "higher criticism" that stressed the book's human, as opposed to divine, origins. Well established among liberal theologians in Europe by the mid-1800s, higher criticism had made inroads into the prestigious divinity schools of the mainline denominations by the late 1800s.[11] Together with the naturalistic understanding of Darwin's theory of evolution that finally achieved cultural dominance after the Scopes Trial of 1925, this new anthropomorphic approach to the Bible presented a profound challenge to the traditional orthodox theology upon which the missionary project had rested. If, for instance as some influenced by higher criticism assumed, the miracles of the Bible did not really happen, if they were, therefore, just literary devices or examples of a pre-scientific worldview, then the historical foundation for Christianity crumbles. Among other things, Jesus could not have been the literal Son of God and could not have been resurrected from the dead. Without these miracles, the traditional Christian meaning of the cross is lost, and with it any justification for the evangelical missionary project.[12]

If these naturalistic ideas challenged Christianity's intellectual foundations, World War I—an almost indescribably brutal conflict largely between Europe's historically Christian countries—appeared to be equally devastating to Christianity's claim to moral superiority. The resulting crisis of confidence among Christians in Europe, and to a lesser extent America, was palpable.[13] And yet, ironically, perhaps most devastating to the mainline missionary project was the missionary experience itself.

---

10 Bays and Wacker, "Introduction," 3–4; Oren, *Power, Faith, and Fantasy*, 216–19, 287.
11 Marsden, *Fundamentalism and American Culture*, 17–18.
12 Hollinger, *Protestants Abroad*, 295.
13 Showalter, *End of a Crusade*, 17–32.

David Hollinger has observed that for missionaries, "[t]he impact of foreign experience was far from unmediated. What people took from the encounter varied to some extent according to the mentalities they brought to it."[14] No longer confident in Christianity's supernatural foundations and demoralized by the effects of the Great War, but alive to the richness of the foreign cultures they were encountering, many missionaries of the inter-war period were less likely to view indigenous populations as the "heathen" other, and more likely to be critical of their own culture and the beliefs and values that undergirded it. During the 1920s, a host of current and former mainline missionaries wrote influential and often critical assessments of the missionary project. Led by E. Stanley Jones' *The Christ of the Indian Road*, Frank Laubach's *The People of the Philippines*, and A. K. Reischauer's famous Princeton lecture series, mainline missionaries openly questioned the traditional view of missions and Christianity's claim to universally applicable truth. This sustained critique culminated in the Hocking Report of 1932. Funded by John D. Rockefeller and supported by many in the mainline establishment, *Rethinking Missions*, as the report was entitled, rejected soul winning in favor of education and philanthropy.[15] In doing so, it accepted as normative the sentiment expressed by the former missionary and President of the American University of Beirut which denied that "Christianity is the sole channel through which divine and saving truth has been conveyed."[16] Of course, the idea that God's truth was imbedded in creation, and to relative degrees, in human culture, was not earth-shattering. Orthodox Christians throughout the ages had agreed with this Pauline conviction. The implication, however, that eternal salvation could be found outside of Christ represented a death-knell for the traditional missionary project.

If William Borden represented the end of an era of evangelical consensus in mainline Protestantism, Pearl S. Buck represents the liberal ascendency of the interwar period. The Nobel Prize winning author of *The Good Earth*, Buck had been raised in China by mainline missionary parents whose theological journey mirrored that of their modernist peers. Although already cynical regarding the missionary project, Buck's love of China and the pleas of her parents brought her back to her adopted home as a missionary herself from 1914 to 1932. Buck's own adoption of the liberal social gospel pushed her to conclusions that went beyond the

---

14 Hollinger, *Protestants Abroad*, 15.
15 Hollinger, 61–69.
16 Bliss, "Modern Missionary," 666.

Introduction

moderate liberalism of her parents. When the *Hocking Report* came out in 1932, the same year that *The Good Earth* was published, Buck was one of its most vocal champions. Over the next forty years, Buck's life followed the increasingly well-worn path from theological moderation to liberalism to post-Protestant secularism.[17] Buck personified the trends in American establishment Christianity of the day. As Hollinger points out, the liberal ecumenical Protestantism of this period was, "subject to a powerful impulse to include, but struggled to define what it was into which diverse peoples were being included."[18] To be sure, many in the mainline denominations did not leave the faith altogether, but as Hollinger concludes, "those who stayed with the faith struggled mightily to decide just what it was [they were staying for.]"[19]

Despite these internal tensions, at the dawn of World War II the mainline denominations appeared to represent America's religious future, and that future suggested a long and unmistakable retreat from the traditional conception of foreign missions. For the most part, evangelically minded mainline Christians like Borden had been squeezed out by the modernist-fundamentalist culture war and banished, along with the separatist fundamentalists, to the cultural margins. Like the former presidential candidate, and once revered, William Jennings Bryant, evangelicals and fundamentalists were largely seen as an embarrassing relic of a less enlightened past.[20]

Circumstances at the end of the Second World War, however, redirected America's cultural trajectory. Financially the war helped to revitalize an economy that had struggled since the Wall Street Crash of 1929. A now booming American economy had replaced the Great Depression and appeared to be positioned to dominate the global financial market for years to come. Similarly, unlike the demoralizing aftermath of World War I, America's central role in defeating the clear evil of Nazi totalitarianism had resuscitated the nation's temporarily flagging moral self-belief. Even the pain felt by the millions of Americans who had lost loved ones in the war was experienced through the galvanizing lens of moral heroism.[21] The economic and moral confidence felt by so many post-war Americans was also reflected in the spiritual life of the nation.

---

17 Hollinger, *Protestants Abroad*, 33–46, 89–90.
18 Hollinger, 82.
19 Hollinger, 81.
20 Marsden, *Fundamentalism and American Culture*, 132–35.
21 Patterson, *Grand Expectations*.

American Evangelicalism and the Religious Cold War

Throughout the Cold War, America was noteworthy for its religious vitality, experiencing what William McLoughlin termed a "religious awakening."[22] Leading the way during this spiritually dynamic time was the nation's resurgent evangelical Christian community.[23] Indeed, while the rapid growth of mainline Protestantism during the initial post-war period was losing momentum by the late 1950s, evangelical Christianity continued its dramatic growth throughout the entire Cold War. Between 1970 and 1985, for instance, the conservative Southern Baptist Convention grew by two million members. Even more dramatic was the explosive growth of many smaller evangelical groups such as the Evangelical Free Church which tripled during the same period, and the Assemblies of God which surpassed even this rapid rise in membership. By 1980, the evangelical Christian community numbered around forty million and had largely exceeded the level of political and cultural activity long practiced by their mainline Protestant counterparts.[24]

Contrary to popular stereotype, Cold War era evangelicals were not a monolithic bloc. To be sure, most evangelicals and their missionaries were theological and political conservatives. They were also, generally speaking, poorer and less educated than the average American. Nevertheless, throughout the early Cold War there were increasing indications of an intellectual and cultural resurgence among evangelicals. Between 1960 and 1972, for instance, the percentage of evangelicals going to college tripled. The increasing economic and intellectual diversity within the evangelical community was mirrored in the political sphere, where on issues such as civil rights, funding for public schools, nuclear disarmament, and the Equal Rights Amendment a sizeable minority of American evangelicals during the second half of the twentieth century could have been classified as "liberal."[25] In short, the evangelical label during most of the Cold War was not primarily an intellectual, cultural, or political one. "Evangelical" was, first and foremost, a theological label, applied to those Protestants committed to a set of traditionally orthodox Protestant beliefs.

---

22 McLoughlin, *Revivals, Awakenings and Reform*.
23 Marty, *Modern American Religion*; Marty, *Modern American Protestantism*; Marsden, *Fundamentalism and American Culture*; Noll, *One Nation Under God*; Herberg, *Protestant, Catholic, Jew*; Wuthnow, *Restructuring of American Religion*.
24 Wuthnow, *Restructuring of American Religion*, 192.
25 Schwartz, *Moral Minority*, 2–16. The political and social diversity of American evangelicalism is convincingly demonstrated in, Schäfer, *Countercultural Conservatives*.

Introduction

The British historian David Bebbington has identified what many agree are four core components of evangelicalism: conversionism (a stress on an individual's life-changing spiritual and moral rebirth); crucicentrism (the conviction that this spiritual conversion must be rooted in the historical death and resurrection of Jesus Christ as atonement for each person's sin); Biblicism (a commitment to the Bible as the ultimate authority in a person's life); and activism (the belief that sharing your faith is an essential part of Christ's universally applicable commandment to love your neighbor as yourself).[26] The missionaries who populate our story fit firmly within these transnational theological parameters. However, they were not just evangelicals. They were also Americans, and as such, typically embodied values that were particularly pronounced within American evangelical experience such as: individualism (resulting from the emphasis on interpreting the Bible for oneself), volunteerism (inherent to the "opt-in" nature of the Protestant confessional tradition), and egalitarianism (resulting from the "priesthood of all believers" principle). Also linked to American evangelicalism are the prevalence of entrepreneurial religious practices (the willingness to adapt practices to the changing needs of the context) and a heightened emphasis on the separation of church and state.[27]

American evangelical missionaries of the Cold War were, therefore, a particular sort of missionary whose work on the field was driven, primarily, by a biblically rooted spiritual worldview and a desire to share the Christian gospel to those who had never heard the message. Most of them were not self-consciously political, indeed many tried very hard to engage the world in apolitical ways. And yet their efforts were often flavored by a set of peculiarly American perspectives and concerns—concerns that sometimes had geopolitical consequences.

Traditionally reluctant to get involved in "worldly" politics, this increasingly influential community had been awakened by the global rise of "atheistic" communism. Indeed, when Billy Graham argued in 1949 that communism was "inspired, directed, and motivated by the Devil himself," he was not simply articulating the religious sentiment of America's heartland, he was making a spiritual case for Cold War interventionism that was to remain influential within American evangelicalism throughout the conflict.[28]

---

26 Bebbington, *Evangelicalism in Modern Britain*, 2–19.
27 Noll, *Scandal of the Evangelical*, 59–81.
28 Pierard, "From Evangelical Exclusivism," 166.

Evangelicals were not the only Americans who saw the Cold War in religious terms. In the early years of the conflict especially, both Democrats and Republicans spoke explicitly, and with equal conviction, of a spiritual battle with communism rooted in a fundamentally religious mythology.[29] "The defense of mankind against these attacks," argued the nominally Baptist Harry Truman, "lies in the faith we profess."[30] Truman's successor, the Presbyterian Dwight D. Eisenhower, was even more explicit. "What is our battle against communism," he declared, "if it is not a fight between anti-God and a belief in the Almighty."[31]

As the country entered a period of religious and cultural upheaval, similar sentiments could be heard by the successive generations of Cold War presidents. Even the language of the relatively non-religious Catholic John F. Kennedy was often indistinguishable from his Protestant predecessors. In his inaugural address, it was Kennedy who stated that the battle was between those who believe that the rights of man come from "the state" and those who believe they come from "the hand of God."[32] Despite some ebb and flow, this religiously infused anti-communist rhetoric continued to fill the American political landscape throughout the 1960s and 1970s culminating in Ronald Reagan. Summing up more than four decades of spiritually inspired American anti-communism, Reagan declared in 1984 that the Cold War was, "not ultimately a test of arms or missiles, but a test of faith and spirit."[33]

Some of the presidents who spoke these words were deeply religious themselves, giving added significance to the rhetoric. But even for those presidents whose religious beliefs were more or less cosmetic, it is a mistake to dismiss the rhetoric as devoid of political significance. Indeed, if anything, the fact that even relatively non-religious presidents felt the need to publicly situate the Cold War within an explicitly religious context makes their rhetoric all the more significant. For whatever may have been the substance of their personal beliefs, these political leaders knew that the American people saw themselves as a religious people, and that spiritual language resonated and inspired in a way that appeals to mere material concerns could not.[34]

American religious vitality during the Cold War is only one half of the story. Simultaneously, many of the nations with which America was seeking to develop healthy relations were experiencing remarkable

---

29 Balmer, *God in the White House*; Gibbs and Duffy, *Preacher and the Presidents*; Inboden, *Religion and American*; Preston, *Sword of the Spirit*, 411–64; Silk, *Spiritual Politics*.
30 Truman, "Address at a Luncheon," 11 November 1949, *Public Papers: Truman*.
31 Inboden, *Religion and American*, 259.
32 Kennedy, "Inaugural Address," 20 January 1961, *Public Papers: Kennedy*.
33 Reagan, "Address before a Joint Session," *Public Papers: Reagan*.
34 Inboden, *Religion and American*.

religious reorientations of their own. This was the case across the non-Western world, but particularly in Africa, where already deeply religious societies were undergoing an unprecedented cultural transformation in the form of mass conversions from traditional folk religions to either evangelical Christianity or Islam—a transformation Philip Jenkins would later call "the largest quantitative change in the whole of religious history."[35] In sub-Saharan Africa, for instance, between 1910 and 2010 Christianity grew from approximately 8.5 million (or 9 percent of the population) to approximately 516 million (or 63 percent of the population) with the majority of that growth taking place during the Cold War.[36] While a lively debate has developed regarding the consequences of this religious transformation, most scholars agree that the global religious revival during the second half of the twentieth century was nothing short of revolutionary—restructuring the political, economic and cultural identity of the nations involved and, significantly, reconfiguring the dynamics upon which these nations would relate to others.[37]

The Evangelical Missionary Movement During the Cold War

Contrary to the expectations of the *Hocking Report* and its mainline supporters, the ideologically and religiously charged context of the global Cold War witnessed the greatest surge of Christian missionaries in world history—with Americans leading the way.[38] While the Great Depression and the World Wars had limited American missionary activity between 1914 and 1945, by 1956 the number of full-time North American missionaries

---

35 Beaver, "Missionary Motivation"; Latourette, "By Way of Inclusive"; Sanneh, *Whose Religion Is Christianity?*; Jenkins, *Next Christendom*, 4; Barrett, Kurion, and Johnson, *World Christian Encyclopedia*; Walls, *Missionary Movement*; Sanneh, *Translating the Message*.
36 Pew Research Center, "Global Christianity."
37 Huntington, "Religious Persecution"; Gifford, *New Crusaders*; Brouwer, Gifford, and Rose, *Exporting the American Gospel*; Harrison and Huntington, *Culture Matters*; Freston, *Evangelicalism and Politics*; Ranger, *Evangelical Christianity and Democracy*; Huntington, "Clash of Civilizations?"; Ajami, "Summoning"; Weeks, "Do Civilizations Hold?"; Bartley, "Case for Optimism." These important studies have also encouraged a more balanced and nuanced reconsideration of missionaries in general and American missionaries in particular. Building on the work of Andrew Walls and Lamin Sanneh (on Christian missionaries generally), Brian Stanley and Andrew Porter (on British Protestant missionaries) and Joel Carpenter, Daniel Bays, Grant Wacker, William Hutchison, and Dana Robert (on American missionaries, both mainline and evangelical) these studies of Christianity's explosion in the Developing World have complicated the stereotype of the missionary as arrogant cultural imperialists created, in part, by Arthur Schlesinger Jr. in "The Missionary Enterprise and Theories of Imperialism."
38 Pierard, "Pax Americana," 158; Carpenter, "Preface," xii; Pierson, "Rise of Christian Mission," 160–69; Mead, *Special Providence*, 142. It should be noted that mainline religious elites in America continued to assume, as Stephen Neil stated in 1964, that "the age of missions [was] at an end." Smith, *Freedom's Distant Shores*, 1.

working overseas had grown from approximately 14,000 in 1925 to 23,000—roughly two-thirds of the world's Protestant missionary contingent. By 1969, the numbers had risen even further to over 33,000—a figure accounting for three-quarters of Protestant missionaries active globally.[39]

Caricatured as the slightly less embarrassing cousins of the separatist fundamentalist movement, it was the resurgent evangelical community that was driving this new wave of missionary activity. By 1960, evangelical mission agencies had overtaken the mainline churches in numbers of missionaries working overseas, accounting for nearly 66 percent of the over 29,000 American Protestant missionaries abroad. And by the 1980s approximately 90 percent of the 69,000 American Protestant missionaries were evangelical.[40] Standing behind this evangelical army throughout the Cold War was a sprawling and engaged grassroots network of individual Christians and evangelical institutions; as well as nationally prominent groups such as the Billy Graham Evangelistic Association and the National Association of Evangelicals and the financial resources they represented.[41]

The size of the evangelical missionary movement, and the increasing influence of this sub-culture on Cold War American domestic politics were, perhaps, eclipsed in significance by the quality of evangelical missionary experience. Unlike both the military (who were largely sequestered from the people of the nations they served in) and the diplomatic corps (whose stay in a given country rarely exceeded two or three years), evangelical missionaries like the McClures often had long-term and intimate interaction with foreign cultures. Living for decades at a time in one location meant that their knowledge of foreign languages, politics, and cultures was often unparalleled. Furthermore, because evangelical missionaries often went to nations that were not of paramount interest to either the public or policy making elite, they regularly acted as the primary source of American

---

[39] Pierard, "Pax Americana," 158. Some of the evangelical organizations not directly tied to a denomination that were particularly active in sending American missionaries abroad after World War II include: Wycliffe Bible Translators, Campus Crusade for Christ, Youth for Christ, the Navigators, African Inland Mission, and Sudan Interior Mission.

[40] Carpenter, "Preface," xii. This number of 69,000 is divided into 39,000 "career" missionaries and 30,000 "short term" missionaries. These numbers do not include the large additional numbers of American Christians working for evangelical NGOs such as World Vision, Compassion, and Samaritan's Purse. When those individuals are included the number of evangelicals active in missionary activity abroad during the 1980s rises to well over 100,000 per year. See Pierson, "Rise of Christian Mission," 169; Monsma, "Faith-Based NGOs"; Nichols, *Uneasy Alliance*. The sharp decline in "mainline" missionary activity is likely a result of evangelicals within mainline churches joining independent mission agencies instead of their own mission boards as their denominations became less "evangelical."

[41] Amstutz, "Faith-based NGOs," 180.

knowledge about that country—giving them an extraordinary power to influence both popular and elite opinion if, or when, these nations moved into the Cold War spotlight.[42] Finally, their relatively large and influential presence in nations many American policymakers considered peripheral also meant that some evangelical missionaries regularly interacted with the elites of the nations in which they worked. The close relationships that sometimes developed between the evangelical missionaries and foreign elites made the missionaries an obvious and important potential link between the governments of their own nation and that of their adopted homes.

A Preview and the Parameters

Accidental Diplomats argues that during the Cold War American evangelical missionaries played a significant, and at times central, role in US relations with three of the region's most politically significant nations: Ethiopia, the Congo/DRC, and Kenya.[43] Several criteria were used to select these countries. First, to best distinguish between what might be universal and what is particular within the story of American evangelical missionary influence, I have selected nations that can boast of divergent cultural and political histories. Ethiopia, for instance, is one of only two sub-Saharan African nations which remained essentially free from European colonial control. Additionally, it can make a claim, unique in sub-Saharan Africa, of being home to an indigenous Christian tradition as old as that of Western Europe. The Congo/DRC has the equally unique distinction of being the only African nation to move from being the personal property of a European monarch to that of an official Belgian colony in which the Catholic Church held a position of privilege. Its status as home to the region's largest deposits

---

42 This was especially true before the size of the State Department caught up with America's international involvement in the 1960s. Bays and Wacker, "Introduction: The Many Faces," 2–4.

43 While this is the first study to look specifically at the influence of American evangelical missionaries on US-African relations during the Cold War, this work rests on the already rich literatures in a number of related fields and sub-fields, including the broad fields of Cold War History (Gaddis, Lefler, et al.); American Religious History (Stout, Marsden, Noll, et al.); twentieth century Protestant missions (Hollinger, McAlister, Robert, Walls, Carpenter, Shenk, Wacker, and Bays, et al.); and the recent literatures related to the cultural, affective, and transnational turns in diplomatic history (McAlister, Rotter, Iriye, etc.) More specific to this study has been the relatively recent interest in the intersection of religion and foreign relations seen most notably in the work of Preston, McAlister, Rotter, Mead, Fogelsong, Ribuffo, Inboden, Kirby, and others. There is also a growing body of literature in International Relations that is concerned with the intersection of religious freedom and foreign relations, including Farr, Johnston, Birdsall, etc. Finally, there is, of course, the rich literatures for each of the African nations included in this study, as well as the fields related to the African diaspora, African independence, and post-colonialism.

of mineral wealth also makes the Congo conspicuous among its neighbors. Finally, Kenya stands out as an example of a quintessentially British colony, with a large population of European colonists and a relatively high degree of religious liberty. These three countries were also selected based on a second key criterion—the relative strength of the American missionary presence. Ethiopia, Congo, and Kenya were consistently the three countries in the region with the largest numbers of American missionaries active in them during this period. Third, and finally, these countries were selected because of their geopolitical significance. Each can make a claim to have been among the most important battlefields in the African theater of the global Cold War.

The book's argument is laid out in three parts, one for each case study nation. Part 1 looks at the influence of American evangelical missionaries on US-Ethiopian Cold War relations. Chapter 1, "Romance in a Marriage of Convenience," chronicles the development of ties between the two countries from the arrival of American evangelical missionaries in 1918 to the failed coup attempt of 1960. Chapter 2, "The Great Reversal," covering 1960 to 1991, considers the direct influence of evangelical missionaries on US-Ethiopian relations both during the build-up to the revolution of 1974 and through the era of the radically Marxist government that came out of that revolution.

Part 2 considers the influence of American evangelical missionaries on US Cold War relations with the Congo, focusing on the short but pivotal period surrounding Congolese independence from 1960 to 1967. Chapter 3, "Accidental Diplomats," considers the influence of American evangelical missionaries on US-Congolese relations during that nation's turbulent post-independence period (1960–1963), including the lengthy history of missionary influence in the build-up to independence. Chapter 4, "Red and Yellow, Black and White," explores the influence of many of these same missionaries during the rise and fall of the Simba Rebellion (1963–1967).

Finally, part 3 explores the influence of American evangelical missionaries on US-Kenyan Cold War relations. Chapter 5, "Constructing a Pro-Western Kenya," covers the period from the arrival of American missionaries in 1895 up through independence in December of 1963, and explores the role of evangelical missionaries in producing the political and cultural foundation that, upon Kenyan independence, made that nation the most politically moderate and openly pro-Western nation in the region. Chapter 6, "A Broad Popular Consensus," argues that independent

Introduction

Kenya's consistently pro-Western geopolitical orientation can be traced back to the influence of these missionaries on both the people and the principal architects of the nation's foreign policy.

The timeframe is the Cold War, defined as the end of World War II to the break-up of the Soviet Union in 1991. However, in order to understand the influence of the American missionaries during the Cold War in each country, it is essential to appreciate the nature and extent of their ties to each nation prior to the Cold War and/or the achievement of independence. For this reason, as has already been noted, in each case study, the story begins to build with the arrival of the first American missionaries in that country—which was during the last two decades of the nineteenth century in the cases of the Congo and Kenya, and for Ethiopia, in the second decade of the twentieth century.

The choice to explore the influence of one group of American missionaries to the relative exclusion of others—such as American mainline Protestant, Catholic, and Mormon missionaries—was made for both practical and historically significant reasons. First, the entirety of the American missionary enterprise during the Cold War, even when focusing on only three nations, is too vast to adequately cover in a single study. Practical considerations, therefore, demanded a narrow focus. Second, as the largest group of missionaries, and as the one that best reflected the dynamic religious ethos of Cold War America, the story of the evangelical missionaries appeared to me as the most theoretically significant and intellectually intriguing of the various subsets of American missionaries.

Virtually all the American non-denominational mission agencies which populate this book fit squarely within the evangelical camp. However, it is important to note that a majority of the American missionaries working under the auspices of mainline denominations such as the Presbyterians and the Methodists, at least prior to the 1960s, would have also subscribed to Bebbington's evangelical "quadrilateral."[44] As a result, in the case of the Congo, for instance, I have included the mainline missionaries of the Presbyterian and Methodist churches working there because the vast majority of these mainline missionaries

---

44 "Mainline" can be as slippery a category as "evangelical." However, the generally accepted usage, and the one that will be employed in this book, defines "mainline" as those older and well-established denominations such as the Congregationalists, Episcopalians, Methodists, Presbyterians, Quakers, and Unitarians, who generally filled positions of influence in American political and cultural life, and whose theology became increasingly liberal in response to the influence of higher criticism and Darwinian scientific naturalism during the late 1800s and early 1900s.

were theological conservatives, often hailing from the predominantly evangelical wings of their denomination's southern branches.

Similarly, I have included within this study the Quaker and the Mennonite missionaries active in Kenya and Ethiopia respectively prior to World War II as the missionaries from both groups also came out of the evangelical wings of their respective denominations.[45] Outside of acting as a foil to their evangelical counterparts, I have chosen not to include mainline missionaries working in Africa after 1970 for the reason that the tiny number of mainline missionaries remaining on the mission field at this point generally reflected the now firmly established liberal theology of their denominations; and, therefore, fall outside the parameters of this study.[46]

Having placed the American evangelical missionaries of the Cold War in their larger historical context, and having outlined the parameters of this study, we can now turn to the story itself.

---

45 The fact that a number of the missionaries working within the mainline denominations prior to the mid-1960s were evangelicals should not be surprising. Generally speaking, the work of traditional missionaries—preaching, evangelism, Bible translation, and theological education—assumed an evangelical theological foundation. As one Presbyterian missionary who worked in the Congo in the 1960s and 1970s noted, "the bulk of the Presbyterian missionaries [in the Congo] were pretty conservative" for, as another Presbyterian missionary stated, "the ones who didn't have that commitment [to the importance of a 'born again conversion'] didn't last ... which was alright." John and Joanne Ellington, interview with the author, 29 June 2009; David Miller, interview with the author, 30 June 2009.

46 The only two organizations included in this study that do not fit neatly into our definition of evangelical missionaries are International Christian Leadership (ICL, later referred to as the Fellowship) and Moral Re-Armament (MRA). While ICL is not, strictly speaking a missionary organization, it is included as an American domestic evangelical organization whose international network often complemented the influence of their evangelical missionary cohorts abroad. In contrast, while having organizational similarities with ICL, MRA could at best claim only a loose association with American evangelicalism. As a result, MRA is used in this study primarily as a foil for the more traditional efforts of the evangelical missionary efforts in the region.

PART 1

Influence of American Evangelical Missionaries on US-Ethiopian Cold War Relations

CHAPTER 1

Romance in a Marriage of Convenience[1]

The Missionary Factor in Early Cold War US-Ethiopian Relations, 1918–1960

Marching bands boomed and flags waved as a blizzard of confetti poured down on the crowd of over a million New Yorkers who had come to catch a glimpse of the fabled Ethiopian Emperor. The ticker-tape parade that greeted Haile Selassie as his motorcade slowly made its way up Broadway came on the back of a remarkable week. Among other things, Selassie had made the first address to a joint session of Congress by an African head of state, met privately with President Eisenhower, and had been an overnight guest at the White House.[2]

The warm welcome Selassie received throughout his two-month state visit to the United States in 1954 reflected the close relationship that had been growing between the two nations for at least a generation. As early as 1944, the United States had chosen to creatively interpret the language of the Lend-Lease program in order to provide aid to an Ethiopian nation recovering from a hostile five-year Italian occupation.[3] The next year Franklin Delano Roosevelt (FDR) and Haile Selassie held meetings in Egypt that helped establish the foundation for Ethiopia's inclusion in the Point Four Agreement (1952), a pivotal mutual defense agreement in 1953, and multiple additional development pacts.[4] By the 1960s, Ethiopia had become the single largest recipient of American aid in sub-Saharan Africa.[5]

---

1 This chapter was first published in Diplomatic History, Volume 35, Issue 5, November 2011, Pages 949–959, https://doi.org/10.1111/j.1467-7709.2011.00999.x. Revised and used with permission.
2 Schumach, "Visiting Emperor Hailed"; "Text of Haile Selassie's"; Vestal, *Lion of Judah*, 1–3.
3 Zwede, *History of Modern Ethiopia*, 184.
4 Bolton, *Report of the Special Study*; Wrong, *I Didn't Do It*; White, *Holding the Line*, 41–66; Zwede, *History of Modern Ethiopia*; Spencer, *Ethiopia at Bay*; Kisse, "Politics of Famine," 113–31; Duignan and Gann, *United States and Africa*; Ambassador Shinn's remarks at Howard University on "A Tale of Two Nations" (26 March 2004); Marcus, "American Security and Ethiopia."
5 Duignan and Gann, *United States and Africa*, 317.

In the context of the early Cold War, a limited and pragmatic relationship between Ethiopia and the United States made sense.[6] Yet while geopolitics help explain why a Cold War marriage of convenience developed between the two nations, it does not adequately explain the extent and intimacy of that relationship. Indeed, relative to the intensifying Cold War battle for Europe, rising tensions in the Middle East and the Indian subcontinent, and conflict on the Korean peninsula, Ethiopia's privileged place in US relations during this period continues to seem disproportionate to its Cold War significance and has remained a matter of incredulity to observers.

Similarly, Haile Selassie's enduring enthusiasm for the United States seemed to fly in the face of opposition from many Ethiopian elites and to contradict centuries of deeply-held anti-foreigner sentiment within its culture. Yet, as the Emperor's long-time American political advisor noted in his memoirs, "[T]hroughout his reign, as automatically as a compass needle drawn towards the magnetic Pole, His Majesty turned towards the United States. Even in retrospect, I cannot be confident of correctly ascribing the reason for that steady and incontestable attraction."[7] This chapter will contend that the otherwise inexplicably close relationship that developed between Ethiopia and the United States in the early Cold War period makes the most sense when the influence of American evangelical missionaries is taken into account.

"Dating," 1918–1941

The influence of American evangelical missionaries on early Cold War US-Ethiopian relations does not begin with the missionaries' arrival near the beginning of the twentieth century, but with a set of shared religious memories. Despite being separated physically by a still vast ocean and culturally by sixteen hundred years of Ethiopian isolation, the worldviews of the Ethiopian Amhara and the American evangelical held important elements in common. Most significantly, both were rooted in the authority of the Bible. For each community, biblical stories were much more than guiding myths, they were sources of identity and a trustworthy description of the transnational grand narrative in which God called them to play a part.

Two biblical accounts simultaneously formed the very heart of the ancient Ethiopian national identity and created a powerful symbolic link between these otherwise dissimilar communities. The first, the Old

---

6 National Archives II, "Confidential Report," 7 October 1943, National Archives II (NARA) RG165/Entry 77/Box 777; Iyob and Keller, "US Policy in the Horn," 102–3; and Zwede, *History of Modern Ethiopia*, 185.

7 Spencer, *Ethiopia at Bay*, 102.

Testament relationship between King Solomon and the Ethiopian "Queen of Sheba," and the related prophecy of Psalm 68 stating that, "Ethiopia would soon stretch out her hands unto God," tied Ethiopia theologically, historically, and (Ethiopian Orthodox tradition suggests) genetically to the Jewish people.[8] Likewise, the well-known New Testament story of the Ethiopian Eunuch's conversion to Christianity through the testimony of Philip, a Jewish convert to Christianity, grafted the African kingdom into the story of Christianity from its very beginning.[9]

Over the next two thousand years, the experience of being an island of Christianity within a rising and hostile tide of animism and, later, Islam in the region, so conflated Christianity and Ethiopian nationalism that, as one scholar put it, "the cardinal criteria for being Ethiopian was acceptance of the Orthodox creed."[10] Despite its relative isolation from the rest of Christendom for over a millennia, Ethiopia remained a highly potent symbol for all Christians, and in particular, Protestants like Martin Luther who regarded it as the first and most authentic Christian kingdom.[11]

Thus, as the twentieth century dawned, there already existed a powerful, if still largely dormant, biblically-inspired bond between Ethiopia and the American evangelical community.[12] It is not surprising,

---

8   1 Kgs 10 (NIV); Kihss, "Ethiopia's Emperor Lands."

9   Acts 8:26–40 (NIV); Ps 68:31 (KJV). Christianity did not become the official religion of Ethiopia until AD 341, but this is still prior to the Edict of Thessalonica, AD 380, when Christianity became the official religion of the Roman Empire. Munro-Hay, *Aksum: An African Civilization*, 77.

10 Eide, *Revolution and Religion*, 36. Yet, Ethiopian allegiance to Christianity did not necessarily make it natural allies with Christian Europe. In fact, when Catholic and Protestant missionary outreach to Ethiopia after the sixteenth century was regularly followed by military efforts, Ethiopia's deep suspicion of foreigners was extended, at least to some degree, to non-Orthodox European Christians and remained deeply entrenched as the twentieth century dawned. Hanson and Hanson, *God and the Emperor*, 11.

11 Daniels, "Martin Luther's Fascination."

12 It is important to note, and this will be developed much more in chapter 2, that despite (and perhaps because of) the important religious connections between the two Christian communities, the relationship between the American evangelical missionaries and the Ethiopian Orthodox Church (EOC) was uneasy from the beginning. Many of the missionaries, while enamored with the Ethiopian church's historical ties to both the biblical Israelites and the first century church, were often highly critical of what they considered to be the EOC's rigid traditionalism and extra-biblical theology. This blend of admiration and contempt is found throughout the accounts of their experiences in Ethiopia. (See among others, "Church in Ethiopia," and Barnhouse, "In the Emperor's Palace.") For their part, the EOC hierarchy, almost without exception, viewed the American missionaries as unwanted intruders, and a threat to their cultural, political, and religious dominance. In fact, it was the EOC, and not the Muslim or animist populations, that exhibited the most virulent antagonism towards the American missionaries and their evangelical converts. (See "Visit to Anglo-Egyptian," as well as a summary by US intelligence of an intercepted letter dated 9 November 1943 from an American missionary in Ethiopia to another based in Egypt, NARA/RG165/77/776.)

then, that the increasing political threat represented by Muslim and animist minorities on the country's periphery, coupled with Ethiopia's need to modernize, pushed the monarchy to seek out transnational allies in the form of Protestant missionaries from countries not closely associated with colonial ambitions in Africa—first Sweden and then the United States. Beginning with the Presbyterians (1918) and building with the Seventh Day Adventists (1921), the Sudan Interior Mission (1928), and a number of other organizations in the 1930s, American evangelicals responded enthusiastically to Ethiopia's openness to missionary involvement, setting up mission stations, churches, schools and hospitals across the country.[13]

Living for years at a time amongst the Ethiopians, becoming fluent in their languages, eating their foods, sharing their stories and absorbing their history, by the 1930s approximately one hundred evangelical missionaries had developed an unparalleled understanding of Ethiopian cultural and political dynamics.[14] To be sure, a considerable cultural gap remained between the missionaries and the Ethiopians they worked amongst, and this gap did sometimes produce errors in perception. Nevertheless, during this period no other group of Western expatriates, American or otherwise, could begin to boast of anywhere near the same level of familiarity with Ethiopia.[15]

As fellow Christians and, theoretically, apolitical agents of the modernization he hoped to initiate, Haile Selassie had made a point of closely following the progress of their work and had met with virtually every American missionary working in Ethiopia prior to the Italian

---

13 Cotterell, *Born at Midnight*, 11.

14 The exact number of American missionaries working in Ethiopia in the 1930s is unknown. We do know that by 1936, the largest mission, SIM, had fifteen stations. Some stations might have been as small as a missionary couple or two single missionaries, while others, such as schools and hospitals, likely had larger missionary numbers. A conservative estimate is, therefore, that the average mission station had three missionaries. The other two missions most active by the 1930s were the Presbyterians who had a long history in Ethiopia, and the Seventh Day Adventists. While smaller, the two missions combined likely had at least the same combined number of stations as SIM. Therefore, when you add together the three larger missions and the several smaller and newer missions that came in the 1930s, we have an approximate number of 35 stations and 105 missionaries. Hege, *Beyond Our Prayers*, 37.

15 Indeed, as we shall see later, their "American eyes" did promote a vision of Haile Selassie that appears to have been at least partially at odds with reality. Among multiple examples of missionary awareness of these challenges see the essays in Winter and Hawthorn's, *Perspectives on the World Christian Movement: A Reader*. Also see the well-known critique by Edward W. Said, *Orientalism*. In addition, as we shall see later, between 1909 and 1943 there were also small numbers of African Americans in Ethiopia: see Joseph E. Harris, *African-American Reactions to War in Ethiopia, 1936–41*. For a description of the intimate interaction of the American evangelical missionaries with the Ethiopian peoples and cultures, see: Hanson and Hanson, *God and the Emperor*; F. Peter Cotterell, *Born at Midnight*; Charles Partee, *Adventure in Africa*; and Don McClure, *Red-headed, Rash, and Religious*.

invasion in 1935.[16] In the process, a number of these working relationships developed into genuine friendships. Dr. Thomas Lambie was just one notable example. Since arriving as an energetic young medical missionary in 1918, Lambie had built four hospitals and been embraced by the Emperor who the *NY Times* described as "an intimate friend."[17] Lambie's commitment to his Christian calling and to the Ethiopian people was such that in 1934, in order to purchase land for another hospital, he renounced his American citizenship and pledged his allegiance to Haile Selassie.[18] When Italy invaded in 1935, Lambie led the Ethiopian Red Cross and was (along with several other American missionaries) the source of much of the information the outside world received regarding the Italian atrocities prior to their occupation.[19] His commitment to Ethiopia, and friendship with the Emperor, made a deep impression on Haile Selassie that was only partially compromised by events during the Italian occupation.[20]

Lambie's decision to continue to work as a missionary under the occupation required at least a partial recanting of the damaging claims he had made concerning the Italian use of mustard gas during the invasion.[21] Fortunately for the American missionary community, the resulting rupture of Lambie's relationship with the Emperor was more than balanced by the reaction of the rest of the American missionary community to the threat of the invasion. Responding to the official request from the US government to evacuate before the invasion, a spokesman for the Sudan Interior Mission (SIM) stated publicly that "While we thoroughly respect our Government's attitude in their request for evacuation, the obedience

---

16 Hanson and Hanson, *God and the Emperor*; Friederichsen, *Dr. Bob Hockman*; Willmott, *Doors Were Opened*; and many others.
17 Associated Press, "Missionaries to Stay."
18 Cotterell, *Born at Midnight*, 79.
19 According to Haile Selassie's American legal advisor John Spencer, American missionary, J. L. Rohrbaugh wrote for the *Times of London*. Spencer, *Ethiopia at Bay*, 65, 68. Articles that were almost certainly his or the result of his work include the feature article "The Bombing of Daggah Bur," 19 December 1935. Articles that credit Hockman as the source include, "Missionary Tells First-hand Story of Ethiopian War," in the *NY Herald Tribune*, 18 November 1935; and others in *The Chicago Tribune*, 26 September 1935; and *The Chicago Daily News*, 17 October 1935. Dr. Lambie is credited with writing reports that "aroused expressions of outrage, especially in Britain." Spencer, *Ethiopia at Bay*, 49.
20 Spencer, *Ethiopia at Bay*, 49.
21 For instance, after pledging allegiance to Italy for the fifteen stations of the Sudan Interior Mission, Lambie is quoted in an AP press dispatch on 30 May 1936 that, "We have never entered politics as a Mission and never will. If the Government is Italian, we shall support the Italian Government—even as the Lord said, 'Give unto Caesar the things that are Caesar's and unto God the things that are God's.'" SIM/ SIM EA/1/7.

of the missionary is to a higher power."²² A *New York Times* article later that year confirmed their continuing commitment to stay in the face of the invasion. "The missionary call [was] supreme" one missionary quoted by the *Times* stated, "[and] that disregard of it in Ethiopia's hour of greatest need would be unworthy of Christians."²³

This spiritually inspired transnational loyalty was supported by individual acts of missionary bravery on behalf of the Ethiopian Emperor and his country. Among many similar examples, one American missionary couple in northern Ethiopia, at great personal risk, housed and fed Selassie for two days along the battle front during his last major stand against the Italians.²⁴ It was, however, the tragic story of a young American missionary doctor, Robert Hockman, that was to have the greatest ramifications for US-Ethiopian relations.

Born in Szechwan, China to missionary parents, "Red" Hockman went on to attend the China Inland Mission's Chefoo School before returning to attend the Presbyterian Muskingum College in Ohio. At Muskingum, Hockman met Melaku, a relative of Haile Selassie's who had been sent by the Emperor to the US with the hope of his becoming Ethiopia's first modern physician. The budding friendship between the two aspiring doctors, in turn, planted seeds of interest in Ethiopia in Hockman.²⁵

"Clean cut" with a "chest like a barrel" and the epitome of "wholesome fun," the deeply religious Hockman excelled at both Muskingum and Northwestern medical school, where he finished at the top of the Illinois medical board examinations in 1932 with the second highest score in state history to date. Despite abundant opportunities to start a lucrative practice in the US, Hockman instead applied to the United Presbyterian mission board and, together with his young wife, accepted the call to begin their ministry in Melaku's Ethiopia, setting sail for Africa in October of 1933.²⁶

Upon arrival in Ethiopia, the dedicated young couple wasted no time getting to work, opening up a new lab at the Presbyterian hospital in the capital alongside honored guest Emperor Selassie. This event was followed

---

22 "Statement Given—7/7/35," SIM/SIM EA/Box 1/Folder 6. SIM is now called, "Serving in Mission."

23 The Associated Press, "American Missions to Stay."

24 "Greater Love," 17–18. After they were expelled by the Italians, the exiled Selassie showed his affection and appreciation for the missionary couple in question, the Ogilesbys, by entertaining them in Bath, England where they stopped on their way home to the United States. See handwritten notes on "alphagraphics" stationary, SIM/ SIM Gen 04/ Ethiopia Research. At least three American missionaries died in Ethiopia at or around the time of the Italian invasion. "SIM Missionaries in Ethiopia—1927–36," SIM/SIM EA/1/13.

25 Friederichsen, *Dr. Bob Hockman*, 11–16.

26 Friederichsen, *Dr. Bob Hockman*, 19–30.

by several additional meetings with the Ethiopian monarch where they discussed Melaku and his progress in America.[27] Hockman's influence in Addis Ababa was immediate and positive. Already the influential head of the Presbyterian Hospital and someone who appeared to have the ear of the Emperor, admiration for the "popular" and "deeply respected" missionary only grew when he joined the majority of American missionaries in choosing to stay in Ethiopia despite rumors of an impending Italian invasion.[28]

When the invasion did begin later in 1935, Hockman was asked to lead the Ethiopian Red Cross team closest to the front. From there Hockman's letters and cables to mission headquarters and family in America, as well as to his pregnant wife on bed rest in Egypt, became a primary means through which specifics on the Italian invasion reached the American media and public. These cables generally detailed conditions on the front and the bleak prospects of the ill-equipped Ethiopian defenders in the face of Italy's modern war machine.[29] But Hockman's communication also reflected the young doctor's zest for life and his American patriotism. "I played Sousa's marches on the Victrola," Hockman wrote in one letter to his parents, "Grand they were! My blood ran faster through the veins as I had the trombones play their part in 'Stars and Stripes Forever.'"[30]

On October 30, 1935, while still at the front, Hockman received the news he had been waiting for. His first child, a daughter, had been born in Egypt. Hockman immediately requested leave to go to Egypt to see his wife and baby, but the Ethiopian government and the Red Cross pleaded with him to stay, arguing that the vital medical support there would collapse otherwise.[31] Ultimately Hockman decided that "this is where I am supposed to be" and made the agonizing decision to stay at the front at least until the new year.[32] On Friday, December 13, 1935 when an undetonated Italian bomb he was trying to disarm exploded, Hockman was killed instantly.

Because of the media's rising interest in the Italian invasion and Hockman's role in bringing the world's attention to the conflict, word of his death made it to the wires quickly and spread across America where

---

27 Friederichsen, 34–38.
28 Associated Press, "Missionaries to Stay"; Wireless to the *New York Times*, "Death of Hockman."
29 Billy Graham Center Archives (BGCA), CN 200, Box 1, Folders 1–6.
30 BGCA, CN 200, Box 1, Folders 1–6; Friederichsen, *Dr. Bob Hockman*, 66.
31 Wireless to the *New York Times*, "Death of Hockman."
32 Friederichsen, *Dr. Bob Hockman*, 71.

Hockman, as the first American killed in the developing global conflict, became a symbol of a deepening and religiously-inspired transnational bond between the United States and Ethiopia.[33] The *New York Times* quoted sources calling the vibrant young medical missionary the "best worker in Ethiopia" who had sacrificed his own life for the lives of the Ethiopians he had come to serve.[34] Another reporter covering the front for UP spoke for many others when he wrote, "Somehow I would like to pay some sort of real tribute to a man who gave his life in service. Until now, the war in East Africa was just another news story to me, but now it has become a hateful thing, which killed a friend and one of the few men I really admired."[35] Selassie's response appears to have been equally heartfelt. Even in the chaos surrounding the final Italian advance on Addis Ababa, the Emperor took the time to send Hockman's parents a cable in which he shared his personal grief at the death of their son and thanked them for his dedication to the Ethiopian people.[36]

Less than a month later, another "missionary kid" from China, and a fellow recent product of the intimately connected Chefoo School diaspora, *Time* and *Life* publisher Henry Luce, made Ethiopia's Christian Emperor *Time's* "Man of the Year." Perhaps as much as any other single event, this choice solidified the religiously inspired bond that had begun to develop between the ancient Christian kingdom and the United States and helped ensure that Ethiopia would remain in the American public eye for a time. Six months later, riding on the back of this publicity, Haile Selassie gave one of the most important speeches delivered before the League of Nations decrying the Italian occupation of his country and challenging the international community to live up to its commitment to collective security.[37] In doing so, Selassie became the first and only head of state to address the forerunner to the United Nations and an enduring symbol of African self-determination.[38]

In the years leading up to the Italian occupation there had been almost no meaningful official relationship between the United States and Ethiopia. There had been a visit by a US envoy in 1903 that established relations

---

33 Almost every major paper in the United States carried the story of his death under headlines such as, "Dr. Hockman, First U.S. Casualty," *Pittsburgh Sun-Telegraph*, 14 December 1935; and "Dr. Hockman's Death by Bomb Stirs Ethiopia," *New York Herald Tribune*, 14 December 1935.
34 Wireless to the *New York Times*, "Death of Hockman."
35 As quoted in Friederichsen, *Dr. Bob Hockman*, 95.
36 Hockman to Haile Selassie, 24 December 1935, BGC/CN 200/1/8; Cotterell, *Born at Midnight*, 85–86.
37 Selassie, "Appeal to the League," June, 1936.
38 Vestal, *Lion of Judah*, 4.

between the two countries. And there was a sporadic and numerically tiny official US presence that followed.[39] But whatever relationship that did exist prior to 1941 was almost entirely due to the work of American evangelical missionaries; and in particular, the growing relationships that their work and sacrifices produced between themselves, the Ethiopian Emperor, and as we will explore later, segments of the American public.

The Proposal, 1941–1945

On May 5, 1941, Ethiopia became the first nation freed from Axis control. When Haile Selassie returned to Ethiopia to considerable media acclaim, the largest group of non-military expatriates there to greet him were American evangelical missionaries. In addition to several missionaries who had remained in Ethiopia in spite of considerable Italian persecution, a number of others had played a role in the Allied force that liberated Ethiopia and stayed on in prominent secular positions to help Ethiopia rebuild itself.[40] Thus, as US-Ethiopian relations began a new chapter, it seemed inevitable that American evangelical missionaries would continue to play a central role. If the initial "dating" period was noteworthy for the role that American evangelical missionaries played in encouraging the Ethiopian monarch to see America as a natural and trustworthy ally, the "proposal" period demonstrates the influence of the same missionaries on their own government's perspective toward Ethiopia.

Prior to the Italian occupation, when Addis Ababa was a relatively obscure diplomatic outpost, social interaction amongst the tiny expatriate community was frequent and people from radically divergent social strata regularly developed close friendships. It was in this context that a pattern of interaction between the evangelical missionaries and the American and international diplomatic communities developed. For instance, in one of many similar accounts, a missionary's report to their American headquarters described as typical a diplomatic reception given by the American representative for Selassie's coronation in 1930 in which "we all [the missionaries] had a lovely time."[41] The same report later describes

---

39 McVety, "1903 Skinner Mission," 187–212.
40 Cotterell, *Born at Midnight*, 101–3. It should be noted that at least one of these SIM missionaries serving with the British Army was not an American citizen. In fact, a number of SIM missionaries have always come from the UK, Canada, Australia, and New Zealand. That said, by the 1940s SIM was dominated by Americans and this continued to be the case throughout the period in question. Associated Press, "American Missions to Stay."
41 "Ceremonies in Connection," 2, 2 November 1930, SIM Archives/Collection—SIM EA/Box 1/Folder 6.

several additional diplomatic functions in which missionaries played a prominent social role. In one such reception given "in honor of all the foreign delegates," Ambassador Addison Southard asked two American missionary couples "to assist in receiving."[42] Complimenting these formal social engagements between the two American communities were shared family picnics, games of tennis, and hunting trips.[43] In short, like a small and isolated town where divergent personalities and social strata regularly intermingled, the pre-Cold War Ethiopian expatriate community naturally nurtured a pattern of interaction that produced a regular flow of information between the American missionary community and its diplomats.[44]

One unexpected but consequential biproduct of this intimate social context was the association of the evangelical missionaries with American intelligence agents. While this phenomenon was a relatively short-lived anomaly, intelligence gathered through this interaction helped create the analytical spectacles through which US policymakers interpreted Ethiopian affairs during the critical early years of the Cold War. More specifically this information appears to have been heavily relied upon in the production of the briefing on Selassie given to FDR prior to his consequential meeting with the Ethiopian leader in 1945—a meeting that laid the foundation for the next thirty years of US-Ethiopian relations.

There are several reasons why this unlikely and short-lived relationship between US intelligence and evangelical missionaries developed in Ethiopia at this time.[45] Foremost among these was the need for quality

---

42 "Ceremonies in Connection," 5, 2 November 1930, SIM Archives/Collection—SIM EA/Box 1/Folder 6.

43 BGC/CN 200/Box 1/Folder 3. Another example of this familiar social relationship is found in Hanson and Hanson, *God and the Emperor*, 55. On the day of the infamous Graziana massacre in Addis Ababa, the US Ambassador and his family were coming to the Seventh Day Adventist mission on the city's outskirts for a two-day visit. This visit never happened because of the political fallout, but others like it did.

44 "Letter from Dr. Bob Hockman to family members on January 28, 1934," BGC/CN200/Box 1/Folder 2; SIM/SIM EA/Box 1/Folder 6; Correspondence with retired missionary Jim Keefer, 13 December 2007.

45 A direct, formal, and political relationship between evangelical missionaries and US intelligence is in some ways difficult to imagine. Unlike their mainline Protestant equivalents (Episcopalians, Congregationalists, Unitarians, liberal Methodists and liberal Presbyterians) whose belief system and cultural tradition intersected regularly with the sphere of "worldly" elite politics, the theology of evangelical missionaries was much more likely to view the world in Manichean (good versus evil) and Platonic (material versus spiritual) terms. Add to this mentality the separatist orientation of evangelical Christianity and the American tradition of church-state separation, and you have the recipe for an almost entirely apolitical and spiritually driven missionary endeavor. As early as the 1920s many evangelical mission groups such as SIM had written constitutions explicitly prohibiting them from direct and formal ties to government agencies. "Confidential

intelligence resulting from the perceived growing strategic and symbolic importance of Ethiopia to American interests both regionally and globally. Complementing the increased need for quality intelligence on Ethiopia was the unique ability of the missionaries to satisfy that need. Unlike the tiny number of US representatives in Africa during this period, who were largely political appointees with "little knowledge of Africa and even less contact with Africans," or the small number of short-term African American emigres to the region, the missionary experience in Ethiopia could boast of depth, breadth and longevity.[46]

Finally, while evangelical theology and mission policies typically forbade this sort of interaction, the patriotic fervor that had engulfed the globe during WWII seems to have also made some missionaries less likely to see interaction with US intelligence as a compromise of their spiritual aims in Ethiopia and more likely to see it as an act of American, and indeed Ethiopian, patriotism. This was especially the case after 1941, when Ethiopia actively sought out cooperation with the United States as an alternative to the quasi-colonial powers enforced by the British during the remainder of the war.[47]

In sum, with no equally promising alternatives, and with a group of knowledgeable missionaries caught up in the patriotic fervor of the war ready at hand, contact between US intelligence agents and American missionaries became frequent. In 1943 and 1944 alone, at least eight different missionaries are named in restricted or confidential US intelligence reports. In addition to supplementing the well-known admiration of Haile Selassie within

---

report from Addis of March 1, 1929," SIM Archives/SIM EA collection/Box 1/Folder 6. This judgment is based on the author's correspondence with missionaries from this period, as well as the extensive discussion of the interaction between missionaries and US intelligence agencies during the debate surrounding the Hatfield Bill of 1976, in which evangelical organizations revealed explicit mission policies requiring no official contact with US government agencies and expressed their conviction that these policies had been overwhelming adhered to by individual missionaries. For an extensive discussion of this debate see the Billy Graham Center Archives (BGC)/CN 165/Box 208.

46 Noer, *Cold War and Black*, 35; "Conditions in Ethiopia," 23 February 1942, NARA/RG 165/Entry 77/Box 778; Cotterell, *Born at Midnight*, 101, 108. It appears that from the handful of African Americans who had emigrated to Ethiopia before the Italian invasion, one or two individuals also remained in the country throughout the occupation. This story is fascinating in its own right, but for our present purposes, there appears to have been no attempts by American intelligence agents to contact these individuals, making the substantially larger missionary community the primary information source for American intelligence and policymakers. For information on the level of African American presence in Ethiopia during the Italian occupation see Harris, *African-American Reactions*, 142–59.

47 The reputation of evangelicals for enthusiastic patriotism both during and after WWII has been well established by a number of scholars including Pierard in "Pax Americana" and Carpenter and Shenk in *Earthen Vessels*.

the missionary community, these reports provided information covering analysis of Ethiopian politics and culture, agricultural and commercial potential, the level of sophistication and freedom in the press, and the extent and quality of the nation's educational and health care systems.[48]

In one report Presbyterian missionary Duncan Henry bolstered the Ethiopian Emperor's image as a capable and willing ally by informing American military intelligence of Haile Selassie's "desire to assist the Allied nations by producing and shipping a surplus of grain and wild rubber." In that same report Henry also added to the American understanding of Ethiopia's internal political dynamics by assessing the causes of a minor rebellion against Selassie that had recently been put down in Northern Ethiopia.[49] In addition, the Baptist missionary James Luckman's proficiency in Amharic and Arabic was utilized by US intelligence officer Francis Colby in assessing the content and quality of the Ethiopian newspapers, as well as in judging the relative amount of freedom allowed to the press by the Ethiopian government.[50]

Other missionary reports describe the terrain of rural Ethiopia, the condition of the roads, the implications of new Ethiopian laws, and the desperate need for an educated middle class.[51] Beyond the substantial nature of the intelligence provided by the American missionaries, what stands out from these reports are both the number of missionaries approached and the close personal relationship that apparently existed between many of them and the primary intelligence agent, Colonel Francis Colby. The otherwise non-religious Colby remarks on several occasions of attending church services and informal dinner engagements with the missionaries, and his own personal attachment to at least one, whom he called "an old friend of mine."[52]

Generally speaking, the reports do not include political intrigues, and none suggest that the missionaries were themselves intelligence operatives, yet they remain noteworthy because they illustrate the role

---

48 "Report numbers: 327, 622, 626 & Informal Reports of 3/8/1944 and 3/14/1944," NARA/RG 165/Entry 77/Box 776.
49 "Report number: 327, 10/7/1943," NARA/RG 165/Entry 77/Box 776. Duncan Henry's story is particularly interesting in that the Presbyterian missionary had previously been accused of spying and was imprisoned with his son for a month by the Italians during their occupation. The fact that he was clearly sought out by US intelligence in 1943, and the familiarity they had with him, suggests that the Italians might have been correct.
50 "Report number 622, 3/6/1944," NARA/RG 165/77/776.
51 "Cross Reference Sheet Synopsis," NARA/RG 165/77/776. "Postal and Telegraph Censorship, London," 24 August 1943, NARA/RG 165/77/776.
52 "Report of March 8, 1944," NARA/RG 165/77/778.

that missionaries played in creating the vital "first impression" of Ethiopia that helped to shape the way US policymakers understood and related to Ethiopia during the early Cold War years.[53] Indeed the tone, and to a large extent the content, of these reports closely mirror the briefing on Haile Selassie prepared for FDR before the two met in Egypt in 1945.[54]

The Long Engagement, 1945–1952—Part One: Growing Intimacy between Selassie and the American Missionary Community

The meeting between Haile Selassie and FDR, in which the perspectives of both leaders towards the other had been substantially influenced by American evangelical missionaries, was "exceptionally cordial and agreeable" and produced not only a continuation of the Lend-Lease program, but an invitation to the Ethiopian Emperor for an official visit to the US.[55] The potential momentum in US-Ethiopian relations stalled, however, with FDR's death just two months later and the understandable pre-occupation of his successor, Truman, with the rapidly emerging European Cold War.

This is not to say that official US-Ethiopian interaction ceased entirely during this period. Ethiopia did, for instance, become a charter member of the US-driven United Nations project in 1945 and supported US and UN efforts in Korea by sending over one thousand troops to the conflict. In terms of bilateral relations, Ethiopia also successfully pushed for inclusion in the Point Four Program, signed a modest economic amity agreement with the US in 1951, and received US support for its claim to Eritrea. All of this was at least partially linked to the continuing use by the US of a communications facility in the country that had been vital to US intelligence gathering during World War II and into the early Cold War. Yet these interactions remained outliers in an otherwise sleepy diplomatic relationship that had appeared to hold such tremendous promise in 1945.

While progress in official relations did experience something of a hiatus between 1945 and 1952, the principal informal, and usually unintentional, driver behind US-Ethiopian relations continued to quietly flourish. American missionary engagement in Ethiopia grew substantially during this period, preparing the soil for the significant US-Ethiopian Cold War

---

53 That is apart from Duncan Henry who might have been working directly for a US intelligence agency.
54 "Pen Portrait of Emperor of Ethiopia," NARA RG 59/3109/67d226/Folder 13a. The missionary-based intelligence reports added to the widespread sentiment that Ethiopia was a nation of some economic potential being led by a benevolent and pro-American monarch. This is also the essence of the FDR briefing.
55 Vestal, *Lion of Judah*, 37.

relationship that was to blossom in 1953 and 1954.[56] Building on the pattern that had developed prior to the Italian invasion, personal relationships between Haile Selassie and the American missionary community remained at the center of the growing affection between the Ethiopian monarchy and the United States.

The most remarkable of these relationships was Selassie's working friendship with the Seventh Day Adventist missionary Della Hanson, who in 1941 began a fourteen-year stint as the coordinator of Selassie's palace. On first glance, a close working relationship between the sophisticated Ethiopian monarch and an unassuming, middle-aged, Scandinavia-American missionary wife seems odd.[57] Hanson had none of the credentials that might have otherwise recommended her as the palace coordinator. She had no formal administrative experience, was not a trained chef, and lacked any notable educational or cultural pedigree. She was, however, a loyal, deferential, and hard-working American evangelical Christian who embraced the traditional domestic role of women that both American conservative Christianity and Ethiopian custom encouraged.[58] Thus from the vantage point of both Haile Selassie and the missionary community, these attributes made Hanson a reasonable choice.

By all accounts, the relationship that developed between Hanson, the Emperor, and the royal family was extraordinarily personal.[59] Beyond her official duties, "Mrs. Hanson" had a regular place at the royal family's dinner table, kept a room at the palace, and occasionally vacationed with

---

56 Exact numbers are hard to determine. A few other American missionaries remained in the rural areas, but we know that the number of missionaries remaining in Addis Ababa when the Allies freed it from Axis control was relatively small, likely no more than five. "Conditions in Ethiopia," NARA RG165/77/778. By the 1950s, however, the number of American missionaries in Ethiopia was likely approaching five hundred. This is based on knowing that SIM alone had 228 missionaries in Ethiopia in 1957. *Sudan Witness*, 1957, Vol. 33, No. 1; Cumbers, *Living with the Red*, 4.

57 *Life Magazine*, "Haile Selassie's Housekeeper." As is clear from the article text, this strange confluence of cultures was certainly part of what attracted *Life* to feature Della Hanson's story.

58 Letter from Haile Selassie to Mrs. Hanson, August 1955, reprinted in Hanson, 187–88. See also Della Hanson's own description of her motivation and the circumstances surrounding her appointment to the palace in the chapter "Called to the Palace," *God and the Emperor*. It should also be noted that, while Hanson represents one face of American evangelical missionary women, other scholars such as Dana Robert have found compelling evidence that women of equally conservative theological stock have used the space created by the cross-cultural missionary experience to expand the parameters of female agency and responsibility, with important consequences for the evolution of the role of women in American evangelicalism. See Robert's, "Influence of American Missionary," 59–89.

59 Letter from Haile Selassie to Mrs. Hanson, in the fall of 1955, reprinted in Hanson and Hanson, *God and the Emperor*, 188. See also multiple anecdotes and quotations throughout this memoir.

the Emperor and Empress.[60] She also was seen as a trusted mentor and beloved auntie by the children of the palace, including the Emperor's favored grandson and future political confidant, Alexander Desta, who was a regular at the Hanson home.[61] When Selassie's daughter was engaged to be married, it was Hanson who not only organized the wedding but threw a private bridal shower with the ladies of the royal family and the missionary community. And after the tragic death of the same princess only months after her wedding, it was Hanson who grieved with the royal family and listened to the private pain of the Emperor.[62] Without hyperbole, Hanson could write in her memoirs that Selassie was "like a father to me."[63]

But the warm relationship between Mrs. Hanson and Haile Selassie contained more than just an uncomplicated narrative of religious affinity and traditional gender roles. By placing Hanson at the heart of his empire, Selassie also revealed a great deal about his vision for Ethiopia's future. Historians of Ethiopia have long been confounded by the simultaneous presence in the Emperor's governance of both modernizing and traditionalizing elements. Indeed, so strong and apparently contradictory have these two themes been, that for the sake of coherence many observers have simply designated one of the two as a chimera.[64] Hanson's role in Selassie's palace, as well as anything in the history of his rule, presents us with a picture of how he sought to reconcile the seemingly inherent antagonism between tradition and change.

While the introductions of strawberry shortcake and potato salad to the palace menu hardly seem like transformative historical moments, these trivial changes nevertheless hinted at the conservative-minded modernization project that Selassie wanted to initiate both within his own family and throughout his nation.[65] In addition to her role of introducing American food and clothing to the royal family, Hanson was put in charge of the day-to-day running of the palace, all state dinners, and the complete redecorating and refurnishing of the palace in line with the modern

---

60 Hanson and Hanson, 114, 146–47, 170; *Life Magazine*, "Haile Selassie's Housekeeper."
61 Hanson and Hanson, 166–68. During the aftermath of the 1960 coup attempt (see ch. 2) the US Embassy considered Desta a trusted bridge between the US and Selassie noting that Desta, "sees HIM daily and frequently expresses HIM's thoughts." "Secret," Ambassador Richards to Assistant Secretary for African Affairs, 3 January 1961. NARA RG84/2438/350.
62 Hanson and Hanson, *God and the Emperor*, 134, 140–45.
63 Hanson and Hanson, 113.
64 Observers concluding that modernization in Selassie's Ethiopia was a myth nurtured by an Emperor in pursuit of the aid needed to ensure the stability of his throne, include, among others Selassie's American legal advisor John Spencer. Spencer, *Ethiopia at Bay*.
65 *Life Magazine*, "Haile Selassie's housekeeper."

American aesthetic.⁶⁶ As part of this refurnishing project she dramatically updated the domestic appliances of the palace, introducing American electric ovens, refrigerators, water heaters, and washing machines.

Along with modernizing the palace hardware, Hanson was also given the much harder task of creating within the palace culture a workable blend of Ethiopian tradition and American-style pragmatic efficiency.⁶⁷ In sum, like the American evangelical missionaries she represented, it appears that Hanson was embraced by Haile Selassie in large measure because she represented a morally conservative and spiritually infused version of modernity that complemented the Emperor's otherwise seemingly contradictory traditionalizing and modernizing aims. If this was the rationale behind Selassie's peculiar choice of the Minnesotan missionary wife, Mrs. Hanson delivered. In her fourteen years at the palace, Hanson managed to significantly modernize the institution that was the cultural and political heart of the country. And she did it without appearing to undermine the foundations of imperial authority.⁶⁸

Although certainly unique in its level of intimacy, the same natural affinity seen between Selassie and Hanson was evident in several other relationships between the Ethiopian Emperor and American missionaries.⁶⁹ While Selassie was known for granting foreigners private meetings, the regularity with which otherwise insignificant missionaries met with the Emperor is conspicuous. Virtually every missionary memoir from the period describes multiple personal audiences with Selassie.⁷⁰ Beyond their role in encouraging his conservative-minded modernization project, for Selassie, these private meetings had multiple purposes. For one, as a master of international diplomacy, he knew that granting these audiences

---

66 Hanson and Hanson, *God and the Emperor*, 180–85.
67 Hanson and Hanson.
68 While not relevant to our central point here, Hanson herself became an important part of the public image of US-Ethiopia relations in 1943, when Henry Luce's *Life* magazine did a cover story on "Haile Selassie's Housekeeper," which included pictures of Hanson comfortably interacting with the royal family and calling her "Housekeeper, lady in waiting, and advisor on American affairs to the Negus Haile Selassie … [and] virtually the third most important person in Ethiopia." "Haile Selassie's Housekeeper," 1943, NARA/RG 165/77/778. While the article goes to lengths to show the importance of Hanson to the Emperor, the image of a White American acting as a servant for an African leader is an interesting one in the context of an America still living under Jim Crow. It was almost certainly noticed by the African American community.
69 Selassie's relationship with Don McClure, while of an entirely different nature and not as close, is still another case of a strong bond forged between Haile Selassie and an American missionary during this period. See McClure, *Red-Headed, Rash and Religious*; and Partee, *Adventures in Africa*.
70 Hanson and Hanson, *God and the Emperor*; McClure, *Red-headed, Rash and Religious*; Hege, *Beyond Our Prayers*.

was likely to create goodwill among the missionaries' American support base; and it is reasonable to assume that he hoped evangelical goodwill might influence US public opinion, and thus US policy, in Ethiopia's favor.

The Emperor also used these audiences as a means of gaining information about areas of his nation almost entirely isolated from Ethiopia's cultural and political center, and about which his government had little reliable knowledge. Towards this end, some missionary audiences took on the feel of an intelligence briefing. In letters to family and supporters, the Presbyterian missionary Don McClure described lengthy meetings with Selassie and his private secretary in which McClure answered their questions concerning "the customs, numbers, [and] political system" of the Anuak people, while the private secretary took "copious notes."[71]

In another incident with the same missionary, the Emperor "wanted to know of the inroads of Islam and communism in the [Ethiopian] west."[72] And in another meeting still, McClure related to the Selassie's private secretary that the tribe he worked amongst "had become ... resentful of the imperial government" because of the government's refusal to allow them to be taught "in their own language."[73] In short, it is likely that Selassie believed frequent contact with American missionaries would have a positive effect in his relationship with the US; and it is certain that he gleaned valuable information about remote parts of his nation from these audiences.

Yet, there is another explanation that also helps to shed light on the frequency of these meetings. In reading the missionary accounts of these audiences, the most striking theme is the relatively guileless discussion that took place concerning spiritual issues. In one sense, this is not surprising. The evangelical missionaries were in Ethiopia for religious reasons, and the Emperor was a practicing Christian. Yet in the context of the notoriously reserved Ethiopian culture, personally candid discussions of this nature were unusual.[74] It is, therefore noteworthy that in Selassie's meetings with American missionaries he displayed a remarkable level of openness and vulnerability. For instance, he confessed his own sense of weakness to Hanson by saying that the only way he managed to handle the demands of his position was his reliance on God. "If God didn't help me," he explained, "I could do nothing."[75] The same expression of personal fragility was made in 1945 to the prominent Presbyterian minister and Billy Graham mentor,

---

71 Partee, *Adventures in Africa*, 268.
72 Partee, 270.
73 Partee, 306.
74 Lockot, *Mission: Life, Reign*, 51.
75 Hanson and Hanson, *God and the Emperor*, 177.

Donald Barnhouse, when Selassie confided that his favorite passage of Scripture was Jesus's promise of rest to the weary and heavy-laden.[76]

The Emperor's willingness to engage in spiritual conversations is a window into his religious worldview and helps explain both the close relationship he nurtured with the American evangelical missionary community and his attraction to the United States more generally. His biographer, Hans Wilhelm Lockot, has described Selassie as having the soul of a mystic, and the evidence of his life bears this out.[77] In addition to his interest in the progress of the missionaries, the Emperor began every day by going to Orthodox Mass, was widely read in Christian devotional literature (both ancient and contemporary, Orthodox and evangelical), was a regular listener to evangelical Christian radio programming in Addis Ababa, and could quote from the Bible at length, verbatim.

When combined with the Ethiopian penchant for melding the worlds of religion and politics, Haile Selassie's personal faith produced a worldview remarkably similar to that of the American evangelical community. In this world, domestic and global political events were visible manifestations of an ultimately more important spiritual war. Whether they were aware of it or not, individuals as well as states took sides in this battle. On one side stood Ethiopia's old nemesis of militant Islam and the rising threat of atheistic communism. On the other side stood Christian believers and the nations that supported them. According to Della Hanson, at the royal family's table "often dinner conversations turned to world conditions and the evil in the hearts of men."[78] Hanson quotes Selassie as saying, "It is the powers of good and evil which are warring against each other."[79] Hanson continued, "He then quoted the words of Paul (the apostle) that evildoers would grow worse and worse in the last days."[80] Another morning at breakfast, after quoting Jesus's reference to the "wars and rumors of wars" that would precede the end of the world, Selassie solemnly remarked, "We are in the end now."[81]

---

76 "Mr. Barnhouse to a Church Group," 15 January 1945. SIM/SIM General/3/Various Early Reports; Graham, *Just as I Am*, 46, 284, 295, and 317.
77 Lockot, *Mission: Life, Reign*, 53.
78 Hanson and Hanson, *God and the Emperor*, 175.
79 Hanson and Hanson. This sort of statement was not unique in Selassie's conversations with missionaries. During an intimate and informal tea with his daughter and four SIM missionaries in Gondar, the Emperor stated in the context of a conversation about the importance of the Bible in people's lives that, "I …… believe man's heart is either the temple of God or of Satan," SIM/SIM General/Box 3/Haile Selassie.
80 Hanson and Hanson, *God and the Emperor*, 175.
81 Hanson and Hanson.

Selassie was a remarkably rational and politically shrewd leader, but he was also a deeply religious person whose beliefs influenced his politics, pushing him—despite consistently strong domestic opposition—into a close relationship with the American evangelical community and the nation they represented. During this period, when official American attention rarely focused on Ethiopia, it was these informal and religiously rooted relationships between Selassie and the missionary community that helped keep the romance between the US and Ethiopia alive.

The Long Engagement, 1945–1952—Part Two: Winning over the Extended Family

The perceptions of American missionaries also influenced a growing cross-section of evangelicals back home. For years, an extensive and grassroots Christian network had been utilizing a variety of means to relay the perceptions and experiences of missionaries in Ethiopia to their American communities. Mission organizations were an important part of this network. Each group had at least one major publication that went out to the individuals and churches across America that supported its work. The Sudan Interior Mission (SIM), for instance, produced the *Sudan Witness*, a quarterly magazine with a readership of at least 100,000 that highlighted, in often dramatic language, the hardships and the triumphs of the mission's work in Ethiopia and around the world.[82] Yet while SIM was the largest evangelical agency working in Ethiopia at the time with over two hundred missionaries, it did not have the most developed communications network of the American missionary organizations working there. Denominationally based agencies such as the Presbyterians, the Eastern Mennonites, and the Seventh Day Adventists likely had a combined network covering a much larger number of people.

Additional news on Ethiopia, albeit less regularly, also came to evangelical audiences through national publications such as the Billy Graham Evangelical Association's (BGEA) *Decision* Magazine, the National Association of Evangelicals' *United Evangelical Action*, and *Revelation*

---

82 *Sudan Witness* did expand to six issues per year at times during the 1940s and 1950s. This estimate is based on the following: (a) according to the IFMA (Interdenominational Foreign Missions Association) SIM had 1,299 missionaries working worldwide in 1960; (b) a conservative estimate of the average number of churches supporting each SIM missionary—either financially or "spiritually" is five per missionary family with an average readership of twenty in each church, through mission committees and other venues. Therefore, 1,299 (SIM missionaries) x 5 (supporting churches per missionary) x 20 (the average readership of SIM's publication per supporting church) = 129,900. The number of SIM missionaries active in Ethiopia in the early 1950s was not substantially below this figure, hence the estimate of "at least 100,000."

magazine.[83] The news found here was complemented by missionary biographies and memoirs such as Kathleen Friederichsen's *Bob Hockman: Surgeon of the Cross*, Thomas Lambie's *A Doctor Without a Country*, and Don McClure's *Red-Headed, Rash, and Religious*. To a lesser, but still significant degree, mission agencies also utilized television and movies to inform the evangelical community about its work in Ethiopia and other parts of the world. In some cases, these organizations produced their own simple short films for use in church mission meetings across America.[84] In other cases, evangelicals formed partnerships with Hollywood to produce relatively sophisticated movies dramatizing a particular missions-related story. The full-color feature film on the Ethiopian revival, entitled "Outstretched Hands" which came out on the eve of the pivotal US-Ethiopian Mutual Defense Agreement (1953), is an example of this second film type.[85]

While undeniably powerful, the missionary-informed evangelical media in America during this period was not the most important factor tying the American evangelical community to Ethiopia. That distinction went to the thousands of intimate meetings that took place between missionaries to Ethiopia and individual evangelicals across America. It is hard to overemphasize the importance of these personal exchanges. In a recent interview, President Jimmy Carter demonstrated just how significant these missionary visits were for evangelicals. The "most famous people in my town were not [people like] the president of the United States," he recalled. "They were missionaries who ... would travel around on their vacation time and come to our church, and they were exalted like saints."[86]

Although it did not always work out as planned, the typical American missionary family was expected to spend approximately four years "on the field," then return for one year of "furlough" before returning to their field. In many cases, the need to raise the funds necessary for the additional years of service meant that missionaries spent most of their furlough crisscrossing the country, sharing their stories with individual supporters and churches in the hopes of inspiring interest and financial support. Some families with especially pressing financial needs (such as those raising funds for a new hospital or school, in addition to four years' living allowance), or who happened to be in particular demand,

---

83 In 1948 the NAE's United Evangelical Action claimed a circulation of their twice-monthly magazine of thirty-six thousand. See *United Evangelical Action*, April 15, 1948. After it began publication in 1956, *Christianity Today* became an influential news source on Ethiopia. See, for instance, *Christianity Today* cover page, 4 February 1957.
84 *Sudan Witness*, 1958, Vol. 34, No. 6.
85 *Sudan Witness*, 1952, Vol. 28, No. 2.
86 Lindsay, *Faith in the Halls*, 30.

might speak to as many as 150 church groups and twenty thousand people within the year.[87] While the average missionary family spoke to numbers considerably smaller than that, every missionary family on furlough was obligated to speak to multiple church groups, in addition to numerous dinners and receptions with friends and supporters. In the 1950s, SIM alone averaged approximately thirty family groupings on furlough from Ethiopia in a given year. When put together with the other evangelical mission groups active in Ethiopia, the number of American evangelicals during this period with personal, and often financial, commitments to Ethiopia easily spills into the hundreds of thousands.[88]

Missionaries in Ethiopia also welcomed influential American visitors who would return and spread the word of their work in the country. One such prominent visitor was the nationally syndicated radio host, Rev. Donald Barnhouse, whose personal audience with the Emperor in 1945 was repeated to numerous congregations across the country over the following year.[89] In short, thanks to this extensive grassroots network, it is almost certain that, regarding Ethiopia, evangelical Christians during the early Cold War period were among the most knowledgeable and engaged sector of the general American populace.

It is notable that the message that spread through this network was one of virtually universal and enthusiastic approval for Ethiopia and its Emperor. Article after article, letter after letter, and speech after speech expressed the firm conviction that Haile Selassie was, at his core, a genuine

---

87 While this was uncommon in the 1950s, it has become the norm in some denominationally based organizations today. Missionaries from the Assemblies of God regularly speak at between 75 and 150 churches, with audiences between fifty and five thousand per service. Based on the author's correspondence with Assemblies of God missionaries working in the Horn of Africa, 7 March 2008.

88 According to *Sudan Witness*, 1957, Vol. 33, No. 6, in 1957 SIM had 228 missionaries in Ethiopia, approximately one-fourth of whom would be on furlough in any given year. However, because approximately 80 percent of these missionaries were married, the number of missionary groupings addressing church groups was not fifty-seven per year, but something closer to thirty-four. If we estimate that the remaining American mission organizations had only a combined number of sixteen missionary groupings on furlough in a given year (which is almost certainly well below the actual number) we have a total of fifty missionary groupings. While some missionary groupings might only have three or four supporting churches, those missionaries connected to a denomination were often encouraged to speak to denominational churches throughout the region, if not the country. If we estimate that each missionary grouping spoke to only ten churches per year, with an audience of one hundred per service (both are likely conservative numbers), we have a total of fifty thousand. Over a four-year cycle that number becomes 200,000. Some missionaries to Ethiopia like the Presbyterian Don McClure spoke so often while on furlough that he often joked he needed to get back to Ethiopia so he could get some rest—this from someone whose work schedule in Ethiopia could only be described as frantic. See Partee, *Adventure in Africa*, 256.

89 Barnhouse, "In the Emperor's Palace," SIM/SIM General/1/Barnhouse.

"born again Christian" and deeply sympathetic to evangelical values and aims. As early as 1946, Gordon Beecham could write in SIM's *Sudan Witness* that in his recent personal interview with the Emperor, Haile Selassie had given a "ringing testimony to his own personal faith."[90] Indeed, the words Selassie used could have come from a Billy Graham crusade: "I know that I am saved," Selassie told Beecham, "not by anything that is of character or the works of the human heart, but by the blood of Jesus Christ alone."[91] In addition, evangelical missionaries could report back home on the personal interest Selassie took in their work as demonstrated by regular visits to their hospitals, schools, and churches. In one extreme case, the Emperor visited a Mennonite school for the blind seventeen times in a year.[92] Through both his words and deeds, Haile Selassie confirmed to Early Cold War American evangelicals their already deep conviction that he was "one of us."[93]

Also clear from these evangelical accounts is the message that Haile Selassie's Christian convictions had political consequences. Not only did the missionaries see the Emperor as a benevolent and progressive leader, seeking to improve the condition of the Ethiopian people through literacy, moral education, and health care, but they perceived the logic of the reforms he introduced as fundamentally in line with the liberal democratic tradition. For instance, while presenting an honorary doctorate to Haile Selassie in 1949 at the influential and staunchly evangelical Wheaton College, Dr. Joseph Evans held up the Ethiopian flag he had received from the Ethiopian ambassador and stated that he hoped the flag would be a, "symbolic expression of our sympathetic understanding [with Ethiopia, and would] remain in our College as a remembrance of H.I.M. Emperor Haile Selassie, the great moral leader of Ethiopia."[94] While uttered in 1966, the statement that nevertheless provides the most succinct summation of evangelical opinion concerning Haile Selassie's politics during the 1940s and 1950s came in Billy Graham's introduction of the Emperor as Selassie was set to deliver a keynote address to the Berlin World Congress on Evangelism. Said Graham:

> Thirty-five years ago there came to the throne Haile Selassie the First. He established a written constitution. He established a parliament, a modern system of communication, built roads, hospitals, schools and universities. And then ... during the heroic

---

90 Beecham, "Testimony of His Imperial," 5.
91 Beecham, 5.
92 Hege, *Beyond Our Prayers*, 73.
93 "King Came," 24; "In the Emperor's Palace," *Revelation Magazine*, August 1946; among others.
94 "Honorary Degree Is Conferred," 1, BGC/CN363/1/3.

days of the war ... when he returned to his country on May the 5th, 1941, he announced to the world that in Ethiopia, Christian ethics in government, liberty of conscience, and democratic institutions would prevail in his country. The Emperor of Ethiopia is a man who goes to church and is a worshipper of Jesus Christ as Lord and Saviour.[95]

In short, Haile Selassie was White evangelical America's type of leader and in the religiously infused context of the global Cold War, this religious and ideological affinity mattered. There was, however, one other group of Americans that could boast a similar level of interest in Ethiopia.

The Long Engagement, 1945–1952—Part Three: Evangelical Religion and "Enchanted Internationalism" in Black America

Although their aims were usually secular, and their numerical presence on the ground was significantly smaller and far less consistent than their White evangelical missionary counterparts, the African American community could also claim a long and spiritually inspired engagement with Ethiopia. Soon after the countries began official diplomatic relations in 1903, an African American businessman visited Ethiopia on behalf of the US government. This visit was followed by the emigration of at least one African American to Ethiopia in 1909, a small and colorful handful of other short-term emigres during the 1920s and 1930s, and a two-year effort to help rebuild the country by almost one hundred African American professionals between 1944 and 1946.[96]

Ethiopia was not, of course, the only African nation to garner attention from Black America. Based on their proud and ancient past, their previous connections to the slave trade, and a history of relative independence from European colonial control, by the middle of the twentieth century, Mali, Ghana, Liberia, Sudan, and Egypt could all claim positions of relative symbolic prominence within the Black community. Despite its lack of connection to the slave trade, Ethiopia, however, stood apart from the others. The principal reason for Ethiopia's preferential status was religious.

The story of this spiritually inspired bond between Black America and Ethiopia begins with the first and second Great Awakenings. As had been true for much of America, these nation-wide revivals transformed the religious landscape for African Americans. The social and emotional force of the evangelical Christian salvation narrative, along with its explicit message that all people are equal before God, brought large numbers of Black

---

95 "Address by Haile Selassie," 26 October 1966, BGC/CN14/Tape 1, Side 2.
96 Harris, *African-American Reactions*, 2, 6–18.

Americans into the churches during the First Great Awakening (1730–1750), a trend that continued during the Second Great Awakening (1790–1840) in the form of new Black denominations and the Abolitionist movement.[97] So pivotal was this turn to Christianity within the Black community, that Frey and Wood have called it, "the single most significant event in African American history ... the principal solvent of ethnic differences and the primary source of [African American] cultural identity." It provided, they concluded, "Afro-Atlantic Christians with an ideology of resistance and the means ... that turned Africans into African Americans."[98]

Like its White evangelical counterpart, Black evangelicalism was rooted in the authority of the Bible. However, when interpreted through the experience of slavery and discrimination, the biblical themes of equality before God, emancipation from sin and slavery, and justice for the oppressed, upended the political status quo and at times pushed Black evangelicals towards very different conclusions from their White evangelical counterparts. In the same way, the images of Ethiopia in the Bible, which had significance for all Christians, took on additional symbolic importance for Black Christians. This was true to such an extent that, from at least the nineteenth century, Ethiopia had become for African Americans a "shorthand" for the "exaltation of all African peoples ... [and the] reversal of their collective fortunes."[99]

While some, like Blyden and Garvey, who went on to lead the "Ethiopianist" and "Back to Africa" movements were not traditional evangelicals, it was nevertheless this biblically inspired vision that animated their message and gave the Ethiopia metaphor its resonance. And this metaphor had real-life consequences. Throughout the nineteenth and twentieth centuries the most quoted biblical passage in African American letters and sermons was a prophecy from Psalm 68 that, "Ethiopia shall soon stretch out her hands unto God."[100] During the first half of the twentieth century, Black Americans started to reach back, making their way in small numbers to Ethiopia.[101]

It has been said that "we define our reality in terms of metaphors and then proceed to act on the basis of metaphors."[102] The problem with this is that metaphors, by definition, aren't the real thing. For many early

---

97 Callahan, *Talking Book*, 3.
98 Frey and Wood, *Come Shouting to Zion*, 1; Callahan, *Talking Book*, xi–6.
99 Callahan, 139.
100 Ps 68:31 (KJV).
101 "American Negroes in Ethiopia," 4 January 1943, NARA RG 165/77/776; Harris, *African-American Reactions*.
102 Lakoff and Johnson, *Metaphors We Live By*, 5.

African American emigres to Ethiopia, the gap between the metaphor and reality became painfully clear. On the eve of the single largest influx of African Americans to Ethiopia in 1944, one US intelligence report expressed concern about the continuing idealization of Ethiopia saying, that previous emigres had pictured Ethiopia as, "a paradise in the African highlands, where any colored person, free from any discrimination, would feel entirely at home, enjoy respect and be given opportunities to attain high posts and influence."[103] But on a number of levels this simply wasn't true. In the first half of the twentieth century, Ethiopia remained largely mired in political, cultural, and economic feudalism, resulting from sixteen hundred years of self-imposed isolation.[104]

In addition to their surprise at the "backwardness" of the country, the report noted the "unsympathetic reception" previous emigres had been given by all ranks of Ethiopian society. Ethiopians, the report continued, "with the conviction they have of themselves of a super-race of Africans ... equal to any white race, treated them [Black Americans] as members of the lowest racial groups, in no way better than the slave element in the country."[105] This observation was supported by none other than Marcus Garvey who, upon feeling snubbed by Haile Selassie during the Emperor's exile in England in the late 1930s, had called the Ethiopian monarch the, "snobbish Lion of Judah ... ruler of a country where black men are chained and flogged."[106] Not surprisingly, when their two-year contract expired in 1946, all but a small handful of the African Americans working in Ethiopia returned to the US, dampening a potentially significant ongoing partnership between the ancient Christian kingdom and the biblically-inspired African American community.[107]

Yet, disappointment by a few with the real Ethiopia did not meaningfully weaken its power as a metaphor. In the lead up to the pivotal 1953–1954 period, biblical references to Ethiopia and praise for its revered Emperor, continued to have a prominent place in African American sermons, civic rights rhetoric, and in the writings of Black intellectuals. Ironically, the non-

---

103 "American Negroes in Ethiopia," 4 January 1943, NARA RG 165/77/776.

104 This was a conviction also shared by many Ethiopians as seen in the scathing public critique of Ethiopia by the Crown Prince during a failed coup attempt in December of 1960. Quoted in diplomatic cable, "Amembassy Addis Ababa to Secstate Washington," 14 December 1960. NARA RG684/2438/350.

105 "American Negroes in Ethiopia," 4 January 1943, NARA RG 165/77/776. This assessment, which references the culturally dominant and ruling Amhara people is largely supported by scholars of Ethiopia; a summary of scholarly opinion on Ethiopia and race can be found in Sorenson, *Imagining Ethiopia*, 12–29.

106 Sorenson, *Imagining Ethiopia*, 25.

107 Harris, *African American Reactions*, 150.

religious African American playwright and activist, Lorraine Hansberry, perhaps best symbolizes the intersection of the spiritually infused Ethiopia metaphor with the ongoing work of White evangelical missionaries in early Cold War Ethiopia. For it was Hansberry's father, Leo, who co-founded the influential Ethiopian Research Council with Melaku Bayen; and it was Melaku whose time at the conservative Presbyterian, Muskingum College had inspired the martyr Bob Hockman to begin his missionary work in Ethiopia.[108] "We had been saying for a long time," Hansberry recalled from her childhood, that "Ethiopia will stretch out ... her hands!" Speaking for many in the Black community Hansberry concluded, "I didn't know anything about Spain, but I certainly did know about Ethiopia."[109]

In sum, the "Long Engagement" period between 1945 and 1952 was relatively quiet as far as official US-Ethiopia relations are concerned. Nevertheless, behind the scenes, continuing engagement in Ethiopia by spiritually-inspired Americans—White and Black—had produced a field ripe for the diplomatic harvest. As we have just seen, the biblical connection between the Black community in America and Ethiopia had turned the East African nation into a powerful metaphor that resonated well beyond the walls of Black evangelical congregations. Similarly, thanks to the remarkably close relationship of their missionaries to the Ethiopian Emperor, and the effectiveness of their sprawling grassroots news network, the large and rapidly growing White evangelical community had become strongly pro-Selassie, and therefore, pro-Ethiopia. Thus, on the eve of the 1953 Mutual Defense Assistance Agreement and Haile Selassie's state visit in 1954, a sizable portion of the American public were, as one scholar put it, "eager to be impressed."[110]

The Wedding (1953–1954)

By almost any measure, 1953–1954 represented a substantial advance in US-Ethiopian relations. For Ethiopia, the Mutual Defense Assistance Agreement of 1953 was a game-changer. As a legal document, it pledged the US and Ethiopia to defend the other in the event of a hostile attack and committed the US to future investment in Ethiopia's modernization and internal security. Most important for the Americans was the accompanying agreement that gave the US military complete control of the key intelligence station at Kagnew. Together, these 1953 agreements were the consummation

---

108 Harris, 155.
109 Callahan, *Talking Book*, 175.
110 Vestal, *Lion of Judah*, 192.

of a surprisingly close relationship between a poor and relatively isolated African country and the world's greatest superpower.[111]

If the 1953 agreements represent the diplomatic equivalent of a marriage certificate, Selassie's state visit to the US in 1954 was the party—and it was a big one. In addition to the ticker tape parade in Manhattan, his meetings with Eisenhower, and the official state dinner and night in the White House, over the next two months, Selassie and his camera-friendly entourage covered virtually every corner of the continental US.[112] In his capacity as the salesman for economic investment in Ethiopia, the Emperor toured auto-plants in Michigan, stockyards in Chicago, the Grand Coulee Dam in Washington state, oil refineries in California, farmlands in rural Minnesota, and a leading agricultural college in Oklahoma. As a champion of modern education in Africa, he visited, among other universities, Harvard, Princeton, Columbia, the University of Michigan, and Howard—the latter three of whom bestowed on him honorary degrees. Demonstrating his appreciation of American pop-culture, Selassie also took in a game at Yankee Stadium, where he was given a glove by famed manager Casey Stengel and visited the Twentieth Century Fox movie studios in Hollywood. Wherever he went, Selassie was lauded, as he had been by President Eisenhower, as a "defender of freedom and a supporter of progress."[113]

Less prominent in the national press, but dominating the African American papers, were Selassie's interactions with Black America, in particular, his extended tour of the segregated South and his visits to several African American congregations in Harlem and Chicago.[114] For the African American community, the significance of Selassie's state visit would have been immense under any circumstances, but his arrival happened to correspond with one of the most significant moments of the twentieth century for Black Americans. Less than two weeks before he landed in the US, the Supreme Court had handed down their verdict in Brown v. Board of Education, a unanimous ruling determining that racial segregation in public schools, and by extension likely all "separate but equal" laws, was unconstitutional.

The Brown decision included considerable risks for the United States, both domestically and internationally. Domestically the decision risked plunging a divided nation into open and racially rooted conflict.

---

111 Baissa, "United States Military Assistance," 53.
112 Selassie also visited Canada and Mexico briefly during this time, including an address to the Canadian parliament in Ottawa.
113 Vestal, "Emperor Haile Selassie's," 133–52. Schumach, "Selassie at Ball Park."
114 Chicago Defender, "Hail Haile Selassie."

Internationally, Brown could either weaken the country's claim to moral leadership, by reminding the world of its history of slavery and racial injustice, or it could act as evidence of a free nation's ability to conquer its demons. The Cold War implications of the decision were not lost on US policymakers. In an Amicus brief the government had argued that the Court needed to view the case from the "context of the present world struggle between freedom and tyranny." American racial discrimination, as seen in Jim Crow laws, they argued, "has an adverse effect on our relations with other countries [and] furnishes grist for the communist propaganda mills."[115]

It was into this moment, with America and the world watching, that Africa's most potent symbol of independence stepped. Ignoring America's checkered history would alienate the Black community, some of whom worried that "the Emperor did not wish to be identified with American Negroes" and undermine his own moral stature.[116] On the other hand, a censorious focus on that history would embarrass his host and throw the young diplomatic marriage between Ethiopia and the United States into crisis. He did neither. Instead, in a diplomatic masterclass, Selassie skillfully utilized the Brown decision to identify with the cause of Black America while simultaneously praising the moral leadership of the United States.

Speaking at the historically Black Howard University, Selassie presented an empowering message, arguing that it was the advances of Black Americans which were forcing the world to "recognize the important contributions made by colored peoples everywhere" and that "[e]vents of recent days, here in the U.S., have brilliantly confirmed before the world the contributions that you have made to the principle that all men are brothers and equal in the sight of God." These words, and others like it during his tour of the US, confirmed Selassie's revered place in the Black community to such an extent that the *Chicago Defender* approvingly quoted one observer to the effect that the Ethiopian monarch had become, "the king of colored people." The State Department appeared to be no less pleased. Capitalizing on numerous remarks by Selassie suggesting that the "historic" Brown decision would, "win the esteem of the entire world," the government took every opportunity to highlight the accomplishments of Black Americans during the Emperor's visit.[117]

Also hidden in the glitz and glamour were Selassie's meetings with American evangelical groups and especially those with connections to his

---

115 Nathaniel, *50th Anniversary*, 125.
116 *Chicago Defender*, "Hail Haile Selassie."
117 Nathaniel, *50th Anniversary*, 126.

missionary friends. For instance, upon arrival in the US, the first group he met with were not political or economic leaders, but an intimate reception hosted by the deeply religious American Ambassador to Ethiopia that included "nine officials of Lutheran church organizations."[118] Similarly symbolic of this dynamic was the Emperor's visit to Della Hanson's modest family home in California on the back of his trip to Hollywood. Well out of the public spotlight, this visit was clearly personally meaningful for the Ethiopian monarch. Seeing Hanson immediately upon his return to Ethiopia, "his dignified look turned to smiles" Hanson recalled, as "He told me he had seen my mother, sister, and brother" who, he assured her in typical Ethiopian fashion, "were in good health."[119]

As important as these events and interactions were in building an affective bridge between the American people and Ethiopia, the most symbolically and politically significant moment of Selassie's six-week trip was his address to a joint session of Congress on May 28th. It was here, with the entire nation listening, that Selassie had the chance to make Ethiopia's argument for an ongoing and intimate partnership with the United States. Reproduced the following morning by the *New York Times*, the speech was extraordinary.

Selassie began by making his admiration for the United States clear, calling America's rise to global prominence "unparalleled in world history," before deftly portraying "profoundly African" Ethiopia as a land of boundless and untapped economic potential, and a willing partner in America's vision for a free and prosperous world. As he did so, the Emperor effectively positioned Ethiopia at the center of the coming Cold War struggle for the global south, claiming for his nation a uniquely strategic "link between the Middle East and Africa" where the United States needed a trusted partner. Then, at the heart of his speech, Selassie laid out what he believed to be the foundation for a US-Ethiopian partnership.[120]

Recalling his nation's ancient Christian heritage, Selassie argued at length that it was Ethiopia's Christian "ideals and principles" that "alone" explained his nation's "profound orientation towards the West." Confirming the claims of his American missionary friends, Selassie anchored his Cold War politics in the presumption of a transnational religious kinship. "We read the same Bible," he continued, "We speak a common spiritual language." As he concluded his historic address to Congress, Selassie again

---

118 Kihss, "Ethiopian Emperor Lands."
119 Hanson and Hanson, *God and the Emperor*, 183–84.
120 "Selassie's Address to U.S. Congress."

returned to this theme. It is "our common Christian heritage [that] unites two peoples across the globe in a community of ideals and endeavor."[121]

The Honeymoon, 1955–1960

The glow of good feelings surrounding the Emperor's 1954 state visit lingered and helped to produce a steady stream of generally positive interactions between Ethiopia and the United States up through the end of 1960. The increased American money and personnel that began flowing into the country because of the 1953 agreements was followed by a steady stream of high-profile visits to Ethiopia, including the first Congressional visit led by a woman, Francis Bolton, in 1955, and an official state visit by Vice President Nixon in 1957. Both visits were highly successful and bore the marks of the missionary-inspired good feelings between the nations. In her trip summary, Frances Bolton, for instance, spoke highly of the "many consecrated missionaries" she had met along the way and highlighted Ethiopia's role as the vanguard of a free and independent Africa. Unlike most of Africa, she said, where "freedom is as yet only a dream," "His Imperial Majesty" had recently adopted a new constitution (1955), which would "build a more democratic government."[122] For his part, Vice President Nixon praised the hospitality of the Emperor and returned the favor in 1969, when Selassie was the first foreign head of state to be welcomed to the White House by the newly elected President.[123]

Behind the scenes, the close relationship that Selassie enjoyed with the evangelical American missionary community continued more or less unchanged. The most notable change in this otherwise steady relationship was the introduction of evangelical elites in the form of International Christian Leadership (ICL) and the Billy Graham Evangelistic Association (BGEA). By 1955, ICL in America was associated primarily with the Bible study groups it facilitated on Capitol Hill and the National Prayer Breakfast it organized annually. While the well-connected group's primary aim was to encourage a personal Christian faith in politically prominent individuals, ICL's transnational network of international leaders sometimes acted as a channel for backchannel diplomacy.[124] This was certainly true in the case of Ethiopia.

---

121 "Selassie's Address to U.S. Congress."
122 Bolton, "View of Africa," 122, 125.
123 "Remarks of Welcome," *Public Papers: Nixon*, 1969, 494.
124 Vereide to Ambassador Joseph Simonson, 26 March 1957, BGC, CN 459, Box 209, Folder 6. Also see Getter, "Showing Faith in Discretion." This article provides evidence linking ICL to an anti-communist film used by the Pentagon throughout the world in the 1950s, a significant role in the Camp David Peace accord of 1978, effective "backchannel" diplomacy leading to a cease-fire between the DRC and Rwanda in 2001 and

The Addis Ababa chapter of ICL was initiated in 1955 by none other than the American ambassador soon after Selassie returned from the United States. In addition to Ambassador Simonson, the first exploratory meeting included the Ethiopian ambassador to Italy, the Greek ambassador to Ethiopia, other members of the Italian and American diplomatic missions, several ranking members of Haile Selassie's government, and leaders of the international business and academic communities.[125] Over the next five years, ICL in Ethiopia became an important point of contact between the Ethiopian elite, the American evangelical missionary community, and US policymakers in Ethiopia and Washington.

Between 1956 and 1960, the leadership committee of ICL in Addis Ababa was active and included members of each of these three groups. Joining Dr. K. M. Simon, the missionary who had taken over leadership of ICL on the departure of Ambassador Simonson, were at least two additional members of the US diplomatic corps and a large number of the Ethiopian elite, including Prince Asrat Kassa (the vice president of the senate), Endelkachew Mekonnen (a future prime minister), Prince Eskender Desta (commander of the Imperial Navy and the favored grandson of the Emperor), and several of Haile Selassie's Imperial Cabinet.[126] In addition to acting as ICL's official patron and encouraging influential Ethiopians to join the group, the Emperor donated two thousand square meters of land near the center of the city as a potential meeting place for the group.[127]

Interaction between the Ethiopian chapter of ICL and the Washington congressional chapters was frequent. Eisenhower's right-hand man, Senator Frank Carlson of Kansas and other leading ICL men corresponded regularly with ranking members of the Ethiopian government. The Ethiopian ambassador to the United States was also a regular at ICL conferences in

---

a host of other foreign policy interventions. Additionally, it should be noted that Frank Carlson, the leader of the Senate chapter of ICL and one of the people most involved in the developing Ethiopian chapter, had been Eisenhower's campaign manager, and was close to the president—a fact that might help explain why Haile Selassie was invited on an official state visit in 1954 over the objections of Secretary of State Dulles (along with the push for a state visit by the current US Ambassador Simonson [the founder of ICL in Ethiopia]). See "Breakfast with the President"; and Spencer, *Ethiopia at Bay*, 268.

125 "Minutes of first ICL meeting taken by Dr. Thomas Melady," 6 October 1955, BGC/459/209/5.

126 Multiple sources within BGC/CN 459/209/5 and 6. There are no records indicating that Haile Selassie ever attended the meetings, but this would have been extremely unusual considering the strains such an involvement would have placed on the highly symbolic etiquette of Imperial Ethiopia. There is, however, abundant evidence that he was an enthusiastic supporter of the project.

127 Coe to Ambassador Richards, 21 July 1960, NARA/RG84/2438/570.3.

Washington, and members of the Ethiopian chapter were often invited to ICL events in Washington and elsewhere.[128] These relationships led to both public and private calls for even closer ties between the two countries. For instance, on the eve of Vice President Nixon's widely publicized trip to Africa in 1957, ICL chose a recently retired US diplomat to Ethiopia, Dr. Thomas Melady, to address their annual Washington conference on the topic, "Africa: Challenge to America." Not surprisingly in his speech to the well-connected group, Dr. Melady singled out Ethiopia as a critical battle ground in both the spiritual and political global Cold War.[129]

Like the relationships that developed between American missionaries and the US diplomatic community during this period, links between ICL's relational network and American or Ethiopian policy were rarely formal or explicit. That said, as a conduit of "enchanted internationalism," a significant number of American political and diplomatic elites received favorable views of Ethiopia in the late 1950s as a result of this evangelical organization's work.[130] Indeed, the strength of the relationship between the US and Ethiopia during Ambassador Simonson's tenure in particular can be at least partially explained by the personal relationships Simonson, Melady, Carlson, and others had been able to nurture with the Emperor and many of the Ethiopian elite through ICL.[131]

The case of Billy Graham is a second example of the American evangelical elite influence on US-Ethiopia relations. Graham's widely publicized tour of Africa brought him to Addis Ababa on March 7, 1960. During his time in Ethiopia, Graham and his team met with evangelical missionaries to discuss their work and the state of Ethiopian culture and politics, adding to the extensive background knowledge the organization had accumulated in the build-up to the crusade.[132] In addition to addressing enthusiastic crowds of some twenty-five thousand Ethiopians, Graham also had personal meetings with the American ambassador and his wife, the entire US embassy staff, the Ethiopian Crown Prince, and Haile

---

128 Vereide to Dr. Melady, 21 December 1955, BGC/CN459/209/5; Coe to Ambassador Richards, 21 July 1960, NARA/RG84/2438/570.3; Vereide to Emperor Haile Selassie, 13 April 1956, BGC/CN459/209/5.
129 "Africa: Challenge to America" by Dr. Thomas Melady, Address to the Annual Washington, DC conference of International Christian Leadership, BGC/CN 459/209/6.
130 McAlister, *Kingdom of God*, 12.
131 See multiple documents including letters between ICL leaders and Ambassador Simons, Haile Selassie, Ethiopian Naval Commander Eskendar Desta and others in BGC archives 459/209/5.
132 *Christianity Today*, "Safari's End," 32.

Selassie, which was to be the start of a fifteen year friendship with the Ethiopia Emperor. From statements he made immediately following the trip, and indeed for years to come, it is clear that Graham left Ethiopia deeply impressed with Selassie and convinced that the Ethiopian Emperor would be a trustworthy ally of both evangelical Christianity and American Cold War foreign policy.[133]

Upon his return to the United States, Graham had widely publicized meetings with both President Eisenhower and Vice President Nixon covering, among other things, his experience in Ethiopia.[134] While these meetings are often dismissed as meaningless photo opportunities, by this time Graham had not only come to represent the concerns of the evangelical community—a community beginning to flex its political and cultural muscle—but had forged deep relationships with many in the policymaking community, not least of whom were Eisenhower and Nixon themselves. Well before these meetings Graham had already become an unofficial advisor and close confidant to both men who followed his international meetings with great interest.[135] Indeed, it was Eisenhower who said that Graham was "the greatest Ambassador that America has."[136] The diplomatic potency of Graham's trip to Ethiopia was augmented by the premiere of a feature film on his Africa crusade at the National Guard Armory just two months later, and addresses by Graham on the global threat of communism at ICL prayer breakfasts for both houses of Congress in which over one hundred congressmen and over fifty senators (including Lyndon Johnson, George Smathers and Frank Carlson) were present.[137]

As the personification of American evangelicalism, with its earnest evangelistic internationalism, anti-communist conservativism, and increasing public prominence, Billy Graham's Ethiopian visit is a fitting symbolic conclusion to this religiously infused period in US-Ethiopian

---

133 Among many instances of Graham's public praise of Selassie, perhaps the most notable is his personal choice of Haile Selassie to address the World Congress on Evangelism in Berlin in 1966. See "Address by Haile Selassie I of Ethiopia," 26 October 1966, BGC/CN14, Tape 1, Side 2.

134 New York Times, "Emperor's Kin Hear Graham"; Billy Graham Africa Tour TV Release #10, BGC/CN 54/22/7; "Graham Confers with President," *United Evangelical Action*, May 1960; BGC/CN 360/93, Reel 14, 88–14.

135 Gibbs and Duffy, *Preacher and the Presidents*. The book is littered with astonishing anecdotes of Graham's influence in the Eisenhower and Nixon administrations. The most dramatic examples relate to his relationship with Nixon whose friendship Graham called in 1960 "one of the most cherished I have had."

136 Pierard, "From Evangelical Exclusivism," 174.

137 *Christianity Today*, "Graham Crusade," 31.

relations. As we have seen, between 1945 and 1960, the United States and Ethiopia developed a surprisingly close Cold War relationship that was to make Ethiopia the single largest recipient of US aid to sub-Saharan Africa. While both nations had valid geopolitical reasons for maintaining some sort of partnership, the US-Ethiopian relationship extended well beyond calculated self-interest. This chapter has argued that the affection which characterized US-Ethiopian relations during this period makes the most sense when the influence of American evangelical missionaries is taken into account.

That influence was demonstrated in different ways at each stage in the relationship. Between their arrival in 1918 and Ethiopia's return to independence in 1941, the faith-driven dedication of American evangelical missionaries to Ethiopia sparked a biblically rooted transnationalism that had lain largely dormant during Ethiopia's 1600 years of isolation. The role American missionaries played in inspiring Selassie's trust in the US prior to 1941 was then matched between 1941 and 1945, when the perceptions of American policymakers, most notably FDR, were influenced by these same missionaries. Even during the relative diplomatic hiatus that followed the FDR-Selassie meetings in 1945, the missionary influence on US-Ethiopian relations grew. In large part, this was due to the remarkable personal relationships that had developed between the Ethiopian Emperor and some American missionaries, and the resulting perception by many American evangelicals that Haile Selassie was "one of us," perception shared for similar reasons by many in the African American community.

Together with the increasing involvement of evangelical elites like ICL and Billy Graham after 1954, over forty years of American missionary engagement with Ethiopia produced a potent and religiously inspired transnational bond that exerted significant influence on US-Ethiopian relations, injecting an authentic element of romance into what would have otherwise been a marriage of convenience. Yet, within the glow of good feelings there lingered the potential for disillusionment. Indeed, even as Billy Graham gave his upbeat assessment on Ethiopia to Eisenhower and Nixon in 1960 there were signs that in Ethiopia, beneath the surface at least, all was not well.

CHAPTER 2

The Great Reversal

The Missionary Factor in US-Ethiopian Cold War Relations, 1960–1991

Between 1960 and 1991, Ethiopia experienced virtually every political permutation conceivable within the context of the global Cold War. Beginning the period as an autocratic but reliable American ally, it then flirted briefly with democratic reform before opting for what Odd Arne Westad has called, "the most important Marxist-inspired transformation in Africa."[1] In the end, the Cold War in Ethiopia concluded much as it had around the world, with the collapse of a Marxist regime and the rise of a nominally democratic and pro-American government.

In this politically capricious climate, the direct influence of evangelical missionaries on US-Ethiopian relations was bound to vary considerably. Indeed, as we shall see, with each new twist in US-Ethiopian relations a different aspect of missionary influence came to the fore. This chapter will follow that ebb and flow through three periods: the final years of Haile Selassie's reign (1960–1974), the ambiguous early years of the Ethiopian revolution (1974–1977), and Ethiopia's ambitious experiment with scientific socialism (1977–1991). I will contend that while old patterns of influence remained, a dramatic increase in American government involvement in pre-revolutionary Ethiopia led to an initial decline in the direct influence of American evangelical missionaries; and that, ironically, it was not until the collapse of the evangelical-friendly Emperor and the rise of a radically Marxist regime that the evangelical missionaries returned to a position of relative significance in US-Ethiopian relations.

US-Ethiopian Relations, 1960–1974:
A Decline in the Influence of Missionaries?

The considerable influence missionaries exerted on early Cold War US-Ethiopian relations had been rooted in their relatively large numbers, intimate knowledge of Ethiopia, and personal relationships with both

---

1 Westad, *Global Cold War*, 251.

Ethiopian and American elites. Despite the fact that the number of American missionaries in Ethiopia grew during the 1960s and early 1970s, and that their understanding of Ethiopian culture continued to be extensive, the relative size and importance of the missionary community *vis-à-vis* the official American presence in Ethiopia experienced a significant decline after 1960.[2]

From a handful of embassy staff in the early 1950s, the official US presence in Ethiopia grew into one of the largest diplomatic, military and aid missions in Africa by the mid-1970s.[3] While the missionaries had once played an important role in defining and nurturing a strong affinity between the nations, by the 1960s geopolitical forces had become the primary impetus behind the now established relationship. Ethiopia's precarious political situation, specifically the increasing threats it was facing in the form of Eritrean and Somali nationalism, and the rising hostility from the region's Arab and Islamic nations in the wake of the Arab-Israeli conflict, demanded a powerful ally.[4]

The US also had their reasons for a continuing relationship with Ethiopia. By the late 1950s, America's close ties to the European colonial powers, and growing global disillusionment with its own interventionist policies, had created an opportunity for the Soviets to replace the United States as the champions of African and Arab nationalism.[5] Thus in 1960, with nearly the entire African continent on the cusp of independence, and with Ethiopia representing both a symbol of African self-determination and one of the only proven American friends in the region, the already strong US attachment to Ethiopia seemed destined to grow.

The scale of American investment in Ethiopia up to the death of Selassie in 1975 indicates the importance the United States now placed on the relationship. Between 1950 and 1975, Ethiopia received close to $300 million in military aid—a figure totaling over 80 percent of US aid to Africa.[6] But American assistance to Ethiopia was not exclusively related

---

[2] The SIM, for instance grew from having 228 missionaries in Ethiopia in 1957 to having over 400 in 1973. *Sudan Witness*, 1957, Vol. 33, No. 1; Cumbers, *Living with the Red*, 4. Yet not only were these groups growing but a significant number of new American evangelical groups were coming to Ethiopia during the late 1950s and 1960s including the Southern Baptists—one of the most influential evangelical missions.

[3] The extent of US involvement in Ethiopia during the period will be spelled out in detail in the following pages.

[4] Agyeman-Duah, *United States and Ethiopia*; Marcus, *Ethiopia, Great Britain*.

[5] Duignan and Gann, *United States and Africa*, 290–93.

[6] These figures come from Iyob and Keller, "US policy in the Horn," 103; and Agyeman-Duah, *United States and Ethiopia*, 48–49. Other scholars who come to similar conclusions are Zwede, *History of Modern Ethiopia*, 184–90; and Duignan and Gann, *United States and Africa*, 317.

to security. Among other things, significant resources and personnel also went into supporting Ethiopia's fledgling educational system. By the mid-1960s, American Peace Corps Volunteers (PCVs) could be found teaching in virtually every government school.[7] The approximately five hundred PCVs in the country at any given time made Ethiopia's allotment the largest in Africa.[8]

At the post-secondary level, education in Ethiopia was also increasingly dominated by secular Americans. As many observers have noted, the nation's premier institution of higher learning, Haile Selassie I University, was "indistinguishable" from the American model.[9] American professors and administrators were ubiquitous and American government funds provided books and equipment for the university's programs and significant infrastructure improvements.[10] All told, by the early 1970s at least four thousand American government employees were in Ethiopia at any given time, and the total US government investment in the country (not including the salaries of the Americans working there) was close to half a billion dollars.[11]

Not surprisingly, the rapid growth of America's official presence in Ethiopia resulted in a decline in the direct influence that evangelical missionaries had on US policymakers. No longer reliant on missionary cultural expertise or links to the crown, American diplomatic, military and intellectual elites generally opted to seek their own counsel with regards to US-Ethiopian relations and left the missionaries to whatever it was that they did. This new arrangement also suited the missionary community who had always felt some ambiguity toward a relationship that could easily compromise their primarily spiritual and moral aims.[12] Thus as the 1960s began, historical circumstances found the diplomatic and missionary worlds functioning in increasing isolation from each other.

---

7 Balsvik, *Haile Selassie's Students*, 11; Zewde, *History of Modern Ethiopia*, 189; Duignan and Gann, *United States and Africa*, 337.
8 Duignan and Gann, 355.
9 Shiferaw Wolde Michael, interview with the author, 17 December 2007. See also Zwede, *History of Modern Ethiopia*, 189.
10 Balsvik, *Haile Selassie's Students*, 197.
11 Iyob and Keller, "US Policy in the Horn," 103; and Agyeman-Duah, *United States and Ethiopia*, 48–49.
12 Ambassador Richard Petree to the author, 25 April 2008. The same description of the relationship between the diplomatic and missionary community was found in emails from a number of retired missionaries from this era—notably the correspondence with the author by Ambassador Petree's close friend, the Presbyterian missionary Harold Kurtz, on 25 September 2007.

The First Crisis: The 1960 Coup Attempt and Aftermath

On 13 December 1960, while Emperor Selassie was on a state visit to Brazil, four high-level conspirators and the groups loyal to them, took control of the Imperial Palace, holding hostage the Crown Prince and approximately fifteen other ranking members of Selassie's government. By the next morning, the rebels had secured the majority of the capital city and forced the Crown Prince to make a national radio address proclaiming a new government under his leadership. Critical to the plans of the conspirators was securing support from the national university's students, something they managed to do with relative ease. After a successful meeting with the university's student leaders the same morning, chanting students flooded the streets creating the impression of grassroots support for the unlikely coup.[13]

Within twenty-four hours, however, it became clear that the coup had failed to gain the support of any of the branches of the armed forces, the hierarchy of the Ethiopian Orthodox Church, and the Ethiopian provinces—all of which remained loyal to Selassie. As a result, when fighting began on 15 December, the rebels were routed. After turning their guns on the members of Selassie's inner circle being held hostage, the conspirators fled. Of the coup's leaders, Tsege Dibu was killed in the fighting, Warquenah Gabayahu and Germane Neway (the coup's instigator) committed suicide, and Mengistu Neway (the Commander of the Imperial Bodyguard) was captured, tried, and later hung for treason. On 17 December, Selassie re-entered Addis Ababa to effusive cheers. The coup attempt was over.[14]

But where had it come from? And to what extent was the coup attempt a symptom of underlying dissatisfaction with Selassie and, therefore, a legitimate threat to his rule? The scholarly consensus has been that, while the 1960 coup attempt did not seriously threaten Selassie's rule, it did uncover the seeds of discontent that would eventually prove to be the Emperor's undoing fourteen years later. Ironically, some of these seeds were the product of Selassie's missionary-inspired affection for American-style modernity—an "abiding faith" his long-time advisor John Spencer observed, that "resisted all disappointments and setbacks."[15]

Three things in particular stand out. First, the transnational spiritual bond that had created such trust between Selassie and the missionary community also appeared to produce in the Americans, both missionaries and secular policymakers, a distorted perception of Selassie as a proponent of classic

---

13 Coup details are taken from Clapham, "Ethiopian Coup d'Etat," 495–507; and Marcus, "1960, the Year," 11–25.
14 Clapham, 495–507; Marcus, 11–25.
15 Spencer, *Ethiopia at Bay*, 156.

political liberalism. At the same time, this "enchanted internationalism" inspired extravagant expectations of US support among the Ethiopian elite and, in particular, the Emperor himself. The disconnect between expectations and reality eventually created so much frustration that, in 1959, Selassie had provocatively accepted an invitation to visit Moscow, temporarily upsetting what had seemed to be a stable and intimate partnership.[16]

Second, in sending the best and the brightest to the US for education, Selassie also created an awareness in the next generation of Ethiopian leaders of the sizable gap that existed between their country and the modern world. For Selassie's protégés, who had been steeped in Ethiopian national folklore and the traditionalist Ethiopian Orthodox Church, this realization produced embarrassment and frustration. In one confidential State Department memorandum from 1956, an Ethiopian studying in America expressed the disillusionment he saw among the educated youth with, among other things, the new 1955 constitution (which he called a "façade" meant to keep the status quo intact), the Ethiopian Orthodox Church (which he called "backward," discriminatory, and out of touch), and the Imperial family (which had "betrayed the liberal cause"). Foreshadowing student support for the 1960 coup attempt, the memorandum quotes "Tekle" as saying he would, "be willing to give up his life in a struggle against the excesses of the Imperial family if he could find a cause to which he could rally."[17]

Finally, by encouraging the American missionaries to develop schools in the outlying provinces—especially those not dominated by the Ethiopian Orthodox Church—Selassie had inadvertently ensured that the previously marginalized periphery would be over-represented in the university and would bring with them an outsider's perspective that was fundamentally suspicious of Imperial power and the Amhara dominated center.[18] Among others, these three missionary-related factors served as indirect causes for the 1960 uprising that continued to fester during the remaining fourteen years of Selassie's reign.

As crises often do, the attempted coup in 1960 also acted to temporarily reverse the trend of decreasing interaction between the American missionary and diplomatic communities. For instance, as the American intelligence community scrambled to gain a picture of what a post-Selassie government might look like, missionaries were again seen as an important

---

16 American Embassy, Addis Ababa, "Review of Current Events in Ethiopia," 3 July 1959, NARA RG 59/3109/67/D226, 13a.
17 Department of State, "Memorandum of Conversation, Ethiopia and the US as seen by an Ethiopian Intellectual," 23 January 1956, NARA RG59/3109/67/D226, 13a.
18 Eide, *Revolution and Religion*, 29.

source of reliable information.¹⁹ A secret government memorandum dated 1 September 1961, quotes ten sources in an attempt to paint a picture of the character, ability level, and political sentiments of Selassie's likely successor, the Crown Prince. Next to high-ranking members of the Ethiopian government and the British and American diplomatic communities are the opinions of two unnamed American missionaries, both of whom viewed the prince as a poor replacement for his father.²⁰

Yet, examples such as this were an exception to the prevailing trend away from formal contact between American evangelical missionaries and their government—a trend that suited the missionaries well. Indeed, as dramatic reports of cooperation between Roman Catholic missionaries and the CIA in Latin America began to emerge in the popular press in the 1960s and early 1970s, evangelical missionaries demonstrated renewed concern about the detrimental effects that such contact might have on their work.²¹ By the early 1970s, virtually every evangelical mission agency had created or strengthened policies explicitly forbidding cooperation with US intelligence agents abroad.²² Evangelical politician, Oregon senator Mark Hatfield, led the way in these efforts by introducing legislation at the end of 1975 aimed at making such contact illegal, ultimately forcing the American intelligence community to "prohibit such contact abroad."²³

---

19 This was true as late as the mid-1970s as seen in CIA Director W. E. Colby to Senator Mark Hatfield, 13 September 1975, Billy Graham Center Archives (BGC), CN 165, Box 208, Folder 3.

20 Intelligence report included in Wayne Fredricks to Johnson, 31 August 1961, NARA, RG 59, Box 3109a, Folder 4a. The British Ambassador, an American advisor to Selassie and a Major in the Ethiopian Imperial Bodyguard are among the sources cited in this report. While the report does not specify if these missionaries were evangelical or mainline, virtually all missionaries to Ethiopia at this time were evangelicals—that includes most of the small number of American missionaries from mainline organizations like the Presbyterians. Don McClure, for instance, was a Presbyterian missionary whose theology and outlook were enthusiastically evangelical and who regarded his own mainline denomination as a hindrance to his work. See his edited letters in *Red-headed, Rash and Religious*; and Partee, *Adventures in Africa*.

21 Senator Hatfield to President Ford, 19 September 1975, BGC/CN165/208/3; Hatfield, "Open Letter to President," *World Vision Magazine*, March 1976; Also see, The Assemblies of God, Division of Foreign Missions to the Evangelical Foreign Missions Association (EFMA) on 4 November 1975, BGC/CN 165/208/3. As we shall see later in the chapter, in Ethiopia, stories of missionary collusion with the CIA in Latin America undermined their ability to speak as apolitical humanitarians and made them a lightning rod for anti-American propaganda by the Marxist regime after 1974.

22 Letters from the Conservative Baptists, the Christian and Missionary Alliance, and the Assemblies of God to EFMA are just a few examples of this apparently universal trend. All letters can be found at the BGC/CN 165/208/3.

23 Senator Mark Hatfield, Open letter to the evangelical community, 16 June 1976, BGC/CN 165/208/3.

The Media and Evangelical Elites, 1960–1974

While the direct influence of American missionaries on their policymakers continued to wane, the missionary-informed American evangelical community, nevertheless, continued to play a role in US-Ethiopian relations. During this period, the influence of the evangelical media on American culture was reaching a new peak. Christian radio, television, newspapers, and magazines were ubiquitous and the message emanating from evangelical sources concerning Ethiopia, while perhaps less effusive than it had been, continued to be strongly pro-Selassie.[24] As late as 1966, Billy Graham famously praised the Ethiopian Emperor as a "worshipper of Jesus Christ" and the person responsible for introducing "democratic institutions" in Ethiopia.[25] The numbers of evangelical missionaries working in Ethiopia was also at an all-time high, meaning that the grassroots news network that had been so important in shaping opinion about Ethiopia in the initial post-war period continued to exert considerable force on the American evangelical subculture.[26] Yet even here something had begun to change.

During the initial post-war period the mainstream media had rarely taken notice of Ethiopia; and when it had its coverage usually reflected the pro-Selassie opinions of their evangelical missionary sources on the ground and those of "missionary kid" and *Time/Life* publisher Henry Luce. However, by the 1960s and 1970s, an increasingly secular press was taking significant notice of Ethiopia. *Time*, for instance, published 248 articles on Ethiopia during this period, while the *New York Times* ran an average of 265 articles per year that included the country.[27] No longer shaped by Luce, who had passed away in 1967, or colored by evangelical missionary

---

24 *Christianity Today*, "Haile Selassie in Berlin"; *Christianity Today*, "A Call for Evangelical Unity"; and Doyle, "Famine in Africa."
25 "Billy Graham's Introduction," 26 October 1966, BGC/CN 363/1/3.
26 By 1973 one American-dominated mission agency, SIM, had approximately four hundred missionaries in Ethiopia, and major American evangelical denominations such as the Southern Baptist Convention were beginning to put their considerable financial and media resources behind their growing efforts in the country. See Cumbers, *Living with the Red*, 4; and letter from Jerry Bedsole, Southern Baptist missionary to Ethiopia (1970–1994), 5 April 2008.
27 This number is based on a search in *Time's* online archives for "Ethiopia." Many of these articles were on related topics and only used Ethiopia in a tangential way, but a significant portion were directly related to the evolving political situation in Ethiopia—often in moderately unflattering terms. A similar search of the *NY Times* online archive produced this average. The average of 265 articles per year is an increase from an average of 195 articles per year in the period from 1941–1960. It should be noted that many of the earlier articles were written concerning Ethiopia's role in World War II and its activities with the UN early on in its history.

sentiment, this attention was not always flattering. While the evangelical media maintained its praise of Selassie as a devout Christian, benevolent ruler, and champion of liberal reforms, the mainstream media increasingly portrayed him as an obstructionist, conservative monarch; desperately clinging to an unjust and corrupt feudal order.[28]

This less sympathetic view paralleled a more measured US assessment of Ethiopia in the late 1960s and early 1970s.[29] As early as 1960, coverage in the popular press had become critical of Selassie to the degree that he temporarily refused to allow copies of *Newsweek* and *Time* to be sold in Ethiopia.[30] By the early 1970s, the mainstream media's highly critical view of Selassie had almost completely overwhelmed the evangelical media's previously dominant and flattering image of the Ethiopian Emperor.

The relative decline in evangelical missionary influence on the mainstream media was partially offset by the increasing role of the Washington-based ICL (now referred to as the Fellowship).[31] Through its close relationship both with members of Selassie's inner circle and the American political establishment, the Fellowship acted as an important pro-Selassie undercurrent that strengthened personal and diplomatic ties between the countries in the face of increasing American disillusionment with Ethiopia. From the 1950s, the Fellowship had viewed Christian-led Ethiopia as a potential hub for its activities in Africa. The Organization of African Unity's 1963 decision to place its headquarters in Addis Ababa, and the Christian Emperor's increasingly important role as Africa's elder statesman, encouraged the Fellowship to redouble its efforts in the country—a reality reflected in their 1964 conclusion that "Ethiopia is probably the key country of the African continent from the standpoint of stability and leadership."[32]

With this in mind, Senator Frank Carlson, Eisenhower's close friend and former campaign manager, invited the Ethiopian ambassador to a Senate Prayer Breakfast in May 1965. Following the presentation of Haile

---

28 *Washington Post*, "Ethiopia: The Final Days"; and Walker, "Day the Bribe."
29 Katzenbach to McNamara, 8 May 1967; Telegram from the Department of State to the Embassy in Ethiopia, 12 July 1968; both in *Foreign Relations of the United States, 1964–1968*, Vol. 24, Africa.
30 Among others see *Time*, 6 January 1961.
31 By this time the organization known as "International Christian Leadership" (ICL) had changed its name to "The Fellowship Foundation." As a result, from this point forward all references to "the Fellowship" should be read in the context of the discussion of ICL in the previous chapter.
32 "Recommendations for Ethiopia 1964," BGC/CN459/209/5.

Selassie's greetings by the Ethiopian diplomat, Vice President Hubert Humphrey gave the keynote address.[33] This successful Prayer Breakfast initiated a series of important contacts between the American political center and the Ethiopian government that continued to produce high-level American sympathy for Selassie's government right up to the Emperor's death a decade later.[34] Writing to Selassie concerning the 1965 meeting, Senator Everett Jordan of North Carolina stated:

> This morning one of the most effective meetings that has been held in Washington for a long time took place. Your message was gratefully received by all of us present. Your Ambassador, His Excellency Mr. Dinke, gave an exceptional talk on the great need for a spiritual bond between the leaders of the world. We had with us outstanding men from the United States Senate, the House of Representatives, the State Department, and the military, as well as many other leaders from our government. The Vice President of the United States was very pleased with what took place, and we all felt that the leadership which your country gave on this occasion can be the foundation of a new relationship and the development of good will between the countries of Africa and the countries of this hemisphere.[35]

Soon after, Alexander Desta (an admiral in the Ethiopian navy and Selassie's favored grandson) arranged a meeting between the Fellowship's future leader Douglas Coe and Haile Selassie. Adding diplomatic weight to Coe's Ethiopia trip was the presence of Congressman Ross Adair—a long-time Fellowship participant, member of the house committee on foreign affairs, and future US ambassador to Ethiopia.[36]

During Selassie's informal visit to the United States just four months later the Fellowship continued to actively promote US-Ethiopian relations by hosting an intimate Prayer Breakfast in the Emperor's honor. Among others, the list of American officials who actively participated in the event included Treasury Secretary Henry Fowler, senators Frank Carlson, Mark Hatfield and Frank Lausche (a member of the senate committee on foreign relations), Speaker of the House John McCormack, House Minority Leader Gerald Ford, and Congressman Ross Adair.[37] Writing to the sympathetic

---

33 "Special Senate Prayer Breakfast," BGC/CN 459/210/1.
34 As late as June of 1974 the Fellowship was in regular contact with the new Ethiopian Prime Minister Endalkachew. Douglas Coe to Prime Minister Endalkachew, BGC/CN459/210/16.
35 Senator Everett Jordan to Haile Selassie I, BGC/CN459/209/5.
36 Douglas Coe to SIM missionary Leslie G. Sprenger, 20 November 1965, BGC/CN459/210/1.
37 Seating arrangement, "The Emperor's Prayer Breakfast," BGC/CN459/210/9.

Ethiopian ambassador, Douglas Coe called the meeting "most remarkable" and noted the strong impression left by the Emperor's "wonderful speech."[38] A joint letter from senators Carlson, Jordan, and Hatfield to Selassie confirmed that the meeting had had the desired effect. "The example you have been," the Senators wrote, "not only to the Christian world, but to our country down through the years, has been an inspiration to us all."[39]

Two years later, newly elected President Richard Nixon extended an invitation for an official state visit to the Ethiopian Emperor—it was to be Selassie's fourth state visit and the first invitation extended to a foreign leader under the Nixon administration. Once again, a Prayer Breakfast was held in honor of the Emperor that included many of those in attendance in 1967 plus senators Edward Kennedy and Alan Cranston, Congressman John Dellenback, future Speaker of the House Carl Albert, Secretary of Labor George Shultz, Secretary of the Treasury David Kennedy, US ambassador to Ethiopia William Hall, and senior editor of *Life* magazine David Snell. Easily missed among the political figures were at least two evangelical missionaries to Ethiopia who had acted as important go-betweens in this evolving network: SIM's John Cumbers and Don McClure.[40]

This second meeting eclipsed the first as an effective bridge between the two countries. As Admiral Desta wrote to Senator Hatfield, the Prayer Breakfast "deeply affected all of us, and I know particularly His Majesty, as it was one of the first times he has spoken publicly in English."[41] The effect on the American contingent was no less potent as Ambassador Hall, previously only loosely affiliated with the Fellowship's activities, immediately began to explore ways to strengthen the Ethiopian Fellowship, meeting at length on several occasions with Admiral Desta and remaining active in the group's activities until his tenure as ambassador ended in 1971.[42]

That Haile Selassie viewed the Fellowship as an important diplomatic channel became clear in early 1971 when he installed his future prime minister, Lij Endalkachew, as the new head of the Fellowship's Ethiopian chapter. Almost immediately the group put on its first National Prayer Breakfast with the Emperor presiding. The event received national

---

38 Douglas Coe to Ethiopian Ambassador Aberra, 18 February 1967, BGC/CN459/210/4.
39 Senators Frank Carlson, Everett Jordan, and Mark Hatfield to Selassie on 1 March 1967, BGC/CN459/210/4.
40 "Attachment III: Those who accepted and attended the Prayer Breakfast with H.I.M.," BGC/CN459/210/9.
41 Admiral Alexander Desta to Senator Mark Hatfield, 28 July 1969, BGC/CN459/210/4.
42 Ambassador Hall to Senator Mark Hatfield, 10 September 1969, BGC/CN 459/209/8.

coverage in Ethiopia and was also highlighted by the *New York Times*.[43] A month later Washington Fellowship member, Ross Adair, was appointed as the new US ambassador to Ethiopia cementing the central role that this highly connected Christian network had come to play in the relationship between the United States and Ethiopia.[44] Under the leadership of Lij Endalkachew, the Fellowship continued to gain momentum right up until the Revolution of 1974, as evidenced by the growing numbers at the group's twice-a-month breakfasts, the visit of Oregon congressman John Dellenback, and plans for hosting an African heads of state Prayer Breakfast in Addis Ababa in late 1973.[45]

A Second Crisis: The Famine of 1973–1974

But the influence of traditional evangelical missionaries, while diminished, was not over. The politically consequential famine of 1973–1974 is a second instance of the missionary and diplomatic communities being brought together through a crisis. Famines were a part of the fabric of twentieth century Ethiopian life, and so when rumors of yet another food crisis began to circulate in late 1972, few took notice.[46] The geography of northern Ethiopia also served to delay recognition of the impending catastrophe. Rain shadows created by the mountainous terrain meant that within a five mile radius, one village may receive abundant rain while another would receive nothing.[47] Although the majority of American missionaries were based in the south, those who worked in the north interacted closely with the local communities which meant that they were among the first expatriates to discover the scale of the humanitarian crisis unfolding in 1973 and 1974.[48] Over the next two years, the Sudan Interior Mission (SIM)

---

43 "'New York Times' Features"; Special to the *New York Times*, "Prayer Breakfast Introduced."
44 Senator Frank Carlson (retired) to Haile Selassie, 28 May 1971, BGC/CN459/209/8. The letter emphasizes to the Emperor the new Ambassador Adair's longtime participation with the Fellowship in DC, and in the Fellowship's relationship with Ethiopia; as well as the common bond the new ambassador and the Ethiopian Emperor had as devout Christians.
45 Ambassador Adair to Douglas Coe, 30 October 1972, BGC/CN459/210/13. At this time the group was averaging seventy-five prominent Ethiopian officials and business leaders at each meeting.
46 The regularity of famines in Ethiopia leading up to the 1973-1974 famine is well documented in, Kissi, "Politics of Famine," 113–31.
47 Forsberg and Forsberg, *In Famine He Shall*, 11.
48 News of the famine began showing up in the evangelical flagship periodical *Christianity Today* as early as 14 September 1973, but was being circulated in the magazines of the mission organizations some time before this. American missionaries were not the first expatriates to be aware that a potential famine was developing. Indeed, as early as 1972, the evangelical Ethiopian government minister Ato Emmanuel Abraham, had discretely approached the US government with a request for food aid, but incomplete and inconsistent data, as well as frustration with the Selassie government, kept the American government

in particular became a critical link between the remote villagers facing starvation and the international governments and NGOs attempting to provide assistance.

In the late spring of 1973, Ethiopian evangelists returning to the SIM hospital at Bora Meda in northern Ethiopia reported disturbing signs of widespread malnutrition in the villages.[49] Travelling by four-wheel drive or on foot, two SIM missionaries were immediately dispatched to conduct an extensive survey of the region, concluding that as many as 500,000 people were at risk of starvation.[50] Based on this evidence, SIM dropped most of its usual work, geared up for a major relief effort, and began to publicize the extent of the danger.[51]

Concerned that a traditional relief effort would force remote villagers to leave the support of their local communities, thus compounding the threat of starvation with a short-term sanitation crisis and a long-term internal refugee problem, SIM did an additional survey of the region's road system.[52] In cooperation with the Ethiopian government's food-for-work program, the SIM survey led to the creation of new roads to many remote and at-risk villages, as well as the development of twenty-one airstrips in places where the creation of new roads was a logistical impossibility.[53]

Because they had already established a grassroots food distribution program, as well as a complementary system of temporary clinics, large NGOs and international governments often chose to provide supplies, food, and logistical support for SIM's efforts instead of creating their own programs from scratch.[54] As a result, once again the American evangelical missionary community found itself working closely with the diplomatic community—sharing information and raising American domestic and international awareness.[55] Ironically, the important role that American

---

from seriously exploring the famine until it became public. For information regarding other efforts see, Eide, *Revolution and Religion*, 80.

49 Forsberg and Forsberg, *In Famine He Shall*, 9–11, 49.

50 Forsberg and Forsberg, 17.

51 *Africa Now*, "Famine Relief Complicated," 12–13; Forsberg and Forsberg, *In Famine He Shall*, 25.

52 Forsberg and Forsberg, 17.

53 In areas where the creation of airstrips was impossible, SIM arranged airdrops from a rented Ethiopian Airlines cargo plane. These drops delivered sixty-six tons of corn. *Africa Now*, 11. Also see, Forsberg and Forsberg, *In Famine He Shall*, 56–57.

54 Forsberg and Forsberg, *In Famine He Shall*, 71. The US government use of PCVs and the provision of supplies by the International Red Cross in cooperation with some SIM relief projects are just two examples of this dynamic.

55 Doyle, "Famine in Africa," 48–49; *Africa Now*, "Famine relief complicated," 12–13; Forsberg and Forsberg, *In Famine He Shall*, 25, 46.

missionaries played in raising the profile of the Ethiopian famine ultimately led to a BBC documentary by Jonathan Dimbleby that, by portraying the government of Haile Selassie as callously indifferent to the suffering of its people, became an important cause of the next Ethiopian crisis—the pro-American Emperor's downfall in 1974.[56]

Missionaries and an Initially Ambiguous Ethiopia Revolution, 1974–1976

The violent and ideologically radical nature of the Ethiopian revolution that began after Selassie's initially non-violent overthrow on 12 September 1974 caught most outsiders by surprise.[57] It is true that the student demonstrations, sporadic military mutinies, and numerous labor strikes in the capital during the first months of 1974 were all ominous indicators of trouble ahead; but they did not feel like the end of Haile Selassie's reign or the beginning of a revolution. Indeed, at the end of 1973, Ethiopia seemed securely anchored to its conservative cultural moorings. The Emperor continued to be revered by the vast majority of the rural peasantry (a group that made up over 90 percent of the population) and the political and military leadership had, to date, showed no serious signs of disloyalty.[58]

In retrospect, the revolution owed its success to the unlikely synergy of an extremely complex and often contradictory set of circumstances. Among others, these circumstances included: a severe famine; the rising discontent aroused by the introduction of Western education; a host of threats associated with the fallout from the Arab-Israeli conflict of 1973 (such as inflation, Somali and Eritrean nationalism, and the radicalization of sections of Ethiopia's large Muslim population); American preoccupation with Vietnam and Watergate; and, ironically, the growing influence of the democratically-inclined Ethiopian evangelical community.[59] Remove any one of these factors and it would seem that, at least until the aging Emperor died, life in Ethiopia would have remained more or less the same.[60]

---

56 Zwede, *A Modern History*, 235. A doctored version of this documentary was shown on Ethiopian New Year's by the Derg, in order to increase sympathy for their actions the day before they imprisoned Haile Selassie.

57 Korn, *Ethiopia, the United States*, 105; Senator Hatfield's foreword to Jodie Collins, *Code Word: Catherine*; Zwede *History of Modern Ethiopia*.

58 Donham, *Marxist Modern*, 16–21. There were, of course, grumblings and demands for increased pay, but this was not new. Even after the revolution had begun, most in the military remained loyal.

59 Zwede, 215–35; Korn, *Ethiopia, the United States*, 2–6; and Donham, *Marxist Modern*, 16–18.

60 Korn, *Ethiopia, the United States*, 105.

There were few revolutionaries at the start of the Ethiopian revolution. The rhetoric that initially brought a diverse and influential group together under the banner of change was a combination of mild socialism and liberal democracy. The revolution's first leaders confirmed this impression through repeated proclamations of loyalty to the Emperor, steps towards a separation of church and state, support for a free press, and the liberalization of the country's Amharic-only laws that had symbolized the oppression of minority groups under the Amhara-Orthodox autocracy.[61] In addition, the first chairman of the new government was the moderate and widely respected evangelical Christian General Aman Andom.[62] The pro-American Andom quickly appointed other moderate evangelicals to prominent positions, including the important governorship of Eritrea and the commander of the air force.[63] As a result, the relatively well-educated and pro-democratic Ethiopian evangelical community rallied behind the new government.

This was especially true of the evangelicals influenced by politically moderate Scandinavian and American Lutheran missionaries.[64] Initially, the Ethiopian evangelical Lutherans, the Mekane Yesus Church (MYC), were among the more vocal supporters of the revolution. Even after the creation of the military junta, known as the "Derg," in June of 1974, and November's "Bloody Sunday" assassination of General Andom and sixty Selassie loyalists, the MYC issued a public pastoral letter identifying the church with the plight of the poor and praising the revolution as a step towards "a more just society."[65] Reflecting the increased emphasis on social justice within global evangelicalism on display at the Lausanne Conference of 1974, the majority of evangelicals who came out of the politically conservative American missions like SIM were also initially

---

61 Zwede, *A Modern History*, 234.
62 Korn, *Ethiopia, the United States*, 7–10; Cumbers, *Living with the Red Terror*, 23–29.
63 Cumbers, *Living with the Red Terror*, 23–29.
64 It should be noted that, unlike the other evangelical groups in Ethiopia where American missionaries were dominant, only 5 percent of Lutheran missionaries to Ethiopia in the 1970s were American. The tendency of the Mekane Yesus Church (the Lutherans in Ethiopia) to be more politically involved reflects the inclination of Scandinavian evangelicals to see social and political concerns as inseparable from spiritual concerns. This influence continues to be important today as Ethiopian evangelicals have drawn on this heritage in order to balance the separatist influence of the American evangelicals. That said, even within the Lutheran church in Ethiopia, American missionaries (reflecting the apolitical inclinations of their other American evangelical peers) had a disproportionate influence through the large amounts of money they were able to pour into influential projects like the radio station, The Radio Voice of the Gospel, which played a critical role in the spread of evangelical Christianity throughout East Africa and the Middle East.
65 Eide, *Revolution and Religion*, 148.

inclined to support the revolution, believing that the apparently egalitarian pursuits of land reform and social justice were more in line with biblical precepts than anything they recently had experienced under the Orthodox-dominated Selassie government.[66] Despite their long-standing loyalty to Haile Selassie, even some American missionaries expressed at least muted optimism. As SIM's Ethiopia director reflected some years later, "A lot of us thought [the revolution] showed promise."[67]

The initial openness by some missionaries to the revolution was rooted in their identification with the peoples of political and religious periphery, as well as the revolution's early support for political and religious liberty. While Selassie had been consistently pro-mission, his power base, the Ethiopian Orthodox Church and the Amhara elite, were not. This meant that missionaries were given free reign among the animist and Muslim populations of the periphery but restricted from areas dominated by the state church. In addition, by the 1960s, the rapid growth in number and influence of the indigenous evangelical movement had become a threat to the Ethiopian political and religious center. The result was increasing instances of government sanctioned persecution against Ethiopian evangelicals and, in some cases, the missionaries themselves.[68] In short, while the aging and increasingly fragile Selassie continued to be revered within the missionary community, the same could not be said for the power structure he represented.

Nowhere was the early evangelical support for the revolution more significant than amongst the university students and in the rural south and west of the country.[69] Despite the explicitly apolitical message of SIM and the other American mission groups, the push for modernization and reform they had initiated produced a disproportionate number of evangelicals among the nation's influential secondary and university student populations.[70] Because the young and educated evangelicals hailed mainly from the non-Amhara and politically marginalized regions of the south and west, they were more sensitive to the discriminatory treatment they had received from Selassie's government than their missionary

---

66 For an excellent summary of the Lausanne Conference and its importance as a symbol of the changing currents in evangelicalism, see McAlister, *Kingdom of God*, 85–102; Eide, *Revolution and Religion*, 210.
67 Cumbers, *Living with the Red Terror*, 13.
68 Letter from Ethiopia Director of Security to the Mayor of Addis Ababa, 30 October 1964, BGC 165/198/13. Letter appeal for support from Ethiopian Evangelicals to Dr. Taylor of the National Association of Evangelicals, 23 September 1972, BGC 165/198/13.
69 Donham, *Marxist Modern*, 48; Balsvik, *Haile Selassie's Students*, xiii.
70 Eide, *Revolution and Religion*, 29.

mentors had been. By 1974, many had been radicalized and were pushing for reform. One SIM missionary noted after a meeting with evangelical university students in November of 1974 that they were "without doubt, more pro-Derg than pro-mission."[71] In the first year of the revolution, fifty thousand secondary and university students fanned out across the country, preaching the gospel of revolution and setting up the community-based political organizations (kebele) that secured the revolution in the rural areas.[72]

Even among the older and less-educated rural evangelical populations of the Ethiopian south and west the story was much the same. Although many Ethiopian evangelicals, like the American missionaries they had been influenced by, believed explicit political involvement would compromise their faith, some were nonetheless quick to join in this apparently just and progressive movement.[73] To them the revolution represented an end to Orthodox religious persecution and economic serfdom and an opportunity for some degree of self-determination for the country's many ethnic minorities.[74] As Donald Donham has argued:

> Christian converts made by the Sudan Interior Mission (SIM) became [the revolution's] Jacobins. They provided crucial support and information to the zemecha students in Maale; they helped carry out the most radical actions of the revolution as it occurred locally; and they dominated the leadership of the new peasant cooperatives when they were established ... It is striking that the structure of the new cooperatives ... was an almost exact replica of existing evangelical church organization in southern Ethiopia—down to the same Amharic names for offices ... [The local leaders of the revolution in Maale] all had attended SIM schools and were, at one time, Christians.[75]

It was not until Selassie's mysterious death in September of 1975, when it started to become clear that the revolution had simply replaced one form of oppression with another, that evangelicals began to distance themselves from the Derg. However, by this time the revolution was largely complete, and evangelicals had been instrumental in securing it.[76]

---

71 Cumbers, *Living with the Red Terror*, 19.
72 Donham, *Marxist Modern*, 34.
73 Ato Mamo Gebremeskel, Former Chairman of the Kale Heywet Church and retired General Manager of the Ethiopian Petroleum Corporation, interview with the author, 17 December 2007; Donham, *Marxist Modern*, 39.
74 Dr. Paulus Dubale, interview with the author, 14 December 2007; Eide, *Revolution and Religion*, 14, 15, 70.
75 Donham, *Marxist Modern*, 82, 48, and 153.
76 Donham, 36, 82.

The Turn Towards the Soviet Union, 1976–1978

Odd Arne Westad, Donald Donham and others have persuasively argued that the revolution in Ethiopia was a battle between Western and Soviet versions of modernity.[77] Until 1974, Haile Selassie had championed a conservative version of American-style modernity, and his most effective agents had been the large numbers of American evangelical missionaries who had poured into the country from 1918 onwards. By the early 1970s, however, the forces of modernity in Ethiopia, including many evangelical Christian converts, were seeking changes that went well beyond what was possible within Selassie's traditional Ethiopian cultural paradigm.

As long-standing and vocal allies of the Emperor, both the US government and the American evangelical missionary community were intimately associated with the actions of Selassie and his government—actions that by this time were seen as corrupt obstacles to much-needed reforms.[78] While the US government had been quietly pushing for reforms from the Kennedy administration onward, the American evangelical missionary community (to many Ethiopians the public face of American policy) had remained largely silent on political and economic concerns. This silence exacerbated the partially inaccurate impression that their politics mirrored those of the Emperor.[79] As a result, when demands for change boiled over in 1974, moderate pro-American reformers had been largely discredited and Ethiopia's elite turned instead to scientific socialism.

Yet Ethiopia's turn towards the Soviet Union was not simply a reaction against Selassie or the Americans. In several important ways, the Soviet model had considerable salience for Ethiopia's would-be revolutionaries. Both revolutions grew out of cultures deeply steeped in the values and traditions of Orthodox Christianity—values that encouraged a highly centralized and authoritarian political model. As American analysts noted early on, this ironic but potentially potent religious connection was not lost on Soviet policymakers who had been exploiting this bond as early as 1960 by sending Russian clerics to Ethiopia on ecumenical missions.[80] In addition, both the Russian and the Ethiopian revolutions occurred within ethnically diverse empires, ruled by a tiny feudal nobility, but numerically dominated by a rural and traditionally servile tenant-farming peasantry.

---

77 Westad, *Global Cold War*; Donham, *Marxist Modern*.
78 "Report on Ethiopia," 1 November 1961, NARA/RG59/3109a/4a; Cumbers, *Living with the Red Terror*, 36, 38; and Balsvik, *Haile Selassie's Students*, 197.
79 "Confidential Memorandum" J. Beard to J. Root, 6 November 1961, NARA/RG59/3109a/4a; Cumber, *Living with the Red Terror*, 63.
80 Melady, "Eyes of Africa."

Finally, both nations experienced initially ambiguous revolutions violently co-opted by radical ideologues. In short, both revolutions were heirs of Byzantium and produced a unique strain of socialism that reflected the influence of their surprisingly similar cultural heritages.[81]

Ethiopian revolutionaries and their Soviet backers quickly seized upon these striking parallels as evidence of a natural ideological affinity between the two governments.[82] In particular, the historical and cultural parallels convinced the Soviets that they were not just witnessing another example of opportunistic Cold War socialism, but instead were seeing their own revolutionary experience being repeated in Africa.[83] Indeed, without taking this ideological and cultural kinship into consideration, it is difficult to explain why the Soviet Union was willing to sacrifice its $400 million military investment in Somalia, abandon the Marxist rebellions it had supported in Tigray and Eritrea, risk the alienation of anti-Ethiopian Arab regimes in the region, and, above all, pour the astronomical sum of eleven billion dollars' worth of arms into Ethiopia between 1977 and 1989.[84]

The American Response to the Ethiopian Revolution, 1974–1978

One of the remarkable sub-plots within the Ethiopian revolution was America's persistent belief, despite consistent evidence to the contrary, that Ethiopia would ultimately remain a loyal American client. Although the first two months of the revolution provided some hints that the revolution might be inclined toward the United States, those impressions should have been destroyed in late November 1974, when the Derg executed fifty-nine members of Selassie's former government and assassinated its own popular and moderately pro-American chairman.[85]

Less than three months later, and in the context of continuous and explicitly anti-American rhetoric, the Derg announced one of the most radical redistributions of property in the twentieth century—abolishing all forms of private land ownership and beginning the process of nationalizing all foreign business initiatives, usually without compensation of any kind.[86] Then in 1976, while the dust was still settling from the revolution's radical property initiatives, the Derg announced the signing of a significant

---

81 Clapham, *Transformation and Continuity*, 79. For similar arguments also see Zwede, *A Modern History*, 229; Donham, *Marxist Modern*, 130; and Westad, *Global Cold War*, 253.
82 Westad, *Global Cold War*, 265–70; also see Remnek, "Translating 'New Soviet Thinking.'"
83 Westad, 253, 265, 270; Remnek, "Translating 'New Soviet Thinking,'" 154.
84 Korn, *Ethiopia, the United States*, 29; Remnek, "Translating 'New Soviet Thinking,'" 154.
85 Cumbers, *Living with the Red Terror*, 22; Korn, *Ethiopia, the United States*, 10; Zwede, *A Modern History*, 250; Westad, *Global Cold War*, 268.
86 Korn, *Ethiopia, the United States*, 51; Zwede, *A Modern History*, 242.

aid agreement with the Soviet Union and began a clearly orchestrated assassination program targeting all persons deemed to be enemies of the revolution.[87] By mid-1976, the revolution's disastrous human rights record and its radical socialist and anti-American rhetoric had made US-Ethiopian relations a campaign issue in the American presidential race.[88]

And yet throughout this period, US policymakers not only continued to believe that pro-American sentiment would ultimately win the day, they backed up that belief by continuing to supply Ethiopia with staggering amounts of military aid. Between 1974 and 1978, US military aid to Ethiopia totaled approximately one and a half times everything it had given Selassie up to 1974—an astonishing figure considering Ethiopia's status as the largest recipient of US military aid in sub-Saharan Africa from 1950–1973.[89] At best, this revolutionary-era aid must be viewed as a calculated gamble by US policymakers. At worst, it demonstrated their inability to alter deeply rooted and missionary-inspired stereotypes to match the changing dynamics on the ground.[90]

The American perception of Ethiopia as a haven of pro-American sentiment was rooted in the early Cold War assessment by evangelical missionaries and US diplomats that Haile Selassie's Christian beliefs were largely in line with American economic and political values.[91] However, two flawed inferences from this initial impression also became part of the generally held American perception of Ethiopia. First, Haile Selassie's dominance of the Ethiopian political scene meant that in American diplomatic language, and eventually in their minds, US policymakers incorrectly came to equate the Emperor's opinion with Ethiopian opinion, creating the false perception that because its Emperor was fundamentally pro-American, so was the country.[92] Second, American policymakers incorrectly assumed that the Orthodox Christianity that dominated Ethiopian culture and politics was roughly on par with its American

---

87 Westad, *Global Cold War*, 270; Zwede, *A Modern History*, 247.
88 Jackson, *Jimmy Carter*, 5–6.
89 Korn, *Ethiopia, the United States*, 21.
90 Immerman, "Psychology," 116.
91 "Pen Portrait of Emperor of Ethiopia," NARA/RG165/77/776; NARA/RG59/3109/13a. Also see, *Sudan Witness*, "Testimony of His Imperial," 5; *Sudan Witness*, "King Came," 24. The "Pen Portrait" created for FDR in advance of his meeting with Selassie stressed Ethiopia's Christian history and placed the Christian Emperor's desire to achieve a closer relationship with the United States in the context of his hard-working and "enlightened" character, and his having "the interests of his people at heart."
92 The extent to which this misconception had become deeply rooted is clear when, even after Ethiopia's unmistakable turn towards Moscow, the NSA's Ethiopia expert, Paul Henze was adamant that the US could salvage its relationship with Ethiopia. Henze to Brzezinski. 8 February 1978, Jimmy Carter Presidential Library (CPL), NSA, Horn, Box 1, 2–78.

Protestant equivalent and, therefore, unlikely to gravitate towards the atheistic socialism of the Soviets.[93]

These erroneous judgments were evidently so deeply ingrained that even well after the revolution had shown itself to be unmistakably Marxist-Leninist in sympathy, American charge d'affaires David Korn could reasonably claim that "Ethiopia would seem a wildly improbable candidate for conversion to Marxism-Leninism. It is a country with a population that for the most part is deeply religious and whose intellectual and cultural ties with the outside were, until the mid-1970s, anchored strongly and almost exclusively in the West."[94]

Evangelical Missionary Activism in Revolutionary-Era Ethiopia, 1974–1991

Between 1974 and 1978, the divide that had grown between the American missionary and diplomatic communities narrowed considerably. The dramatic decline in the size of the official American presence in Ethiopia encouraged this renewed relationship. So did the intensity of the situation. It was not uncommon, for instance, for American diplomats and missionaries driving their children to school in the mornings to pass stacks of bullet-strewn bodies piled on street corners from the previous night's wave of assassinations.[95] In one case, approximately one thousand students were gunned down in front of a young American missionary mother. As she sat stunned in her Volkswagen Beetle,

> hundreds of uniformed, armed soldiers ran in all directions with their rifles blazing. The noise was deafening. I began to feel sick [to] my stomach and dizzy with fear. Traffic stood still, pedestrians fled in all directions ... the students, like limp rag dolls, began slumping onto the ground in scarlet pools of blood ... Suddenly it was silent ... Soldiers were lifting the limp, bloody bodies and throwing them carelessly into the trucks ... I opened the car door and sour vomit spewed over the curb beside me.[96]

By virtue of their now relatively large numbers, evangelical missionaries between 1974 and 1978 were necessarily involved in meetings concerning evacuation plans and were an important resource as the embassy sought

---

93 Korn, *Ethiopia, the United States*, 169.
94 Korn, 169.
95 Collins, *Code Word: Catherine*, 121. Collins was a Southern Baptist missionary.
96 Collins, 25–26. This event was confirmed by multiple human rights organizations including Save the Children who estimated that approximately one thousand students were killed in the massacre. Korn, *Ethiopia, the United States*, 26.

to evaluate the politically fluid situation and ensure the protection of its citizens. The experience of SIM administrator John Cumbers is a case in point. At the peak of the initial tensions in February of 1975, Cumbers was receiving high-level diplomatic phone calls, often from the American or Canadian ambassadors, "seven or eight times a day."[97] This revitalized relationship continued into the late 1970s, as evidenced by regular "off the record" briefings with missionaries at the American embassy and increasing social interaction between missionaries and diplomats.[98]

One example that hints at the dual purpose of the renewed social interaction between the two American communities was the celebration of SIM director John Cumbers' birthday in January of 1977 at the home of one embassy official. Concerning the host who had worked particularly closely with SIM personnel, Cumbers noted, "none of us were quite sure what 'Benny' did at the US embassy, but it was through him we obtained the two-way radio which made all the difference to our handling of emergencies."[99]

Much to their chagrin, the profile of American evangelical missionaries also grew because of the revolution. As early as 1975, official radio broadcasts and newspaper headlines had singled out missionaries as agents of American imperialism, CIA operatives, and oppressors of the people.[100] Thanks to this propaganda, the threat to American evangelical missionary personnel and property had become acute. Although during the first years of the revolution this translated into very little action by the central government, at the local level the government accusations created rising tensions that ultimately boiled over into attacks on rural mission hospitals, schools and churches; as well as to the confiscation of a great amount of missionary property and personal goods.[101] By the first part of 1977, virtually every SIM station had lost some or all of its property to the local kebele (farmers' associations).[102] In addition to these continuous threats of violence, missionaries were regularly imprisoned without trial.[103]

---

97 Cumbers, *Living with the Red Terror*, 51.
98 Letter from Jerry Bedsole (Southern Baptist Missionary to Ethiopia, 1970–1994) on 5 April 2008; Letter from Ed and Sue Erickson, Baptist General Conference Missionaries to Ethiopia, not dated, 2007.
99 Cumbers, *Living with the Red Terror*, 116.
100 Among others see, "Report from Ethiopia," 28 June 1976. SIM Archives, SIM General 03, "1966–1977, Publicity Section Files"; Cumbers, *Living with the Red Terror*, 167.
101 *Africa Now*, "Crisis Builds."
102 Cumbers, *Living with the Red Terror*, 138–39. Evidence that this phenomenon included all American evangelical mission groups is found in letters from long-time Presbyterian missionary to Ethiopia, Harold Kurtz on 25 September 2007, and an anonymous Southern Baptist missionary to Ethiopia, 7 April 2008.
103 Cannata and Cannata, *Truth on Trial*; Dortzbach and Dortzbach, *Kidnapped*.

Evangelical missionaries were also vulnerable to attack by rebel groups. In one highly publicized case, a young American missionary nurse was kidnapped by the insurgent Eritrean Liberation Front (ELF) and held for four weeks as the ELF unsuccessfully sought ransom from her husband and their mission.[104] For the vast majority of American evangelical missionaries who saw their work in strictly spiritual and humanitarian terms, and who had developed deep friendships within the local Ethiopian communities, this was an emotionally painful period.[105] However, for American officials desperately trying to engage in a dialogue with the new regime, these attacks on Americans and their property also represented an additional obstacle to their diplomatic aims.[106]

In some cases, American evangelical missionaries complicated things even further by actively, if unintentionally, sabotaging US diplomatic efforts. Occasionally maverick missionaries, spurred on by an aversion to the socialist revolution or by loyalty to the people they worked amongst, became politically active. In several instances, missionaries acted as messengers for royalist rebels seeking dialogue with the US embassy.[107] And in another instance, an evangelical missionary director working in Eritrea was deported by the new regime in 1975 because a van linked to an evangelical group had been caught allegedly shuttling guns and ammunition for a rebel group.[108]

Perhaps the most remarkable example of American missionary activism during this period came in 1977, when a young Southern Baptist missionary couple escaped under a shroud of secrecy to Kenya with ten of the former Emperor's great-grandchildren and the daughter of a prominent rebel group leader. When word of a possible escape had reached the embassy in Addis Ababa, the American charge d'affaires had been furious to the point of threatening to have the missionary couple removed from Ethiopia and warning American embassy personnel against any attempts to aid in the plans. After the missionary couple defied the embassy and went ahead with the escape, their actions were considered so diplomatically explosive

---

104 Dortzbach and Dortzbach, *Kidnapped*; Blau, "Nurse Kept Faith."
105 "Report from Ethiopia," 28 June 1976, SIM/SIM General 03/ "1966–1977 Publicity Section Files"; also see letter from an anonymous Southern Baptist missionary, 7 April 2008.
106 While David Korn does not mention missionaries explicitly, he does on several instances discuss the issue of compensation for "nationalized" American property as an unnecessary but significant obstacle in US-Ethiopian relations during the 1980s. Korn, *Ethiopia, the United States*, 51.
107 Lindholm and Lindholm (Southern Baptist missionaries to Ethiopia, 1969–1983) to the author, on 10 November 2007; Letter from a source which, for reasons of personal safety, must remain anonymous to the author, 7 April 2008.
108 Cumbers, *Living with the Red Terror*, 56, 58.

that President Jimmy Carter, Secretary of State Cyrus Vance and National Security Advisor Zbigniew Brzezinski gave the US embassy in Nairobi the highly unusual order to reject any appeals from the American family for embassy assistance.[109]

This uncharacteristic political activism by a few evangelical missionaries became such a concern that the largest Ethiopian evangelical denomination sent SIM a letter pleading with it to mute its vocal disapproval of the Derg.[110] In the end, while these instances of political activism created considerable tension between the missionary community and the US embassy, in general, the revolutionary crises had the effect of increasing the cooperation between the two American communities. This increased cooperation inevitably included the sharing of information that influenced the way US diplomats viewed the evolving situation on the ground and, thus, helped to shape American responses to these events.

By the time the Red Terror ended in 1978, Ethiopia was completely in the hands of the Derg's enthusiastic Soviet apostle, Lieutenant Colonel Mengistu. The Soviet bloc's now ubiquitous presence (which included approximately one thousand Soviet advisors, two South Yemeni armored battalions, and over eighteen thousand Cuban troops and advisors) stood in dramatic contrast to the official American presence (which had fallen from a high of over four thousand in the early 1970s to well under one hundred by May of 1977).[111] The Ethiopian revolution had become one of the Cold War's most startling reversals and, as such, had important consequences for US-Soviet relations. Indeed, the massive Soviet intervention in Ethiopia's 1977 war with Somalia so fundamentally upset the balance of power in the region that Carter's national security advisor, Zbigniew Brzezinski, was prompted to declare that detente had been "buried in the sands of the Ogaden."[112]

In the midst of these events, the American evangelical missionary community had also been decimated. The largest American-based evangelical mission, SIM, saw its presence in Ethiopia fall from approximately four hundred in 1974 to thirty-seven by 1978.[113] Other American evangelical missionary groups were also affected, leaving the

---

109 Collins, *Code Word: Catherine*; "Kin of Selassie"; "Great-Grandchildren."
110 Cumbers, *Living with the Red Terror*, 66.
111 Westad, *Global Cold War*, 276; Jackson, *Jimmy Carter*, 52.
112 The Ogaden is a desert in the eastern portion of Ethiopia that borders Somalia. It is where much of the conflict between Somalia and Ethiopia during 1977–1978 took place. Brzezinski's remark was an indictment of the willingness by the Soviets to pour tremendous amounts of military aid into the region—first into Somalia and then into Ethiopia—in the hopes of creating a foothold in the Horn of Africa. Jackson, *Jimmy Carter*, 3.
113 Cumbers, *Living with the Red Terror*, 4, 75.

total number of American missionaries in Ethiopia at approximately one hundred by the end of the Red Terror.[114]

Nevertheless, these changes only altered the role that the missionaries were to play in US-Ethiopian relations; they did not end it. In fact, harassed by a politically hostile regime, the once-strong sense of camaraderie between the missionaries and the now small embassy staff continued to revive. The embassy cafeteria, swimming pool and sports facilities were opened up to the missionary community, "off the record" exchanges were "extensive and detailed," and close personal relationships between missionaries and higher-level diplomats became common.[115] Once again, the US embassy needed the missionaries in a way that they had not since the 1950s.

Ironically, the Marxist government also came to rely heavily on the American evangelical missionaries. Despite its own efforts, and those of its monarchical predecessor, Ethiopia in the 1970s and 1980s remained incapable of providing for the basic needs of its people. Making matters worse, their own effective propaganda had ushered in a level of expectation among the people that was impossible to meet.[116] In order to fill the gap between expectations and the harsh realities on the ground, the Derg turned to the missionaries. While they severely curtailed explicitly religious work, the Marxist regime did seek out missionary aid in meeting its secular and humanitarian objectives—in fact, they often demanded it. As hard as they made it for American evangelicals to stay, the Derg often made it more difficult for them to leave. Passports were regularly confiscated, or retroactive tax schemes were applied to missionary agencies that had to be paid in full before anyone from that organization could leave the country.[117]

---

114 This is a rough estimate based on the number of SIM missionaries (thirty-seven—the majority of whom would have been American) as well as the continued, albeit smaller, presence of the Southern Baptists, the Bible Baptists, the Baptist General Conference, the Presbyterian Mission, the Orthodox Presbyterians, the Eastern Mennonites, the Seventh Day Adventists and others as evidenced in Hege, *Beyond Our Prayers*, 17-29; Cumbers, *Living with the Red*, 75; Dortzbach and Dortzbach, *Kidnapped*; Collins, *Code Word: Catherine*, 323-25; Letters from Presbyterian missionary, Harold Kurtz, 25 September 2007, Southern Baptist missionary, Jerry Bedsole, 5 April 2008, and Baptist General Conference missionary Ed Erickson (2007, not dated). The number of American evangelical missionaries in Ethiopia at any given time between 1978 and 1991 would never have been less than fifty but would likely have not exceeded five hundred.

115 Cumbers, *Living with the Red Terror*, 56. Also see letters from Southern Baptist missionary Jerry Bedsole, 5 April 2008; Presbyterian missionary Harold Kurtz, 25 September 2007; and Ed Erickson, 2007 (not dated).

116 Letter to the author from Baptist General Conference missionary, Ed Erickson, 2007 (not dated).

117 Collins, *Code Word: Catherine*, 224; Cumbers, *Living with the Red Terror*, 142.

Beyond the valuable humanitarian assistance they provided, the Derg had an additional incentive for keeping the American evangelical missionaries in Ethiopia. As the years began to drag on and as life in Ethiopia grew increasingly bleak, the Marxist regime needed a scapegoat, and the American missionary community was ideal for the role. Both visible and generally pliant, the American missionaries were ready-made symbols of everything the Derg blamed for Ethiopia's woes—American imperialism, individualistic capitalism and a culturally-invasive foreign religion. To this end, official government radio and television broadcasts, including speeches by Mengistu himself, regularly highlighted supposed corruption at SIM clinics, luxurious living conditions of American missionaries, and their alleged role as undercover CIA operatives.[118]

In short, in the American evangelical missionaries the Derg received both a valuable group of contributors to the nation's development and a powerful propaganda tool. Yet the work of the American evangelical missionaries did not always fit neatly into the designs of the Ethiopian regime. Indeed, the missionaries did significant harm to Ethiopia's defiantly anti-American government. Perhaps the most important way they undermined the communist Derg was indirect—in the form of the exploding size and influence of the Ethiopian evangelical community.

During their first twenty years in Ethiopia (1918–1938), American evangelical missionaries laid an important foundation for their message but saw very few Ethiopian converts. Indeed, by 1938 the largest American mission could claim only 150 converts.[119] However, during the war period, the evangelical message began to take root and by 1942–1943 the evangelical population in the south of the country was estimated to have risen to as many as twenty-five thousand.[120] From that point up until the early 1970s, the evangelical population essentially doubled every five years, increasing to almost one million.[121] This astonishing growth accelerated even further during the intense persecution by the Communist regime from 1976–1991, and by the national census of 1994 the number of evangelicals was estimated to be close to six million.[122]

---

118 "Report from Ethiopia," 28 June 1976, SIM Archives, SIM General, Box 03, Folder "1966–1977, Publicity Section Files"; *Africa Now*, 8–9.
119 Cumbers, *Living with the Red Terror*, 4.
120 This figure is an average of figures for this period given in the memoir of Davis, *Fire on the Mountains*, 109; Cotterell, *Born at Midnight*, Appendix A; and Cumbers, *Living with the Red Terror*, 4.
121 Cotterell, *Born at Midnight*, Appendix A.
122 Eshete, *Evangelical Movement*, 2. Many Evangelical leaders believe that the real number

The growth of evangelical Protestantism in Ethiopia from less than one thousandth of a percent of the total population in 1929 to more than 10 percent of a rapidly growing population at the end of the Cold War was remarkable. Yet even these numbers do not sufficiently reflect the rising political force of evangelicalism in Ethiopia from the 1970s onward. Indeed, by 1971, the CIA was already noting that despite their still relatively small numbers, evangelicals were "more important than their numbers warrant."[123]

The reasons for their disproportionate political potency lay in the values and practices of the largely American brand of evangelical Christianity to which they had converted. Because Protestantism generally placed such a premium on the need for individuals to read the Bible for themselves, the American missionaries had made education a critical part of their work from the very beginning. The result was that up until the communist era, when almost all schools were nationalized, the school system established by the American missions dominated large swathes of Ethiopia—especially, as we have seen, the south and west of the country.

For instance, on the eve of the Revolution of 1974–1975, SIM and the Ethiopian church that had grown from its work were employing over twelve hundred teachers in the running of 676 learning institutions that were educating almost sixty thousand students, including a number of the country's premier schools.[124] For other American evangelical organizations,

---

is now well over 12 million. Their reasoning is that the census-takers asked Ethiopians if they were "Protestant" or "Christian." The problem with these designations is that evangelical Christianity in Ethiopia has never used the term Protestant, and thus, the argument goes, many rural evangelicals, not knowing what a "Protestant" was, simply said that they were Christian. The CIA estimated that Protestants made up "no more than 1 percent of the Ethiopian population" in 1971. It should be noted that in Ethiopia, "Protestant" is equated with "evangelical." This is partially because of the tremendous influence on evangelical missionaries but equally because the evangelical beliefs, ethos, and style of worship resonated with even those Ethiopians who had converted through the small number of mainline missionaries in Ethiopia. "National Intelligence Survey—Ethiopia, November 1971," NARA/RG263/A1-48/260. The highly respected *World Christian Encyclopaedia* put the total in 1970 at 2.9 percent of the Ethiopian population. Barrett, *World Christian Encyclopaedia*. It should be noted that the State Department, evidently still using the statistical data from the haphazard 1994 census, still puts the number of evangelicals in Ethiopia at only 5 percent.

123 "National Intelligence Survey—Ethiopia, November 1971," NARA/RG263/A1-48/260.
124 Cumbers, Appendix C; Dr. Tesfaye Yacob, General Secretary of the Kale Haywet Church, interview with the author, 14 December 2007. KHC stands for *Kale Heywot Church*, which translated means, *Word of Life Church*. This was the denomination that came out of SIM's missionary efforts. The KHC and SIM continue to work together in a complementary, albeit independent, relationship. Rev. Alemu Shetta, General Secretary of the Evangelical Churches Fellowship of Ethiopia, interview with the author, 18 December 2007.

the story was largely the same. The Mennonite Nazareth school, for instance, was able to boast a 100 percent pass rate on the government's university entrance exam at a time when only a small percentage of students sitting the exam were allowed to continue.[125] This impressive track record was mirrored in the mission's technical and vocational training as well. The institute for training nurses and medical assistants run by the American Mennonites at their hospital in Nazareth produced over one thousand graduates between the years of 1946 and 1978—graduates who then spread out across the nation bringing their knowledge and culture of agency with them.[126]

Perhaps even more significant than the size and relative quality of the American missionary educational system was the philosophy and content of the curriculum. In stark contrast to the Orthodox Church's limited educational system, whose primary purpose had been preserving tradition through the use of memorization and rote learning, the aim of missionary education was to produce students who could read and interpret the Bible for themselves. This required critical thinking. This is not to suggest that the missionaries were advocates of radical free thought. Not at all. In their teaching and in their approach to the text, the evangelical missionaries proceeded from the foundational premise that the Bible was divinely inspired and, therefore, true and authoritative. Nevertheless, even if the essential truth of the Bible was not up for debate, the very process of learning to read and interpret for oneself meant that the dangerous "why" questions were never far from educational practice of the missionaries and the Ethiopian teachers who had trained under them. The result was a noticeable and politically consequential intellectual independence among Ethiopian evangelicals.[127] As one Ethiopian leader from the south stated, "even the thinking process [was] different between the south and the north based on our religion."[128]

The American educational system, and the missionaries who initiated and oversaw that system, also explicitly promoted the democratically-friendly values of individualism and egalitarianism—another explicit contrast to the hierarchical values of the Ethiopian Orthodox Church. Significantly, these values were also modelled in the culture and governing systems of the evangelical churches in the country.

---

125 Hege, *Beyond Our Prayers*, 81.
126 Hege, 78.
127 Balsvik, *Haile Selassie's Students*, 16; Eide, *Revolution and Religion*, 29.
128 Dr. Nigatu Chuffo, interview with the author, 14 December 2007.

For instance, as early as the 1940s, the Ethiopian churches associated with SIM were beginning to formalize an organizational scheme that was indistinguishable from the highly democratic church structures found in evangelical denominations across the United States. Nominations for leaders were taken from the congregation, followed by a free election between the nominees. The winners of the election would be presented as the church leaders for three-year terms, to a maximum of two terms each. This process of electing local congregation leaders was then repeated at the sub-district level (a group of several local churches), the district level (a group of several sub-districts), and the zone level (a group of several districts), all the way up to the General Assembly, which acted as the denomination's national parliament, composed of 120 members from across the country, and responsible for electing the General Secretary.[129] In scale and substance, nothing remotely comparable to this model of modern democracy existed anywhere else in Ethiopia.

Acting as the ultimate authority over this remarkably democratic process was yet another bedrock of the American political system, a written constitution. With the political equivalency of the scriptural authority given by evangelicals to the Bible, the written constitution provided accountability and order for the evolving democratic ethos of SIM's Ethiopian churches.[130] The churches influenced by SIM were not unusual in this regard. Indeed, similar practices could be found wherever American mission groups were active.[131]

As a result of the values, structures and practices established by the American missionaries and indigenized by the Ethiopian evangelicals, by the 1970s this still small minority was a potent political force. As we have already seen, in the early days of the revolution, prior to its radical Marxist turn, evangelicals were among its most vocal and politically effective sympathizers. However, when it became clear that the revolution had not just replaced one form of authoritarianism with another, but that the new totalitarian regime was, in fact, far more antagonistic to their faith than

---

[129] Ato Kursie Shefano, interview with the author, 18 December 2007.

[130] It is almost certain that the first written constitution to be created in Ethiopia by grassroots Ethiopians (beyond the largely symbolic national constitution that Haile Selassie created in 1930 and revised in 1955—which of course was created primarily by Western advisors) was that created in 1957 by the SIM Darassa Church. This constitution became the model for other regional church groups and ultimately for the SIM-initiated Ethiopia church's national constitution which was finalized in 1966. The text of the 1957 constitution is included in Cotterell, *Born at Midnight*, Appendix D.

[131] Hege, *Beyond Our Prayers*, 142.

the evangelical-friendly Selassie had been, many evangelicals began to actively resist the dictates of the Derg.

Ethiopian evangelical resistance to the Derg was rarely explicitly political, but it was political nonetheless. Instead of directly confronting the communist regime, the evangelical churches went underground, forming thousands of "invisible" house groups where the Christian gospel flourished alongside a message of non-violent non-participation. In addition to various forms of civil disobedience, the house church movement also produced a new form of protest music that quickly spread throughout the country's urban centers. By proclaiming allegiance to God over the state, this new evangelical music gave meaning to the evangelical silence and, thus, represented a direct challenge to the Derg's totalitarian claims of authority.[132] The extent to which the Derg felt threatened by the movement was quickly apparent. By 1977, the regime had begun to unleash a systematic and often brutal fourteen-year campaign of religious persecution against the evangelical community. During this period most evangelical churches were closed, church property and programs were nationalized without compensation, and thousands of evangelicals were imprisoned, tortured, or killed.[133]

The experience of Jallataa Nagarii was common: "I was hung over a pole with my feet up for three hours at a time. They beat me under my feet until I couldn't walk."[134] Others were placed in tiny cells, packed well beyond capacity, with disease-ridden and malnourished prisoners for months or years at a time. Many were simply executed.[135] Remarkably, the persecution seemed to produce an even more dynamic evangelical community whose numbers and influence continued to defy the odds. As already noted, between 1974 and 1991, the Ethiopian evangelical population grew by more than 600 percent from just under one million to approximately six million.[136] In short, thanks to their evangelistic efforts, and especially the efforts of their zealous early Ethiopian converts, American missionaries

---

132 Eshete, *Evangelical Movement*, 273–99.
133 "Ethiopia Political Imprisonment." SIM/SIM 1/32/9&10; a compilation of testimonials from evangelicals can be found in Cumbers, *Count It All Joy*; Bascom, *Hidden Triumph in Ethiopia*; Hege *Beyond Our Prayers*. All three accounts rely on the testimonies of Ethiopian converts.
134 Eide, *Revolution and Religion*, 239.
135 "Report from Ethiopia, 28 June 1976," SIM/SIM General/03/1966–1977 Publicity Section File; "Campaign to Root Out"; Cumbers, *Count It All Joy*, 111; Eide, *Revolution and Religion*, 222.
136 Barrett, *World Christian Encyclopaedia*.

inadvertently helped produce a movement with considerable political force—a force that historian Tibebe Eshete called, "one of the biggest roadblocks" to the success of the Ethiopian communist revolution.[137] As Eshete noted, by "choosing the path of suffering, and adopting indirect forms of resistance including the creation of underground structures, evangelicals promoted a storm frontier to challenge the regime."[138]

Another way in which some missionaries actively, and this time directly, undermined the Derg was through their role in quietly bringing international attention to the atrocities being perpetuated by the regime against the Ethiopian evangelical community. This was not a course that all missionaries supported. In fact, for long periods some groups like SIM argued that international attention would only serve to further antagonize the government and thus increase the persecution their Ethiopian colleagues were experiencing. Nevertheless, by the late 1970s representatives for American evangelical mission groups were discussing the most effective means for bringing attention to the plight of the Ethiopian evangelicals. Ultimately their strategy called for "discrete publicizing of the persecution ... released through a secular ... non-American source [consisting only of information] factual and accurate in every detail."[139] As groups like Amnesty International began to take part in the meetings, and news began to filter out into the mainstream media, international pressure began to mount, turning the Soviets' prized jewel into an object of global derision.[140]

Coinciding with the international condemnation of the Ethiopian regime was the onset of what turned out to be one of the greatest humanitarian disasters of the twentieth century: the Ethiopian famine of 1984–1985. The exodus of the Western diplomatic and aid communities from Ethiopia between 1975 and 1980 meant that the remaining evangelical missionaries were once again a key link between the events unfolding in rural Ethiopia and the outside world.[141] Ethiopian evangelicals were now the primary implementers of relief and development work in the country

---

137 Eshete, *Evangelical Movement*, 277.
138 Eshete, 298.
139 "Confidential Report on ad hoc meeting at Philadelphia, 21 August 1979," SIM/SIM General/05/04.
140 *Christianity Today*, "Campaign to Root Out"; *Toronto Star*, "Ethiopians Get 15 Days"; BBC Television News, 15 June 1979; *London Times*, 15 November 1985; Amnesty International, "Ethiopian Political Imprisonment," 4–8.
141 As a result of harassment by the Derg and continuing human rights abuses, American development assistance to Ethiopia was cancelled on 5 July 1979. Korn, *Ethiopia, the United States*, 53.

but American missionaries continued to be an integral part of the work, not only by providing highly skilled labor and training expertise, but also through their role as a primary news source on the disaster for the Western world.[142]

As early as August of 1980, the American evangelical media were describing famine conditions in the south and west of the country as comparable to the famine of 1973–74.[143] These reports continued to build in intensity through 1983 when SIM reported that 4.5 million Ethiopians were at risk of starvation.[144] Because of SIM's partnerships with large American evangelical NGOs such as World Vision, their news quickly reached the mainstream media. Despite the secular media's initial skepticism, by 1984 and 1985 images of starving Ethiopians were ubiquitous on Western television sets and were spread across virtually every major magazine and newspaper in the United States, sparking a massive outpouring of American, and indeed global, philanthropy.[145]

Even in advance of the media frenzy that ensued, and despite the continuing hostility of the Marxist regime in Ethiopia, the US government had begun to provide significant famine relief as early as 1983 ($11 million). By the peak of the famine in 1985, the US government was giving $280 million of food aid per year to Ethiopia—an amount almost equal to the efforts of the rest of the world combined.[146] Although the government-controlled press in Ethiopia paid scant attention to US assistance, the aid effort does appear to have been a watershed for US-Ethiopian relations. From 1986 onwards, the stance of the previously defiant Ethiopian regime towards the United States softened considerably and limited reforms began to be introduced.

In addition, by defying the Ethiopian government and providing substantial aid to rebel-held areas in the north, the US government also established strong relations with the Tigray People's Liberation Front (TPLF), the group who would claim control of the country only four years

---

142 *Africa Now*, "Ethiopia: Land of the Lion," 2–9.
143 *Africa Now*, "Ethiopia: SIM sends food," 12.
144 *Africa Now*, "Church, mission thriving," 12; *Africa Now*, "SIM provides more," 13; *Africa Now*, "Ethiopia: Famine conditions build," 12; *Africa Now*, "Ethiopia: Famine conditions," 12.
145 David Korn, the US Charges d'Affaires in Ethiopia during this period, claims he told reporters from the *Washington Post* and the *New York Times* of the impending crisis during their visit to cover the tenth year celebration of the Ethiopian Revolution in the summer of 1984, but they basically ignored his comments believing them to be politically motivated. Korn, *Ethiopia, the United States*, 124.
146 Korn, *Ethiopia, the United States*, 126. Also see Korn, *Ethiopia, the United States*, Appendix III, which includes the figures produced by the UN.

later. Finally, through its negligible aid to its once model client, the Soviet Union betrayed both its inability to adequately meet the challenge posed by the famine, as well as its growing disillusionment with the slow progress of Mengistu's socialist regime.[147] In 1991 a regime that just a few years earlier had appeared to be in complete control of the country unraveled much like its Soviet patron and was overthrown by the formerly Marxist, and now pro-American, TPLF.

Conclusion

Between 1960 and 1991, Ethiopia was as volatile as it was geopolitically significant. America's willingness to make Haile Selassie's nation the largest recipient of American military aid between 1950 and 1973, not to mention its readiness to risk astonishing amounts of military aid in an attempt to sway an apparently anti-American revolutionary government, belied the American convictions that Ethiopia was both essentially pro-American and of tremendous strategic value. The actions of the Soviet Union from 1976 to 1991 are even more startling. As Odd Arne Westad has noted, their massive intervention on the side of Ethiopia in the Ogaden in 1977 was "the most important Soviet-led military operation outside the area of the Warsaw Pact since the Korean War"—a truth resoundingly confirmed in their $11 billion provision of military aid to Mengistu's regime between 1976 and 1991.[148]

It is understandable then, that in the high stakes Cold War drama that was Ethiopia between 1960 and 1991, the role of American evangelical missionaries would have been ignored by historians. And indeed, relative to its surprising strength in the initial post-war period (1941–1960), the direct influence of American evangelical missionaries on US-Ethiopian relations did experience a moderate decline during these years. Nevertheless, as we have seen, American evangelical missionaries continued to play a substantial role in US-Ethiopian relations.

In keeping with patterns established before World War II, American evangelical missionaries remained an important source of both formal and informal intelligence for American policymakers during this period. In addition, prominent American evangelicals, such as Billy Graham and those participating in the Fellowship, continued to be an influential pro-Selassie voice in Washington right up until his death in 1975. Although

---

147 Korn, *Ethiopia, the United States*, 121–26.
148 Westad, *Global Cold War*, 277; Remnek, "Translating 'New Soviet Thinking,'" 154.

it was not direct, but instead came through the political activism of the Ethiopian evangelical community, American missionaries also played a major, if ironic, role in both the early success of the communist revolution during the mid-1970s and its ultimate demise.

Finally, through their critical role in the politically transformative famines of 1973–1974 and 1984–1985, and their uncharacteristic political activism during the years of the Marxist regime, American evangelicals poked and prodded American policymakers in directions that they may not have otherwise taken. If the ultimate test of historical importance is trying to imagine similar results without including a given variable, then even during this period of declining influence, the American missionaries active in Ethiopia remained historically significant. Indeed, remove any one of their activities listed above and the story of US-Ethiopian Cold War relations looks very different.

PART 2

Influence of American Evangelical Missionaries on US-Congo Cold War Relations

CHAPTER 3

Accidental Diplomats[1]

The Missionary Factor in US-Congo Relations, 1959–1963

In August of 1959, the newly appointed CIA Chief of Station was talking with a colleague in Washington about his upcoming tour in the Belgian Congo. While aware that all was not well, the unmistakable impression Larry Devlin was given of the Congo was one of a generally placid "diplomatic backwater." "There are a lot of black-tie dinners" warned his colleague. "Take two tropical dinner jackets so you can have one at the cleaners at all times. And, by the way, you'll be on the golf course by two o'clock every afternoon."[2] As things turned out, Devlin wouldn't have much time for golf. By the time he arrived in July of 1960, the once sleepy colony had already begun a startling descent into anarchy that would catapult the new nation to the forefront of the world's attention and make it the African focal point in the global Cold War.

Although he did not recognize it then, it was entirely appropriate that the first Americans Devlin would meet upon entering the Congo were evangelical missionaries.[3] For although they had starkly contrasting goals and methods, the CIA and American missionaries proved to be equally critical to their nation's Cold War triumph in the Congo. This chapter will follow the influence of American evangelical missionaries during the turbulent independence period, from 1959 to the end of the Katangan secession in January of 1963, and will argue that they played a major role in US-Congolese relations in three important ways: by helping to influence Congolese public opinion in a generally pro-American direction, by informing and influencing American public opinion on the Congo and, finally, by acting as an important diplomatic bridge between Congolese and American policymakers.

---

1 This chapter was originally published in Bevan Sewell and Maria Ryan, eds., *Foreign Policy at the Periphery*, Lexington: University Press of Kentucky, 2017. Used with permission.
2 Devlin, *Chief of Station, Congo*, ix.
3 Devlin, 3.

The Context of Independence-Era Congo

There are a number of reasons why the Congo became a Cold War focal point. Natural resources were near the top of the list. In addition to its potential as a world-leader in the production of industrial diamonds, by the 1950s the Congo was producing 10 percent of the planet's copper, the majority of Belgium's zinc, and approximately two-thirds of the world's cobalt.[4] Complementing the Congo's remarkable mineral resources was its size, strategic location, and potential for hydroelectric power, which, according to a 1959 CIA report, equaled 20 percent of the world's potential.[5] Further, as the second largest nation in Africa, located at the heart of the continent, and surrounded by nine economically subservient nations, it was assumed that whoever controlled the Congo would control the economic and political pulse of Central Africa.[6]

Perhaps even more significant, however, was the Congo's status as a genuinely contested space. Despite its history as a colony of a Western nation, there were a number of reasons why Congo's Cold War allegiances were very much uncertain. Prominent here was the Congo's violent history of racially based oppression. Beginning with the foundational period of King Leopold's dominance (1884–1908), the Congo witnessed almost unspeakable levels of violence that included: state-sanctioned mass killings and kidnappings, conscripted labor, and a harsh quota system of rubber harvesting that included the liberal use of the *chicotte* (whip).[7]

The long-term damage to the people of the Congo is incalculable. According to a disputed study by Jan Vansina of the University of Wisconsin, between 1890 and 1920 the Congolese population was cut in half.[8] Thanks to the attention brought to the situation by the Black American Presbyterian missionary William Sheppard, by the 1920s racially linked violence was a thing of the past.[9] The race-based colonial

---

[4] Kalb, *Congo Cables*, xxii; *Geographic Intelligence Review*, 5. Significantly, the majority of the Congo's mineral wealth resided in the politically separatist province of Katanga. So vast was the wealth of Katanga that less than a year before Congolese independence, the American intelligence community continued to worry aloud that "No colonial power in Africa ha[d] ever surrendered a prize comparable to the Katanga." *Geographic Intelligence Review*, 1.

[5] *Geographic Intelligence Review*, 6–8.

[6] Wrong, *In the Footsteps*, 68.

[7] Wrong, 47. Hochschild, *King Leopold's Ghost*, 164. Carl and Gladys Becker, interview with the author, 9 July 2009.

[8] Hochschild, *King Leopold's Ghost*, 233. While most of the violence was done by the Congolese themselves, everyone involved knew who had planned, organized, and implemented the system—and they were White.

[9] Hochschild, 164.

hierarchy, however, was not. Despite the Belgian government's attempts to initiate important economic and social reforms after World War II, efforts a CIA report called, "unequaled in other colonial areas of Africa," the profoundly resented racial hierarchy within the colony remained essentially untouched.[10] Right up to the time of independence, Africans were not allowed to walk or shop on the main streets of some Congolese towns and were "treated as second class citizens."[11]

A lack of democratic experience also made the Congo particularly vulnerable to Cold War intrigues. Unlike many British and French colonies, where limited elections and the development of democratic institutions were well underway by the 1940s, the first experience that some Congolese had of democratic participation was in May 1960, scarcely a month prior to independence.[12] Regarding leadership development and intellectual capital, the story was largely the same. Until the 1950s, the Belgian administration made almost no effort to encourage the training of students beyond the level of basic literacy required to serve as clerks or minor functionaries within the colonial economic system.[13] The result was the infamous distinction of having produced at the time of independence approximately one university graduate for every million Congolese and a Congolese elite with virtually no vested interest in the socio-economic status quo. As Eisenhower later remarked, this made "political stability almost impossible."[14]

The region's internal ethnic rivalries created yet another layer of complexity in the Congo. Perhaps by design, almost a century of colonial rule had done very little to break down the strong loyalties that separated the nation's approximately two hundred tribes and three hundred linguistic groupings. As a result, the Congo lacked a political and cultural center and was, therefore, particularly vulnerable to tribally based upheaval. As one

---

10 *Geographic Intelligence Review*, Number 58, CIA, RR MR 59-2, July 1959, 1.
11 Carl and Gladys Becker, interview with the author, 9 July 2009.
12 Although there were limited local elections in some areas as early as 1957, the May 1960 national election was the first that would have included a large percentage of Congolese. Devlin, *Chief of Station, Congo*, 7. In Kenya, for instance, the practice of selecting African leaders through democratic elections was well in place by the mid 1940s. Date and author of document obscured, National Archives II (NARA), RG84/2844/7; Morton, *Moi: The Making*, 71–73.
13 Williams, *Africa for Africans*, 90–91.
14 Attwood, *Reds and the Blacks*, 191. Further, of the some five thousand management-level positions available in the civil service at independence, a total of five were filled by Africans. Hochschild, *King Leopold's Ghost*, 301. The lack of vested interest by the Congolese elite was a point first brought out by Young, *Politics in the Congo*, 203; Eisenhower, *Waging Peace*, 573.

CIA analyst noted, "Villages ten miles apart might be as distinct as, say, the Italians and the Swedes. To expect large numbers of them to point their guns or spears in the same direction seemed highly unlikely."[15]

In short, the Congo had all the ingredients necessary to become a Cold War hot spot: vast natural resources and a geographically strategic location, a volatile racial history, political inexperience, and internal ethnic rivalry. Yet these ingredients did not guarantee the central place the Congo was to take in the Cold War. In the end it was the startling chain of events that transpired in the Congo between 1959 and January 1963 that turned this potentially combustible "diplomatic backwater" into the most important theater of the early Cold War in Africa.

Arguably the pivotal moment in modern Congolese history, and the spark that touched off the wildfire that was independence-era Congo, was the speech delivered by the newly elected Congolese prime minister at the nation's independence ceremony on 30 June 1960. In front of the Belgian king and a host of international diplomats and media, the mercurial Patrice Lumumba rejected reconciliation with his former colonial rulers and instead angrily denounced the "ironies, insults, and blows which we had to undergo morning, noon and night because we were Negroes."[16]

Igniting their latent anger, Lumumba's speech resonated deeply with many Congolese listening to it on the radio.[17] It also sparked extravagant expectations for what independence would bring. Within a week, when their expectations for immediate promotion and privilege went unheeded, a section of the Congolese army in Thysville mutinied. On 6 July, the mutiny spread to the capital city of Leopoldville, and then on to other areas of the country, where often intoxicated and leaderless soldiers perpetuated a series of violent attacks on European residents that induced widespread lawlessness and an economically destabilizing mass exodus from the Congo by the expatriate community.[18] Less than a week later the nation's

---

15 Adams, *War of Numbers*, 7.
16 Close, *Beyond the Storm*, 56; *Time*, "Congo: Freedom at Last."
17 This was especially true for members of the Congolese army who could not claim a single Black officer among their ranks and whose meager income was dwarfed by the relatively extravagant living set aside for their Belgian officers. Devlin, *Chief of Station, Congo*, 113–15.
18 Distrust of Lumumba among the army rank and file—most of whom came from tribes hostile to Lumumba's—were also central to explaining the almost instantaneous mutiny. In a letter published in Congolese political journals between the Brussels Roundtable and Congo's independence, representatives from the army wrote ironically but ominously, "Dear Lumumba, friend of the Europeans ... we guarantee you the infernal ruin of your powers as long as you insult us as ignorant and incapable of taking the place of your white brothers." Young, *Politics in the Congo*, 315.

wealthiest province (Katanga) seceded, devastating whatever hopes that remained for a stable and self-reliant Congo.[19]

Between the Katangan secession and the withdrawal of UN forces on 24 January 1963, the Congo saw almost half its provinces temporarily secede, the assassination of its prime minister, multiple tribal conflicts, and almost uninterrupted lawlessness.[20] It was this domestic political chaos, within the larger context of the Congo's economic and symbolic significance, which attracted superpower attention and secured the nation's prominent place in the Cold War. As had been the case in Ethiopia, playing a surprisingly significant role in the midst of this high-stakes Cold War contest were a group of generally unassuming American evangelical missionaries.

Religion and Anti-American Sentiment in the Congo

Ironically, the apparently widespread antagonism towards the West in the Congo was often bolstered by the religious loyalties of its population. By the time of Congolese independence, the effectiveness of both Catholic and Protestant missionaries had helped turn the country into a largely, if often nominally, Christian nation. In a religious Cold War that pitted a theoretically Christian West against an officially atheist East, the Christian-influenced religious vitality of the Congo should have been an important Western asset. However, historic tensions in the Congo between the principally Belgian Catholic and American Protestant missionaries served, in complicated ways, to undermine this Cold War advantage.

As early as the 1890s, American Protestant and Belgian Catholic missionaries were in conflict, with the Catholics supporting King Leopold's administration and the American Protestants acting as the colonial government's most outspoken critics.[21] American anti-colonial rhetoric, and the revolutionary activities of several caustically anti-colonial religious movements with ties to American missions, further exacerbated Belgian-Catholic mistrust of the American missionary enterprise in the Congo

---

19 This was certainly the view of the American policymaking establishment, who almost universally pushed for an end to the secession (despite Tshombe's pro-Western positions). Attwood, *Reds and the Blacks*, 194–95; Devlin, *Chief of Station, Congo*, 170; and Williams, *Tragedy of American Diplomacy*, 89.
20 For the best moment by moment unfolding of this period in the Congo see Kalb, *Congo Cables*.
21 Hochschild, *King Leopold's Ghost*, 102, 125, 165, 172–73, etc. There were significant financial, as well as cultural and religious reasons for the loyalty of the Catholic church to the Belgian colonial administration. For instance in 1926, the de facto colonial support for Catholicism became *de jure* when a law sanctioning state support for religiously based native education prohibited funds from going to Protestant schools. American Presbyterian Congo Mission (APCM) Legal Representative to US Vice-Consul Harry Schwartz, 7 February 1945, Presbyterian Historical Society Archives (PHS)/432/64/21.

during the three decades immediately preceding the Cold War.[22] Throughout the Second World War, this long standing religious antagonism increasingly found an outlet in Belgian-Catholic accusations that American missionaries were, among other things, undermining the colony's de facto color line, avoiding war-time mail censorship, encouraging Congolese opposition to the Belgian war effort, and organizing prayers for an American invasion of the Congo.[23] By 1944, the rumors and formal accusations had progressed to the extent that the American consul was forced to intervene on behalf of the embattled American missionaries and their Congolese converts.[24]

While the religious dimension of the Cold War did begin to create a spirit of Christian ecumenism between Catholic and Protestant missionaries in the Congo, their African converts were slow to discard the mutual animosity that had been so thoroughly woven into the fabric of their new faith.[25] Indeed, such was the political potency of Catholic-Protestant tensions amongst the Congolese that in December of 1960 the Catholic minister of finance in the new Congolese government openly marveled to two visiting US senators at how the United States "with a Protestant majority," could "elect a Catholic President," an event he likened to a "revolution."[26]

---

22 Presbyterian missionary "Ray" to Rev. J. Morrison, 8 September 1944, PHS/432/64/20; Presbyterian missionary Plummer Smith to Rev. J. Morrison, 18 October 1944, PHS/432/64/20.

23 APCM Legal Representative, Rev. J. Morrison to American Consul Patrick Mallon, 24 November 1943, PHS/432/64/19; US Consul General Robert Buell to Rev. J. Morrison, 26 February 1945, PHS/432/64/21; Presbyterian missionary "Ray" to Rev. J. Morrison, 8 September 1944, PHS 432/64/20; Letter from APCM Legal Representative to US Vice-Consul Harry Schwartz, 7 February 1945, PHS/432/64/21; Presbyterian missionary "Ray" to Rev. J. Morrison, 17 September 1944, PHS/432/64/20. Although most of these allegations were not taken seriously at the top of the Belgian bureaucracy, American missionaries, and especially their Congolese converts, experienced what could only be called bureaucratic persecution, with Congolese Protestants regularly being harassed and questioned by Belgian authorities and Congolese Catholics. Growing up as a son of American missionaries in the Congo of the 1930s and 1940s, Carl Becker Jr. recalled "being on evangelistic meetings in villages and the Catholic catechist would come out and chase the villagers away, because these [missionaries] were Protestants." Carl and Gladys Becker, interview with the author, 9 July 2009. For bureaucratic persecution see: unsigned letter to Rev. H. Coxill, 5 October 1944, PHS/432/82/14; and Presbyterian missionary Vernon Anderson to Rev. J. Morrison, 17 October 1944, PHS, 432/64/20.

24 US Consul General Robert Buell to Rev. J. Morrison, 26 February 1945, PHS/432/64/21.

25 For evidence of the improved relations between the Belgian community and the American missionary community see letters exchanged between Presbyterian missionaries Plummer Smith and Vernon Anderson on 29 April and 30 April 1952, PHS/432/64/22; and memo from the US Consul General in Leopoldville to the Department of State, 26 July 1957, National Archives II at College Park (NARA)/RG 84/350/C/60/1/Box 21.

26 Memorandum of Conversation including the Congolese Minister of Finance and Vice President Jean Baptiste Kibwe, US Senator Church, US Senator Moss, and others, 5 December 1960, NARA/RG 84/350/C/60/1/Box 24.

The most explosive ingredient in independence-era anti-American sentiment, however, may have been the mixture of syncretistic religious movements with the population's extravagant hopes for independence. As early as the 1920s, the tendency towards critical-thinking and egalitarianism in American Protestantism had combined with colonial oppression and indigenous religions to produce religio-political movements with a markedly anti-Western flavor. The largest and most significant of these was the Kimbanguist movement which was started in the early twentieth century by a Congolese convert of American Baptist missionaries. By the 1920s, Kimbanguism had become a mass protest movement against Belgian, and by extension White, power in the Congo.[27] In the years leading up to independence, Kimbanguism and other similar religious movements continued to concern both the Belgian authorities and the American missionaries often held responsible for them.[28] As one American mission's annual report from 1949 stated:

> [There were] some troubles in this section [of the Congo] with a new native sect which is a queer mixture of heathenism and Christian practice. It is subversive to both the church and the state. It obviously stems from the Watchtower Movement, and has a tinge of Bolshevism in it ... the Government has outlawed it ... Yet the movement still smolders.[29]

As Congolese independence grew closer, the potency of this religio-political cocktail began to be taken seriously by American diplomats.[30] In one of many other similar examples, Foreign Service Officer Richard Sanger expressed alarm at the success of operatives led by Lumumba confidant Antoine Gizenga in utilizing radical religious sentiment in support of the strongly anti-Western Parti Solidare Africaine (PSA). Sanger noted that in early 1960, the PSA was consciously and successfully building political support upon the Kimbanguist spiritual narrative of a Black redeemer who would drive the Whites from the land, but they did so with one adaptation. In the new storyline, a distinction was made between the "bad" White people (the Belgians and the missionaries who were to be

---

27 Among other descriptions of the origins of the Kimbanguist movement, see Duignan and Gann, *United States and Africa*, 245–46.

28 One example of the many instances of the syncretism alive and well in Congolese Christianity is found in a 1944 American missionary letter from southern Congo in which the missionary writes with marked concern of "our Baluba Bibles being misused by certain natives in a sort of secret cult." "Ray" to the Rev. J. Morrison, 8 September 1944, PHS/432/64/20.

29 American Presbyterian Congo Mission, "Annual Report" 1949, PHS/432/40/34.

30 "Biblical Prophecy of the Independence of the Congo," American Consul William C. Canup, 26 February 1960, NARA/RG84/350/C/60/1/24.

driven out) and the "good" White people (unnamed foreigners who were so rich they didn't need Congolese wealth and would give to the country without strings attached).[31]

Anti-Western sentiment born out of this strange union between racial animus, socialist propaganda and the spiritualization of political independence was not unique to the Kikwit area. Indeed, American missionaries active throughout the Congo during this period told similar stories.[32] In a lengthy memo assessing the causes of the Congo crisis, one US diplomat correctly hypothesized that,

> although the Communists did not cause the present crisis in the Congo, they have been able to capitalize on it to a far greater extent than I had realized ... a project should be set up to interview as many returning American and Canadian missionaries as possible and to correlate their stories regarding the events in their parts of the Congo in July. I think such a report would show that the state of panic which developed among the local Belgian officials and spread to many American and Canadian missionary groups was deliberately intensified by anti-Belgian and anti-Western extremists.[33]

---

31 In the hands of the local spiritualists, this message grew into a transcendent vision of a Black millennium, complete with tractors and farm machinery that would pour out of the ground on Independence Day. If this wasn't enough, for the most faithful followers there would be money-making machines to give them all that they needed. In May of 1960, American missionaries in the area were informed by local Christian converts that the leader of the "Spirit Movement," appropriately named "Machine," had told his followers that if the missionaries were allowed to continue preaching, the blessings of independence would never come. Not surprisingly, when the extravagant hopes of the local populations failed to materialize, Machine quickly and dramatically pinned responsibility on the American missionaries and told his male followers to fast while they sharpened their weapons for war. A series of threats and rumors of violence finally reached a climax in July of 1960 when Christian converts told the missionaries that "the Call" for their deaths had been issued by Machine and that if they wanted "to get out alive" they should "go quickly." Even though the American missionaries were able to return a few months later, a noticeable undercurrent of anti-missionary and anti-Western feeling remained. Richard H. Sanger to Hugh S. Cumming Jr., 22 August 1960, 11, NARA/RG 59/250/63/10/ Box 8.

32 For instance, at exactly the same time, American Baptist missionaries closer to Leopoldville were assaulted by an angry mob and forced to flee ("Chronological Record" PHS/432/14/6). In addition, AIM internal documents during the latter part of 1960 show widespread anti-missionary activity in the Lumumba stronghold of Stanleyville and Orientale and Kivu provinces (Dr. Carl Becker to Sidney Langford, 23 November 1960, BGCA/CN81/10/32; letter from unknown author, December 1960, BGCA/CN81/85/6; and Sidney Langford to "Dear Friends," 28 November 1960, BGCA/CN81/85/6). A further American missionary of the Evangelical Free Church was quoted in *World Vision Magazine* that around independence, "Things got beyond all limit and description ... White people beaten and put in jail, women abused, nobody was safe ... Bayonets were put to ribs, guns pointed at us from all sides, 'Doctor or missionary,' they said, 'it does not matter who you are or what you do. It is your skin.'" "Facts of a Field," 21.

33 Richard H. Sanger to Hugh S. Cumming Jr., 22 August 1960, NARA/RG 59/250/63/10/ Box 8.

Ethnicity, Propaganda, and Anti-West Sentiment

Ethnic loyalties were another unexpected source of anti-American feeling in many parts of the Congo. From the beginning, American policymakers had largely agreed that only a Congo united under a strong central government would be able to produce the stability the US believed was in its interests.[34] Thus, when within six months of independence the Congo had disintegrated into four tribally-based, rival governments, American support for the central government had, by default, pitted several powerful tribes against the US—including, ironically, the otherwise pro-West leadership of the powerful breakaway provinces of Katanga and Kasai.[35] By early 1961, America's perceived complicity in the murder of Patrice Lumumba, and its unwavering support for the moderate Kasavubu/Adoula government, had also unleashed anti-American anger in several additional Congolese provinces.[36] As one American missionary administrator confirmed in a confidential letter shortly after Lumumba's death, "Even though our missionaries have avoided political issues, the very fact that they are Americans has labeled them with the United States Government policy of favoring the Kasavubu regime, which, of course, is violently opposed both in the Kivu and Orientale Provinces."[37]

In this religiously, racially and ethnically anti-American context, it is not surprising that the increasing Communist propaganda in the Congo during the late 1950s and early 1960s found an enthusiastic audience. While Soviet and Chinese attempts at using printed propaganda were often amateurish, their use of the radio was highly effective.[38] In a still largely

---

34 Williams, *Tragedy of American Diplomacy*, 94.

35 To the end of his protracted and violent fight for self-determination, the American-educated and Methodist President of Katanga, Moise Tshombe, could not understand why the United States had failed to support an ardently pro-West provincial government's pursuit of American-style federalism. As he said after the successful UN invasion of Katanga, "I sacrificed myself to Western values and the Westerners have betrayed me." Bouscaren, *Tshombe*, 5.

36 In particular the Kivu and Orientale provinces which were the home of several large American missionary groups. E. G. Schuit to the Rev. Sidney Langford, 11 February 1961, BGCA/CN 81/10/32; General Secretary of the Africa Inland Mission (AIM) to the Rev. Robert S. Wilson of the Church Center Press, 28 February 1961, BGC/CN 81/85/6; E. G. Schuit to the Rev. Sidney Langford, 22 March 1961, BGC/CN 81/10/32.

37 "Confidential" letter from the AIM General Secretary to Rev. Robert S. Wilson, 28 February 1961, BGC/CN 81/85/6.

38 For instance, CIA Station Chief for Congo, Larry Devlin, in an interview with the author Michela Wrong recalled that soon after independence, the Soviet attempted to distribute out-dated and English versions of pro-communist tracts among a Congolese army that was barely literate, and if literate, only in French. Wrong, *In the Footsteps*, 69.

localized and oral society where the spoken word had retained its aura of authenticity, the radio held enormous power to influence Congolese public opinion. Observing the effects of radio propaganda in the Congo crisis, an American missionary doctor, William Close, remarked that he now "understood why politicians and coup plotters go for the radio station like mad dogs go for the throat. Those who control the flow of news and propaganda control the population."[39] As early as the mid-1950s, American missionaries were warning US diplomats that anti-American feeling was being intentionally stoked by the anti-Western rhetoric being beamed into the Congo by Nasser's Radio Cairo.[40] And by January 1960, six months prior to independence, American missionaries in rural northeast Congo were expressing alarm over the unsettling effects that the "extremist propaganda" was having on the Congolese population.[41]

Whether the source was external Communist propaganda or the voices of Lumumba's radical supporters speaking on local stations, the anti-West and anti-White message was often the same. Shortly after independence Lumumba's chief of protocol, Madame Andree Blouin, for instance, was regularly on the radio lambasting Western imperialists and ordering the population to set up roadblocks to intercept Whites fleeing with the country's gold.[42] As one missionary described the early days of independence, "All day long the local radio is broadcasting violent hatred against all whites ... and telling the most stupid stories and flagrant lies, in order to excite the mass[es] against all whites."[43]

While the message on government radio changed with the dismissal of Prime Minister Lumumba by President Kasavubu in September 1960, seemingly ubiquitous and unidentified broadcasts continued to preach the same anti-imperialist and anti-White gospel.[44] One such broadcast after the murder of Lumumba in February 1961, which called for the murder of all Whites in the Congo, so destabilized the population in the northeast that the US Embassy in neighboring Kampala strongly urged the immediate

---

39 Close, *Beyond the Storm*, 119.
40 Memorandum from American Consul General in Leopoldville, James Green, to the Department of State, Undated, NARA/RG 84/350/C/60/1/Box 21.
41 Minutes of the Congo Field Council, African Inland Mission, 7–12 January 1960, BGC/CN 81/36/10.
42 Close, *Beyond the Storm*, 59.
43 Unsigned letter of 15 July 1960, from AIM missionary in Leopoldville, BGC/CN 81/85/6.
44 The perception that many missionaries had of a sudden wave of radio propaganda was not a product of hysterical anti-communism. The reality was that between 1956 and 1961 Soviet radio propaganda in Africa had grown from next to nothing to over 130 hours of programming a week. Lessing, *Africa's Red Harvest*, 120–22.

evacuation of the region's American missionaries.[45] Those missionaries who ignored the evacuation plea and remained in the Congo reported a widespread increase in anti-mission rhetoric, threats of violence from formerly friendly locals, and the sudden arrival of vocabulary that could have been taken directly from the pages of *Pravda*. After visiting a rural church that had been started by his mission, one American reported that "[u]pon our arrival [the entire town] met us with shouts and curses. Africa Inland Mission was but an instrument of the imperialists ... 'Take your Bible, and your lying missionaries, and your Jesus Christ, and get out of our village right now. If you don't, we will kill you!'"[46]

Colonial brutality, institutionalized racial prejudice, historical antagonism between Catholics and Protestants, a potent cocktail of religiously-infused political radicalism, early post-independence US policy, and widespread anti-Western propaganda combined to create a context in which anti-Americanism should have been the default mindset for many Congolese. And yet the story did not play out as one might have predicted. Thanks to the longstanding and intimate relationship between significant portions of the Congolese population and American missionaries, a considerable residue of pro-US sentiment remained—and this would prove to be a critical component in the Cold War battle for Congolese hearts and minds.

The Missionary Factor in the Battle for Congolese Hearts and Minds

The story of American missionary influence can be traced back to the beginning of the Congo's modern history—that is, the inception of King Leopold's Congo Free State in 1884. Because the United States was the first nation to officially recognize Leopold's claim to the Congo, the staunchly Catholic monarch reluctantly opened the colony's doors to American Protestant missionary activity.[47] The Americans did not tarry. In just over a decade there were at least eight different American missionary organizations active in the Congo, including the American Baptists (1886), the American Methodists (1886), the Christian and Missionary Alliance (1889), the Southern Presbyterian Church of the United States (1891), and the Disciples of Christ (1895).[48]

---

45 E. G. Schuit to the Rev. Sidney Langford on 15 February 1961, BGC/CN 81/10/32.
46 Brashler, *Change: My Thirty-Five*, 131.
47 Hochschild, *King Leopold's Ghost*, 79–84.
48 Hildebrandt, *History of the Church*, 168.

Significantly, American missionary activity in the Congo continued to grow over the next several decades as new missionary groups arrived and some children of American missionaries, born and raised in the colony, returned to build on their parent's work. As the records of the US consulate in Leopoldville indicate, as of the 1940s almost all significant American activity within the Congo included Protestant missionaries, of whom virtually all would have been theologically conservative evangelicals.[49] By 1949, the Presbyterians alone could boast of 124 full time missionaries; and by 1960, the total number of American missionaries active in the Congo was well over one thousand, giving the Congo one of the largest concentrations of American missionaries in sub-Saharan Africa.[50]

Just as important as the large number of American missionaries in the Congo was their longevity. In stark contrast with the secular missionaries of the 1960s, who came with the Peace Corps or Crossroads Africa for one- or two-year terms, it was not uncommon for a missionary couple to spend their entire adult lives in the Congo. The Africa Inland Mission (AIM) in the 1960s, for instance, could boast of multiple missionaries who had lived in the former Belgian colony for over forty years, including some children of these missionaries who had returned as missionaries themselves.[51]

If the large number of American missionaries in the Congo and the longevity of their stay there made it likely that their influence on the Congolese people would be significant, the nature of their work made it virtually inevitable. The very presuppositions upon which the evangelical missionary enterprise rested assumed a spiritually rooted and intimate transnational bond with the people. Whatever their personal prejudices, these missionaries believed in a fundamental spiritual equality of humanity under a creator God for whom there was, according to the Apostle Paul, "neither Jew nor Greek, slave nor free, male nor female. For you are all one in Christ."[52] As one missionary writing in the midst of the Congo crisis put it, "regardless of any other factors which might tend to separate us

---

49 NARA/RG 84/350/49/18/Box 2/Folder 131.

50 According to John Crawford, the total number of Protestant missionaries in the Congo in 1959 was 2,608. If previous patterns apply, between 50 and 70 percent of this number would have been Americans. Crawford, "Protestant Missions in Congo," 94. See also, list of Presbyterian missionaries prepared by the Presbyterian Legal Representative for American Consul, 16 September 1949, PHS/432/64/22; Memo to Wayne Fredericks, 6 August 1962, NARA/RG 59/250/63/10/Box 5; Howard Brinton to Dear Friends in the Home Churches, 10 July 1953, United Methodist Church Archives (UMCA)/1121/3-2-25.

51 Carl Becker, interview with the author, 9 July 2009; Brashler, *Change: My Thirty-Five*, 53, 117, 121.

52 Gal 3:28 (NIV).

from our Congolese brethren, may we be truly 'TSHINTU TSIMUE,' one in Christ, made one in redemption by His blood to newness of life, brought together into one by the fellowship of His service for His Church in the Congo."[53]

That is not to say that American missionaries were devoid of a sense of cultural superiority or racial prejudice. Indeed, it appears that some missionaries felt far too at home with the regimented racial categories long in place in the Belgian colony. For instance, one American missionary who arrived in the early 1950s described with disgust a typical Congolese scene: "We sit down to a supper as a missionary group, served by a 40–50-year-old 'boy,' who is summoned for his services by a little hand bell in reach of the hostess." This sort of Old South mentality was endemic in the Belgian colony and was occasionally adopted by missionaries from a variety of nationalities. The same missionary noted a similar spirit of prejudice in a Norwegian missionary who, when offered a cup of coffee by some Congolese, turned to the American in English and said, "Surely you don't drink with these people? Aren't you afraid of getting dysentery?"[54] These instances of missionary prejudice did not go unnoticed by US diplomats. After getting frustrated with American missionary loyalty to the breakaway province of Katanga, one complained to his superiors that "A number of them (particularly those Methodists whose origin is the Deep South) are segregationists in thought and action ... How they have gotten away with this," he continued, "never ceases to amaze me."[55]

Nevertheless, while American missionaries were not immune to the racial prejudice at the heart of anti-Western sentiment in the Congo, generally speaking they stood out as racial progressives in a colony dominated by the color line. Indeed, the willingness of American missionaries to challenge the Belgian racial hierarchy seems to have been a primary cause of much of the mistrust that had existed between the missionaries and their Belgian neighbors well into the Cold War. In one of several similar episodes the American missionary H. E. Griggs was refused

---

53 Letter from Acting Area Secretary for Congo, APCM, Walter D. Shephard, January 1962, PHS/432/80/16.

54 Bayly, *Congo Crisis*, 46–47. It is important to note here the ambiguity of this example. In this case, the action of the missionary can legitimately be viewed as a prudent health measure, and not, as critics would put it, an example of racism. However, the issue here is not necessarily the motive of the missionary but the message it likely sent to the Congolese with whom he was interacting. It is also important to note that the one making the criticism is also a missionary.

55 Lewis Hoffacker, to Sheldon B. Vance, 27 October 1961, NARA/RG59/250/63/10/Box 6.

re-entry into the Belgian Congo by colonial officials precisely because he was undermining the colony's racial hierarchy. In a letter to Mr. Griggs, the American representative of the Congo Protestant Church wrote, "I learn that the Government agrees that your character is above reproach morally, but they insist that you set an unbecoming example in living on a native level economically," a verdict confirmed by the US consul general who told Griggs that according to the colonial administration, "Your manner of life casts discredit on persons of the white race and threatens to compromise public order and security."[56]

The relatively egalitarian perspective of the American missionaries was most explicit in the area of church governance. Well before the Belgians were seriously contemplating Congolese independence, American missionaries were consciously applying the democratic structures and practices they had grown up with to the Congolese church. Soon after World War II, most American missionary groups were holding elections in order to choose African leaders for church leadership. By the mid-1950s even the conservative AIM could, with obvious pride, claim that "The Church is emerging as a separate entity [from the mission] but the Government will not recognize it as such." The document continued, "[o]n all the Councils of the Church, the mission is represented by a minority in an advisory capacity" including the power of the purse, where "The Church has for long been responsible for its own financial matters."[57]

Similar to the case of Ethiopia, the personal practice of democracy that hundreds of thousands of Congolese experienced within American-influenced Protestant congregations not only created a close association between the United States and political independence, it also provided virtually the only training in Western-style democratic institutions available in pre-independence Congo.[58] As the first President of the post-independence Congolese Senate told an American missionary friend, "David ... they just stand up and yell to get the floor! I had to quiet them all down and teach them what we Presbyterians know, that you raise your hand to make a motion ... you talk about things after you are

---

56 H. E. Griggs to the Vice Governor General of the Belgian Congo, 23 June 1947, quoting Vernon Anderson, of the Congo Protestant Church, who, in turn was quoting from an interview Anderson had had with Belgian colonial officials concerning Griggs. NARA/RG84/350/49/18/2.

57 A Memorandum from the Congo Field, September 1957, BGC/CN81/36/10.

58 A Memorandum from the Congo Field, September 1957, BGC/CN81/36/10; David Miller, interview with the author, 30 June 2009; Carl Becker, interview with the author, 9 July 2009.

recognized by the chair."⁵⁹ By the standards of today, many American missionaries in the Congo appear to have been racially insensitive at best; but within the context of pre-1959 Belgian-Congo where Congolese were entirely excluded from positions of leadership and in which, by design, virtually no political education was taking place, the Africanization and democratization of the Congolese Protestant Church initiated by American Protestant missionaries was paradigm altering.⁶⁰

It was, however, the consistent tradition of humanitarianism and the personal relationships that developed over the years between the American missionaries and the Congolese, that gave the egalitarianism and the democratization of the Protestant church their potency. As a future American ambassador to Kenya, Smith Hempstone, observed in 1958, the work of American evangelical missionaries, although principally motivated by the spiritually rooted desire to "win souls," had always included a strong materially based humanitarian component.⁶¹ In the Congo this tradition was principally seen in the medical and educational fields. In almost every case, when a new American missionary group arrived in the Congo their explicitly religious activities were complemented by the building of hospitals and schools. This pattern applied to even the most theologically conservative missions, such as the AIM, whose first hospital, built in 1922, preceded its first explicitly religious school.⁶²

Thanks to their desire to give the Congolese the ability to read the Bible for themselves, American missionaries also poured considerable energy and resources into Congolese education.⁶³ For instance, by 1941, in an official report to the American consul, the Presbyterians could claim to have trained 1,535 Congolese teachers, who were annually educating over thirty-five thousand students.⁶⁴ Just five years later the American

---

59 David Miller, interview with the author, 30 June 2009.
60 There is no more sophisticated analysis of the significant role that the infusion of the Protestant missionary worldview played in pre-independence African cultures like those present in Congo than Sanneh, *Encountering the West*.
61 Letter from Smith Hempstone to Walter S. Rogers of the Institute of Current World Affairs, 22 January 1958, NARA/RG 84/350/C/60/1/Box 21.
62 Hildebrandt, *History of the Church*, 215–16.
63 This apparently minor point is of considerable significance, for it assumes an ultimate intellectual and spiritual independence that was present in neither the pre-Vatican II Catholic church, nor in many traditional African tribal hierarchies. As Lamin Sanneh and others have noted, the quest to teach literacy and to translate the Bible into the local languages was, thus, near the heart of the movement towards political independence in Africa. Sanneh, *Encountering the West*, 17.
64 Presbyterian Mission Treasurer to American Consul, Patrick Mallon, 2 February 1942, PHS/432/64/19.

dominated Council of Protestant Missions of Congo released a report that documented a total of 11,455 Protestant missionary-run schools that were educating almost 350,000 Congolese.[65] Thus by the time of independence it can be conservatively estimated that American Protestant missions were responsible for providing at least a primary-level education to approximately one million Congolese.[66]

Missionary efforts in the area of medicine were equally transformative. One particularly telling example is the work of Dr. Carl Becker. First arriving in the Congo in 1929 with his young family, Becker was immediately confronted with a host of medical challenges. Malaria and blackwater fever were rampant, child mortality was nearly 50 percent, and in some areas of the Congo it was estimated that nearly 40 percent of the population was afflicted with leprosy.[67] While acting to address each of these crises, Becker's work in the field of leprosy treatment is noteworthy. By the onset of World War II, the young American physician had established three leprosy colonies in northeast Congo which not only treated the afflicted, but acted as research centers where Becker and his team of Congolese and American assistants pioneered the cultivation of leprosy bacillus—a process that helped transform the way leprosy was understood and treated around the world.[68]

Driven by deep Christian convictions, Becker typically worked six, fourteen-hour days, but still managed to wake every morning before five for prayer and Bible reading.[69] Becker's belief that all people were made in God's image and worthy of love and dignity also pushed him to fight

---

65 Informational booklet produced by the Council of Protestant Missions in Congo for 1946, NARA/RG 84/350/49/18/2/Box 14/360.

66 This estimate is a conservative number arrived at by taking the number of years that the Protestant missions had been involved in education by the time of independence, the increasing size of that program over the years and the reality that most students would only attend for two or three years of primary level education (grade levels 1–6). If, therefore, in 1951 there were 350,000 students in Protestant schools in the Congo, and that each year approximately one-fourth of those students would be new (85,000), over the fifteen years in which the Protestant educational push was at its peak, there would have been approximately 1.3 million students. This number does not include the large number of Congolese who had received some Protestant education prior to World War II. It should also be mentioned that while American missionaries were widely successful in educating the Congolese at a primary level—that is in basic literacy—they were discouraged from training students beyond the secondary level. The handful of students that went to university prior to independence were, thus, forced to go outside of the Congo for their post-secondary education.

67 Peterson, *Another Hand on Mine*, 128.

68 Peterson, 131–32, 159.

69 Vera Hillis, interview with the author, 9 July 2009.

against the isolating cultural stigmatization attached to leprosy victims in the Congo. Towards this end, large tracts of land given to the mission by the colonial government were converted into small-scale farms where leprosy patients were able to work and provide for themselves and their families.[70]

The moral and medical success of the colony at Oicha was such that by 1951 it was home to four thousand self-supporting leprosy patients and six thousand of their family members, making it the second largest leprosarium in the world.[71] By 1957, Dr. Becker's Oicha operation included not only the leprosarium and a 250-bed hospital, but a tuberculosis sanatorium, a maternity ward, an orphanage, modern operating rooms, eight satellite dispensaries, and even a psychiatric unit.[72] It is no wonder then that the American syndicated columnist Art Buchwald, in writing home from the Congo, observed that "In all of Congo, the man who made the greatest impression on us was an American missionary doctor named Carl K. Becker ... We couldn't help thinking as we left Oicha that America had its own Dr. Schweitzer in Congo."[73]

Becker's accomplishments were unusual both in scale and quality. That said, virtually every American mission in the Congo had a substantial medical program. At the time of independence, for instance, the Presbyterians had eight hospitals and ten dispensaries placed throughout southern Congo, treating over fifty thousand patients a year. Significantly, five of these hospitals were also teaching hospitals responsible for producing over 150 new nurses each year.[74] The activities of the Baptists, the Methodists, the Seventh Day Adventists, and other American missions were much the same. Indeed, as early as 1953, the Protestant missions in the Congo (most of whom were American) could boast of 171 hospitals and dispensaries which, in the previous year, had treated 5,611,688 cases.[75]

Considering the longevity, scale, and quality of the American missionary humanitarian effort in the Congo, it is not surprising that the American diplomatic establishment saw in the actions of these accidental diplomats the potential foundation for a close relationship between the

---

70 Peterson, *Another Hand on Mine*, 131.
71 Vera Hillis, interview with the author, 9 July 2009; Peterson, *Another Hand on Mine*, 132.
72 Peterson, *Another Hand on Mine*, 154.
73 Peterson, 144.
74 Annual Statistical Report included in letter from Vernon A. Anderson to Dr. C. Darby Fulton, Executive Secretary, Board of World Missions, 12 February 1959, PHS/432/41/50.
75 Howard Brinton to Dear Friends in the Home Churches, 10 July 1953, UMCA/1121/3-2-25.

United States and the newly independent nation. In the official American statement congratulating the Congo on its upcoming independence, Eisenhower's representative, Robert D. Murphy, drew special attention to the American missionary tradition in the country. Since 1885, Murphy remarked, "hundreds of American missionaries ... have come to this country to open schools and hospitals and to contribute to the welfare of the people. Through the years they have grown to love the Congo and its people and have created the basis of a lasting friendship between our two countries."[76]

An important biproduct of the humanitarian tradition of the American missionaries was the level of intimacy they enjoyed with significant portions of the population. Unlike the diplomatic and Belgian expatriate communities, missionaries often lived outside of the European enclaves and close to the Congolese. They visited African homes, shared their meals, and learned their languages. Most missionaries had to learn a minimum of two additional languages in order to do their work—normally French and one of the local trade languages (typically Lingala or Swahili). But for the missionary doctors, Bible translators, and rural evangelists, proficiency in one or more of the tribal languages was also necessary. As a result, it was not uncommon for veteran American missionaries to be functionally fluent in four or five languages.[77] For instance, by the end of his thirty-five years in the Congo, the seasoned AIM missionary Peter Brashler could boast of proficiency in French, Bangala, Swahili, Flemish, and Kakwa, the latter of which had been, to that point, an entirely unwritten language.[78]

For Bible translators in particular, learning the local languages involved much more than an academic mastery of a new grammatical structure and vocabulary. The thorough understanding of the local culture they were required to gain in order to create a faithful and culturally relevant translation of the Bible (including a tribal culture's humor, oral history, and subtle word-play) invariably produced deep cultural intimacy.[79] The decades it often took to complete a translation of the Bible also produced profound bonds of loyalty and friendship with the Congolese with whom they had worked. After giving the first copy of a newly translated Bible to

---

[76] Statement by the Honorable Robert D. Murphy, Personal Representative of the President and Head of the American Delegation to the Independence Ceremonies of the Republic of the Congo, 30 June 1960, NARA/RG 84/350/C/60/1/Box 24.

[77] Betty Pontier, interview with the author, 9 July 2009; Brashler, *Change: My Thirty-Five*, 35, 37, 58, 63, 69; John and JoAnn Ellington, interview with the author, 29 June 2009.

[78] Brashler, *Change: My Thirty-Five*, 35, 37, 58, 63, 69.

[79] Sanneh, *Encountering the West*, 16–19.

a Congolese Christian with whom he had worked for sixteen years, one missionary recalled with satisfaction that,

> The whole class wanted to fondle the Bible at the same time. Ofeni's reaction was unforgettable. There were tears in his eyes as he leafed through the Book, some of which fell on the bright new pages. Finally, in a voice thick with emotion he hugged the Bible to his breast and said, "Lord, let now thy servant depart in peace."[80]

In the racially charged Congolese context, the personal bonds and the cultural intimacy that grew between some American missionaries and their African colleagues broke down cultural and personality-based barriers and replaced them with genuine friendships, rooted in mutual respect and affection.

Of course, the American missionaries who worked in the Congo were not there to promote American interests or to create pro-American sentiment. Their aim was religious. And yet, considering the longevity, intimacy, and type of the American missionary involvement in the Congo, it is not surprising that there existed a reservoir of pro-missionary, and therefore often pro-American, feeling amongst the wider population. In the aftermath of independence, the evidence of pro-missionary sentiment was abundant.

Missionaries and Pro-American Sentiment in Independence-Era Congo

At mission stations across the Congo, it was often Congolese Christians, afraid for the safety of their American friends, who first warned the missionaries of impending threats and pleaded with them to flee. Significantly, it was these reports coming in from across rural Congo that gave the State Department a sense of the breadth and scale of the developing crisis.[81] Following the first major missionary evacuation in late July of 1960, additional reports described around-the-clock security patrols being set up by local Congolese to protect the homes and property of the missionaries. As one missionary organization reported, "Pastors and Christians on each of these stations have set up a 24 hour watch to prevent looting of the station and the missionaries' homes."[82] After Lumumba's

---

[80] Brashler, *Change: My Thirty-Five*, 70.
[81] Protestant Council of Congo to American supporters, 26 July 1960, BGC/CN 81/36/9; Richard H. Sanger to Hugh S. Cumming Jr., 22 August 1960, NARA/RG 59/250/63/10/Box 8.
[82] Africa Inland Mission American Home Office to "the Relatives, Churches and Friends of our Congo Missionaries," 26 July 1960, BGC/CN 81/3/25.

murder had forced a second evacuation in February 1961, a reconnaissance trip by a second missionary organization found that "In all the places we visited there are guards in all the missionary residences [and an] ... earnest group of [Congolese] men there who are conscientiously trying to guard all mission property."[83] In the context of widespread looting of European businesses and homes during this period, the contrasting treatment towards the property of American Protestant missionaries is noteworthy.

In addition, the larger local communities, who saw the missionary departure as a loss of medical care and education, were often equally vocal in their calls for the missionaries to stay. In several instances, local officials ordered missionaries to stay or pleaded with missionary administrators for their return.[84] The president of the Congo, Joseph Kasavubu, was only the most prominent official to do so when, in July 1960, he visited the American Baptist Mission to plead with the missionaries to stay despite a recent violent attack on colleagues in the area.[85] Significantly, even when balanced against the rising threat of violence against American citizens, the State Department, as late as 22 July 1960, saw the benefits of a continuing American missionary presence and counseled against a hasty withdrawal stating: "where possible," the State Department contended, the missionaries "should continue occupying mission properties."[86] Finally, despite examples of anti-missionary rhetoric and violence in some areas, the sense of mutual affection and loyalty between the US missionaries and the Congolese people was confirmed as missionaries across the Congo returned—often within several weeks of their initial departure—to a generally, though not universally, warm welcome.[87]

Although at least 70 percent of the American missionaries active in the Congo had temporarily evacuated by August 1960, a significant number of others ignored the risks to stay and continue their work alongside their

---

83 Carl Becker to Sidney Langford, 17 February 1961, BGC/CN 81/10/32.
84 Mr. Stanfield from State Department, 2 February 1961, BGC/CN 81/85/6.
85 AIM American Home Office to "the Relatives, Churches and Friends of our Congo Missionaries," 26 July 1960, BGC/CN 81/3/25. Other examples of Congolese officials supporting a missionary return include a letter from the AIM Congo Field Council "To our Congo Missionaries everywhere," 13 May 1961, BGC/CN 81/85/2.
86 Clyde W. Taylor of the Evangelical Foreign Missions Association (EFMA) to Evangelical Mission Executive, 22 July 1960, BGC/CN 81/85/6.
87 AIM Congo Field Council "To our Congo Missionaries everywhere," 13 May 1961, BGC/CN 81/85/2; Letter from Carl Becker to Sidney Langford, 17 February 1961, BGC/CN 81/10/32; Memorandum from American Consul in Salisbury to Secretary of State, 5 August 1960, NARA/RG 84/350/C/60/1/Box 24; Memorandum from American Consul General in Kampala to Secretary of State, 21 April 1961, NARA/RG 84/350/C/60/1/ Box 27.

Congolese colleagues.[88] And in a few instances, such as that of Dr. Herb Atkinson and his young family, missionaries fought against the current of fleeing expatriates and the strong protests of their missionary boards and the American government in order to enter the Congo.[89] The commitment of this minority of missionaries to stand alongside the Congolese at a time of crisis seems to have further cemented the bond between American missionaries and many within the Congolese population. This is evident in the multiple cases where American missionaries acting in particularly anti-Western regions were given special protection by local rebels.

Regarding the deference given to the few Presbyterian missionaries continuing the mission's work in the Congo, veteran missionary David Miller recalled, "each of us went to an area where we were known, where we had done evangelistic and educational work, so that when the guys with the paint and arrows ... would stop the truck, they would say, 'Oh that's just [the name of the missionary], let him go.'"[90] In another instance, the veteran missionary physician Dr. Becker, who had refused his mission's request to evacuate, was able to travel over one hundred miles, through multiple rebel checkpoints, in order to successfully demand the release of three American missionaries being held captive by a group of drunk and angry rebels. According to his biographer, at one of the many roadblocks Becker and his Congolese assistant encountered "a mob of Africans brandishing spears and bows and arrows rushed the car. Boldly the doctor rolled down his window, stuck his head out and waved at them. Then he thought he recognized a couple of them and called them by name. Immediately their attitude changed."[91]

The special consideration given by the Congolese to American missionaries was not lost on the US State Department, who regularly noted the largely positive reception of returning missionaries to otherwise hostile areas and the mysterious resilience of "goodwill and respect" for the United States in the now predominantly anti-Western Congo. As one US embassy report after Lumumba's death observed:

---

88 By 20 July 1960 the State Department was reporting that roughly 70 percent of Americans (the vast majority of missionaries) had been evacuated from the Congo. Memorandum "Evacuation of Americans from the Republic of the Congo," 20 July 1960, NARA/RG 59/250/63/10/Box 6. The AIM could report at the end of August that 75 percent of AIM missionaries had been evacuated. It appears, then, that the bulk of evacuations were completed by the end of July and that most of those missionaries remaining, around 25 percent, stayed throughout the crisis. Report from Dr. R. T. Davis, "Congo Turbulence," BGC/CN 81/85/6.

89 Peterson, *Another Hand on Mine*, 19.

90 David Miller, interview with the author, 30 June 2009.

91 Peterson, *Another Hand on Mine*, 15.

> While Americans head the propaganda list ... a considerable reservoir of goodwill does exist for Americans. Provincial President Manzikula, who last time was less than friendly, greeted the reporting officer on this trip like a long-lost brother and praised the work of American missionaries. Louis Lumumba, brother of Patrice and influential Provincial Minister of Interior, also praised American missionaries.[92]

In a letter the following month to Congressman Arends, Assistant Secretary of State Brooks Hays noted in specifically Cold War terms that,

> American (and European) missionaries have been doing a most effective job for many years in combating communism in the Congo. It is significant in this connection that a great majority of the Congo's present leaders are markedly anti-communist. This can certainly be ascribed, at least in part, to the fact that many of them were educated by missionaries.[93]

Again, a year later, the American consul working in the breakaway province of Katanga reiterated what by then seems to have been the widespread conclusion that "there still remains ... a reservoir of goodwill which will serve us in the future when the current nastiness of UN/GOK conflict passes. The missionaries must be given credit for this basically charitable attitude among the Katangans."[94]

In sum, as the Congo moved towards independence, a host of toxic forces were acting against the development of a pro-Western and pro-American sentiment within the Congolese population, including a colonial past filled with racially based violence and prejudice, a host of ethnic and religious tensions, a lack of democratic experience, and an effective program of radical and Communist propaganda. As a result, for many independence-era Congolese anti-American feeling was virtually a birthright. Yet in the midst of this hostile context, there existed such a resilient sympathy for the United States among both the grassroots and elite of Congolese society that American diplomats concluded was largely the result of several generations of evangelical missionary work in the country.

---

92 Memorandum from American Embassy in Leopoldville to Department of State, "Current Conditions in Stanleyville," 24 February 1961, NARA/RG 84/350/C/60/1/Box 24.
93 Assistant Secretary Brooks Hays to Congressman L. C. Arends, 9 March 1961, NARA/RG 59/250/63/10/Box 8.
94 Lewis Hoffacker to Charles S. Whitehouse, 24 March 1962, NARA/RG 59/250/63/10/Box 5.

The Influence of American Missionaries on US Public Opinion on the Congo, 1959–1963

American missionaries also played an important role in shaping US public opinion on the Congo. As a general rule, prior to 1959, if an image of the Congo existed at all in the American mind it was a reflection of Joseph Conrad's *Heart of Darkness*. While few Americans may have actually read the classic, its depiction of the Congo as the symbolic epicenter of human depravity, barbarism, and greed had filtered down into the larger American culture. Conscious of the religious appeal of this powerful image, missionaries to the Congo were not above using the metaphor of darkness when appealing to churches and Christian groups for financial and spiritual support.[95] To the extent that they did, missionaries were responsible for perpetuating the vaguely disturbing picture of the Congo that existed in the American psyche and that seemed to be confirmed in the events of independence-era Congo.

However, American missionaries did not just reinforce nineteenth century stereotypes. In fact, prior to 1959, the only significant information available to the larger American public countering Conrad's vision came from missionaries. While their reports often failed to reach a broader public, large numbers of evangelicals were gaining a more nuanced and often positive view of the Congo and its people. Through missionary letters, denominational and missionary organization publications, evangelical radio, and regular talks at Christian gatherings around the nation by missionaries home on furlough, significant numbers of Americans were encouraged to see the Congolese as a part of the universal Christian family and as future leaders in an optimistic vision of the new independent Africa.[96] As a result, when the modern and very real Congo suddenly entered the American public consciousness in 1959 arguably the most informed and engaged sector of the population was the evangelical community.

Generally speaking, the American missionary community was not intentionally political in their communication to their broad network of supporters in the US. As it had always been, their aim was to see the Congolese Church grow and become a self-sufficient and vibrant

---

95 For instance, see references to "the Dark Continent" in the article "International Conference" in the AIM publication, *Inland Africa*, May–June 1959.

96 *Inland Africa*, "International Conference"; "To the Relatives, Churches and Friends of our Congo Missionaries," 3 July 1960, BGC/CN 81/85/6; "Annual Report" of the APCM for 1949, PHS/432/40/34.

Christian community, and while the bulk of missionary news that reached the American public during this time included information relating to the political upheaval, it reflected this primarily religious perspective.[97] The important exception to this rule was the very public, and surprisingly effective, campaign waged by American missionaries on behalf of the critical breakaway province of Katanga.

Missionary Activism in Katanga, 1959–1963

The two principal causes for missionary activism in Katanga were their close identification with the Katangan people and the outspoken anti-communism of the American missionary-educated Katangan leader.[98] For several generations, American missionaries had lived among the Katangans, educating their children, caring for their sick, and preaching the gospel. Like Methodist missionary Howard Brinton, whose childhood playmates included several of the province's key leaders, for many American missionaries the people of the region had become like family.[99] Thus when US-supported UN forces took action on behalf of the ideologically ambiguous central government, and against the explicitly anti-communist Katangan secession, American missionaries, to the considerable displeasure of the US government and their own mission boards back home, aggressively lobbied the American public and political elite for a change in US policy.

Missionary activism took a variety of forms. Missionaries at home on furlough often used speaking engagements to advocate for a pro-Katangan change in US policy.[100] In addition, letters to churches and supporters sent by the numerous American missionaries still in Katanga informed their readers, in often heart-wrenching detail, of American-backed UN violence against both the missionary community and the Katangan people. One such letter written by Seventh Day Adventist missionary Julia Hoel described UN attacks on an American missionary compound in which missionaries

---

97 "To all readers of the Congo Mission News," Letter from the Council of Protestants in Congo, 26 July 1960, BGC/CN 81/36/9.

98 A particularly revealing description of American missionary identification with the Katangans comes in a letter from American Consul, Lewis Hoffacker to Congo Desk officer Sheldon Vance, 27 October 1961, in which Hoffacker claims that American missionaries there regularly referred to Katanga as "our country," NARA/RG 59/250/63/10/ Box 6.

99 "Confidential" Memo to Governor Williams, 18 January 1962, NARA/RG 59/250/63/10/Box 7.

100 Speech by Mr. Fred Lasse to the Keswick convention in New Jersey, September 1960, BGC/CN 81/85/6.

had been wounded and a home had been completely destroyed.[101] Other letters detailed the bombings of a Katangan hospital by the UN, the mounting death toll, and indigenous outrage that the US would return Katangan affection with violence.[102] As one missionary put it, "It made our hearts bleed to think that the American citizens were paying for the killing of these African people who have been standing by the same principles of freedom and self-expression that America has been proud of upholding through the years."[103]

Building on this transnational bond, missionary letters coming out of Katanga often made reference to the American Christian education of some of the province's leaders and, in particular, the Christian faith of President Moise Tshombe. Here the message was clear: he was one of us. In a letter describing the visit of the charismatic Katangan President and three of his cabinet to a Methodist conference in 1961, Everett and Vera Woodcock noted that Tshombe,

> [p]aid high respect to the church, and mentioned how his experience as a lay leader in the annual conference helped prepare him for the problems in his present position. After telling how much his Bible and faith in prayer meant to him and foreign minister Kimba during their arrest by the central government, he appealed to the whole church to work harder than ever and pray fervently for the advancement of God's kingdom.[104]

Missionaries and their supporters in America also were an important component of the powerful Katanga lobby led by Michel Struelens in Washington.[105] This composite of generally conservative opposition to American policy in Congo drew heavily on missionary accounts of pro-American sentiment in Katanga, the UN's use of excessive force, and the anti-communist credentials of the province's American missionary-educated leaders. Together with a successful letter writing campaign to

---

101 *US Congressional Record—Senate*, 25 January 1962. See letter entered in the record by Senator Dodd (D-CT) from Miss Julia Hoel to Mrs. Robert E. Barlett, 6 December 1961.
102 *US Congressional Record—Senate*, 25 January 1962. Letters entered in the record by Senator Dodd (D-CT) including those from Julia Hoel, James Brouwer, and others.
103 Everett and Vera Woodcock to supporters in the US, 13 September 1961, NARA/RG 59/250/63/10/Box 6.
104 Everett and Vera Woodcock to supporters in the US, 13 September 1961, NARA/RG 59/250/63/10/Box 6.
105 For information on Struelens see, *Time*, "Administration: An Abuse of Power." For an excellent example of the impressive Katanga public relations machine and the use of American missionaries as sources for that effort, see the pamphlet written by Ernest Van Den Haag, NARA/RG 59/250/63/10/ Box 5.

policymakers such as Richard Nixon, Senator Dodd of Connecticut, and Senator Russell of Georgia, and UN ambassador Adlai Stevenson, the missionary lobby became a real threat to US policy in the Congo.[106]

The reaction of US diplomats and policymakers to this unusual activism of the missionaries speaks volumes about the perceived threat missionaries posed to US policy in the Congo. One particularly telling example of the tension that had built up between American policymakers and missionaries in Katanga is a confidential letter from the US consul in the province's capital, Elizabethville, to the State Department's Congo desk officer, Sheldon Vance. In it, the consul, Lewis Hoffacker, accused the missionaries of being virtually treasonous and the worst enemies of US policy in the region. "Cowardice and disloyalty to their country," wrote Hoffacker, "are obviously qualities with which they can sanctimoniously live. One hears them speak of 'our country,' which usually means Katanga, not the U.S." Giving "the devil his due," Hoffacker did reluctantly concede that "the American missionaries" work in the educational field has "apparently been good (they have educated not only Tshombe but also Sendwe and other leaders of the province)." Nevertheless, he concluded, something had to be done, and that "conceivably only mission headquarters at home are in a position to do anything constructive in this respect."[107]

The bitter sarcasm of Hoffacker's letter was not the only indication that the missionary lobby was frustrating US policymakers. By 1961, Under Secretary of State George McGhee and Assistant Secretary of State G. Mennen Williams were aggressively courting American mission boards in the US as a means of neutralizing the political threat posed by the missionaries in Katanga.[108] By early 1962, Williams had met personally with every denomination "with any sizable missionary representation

---

[106] Reference to a letter to Vice President Nixon by American missionary P. D. Claar, even before the independence-era crisis, offering advice on Congo policy seen in Memo to William Macomber Jr., 29 February 1960, NARA/RG 59/.855a/411.8-160; For letters to Dodd, of which there were many, see *US Congressional Record—Senate*, 25 January 1962. See letters entered in the record by Senator Dodd (D-CT) including those from James Brouwer; Letter to Mr. Adlai Stevenson from Everett L. Woodcock, 30 September 1961, NARA/RG 59/250/63/10/ Box 6; letter to Mr. Adlai Stevenson from Mrs. Charles R. Johnson, 15 November 1961, NARA/RG 59/250/63/10/ Box 9. George McGee in his memoirs, relates that "I practically lived with Dodd during this period ... I then flew to Georgia to meet with Russell, who had come under the influence of missionaries from his state." McGhee, *On the Frontline*, 154.

[107] Lewis Hoffacker to Sheldon Vance, 27 October 1961, NARA/RG 59/250/63/10/Box 6.

[108] Williams and Assistant Secretary of State George McGhee in "Confidential" memos of 21 December 1961 and 26 December 1961, NARA/RG 59/250/63/10/Box 5.

in Katanga."[109] In addition, Sheldon Vance, Frank Carlucci, and Williams had begun to use division within the missionary community to their advantage, stressing in public comments that, in general, only the Katanga missionaries were staunchly pro-Tshombe while American missionaries in other regions of the Congo were sympathetic to US policy.[110]

The potential influence of American missionaries on public opinion was also a matter of serious concern for Williams and his colleagues at the State Department as they began preparations for congressional hearings on US Congo policy—hearings that were initiated largely by missionary appeals to Senator Dodd.[111] Concerning William's testimony, aide Fredrick Dutton suggested that he stress the missionary divisions in the Congo which "in a public sense ... could be the most critical point in the latter stages of the Congo hearings."[112] Complementing State's strategy of aggressively countering US missionary influence was its effort to secure the testimony of respected Methodist missionary Howard Brinton. A close childhood friend and confidant of the Katangan President, Brinton nevertheless remained cautiously sympathetic to US policy in the Congo and as such was seen as a critical player in the push for Congressional support.[113]

In the main, the influence of American missionaries on US public opinion concerning independence-era Congo was benign and apolitical. Outside of religiously inspired concerns about the increasing instances of communist propaganda in the Congo and dramatic descriptions of their evacuations, in their letters and publications the missionaries continued to focus on humanitarian concerns and the transnational spiritual bond that linked the evangelical communities in the US and Congo. These positive themes helped to balance the image of chaos and barbarism that was the staple of the international media, and implicitly encouraged a continued US presence in the new nation.

The case of the Katanga was, of course, the important exception in the sense that the missionary influence was explicitly political, outspokenly critical, and surprisingly potent. The fact that the breakaway province was

---

109 Williams to McGhee, 9 January 1962, NARA/RG 59/250/63/10/Box 5.
110 Memo on "Congo Hearings" from Sheldon Vance to Williams, 30 January 1962, NARA/RG 59/250/63/10/Box 9.
111 Mahoney, *JFK: Ordeal in Africa*, 135. Mahoney's point here is simply that Dodd initiated the hearings and invited Tshombe, but for some examples of the missionary letters to Dodd, of which there were many, see *US Congressional Record—Senate*, 25 January 1962.
112 Frederick Dutton to Williams, 24 January 1962, NARA/RG 59/250/63/10/Box 9.
113 Sheldon Vance to Williams, 18 January 1962, NARA/RG 59/250/63/10/Box 7.

able to withstand intense American and UN pressure for more than two years was due at least in part to the activism of a small group of American missionaries and their evangelical supporters at home in the United States. However, in the end, the collapse of European support for Katanga, and the decision by the Belgian government to support UN military action against the breakaway province at the end of 1962, led to the collapse of the Katangan government and an initial triumph for US policymakers.

The Influence of American Missionaries on the Perceptions of US Policymakers, 1959–1963

Long before the Congo became a focal point of the global Cold War, American missionaries and diplomats had enjoyed a close and mutually beneficial relationship.[114] Thousands of miles from their home nation, and facing many of the same cross-cultural challenges, it was natural, just as it had been in Ethiopia, that close friendships would sometimes develop between members of the two American communities.[115] The responsibility of the American consulate to care for the safety and interests of its citizens also meant that, regardless of any natural affinity, diplomats necessarily took an interest in missionary activity throughout the colony.[116] Visits by the American consul to American missionary stations in "the bush" were not uncommon and provided an excellent opportunity for American diplomats to both monitor American humanitarian efforts and make an appraisal of the socio-political realities of rural Congo.[117] In the capital of Leopoldville, the historically close relationship between the two groups meant that missionaries often acted as de facto diplomats, hosting VIPs, presiding over formal functions, and enjoying the comradery of the diplomatic elite. As one Presbyterian missionary wrote in 1957:

---

114 The examples of friendships developing between US missionaries and diplomats in the Congo prior to independence are myriad. For instance, see letter from American Public Affairs Officer Gilbert E. Bursley to Rev. Vernon A. Anderson, 4 December 1956, in which Bursley writes, "I've thought a lot about you and the very kind folks of the A.P.C.M. in the hectic weeks since my return to Leopoldville. Your kindness and hospitality are something I will never forget." PHS/432/64/22.

115 J. A. Halverstadt to US Public Affairs Officer William M. Hart, 30 October 1959, PHS/432/64/23.

116 Patrick Mallon to the Legal Representative of the American Presbyterian Congo Mission, 23 December 1941, PHS/432/64/19.

117 David Miller, interview with the author, 30 June 2009; Representant de Poste, Mutoto to Vernon Anderson, 29 April 1952, PHS/432/64/22; Burley to Anderson, 4 December 1956, PHS/432/64/22; A series of four lengthy memos from American Consul General, Leopoldville to State, 26 July 1957, 21 September 1957, 14 December 1957, NARA, RG 84/350/c/60/1/Box 21.

We have had a hectic week ... Admiral Burke came on a visit, and we went to a cocktail party in his honor at the Consulate ... I married a young American couple and at our American Club luncheon we had the New Orleans Wilbur de Paris Jazz Orchestra, and a Major General Hardick, and I keep asking myself, "Is this missionary work?"[118]

This social context facilitated a free flow of ideas, information, and experiences between the American diplomatic and missionary communities that inevitably shaped the perceptions of both.

With the advent of the Cold War in the Congo in 1960, this history of close interaction aided the American effort to make sense of the Congolese chaos. It was, for instance, American missionaries working in southern Congo who first alerted US diplomats to the scale and significance of the inter-tribal violence taking place in that region. Calling the Lulua-Baluba conflict "virtually insoluble" in a report to the US Consulate in Leopoldville, one American missionary described what would now be referred to as "ethnic cleansing," including the widespread burning of Lulua homes by the Baluba, multiple murders, and the mass exodus of the Lulua from Baluba majority areas.[119]

Two months later, in August 1960, after the mass evacuation of most Europeans from the region, it was again missionaries remaining behind who reported to the consul general that large numbers of the Baluba were moving towards areas bordering Katanga, and that this movement was a possible precursor to a politically potent merger between the Lunda (Tshombe's indigenous majority tribe in Katanga) and the Baluba (the politically influential tribe with minorities in Katanga and a majority in Kasai province) against the US-backed central government.[120] In September, it was another American missionary who reported that troops loyal to Lumumba were engaging in massive retaliatory executions of Baluba tribespeople.[121] Close communication between American missionaries and the US Embassy in Leopoldville concerning these events in Kasai, and others across the Congo, continued throughout the period with the US ambassador and other American diplomats sitting in on mission meetings

---

118 "Jack" to J. F. Watt, 7 April 1957, PHS/432/14/5.
119 Memo from the American Consul, Leopoldville to State, 3 June 1960, NARA/RG 84/350/c/60/1/Box 24.
120 Memo from American Consul, Salisbury to Secretary of State, 5 August 1960, NARA/RG 84/350/c/60/1/Box 24.
121 Memo from American Embassy, Leopoldville to State, 23 September 1960, NARA/RG 84/350/c/60/1/Box 24.

and occasionally being shuttled around various Congolese hot-spots in missionary planes.[122]

Just prior to independence, American missionaries were also responsible for drawing US attention to the proliferation of anti-Western and anti-White religious movements across the Congo. Unlike their secular compatriots in the State Department, not only did the missionaries take the spiritualist movements seriously in their own right, but they understood the significant power those movements had to shape Congolese politics. Thus, in June 1960, Mennonite Brethren missionaries in the Kikwit area were the first to report on the potential political consequences of the close relationship between the leftist PSA and a local spiritualist movement.[123] It was likely this intelligence that led to Richard Sanger's report in August confirming in great detail the political threat that the movement, and others like it, posed to US aims in the Congo. It is noteworthy that, like other American analysts trying to make sense of the Congolese chaos, Sanger's investigation had led him to conclude that if the US hoped to make sense of the Congo, missionary knowledge and expertise would continue to be indispensable.[124]

As it became increasingly clear throughout the summer of 1960 that the lives of American missionaries were in real danger, the already significant volume of information exchanged between the two communities grew exponentially. The principal reason for this increase was, of course, the protection of American lives, and in this regard the information flow was largely initiated by the American embassy. For instance, at 1:30 a.m. on the night of 7–8 July, as soon as the embassy had confirmed reports of the spread of the soldier mutiny towards Leopoldville, the ambassador called the missionary head of the Council of Protestants in Congo to his residence in order to develop contingency plans for a mass evacuation of American missionaries in the country.[125]

However, the increased contact with American missionaries also served the additional function of keeping the State Department informed on the movement of various political and tribal factions, as well as the

---

122 "Second Stated Mission Meeting, Luluabourg, 10–19 October 1961," PHS/432/3/9; draft of letter from APCM to "Bulupe Folks," 30 November 1961, PHS/432/9/34; and "Situation in Kasai," Trip Report, 3 March 1962, NARA/RG 84/350/c/60/1/Box 29.

123 Office Memo, American Consul, Leopoldville, 15 June 1960, NARA/RG 59/.855a/ 411.8-160.

124 Richard H. Sanger to Hugh S. Cumming Jr., 22 August 1960, NARA/RG 59/250/63/10/ Box 8.

125 Council of Protestants of Congo to "all readers of the Congo Mission News," 26 July 1960, BGC/CN81/36/9.

ebb and flow of political sentiment in a number of Congolese regions where the US government had almost no reliable sources of information. In the particularly volatile Lumumba strongholds of Orientale and Kivu provinces, for instance, the US embassy in neighboring Kampala remained "in constant contact" with American missionaries which, by December 1960, meant that the missionaries typically spoke with the US Ambassador twice a day.[126] The same level of diplomatic communication was true of American missionaries on the Congo-Sudan border the following year who could also report that they were in "constant touch" with the American Ambassador.[127]

Facilitating this important exchange of information was a highly effective radio network that connected American mission stations across the Congo. Over the years, a variety of American missionary groups had come together to develop a system of radio communication that had allowed them to organize national meetings of the Protestant church, cooperate in handling medical and humanitarian crises, and help each other keep abreast of significant events in the colony. During the independence-era crisis, this missionary radio network also became an indispensable source of information for American policymakers who regularly eavesdropped in order to monitor the fluid political situation in rural areas.

For instance, during the initial crisis of July 1960, mission stations in northeast Congo were making radio reports at designated hours several times daily, each of which was being monitored by the US Embassy in Kampala. According to the US consul there, the missionary radio network had acted as the "main source of [US] information" for that part of the Congo.[128] By December the same US Embassy had set up a radio frequency that would, in case of emergencies, broadcast every two hours from 9 a.m. to 7 p.m., and was regularly utilizing the already established network to provide missionaries with up to the moment information on current events and, if necessary, evacuation instructions.[129]

Exit interviews of fleeing missionaries during the two major evacuation periods (July 1960 and February 1961) also appear to have

---

126 Acting General Field Secretary of the AIM to Mr. Thornberry, circa 1960 (date indistinguishable), BGC/CN 81/36/9; transcription of radio message to AIM headquarters in New York, from Eddie Schuit, 15 December 1960, BGC/CN 81/3/25.
127 Acting General Field Secretary to Rev. Sid Langford, 18 December 1962, BGC/CN 81/36/9.
128 Dr. Carl Becker to Sid Langford, 21 July 1960, BGC/CN 81/10/32.
129 Minutes of AIM Congo Field Council, 13–19 December 1960, BGC/CN 81/36/10; *Inland Africa*, 8–9.

been key as US diplomats scrambled to gain an understanding of the unfolding political chaos. US government and missionary documents show that American officials in Rhodesia, Portuguese Angola, British East Africa, and Congo-Brazzaville were all actively gleaning information from American missionaries, paying especially close attention to evidence of external communist activity.[130] Whether the result of long-standing ties between the two American communities, or the unique demands for immediate information brought on by the independence-era crisis, during this period an extensive exchange of information between US diplomats and missionaries appears to have shaped official American perceptions of events in the Congo.

Missionaries and Formal Diplomacy, 1959–1963

As has been noted, thanks to their long and intimate history with the Congo, missionaries played a critical role in promoting pro-US sentiment at the grassroots level. Perhaps even more significant, however, was the influence that they had on some members of the Congolese political elite. Whether the result of religious, medical, or educational ties, it was not uncommon for these missionaries to be on first-name terms with the nation's new African leaders. As a result, in a manner and to a degree that most official diplomats could not match, a number of American missionaries wielded a considerable amount of political influence.

As early as the Brussels Roundtable leading up to Congolese independence, American diplomats were taking note of the diplomatic potential of the missionary community. US ambassador to Belgium William Burden was particularly emphatic: "I am impressed by [the] surprising effectiveness, importance, and influence of US Protestant missionaries in Congo," and "Believe appropriate use should be made in the future of their knowledge and contacts."[131]

Nevertheless, perhaps because of their generally apolitical perspective, or because of the rigid separation of church and state to which many of the more conservative Protestants generally held, American missionaries rarely sought or accepted prominent roles in formal US diplomacy. There were, however, exceptions. The most important of these was the role played by Methodist missionary Howard Brinton in US attempts to resolve the

---

130 Memo from American Consul, Salisbury to Secretary of State, 5 August 1960, NARA/RG 84/350/c/60/1/Box 24; Telegram from US Consul Luanda to US Embassy Leopoldville, 30 July 1960, NARA/RG 84/350/c/60/1/Box 24; Devlin, *Chief of Station, Congo*, 3.
131 Ambassador Burden to Secretary of State, 23 March 1960, NARA/RG 59/ .855a/411.8-160.

Katangan secession. In January 1962, Brinton surfaced as a major player in the high stakes stand-off between the US backed Congolese government (and the UN forces supporting them), and Tshombe's breakaway province of Katanga.

A number of factors combined to make the Katangan secession the centerpiece in the Congolese independence-era crisis. First and foremost was the immense wealth of the province and the extent to which the Congo's economic and political viability rested upon the inclusion of the province. Early in the crisis both pro-Western Congolese leaders and American policymakers had concluded that a successful Katangan separation would be devastating for Congolese economic stability and dramatically increase the new nation's vulnerability to external Communist influence.[132]

The Katangan secession also represented a major threat to national, regional, and continental political stability. Both the Western powers and the leaders of their former colonies came to agree that if one ethnically-based separatist movement was successful, it could lead to an infinitely regressive Balkanization of the entire continent, with political, economic, and social consequences too dire to contemplate.[133] For American policymakers concerned that any descent into anarchy would create an opening for significant Communist intervention in Africa, this represented a serious threat to their Cold War objectives.

Finally, the Katangan secession was further complicated by the question of race. While African nationalists had often found it convenient to adopt much of the colonial structure, any lingering presence of Europeans in positions of power and privilege within that system was understandably anathema. Therefore, when Katangan President Moise Tshombe elected to retain a considerable number of European functionaries and advisors, he became a potent symbol of neo-colonialism and was easily labeled by domestic political enemies and the communist bloc as a traitor to the cause

---

[132] For instance, a State Department memo of 20 January 1962, quoted Kasavubu, Mobutu, and Adoula to confirm their already well-entrenched fears that an independent Katanga "would mean the end of moderate influence in the Congo." NARA/RG 59/250/63/10/Box 5. Williams, *Africa for Africans*, 94; "Secret" CIA Geographic Intelligence Review, N. 58, CIA/RR MR 59-2, July 1959, 1; Mrs. Charles R. Johnson to US Ambassador to the UN, Adlai Stevenson, 15 November 1961, which refers to Congolese Foreign Minister Bomboko's speech to the UN stressing the critical importance of Katanga to the viability of the Congo, NARA/RG 59/250/63/10/Box 9.

[133] "Confidential" State Department memo of 20 January 1962, quoting multiple Congolese leaders, NARA/RG 59/250/63/10/Box 5.

of African nationalism.[134] Considering America's own racially checkered past, and its historical friendship with the colonial powers of Western Europe, American policymakers were reluctant to forge a close relationship with independent Africa's version of Uncle Tom. In short, the Katangan secession sat at the economic, political, and symbolic nexus of the larger Cold War drama that was independence-era Congo. And at the very center of that crisis stood an otherwise unassuming Methodist missionary.

A number of factors made Reverend Howard Brinton an ideal candidate for the back-channel diplomacy that took place between the US and Tshombe. Having grown up in Katanga as the child of Methodist missionaries and then returning as a Methodist missionary himself, Brinton had an understanding of the language and culture of the province unmatched by any US diplomat, either on the field or in Washington.[135]

Brinton could also claim friendships with many of Katanga's most prominent leaders, including President Tshombe and Congolese Vice Premier Jason Sendwe. Brinton and Tshombe, in particular, were close and life-long friends. Because Brinton's missionary parents had been mentors to Tshombe's parents, the boys regularly "climbed trees, swam, and fished together." And when Moise's father had died, it was Howard's father who buried him and grieved alongside the future Katangan President's widowed mother.[136]

Despite the many years that had passed, these friendships were very much alive as the Katanga crisis unfolded.[137] Finally, and perhaps most importantly from the perspective of Washington, unlike the majority of American missionaries in the province, Brinton's close relationship to the Katangan people and its leaders had not made him antagonistic towards

---

[134] The anger of some Congolese against Tshombe, which was fueled by Communist propaganda, was picked up by both independence-era African leaders from around sub-Saharan Africa and the Africanists in the State Department led by Williams, Wayne Fredericks, and others. For instance, in his memoirs, *Africa for Africans*, G. Mennen Williams referred to Tshombe as "the devil," because of his apparently neo-colonial perspective and policies, Williams, *Africa for Africans*, 87. According to US Ambassador William Attwood, later in the Simba rebellion of 1964, President Kenyatta of Kenya's continuing animosity towards Tshombe was a critical hindrance to negotiations meant to free Western hostages in the rebel-held city of Stanleyville. According to Attwood, at one point Kenyatta told the US, "We can be friends ... only if you stop being friends with Tshombe." Attwood, *Reds and the Blacks*, 215.

[135] G. Mennen Williams from Sheldon Vance, 18 January 1962, NARA/RG 59/250/63/10/Box 7.

[136] Asbury Alumnus, "Brinton Committed to Work," 2.

[137] Memorandum of Conversation including Rev. Brinton, G. Mennen Williams, Robert Eisenberg, and Richard Sanger, 19 January 1962, NARA/RG 59/250/63/10/Box 7.

America's larger policy aims in the Congo.[138] In short, in Brinton both parties had a trusted ally and someone personally invested in seeing a mutually beneficial solution to the crisis.

To American policymakers, Briton consistently portrayed Tshombe as a reasonable and pragmatic pro-Western leader, willing to compromise for the good of the Congo—provided that structures were put in place to ensure that a fair portion of political autonomy and Katangan wealth remained within the province.[139] Stressing the Katangan leader's knowledge of the American system, Brinton also regularly voiced Tshombe's claim that he sought for Katanga only what the federal system in the Constitution had provided for Americans.[140] In a similarly sympathetic manner, Brinton appears to have been a forceful advocate of American good intentions and its willingness to support the legitimate interests of the Katangans within a unified and centralized Congo.[141]

The fact that both sides placed a great deal of trust in Brinton is evident from the virtually unlimited access he had to Tshombe and the host of American diplomats who he interacted with during the prolonged negotiations. Concerning his relationship with Tshombe, American Consul Lewis Hoffacker noted in a confidential memo to Central African Affairs Deputy Director Robert Eisenberg that Brinton,

> [h]as spoken for the US Government during his many interviews with Tshombe and has, I am confident, countered much of the bad advice which constantly permeates the presidential palace ... he has accomplished things which you and I would be unable to do. For example, he can read the riot act to Moise (they are on a modified first name basis with Tshombe calling him Bwana and he calling Tshombe by his first name) and get away with it.[142]

Brinton's access to the American diplomatic and political hierarchy, and the respect he garnered from the conflicting parties within that hierarchy, was no less significant. In addition to regular meetings with

---

138 G. Mennen Williams from Sheldon Vance, 18 January 1962, NARA/RG 59/250/63/10/Box 7.
139 Memorandum of Conversation with Reverend Brinton, 17 January 1962, NARA/RG 59/250/63/10/Box 7.
140 Memorandum of Conversation with Reverend Brinton, G. Mennen Williams, Robert Eisenberg, and Richard Sanger, 19 January 1962, NARA/RG 59/250/63/10/Box 7.
141 Memorandum from Sheldon Vance to G. Mennen Williams, 19 January 1962, NARA/RG 59/250/63/10/Box 7.
142 "Confidential" letter from American Consul Lewis Hoffacker, to Deputy Director at the Office of Central African Affairs Robert Eisenberg, 7 March 1962, NARA/RG 59/250/63/10/Box 6.

Tshombe, the UN, and the Congolese government, between January and September of 1962, Brinton met with a veritable who's who of the US policymaking establishment including, among others, American consul in Katanga Lewis Hoffacker, US ambassador Edmund Gullion, Assistant Secretary of State for African Affairs Mennen Williams, Congo desk officer and future ambassador Sheldon Vance, Senator Thomas Dodd, and US Secretary of State Dean Rusk.[143]

His remarkable ability to engender trust and goodwill from otherwise politically hostile groups was perhaps best seen in the strong support he gleaned from both Senator Dodd (the most outspoken critic of US policy in Katanga) and Williams (a primary architect of that policy). For his part, Williams made sure that Brinton testified before the Gore Committee as it met to discuss the Congo crisis.[144] At the same time, William's nemesis, Senator Dodd, was urging Secretary of State Rusk to meet personally with Brinton, whom Dodd called, "a man of rare wisdom and balance" and "one of the most impressive men I have ever met."[145]

In the end, Brinton's efforts to bring a peaceful solution to the Katangan secession met with failure. American impatience with the pace of African-style diplomacy and its fears of being painted with the brush of neo-colonialism, combined with the withdrawal of Belgian support for Tshombe's government, led to a conclusive US-supported, UN military effort in January 1963 which forcibly reunited the province with the rest of Congo and sent Tshombe temporarily into exile. Nevertheless, the ultimate failure to find a peaceful solution to the crisis should not obscure an important historical reality. For almost a year, American and Katangan policymakers at the highest level had placed much of their hopes for a peaceful resolution to the Congo crisis on an unassuming Methodist

---

143 Howard Brinton to unnamed recipient, 16 January 1962, UMCA/1197/6/2/46; Sheldon Vance to Governor Williams, 19 January 1962, NARA/RG 59/250/63/10/Box 7; Brinton to Dr. Eugene Smith, 5 February 1962, UMCA/1197/6/2/46; Brinton to Dr. Melvin Blake, 11 February 1962, UMCA/1197/6/2/46; Brinton to Blake, 4 March 1962, UMCA/1197/6/2/46; Brinton to Anne Anderson, 10 April 1962, UMCA/1197/6/2/46; Senator Thomas Dodd to Secretary of State Dean Rusk, 11 July 1962, NARA/RG 59/250/63/10/Box 7; Memo from Wayne Fredericks to Secretary of State Dean Rusk, 16 July 1962, NARA/RG 59/250/63/10/Box 7; Brinton to Blake, 18 July 1962, UMCA/1197/6/2/46; Brinton to Blake, 1 September 1962, UMCA/1197/6/2/46; Brinton to Anderson, 6 September 1962, UMCA/1197/6/2/46; Brinton to Anderson, 29 September 1962, UMCA/1197/6/2/46; Brinton to Anderson, 16 November 1962, UMCA/1197/6/2/46.

144 Senator Thomas Dodd to Secretary of State Dean Rusk, 11 July 1962, NARA/RG 59/250/63/10/Box 7.

145 Senator Thomas Dodd to Secretary of State Dean Rusk, 11 July 1962, NARA/RG 59/250/63/10/Box 7.

missionary who, at key moments in that process, came surprisingly close to achieving that unlikely goal.

Conclusion

Between the beginning of 1960 and the end of the Katangan secession in January of 1963, twenty-three African nations became independent. In taking almost everyone by surprise, the rapid decolonization of the continent stoked the flames of the Cold War and produced anxiety within the policymaking establishments of both superpowers—an anxiety evident in Eisenhower's description of African nationalism as a "flood force" and "a torrent overrunning everything in its path."[146] Within this geopolitically turbulent atmosphere the Congo, Africa's symbolic heart and economic treasure, began to unravel. Viewed as a quiet "diplomatic backwater" only months before, the Congo's descent into anarchy seemed to compel superpower intervention and pushed the young nation into the spotlight of the global conflict.[147] In the high stakes conflict-by-proxy that erupted between the two superpowers in the Congo, the usual suspects were joined by an unlikely, and often reluctant, group of accomplices.

American evangelical missionaries played a central role in this unfolding drama. First, as a bi-product of several generations of intimate humanitarian involvement in the Congo, American missionaries nurtured a critical mass of resilient pro-American sympathies within the otherwise anti-Western environment of independence-era Congo.

Second, through their letters home, speeches at American Christian gatherings while on furlough, and the constellation of evangelical publications that carried their stories, American missionaries gave a significant portion of the US public an intimate view of the events transpiring in the Congo that generally helped promote US interests and justify American involvement in the new African nation.

Third, acting out of character, but in line with the spiritually rooted transnational bonds they had developed with the Congolese people, missionaries in Katanga also aggressively lobbied US politicians and public opinion for a change in America's Congo policy, and in doing so became a major threat to US policy objectives in the region.

Finally, and conversely, thanks to their unparalleled understanding of the Congo and a simultaneous loyalty to both the US and the Congo, some American missionaries, such as Howard Brinton, became key players in

---

146 Eisenhower, *Waging Peace*, 572.
147 Devlin, *Chief of Station, Congo*, ix.

the important but unsuccessful attempts to bridge the gap between US interests and the interests of various Congolese factions.

In the sixty years leading up to independence in the Congo, American evangelical missionaries had gone about their humanitarian and spiritual work in blissful anonymity. However, when the Congo unexpectedly burst into the global spotlight (between Congolese independence in 1960 and the end of the Katangan secession in January of 1963) the relational, cultural and political capital that they had accumulated suddenly assumed considerable Cold War significance. Yet as a form of stability returned to the Congo in early 1963, these accidental diplomats quite happily returned to their lives and work among the Congolese people only to find that everything had changed. The Cold War in the Congo was just warming up.

CHAPTER 4

"Red and Yellow, Black and White"

American Evangelical Missionaries and the Rise and Fall of the Simba Rebellion, 1963–1967

> Jesus loves the little children,
> all the children of the world.
> Red and yellow, black and white,
> all are precious in His sight.
> Jesus loves the little children of the world.[1]

On 21 January 1963, thanks to a final decisive push by US-backed UN forces, the controversial and drawn-out Katanga secession was over. That day, a relieved John F. Kennedy confided to Under Secretary of State George McGhee that the administration's Africa team was entitled to "a little sense of pride."[2] Adlai Stevenson, always the consummate multilateralist, was no less pleased, calling success in Katanga the UN's finest hour.[3] For the New Frontiersmen of the Kennedy administration, these were indeed heady times. On the back of the successful end to the Cuban Missile Crisis, the suppression of the Katangan secession seemed to vindicate the pro-nationalist convictions of Africanists like Mennen Williams, Wayne Fredericks, and Ambassador Edmund Gullion. While few believed that all of the Congo's problems were solved, it was hoped that the worst was past and that things were looking up. Moise Tshombe had been humiliated and exiled, an apparently centrist Congolese government was in place, and the Communists remained on the outside looking in.[4]

This sense of satisfaction, however, proved to be short-lived. A year later, on the morning of 23 January 1964, American Baptist missionaries at Vanga, near Kikwit, were awakened by a courier from the nearby Catholic mission carrying a hastily composed message. "Please come over and help us,"

---

1 American evangelical children's song popular during the 1960s, George Root, 1820–1895.
2 Mahoney, *JFK: Ordeal in Africa*, 156.
3 Mahoney, 155.
4 Godley to Williams, 15 January 1963, National Archives II (NARA)/RG 59/250/63/10 Box 6. In this memo Godley appears to express pleasure that Tshombe's "stock has already fallen greatly ... and that if the UN could take Kolwezi by force Tshombe's collapse would be complete."

the Mother Superior had written. "Last night all the priests at the mission were massacred. Terrible!" What the Americans found when they arrived was nauseating. "We passed from cot to cot lifting the shrouds," one missionary reported. "What a ghastly massacre. Mutilations ... legs broken. Some hands chopped off above the wrists leaving a bloody stump. Fingers chopped." Upon returning from the Catholic mission, the Americans notified the Protestant missionary radio network that the massacre appeared to confirm rumors of a disturbing new quasi-religious insurrection. From there, word spread quickly to the US embassy and on to Washington. Congo was back in the global spotlight, and once again American missionaries found themselves at the center of the story.[5]

Continuity—American Missionaries and the Simba Rebellion

Between the Vanga massacre and July 1964, the first chapter of a new period of revolutionary chaos was written in the area surrounding the Kikwit mission. Known as the Kwilu uprising, after the Congolese province where it took place, the revolt was the initial manifestation of the mystifying— and to US policymakers deeply disturbing—Simba rebellion. While there were significant differences between the independence-era rebellion of 1960–1961 and the Simba rebellion of 1964–1965, the two periods held a great deal in common. Alongside continuing Congolese disillusionment with independence, and deeply rooted inter-tribal and racially flavored anti-colonial tensions, was the continuing work and influence of American evangelical missionaries.

Although large numbers of missionaries were evacuated during the turmoil of 1960–1961, by the end of 1963 the American missionary population in Congo was again approaching pre-independence levels.[6] Because many of those who returned did so within a month or two of leaving, the work of the American Protestant missions continued largely unabated in spite of the internal chaos that had engulfed the young nation. This continuity, according to the US embassy in Leopoldville, meant that their impact, while "diffuse" and "not focused on the political process," remained "significant."[7]

---

5 Draft of a report for Congo Mission News, January 1964, Billy Graham Center Archives, Wheaton, IL (BGC)/CN 136/8/9. This horrific missionary report was confirmed by US Ambassador to Congo Edmund Gullion in a confidential telegram to the Secretary of State on 30 January 1964, NARA/RG59/250/7/3-7/1964-66/Box 2713; American Embassy Leopoldville to Secretary of State, Confidential Telegram, "Kwilu Crisis ... Background" 31 January 1964, NARA/RG 59/250/7/3-7/1964-66/Box 2713.

6 Lewis Hoffacker to Secretary of State, "Christian Mission Activities in the Congo," 13 June 1963, NARA/RG84/350/c/59/7/Box 36.

7 Hoffacker to Secretary of State, 13 June 1963, NARA/RG 84/350/c/59/7/Box 36.

By the end of 1963, approximately fifteen hundred American missionaries were partnering with thirty-two thousand Congolese pastors and evangelists in ministry to a Congolese Protestant constituency of almost 2.5 million people.[8] In addition to a vast network of primary schools established during the colonial period, in the first three chaotic years of independence American missionaries also increased the number of secondary schools under their supervision from ten to almost fifty, and were in the process of launching the first Protestant university in the Congo.[9] Overall, by 1964 well over one million Congolese—including a number of prominent political leaders—had been educated in Protestant mission schools initiated and overseen by American evangelicals.[10]

In addition, due to the hasty departure of the Belgian civil service, the public health system had largely collapsed, leaving Protestant missionaries in charge of "virtually all health care in the bush, and perhaps the greater part of it in the cities."[11] Confronted with this increased burden, the response of the missions was impressive. In 1961, for instance, the American-dominated Africa Inland Mission (AIM) alone treated over two million Congolese.[12] In short, despite the destructive chaos of the first three years of Congolese independence, and the repeated waves of racially charged anti-Western sentiment, the spiritually inspired work of American missionaries continued.

Nowhere was the impact of this work more evident than in the Congolese reaction to the death of the veteran missionary physician, Dr. Kleinschmidt, in April 1964. Having served in the remote northeast of the Congo for over forty years, his death was met with an outpouring of affection-laden grief that impressed observers. According to one, "well over 6,000 people" made their way "by truck, car, bicycle, and on foot" to the isolated rural town of Aba to pay their last respects.[13]

Among the mourners was a delegation of government officials accompanied by a military honor guard in full dress.[14] Both the nearby

---

8 Crawford, "Protestant Missions in Congo," 86. It is important to remember that other non-American Protestant missionaries were also active in serving this community, although the British, Canadian, and Australian missionaries (and to some extent the Scandinavians as well) did so within a larger culture of American evangelical Protestantism.
9 Crawford, "Protestant Missions in Congo," 89.
10 Hoffacker to Secretary of State, 13 June 1963, NARA/RG84/350/c/59/7/Box 36.
11 According to Hoffacker, the total number of doctors in the Congo in 1963 was about one hundred with at least fifty of those being American Protestants. Lewis Hoffacker to Secretary of State, 13 June 1963, NARA/RG84/350/c/59/7/Box 36.
12 A.I.M. Congo report 1961, BGC/CN81/18/35.
13 Brashler, *Change: My Thirty-Five*, 117–19.
14 Letter from Rev. Pete Brashler to Rev. Sidney Langford, 30 April 1964, BGC/CN 81/10/33.

Catholic missions and the town's Greek merchants also closed for the day to allow their communities to attend—which they did en masse, "dressed in black and mourning unabashedly."[15] While the presiding African pastor made it clear that because the doctor was now in heaven the funeral was to be a celebration of his life, "silent weeping continued" throughout the service led by the Kakwa chief who "knelt before the casket sobbing with grief."[16] Significantly, neither Dr. Kleinschmidt's story, nor the local response to his life, were unusual. Similar examples of the continuing bond between American missionaries and the Congolese people during the lead up to the Simba rebellion are myriad.[17]

Change—American Missionaries and the Simba Rebellion

In the midst of this continuity were three important changes—in quality and quantity, if not in kind. The first difference between the independence-era rebellions (1960–1961) and the Simba rebellion (1964–1965) was the higher levels of organization and planning initially found in the latter. For an uprising that soon became synonymous with decentralized anarchy, the first months of the Simba rebellion demonstrated a remarkable degree of effective planning, military training and leadership. As one missionary noted, "The youth movement seems better armed than the government forces. [They] know all about explosives, how to mine roads, make Molotov cocktails, etc." Clear indications of an intentional and concerted use of indigenous religious supernaturalism by the rebellion's leadership were also present in the form of widespread rumors of the magical power of the rebellion's leader.[18] Finally, and perhaps most ominously, was the uprising's coherent and effectively communicated message. As the same missionary confided to a colleague,

---

15 Brashler, *Change: My Thirty-Five*, 117–19.

16 Brashler, 117–19.

17 As evidence that this phenomena was noticed by US policymakers see statement by the Honorable Robert D. Murphy, Personal Representative of the President and Head of the American Delegation to the Independence Ceremonies of the Republic of the Congo, 30 June 1960, NARA/RG 84/350/C/60/1/Box 24. See also multiple examples from the independence era of pro-missionary sentiment in the previous chapter of this book.

18 Excerpts from Letter to Rev. Chester J. Jump, Jr. (A.B.F.M.S Regional Representative) from Rev. Norman G. Riddle (A.B.F.M.S. Missionary in the Congo at Vanga Station) 13 January 1964, NARA/RG59/250/7/21/2/Box 3243.

> The workers at the [Agricultural] school kept asking the [missionary instructors] when they were going to Leo[poldville]. The staff members answered ... that they weren't going to Leo. "Oh, yes you are. So are all the white people. Big trouble is coming after the first of the year and your government will take you all away."[19]

These early examples of effective planning and organization by the Simbas were initially matched by considerable attention to detail once the uprising began. By the end of January 1964, American missionary pilots were reporting systematic efforts by the rebels to sabotage the airstrips, bridges, and major roads providing access to the missions stations and strategic towns.[20] As another American missionary reported after a rebel "visit" in January 1964, the Simbas "were quite well organized and asked for gas, motor oil, brake fluid, [our] telephone (radio transmitter set) ... our money box, blankets, etc. Their secretary made a list of the things we gave them so they could report it to their leader."[21] Even the early examples of rebel violence in Kwilu appear to have been carefully orchestrated to produce the maximum amount of fear and intimidation. On several occasions missionaries were threatened by a mob led by a red-robed "executioner" who theatrically and graphically described the death and dismemberment that would come to any who opposed the uprising.[22]

With the notable exception of their continuing success in arms smuggling, this early evidence of rebel organization declined rapidly as the movement grew and spread during the summer of 1964.[23] Nevertheless, the rebel's initial campaign of violence and intimidation was effective. By the end of January 1964, just weeks after the Catholic priests had been murdered, almost one hundred missionaries had fled, the infrastructure of the province had collapsed, and the central government had lost an estimated twenty thousand square kilometers of territory to rebel control.[24]

---

19 Excerpts from Letter to Rev. Chester J. Jump, Jr. (A.B.F.M.S Regional Representative) from Rev. Norman G. Riddle (A.B.F.M.S. Missionary in the Congo at Vanga Station) 13 January 1964, NARA/RG59/250/7/21/2/Box 3243.

20 Fairley, "Three Day Diary," Missionary Aviation Fellowship, 1 February 1964, BGC/CN136/8/9; Jane and Wes Eisenmann to MAF team, February 1964, BGC/CN136/8/8.

21 Mr. and Mrs. Auguste Eicher, Report of American Baptist missionaries on "events taking place during the terrorist uprising of January 1964 in Kwilu Province," 26 February 1964, BGC/CN136/8/9.

22 Mr. and Mrs. Auguste Eicher, 26 February 1964, BGC/CN136/8/9.

23 "Mukedi Evacuated," author was an unnamed American Baptist missionary, 29 January 1964, BGC/CN136/8/9.

24 MAF News Release, 28 February 1964, BGC/CN136/8/11; Jane and Wes Eisenmann to MAF team, February 1964, BGC/CN136/8/8.

The second important difference between 1960–1961 and the Simba Rebellion was the role communism played. While there was not initially a noticeable increase in external influence in the Kwilu uprising, the first three years of independence had created a context in which the anti-colonial rhetoric of communism was even more welcome than it had been in 1960. More specifically, when reality shattered the extravagant expectations for independence held by virtually all Congolese, the US-backed government was naturally held responsible. The effectiveness of anti-Western rhetoric, then, increased in inverse relationship to the increasingly obvious failure of the US-backed Adoula/Kasavubu government.[25]

Adding to the potency of the anti-Western propaganda was the January 1961 assassination of the Congo's first prime minister, the charismatic and mercurial Patrice Lumumba. The fact that he was killed before his government had a chance to fail only served to further romanticize his memory in the Congolese consciousness, and indeed, in the collective memory of sub-Saharan Africa. In the context of strident American opposition to his rule, Lumumba's violent death under mysterious circumstances placed the United States on the wrong side of African nationalistic aspirations. In the years following, the Soviets were particularly effective in exploiting Lumumba's memory. In addition to a continuous stream of hagiography, just days after Lumumba's death was announced, the Soviets renamed a prominent Moscow university after the former Congolese Prime Minister, cementing for many the perception that African nationalism and Soviet anti-colonial communism were fundamentally aligned.[26]

More significant than the symbolic link between the communist powers and Congo were the competing efforts of the Soviets and Chinese to develop effective revolutionary leadership in the Congo. Pierre Mulele, the mastermind behind the initial Simba uprising in Kwilu is a case in point. Tabbed by the CIA as a KGB agent during his short tenure as minister of education, Mulele had abruptly left the country for China after Lumumba's death, only returning in August 1963 after having "secured promises of support from Peking."[27] Evidence of this support was apparent almost

---

25 By Jan. of 1964 the inflation was so high that the 5 February 1964 American Mid-Baptist Mission Report concluded that there was a lot of support for the "red inspired attempt to overthrow the present government," estimating that "[p]robably 80 percent of the Congolese are disgusted" with the US-backed government. 5 February 1964, "Congo News," BGC/CN136/8/8.

26 Attwood, *Reds and the Blacks*, 192.

27 Devlin, *Chief of Station, Congo*, 66; Ambassador Gullion to Secretary of State, 31 January 1964, NARA/RG59/250/7/37/1964-66/Box 2713; Guevara, *African Dream*, xv.

immediately. Despite being unaware of his return, in late 1963, American missionaries in the Kwilu region began to note the disappearance from the villages of large numbers of young men and the accompanying rumors that these men were undergoing military training in the forests.[28] When the uprising in Kwilu began in earnest in January 1964, the appearance of communist rhetoric alongside high levels of organization, and superior arms seemed to strongly suggest external involvement.

Indeed, despite the 1961–1962 Washington consensus that communist influence in the Congo had followed the Soviets into diplomatic exile, by mid-1964 evidence of at least some communist involvement was undeniable. As missionary hostages John Arton and Chester Burk confirmed, Simba references to Chinese or Soviet assistance were ubiquitous. "Plant big gardens," a Simba officer told his men in the missionaries' presence. "Next year people whose skins are different and whose eyes are different, will come. They will buy your produce ... They will give you a good price."[29]

Furthermore, with few exceptions, the rebel leaders had been trained in either China or a Soviet bloc nation, and those who had not were known to have participated in meetings with communist diplomats in left-friendly neighboring nations such as Tanzania and Burundi.[30] Communist propaganda, including both radio and written material, had also become increasingly widespread and influential in Simba held territory—a fact that the missionaries noted in the increasing use by the rebels of distinctly non-indigenous, anti-religious, and anti-capitalist rhetoric.[31] Whether they were card-carrying communists or not, at least at the highest levels, the ideological sympathies of the Simbas were clear. Indeed, even before much of this evidence was available, US Ambassador Edmund Gullion was already reluctantly conceding to Washington that "these are not all hordes of uncontrollable savages but terrorists with varying levels of military training and political indoctrination. Some even call themselves communists."[32]

The third difference between the early independence era crisis and the Simba Rebellion—again in quantity and quality, if not in kind—was the role played by religion. Of course, religious mysticism, ethnicity, and politics had always been tightly interwoven in the Congo.[33] What was

---

28 Missionary Aviation Letter to American Supporter, February 1964, BGC/CN136/8/8. This letter refers to relatively old reports of these rumors.
29 Dowdy, *Out of the Jaws*, 238–39.
30 Guevara, *African Dream*, 7.
31 Sidney Langford to Prayer Partners, 1 October 1964, BGC/CN81/85/7.
32 Ambassador Gullion to Secretary of State, 31 January 1964, NARA/RG59/250/7/37/1964-66/Box 2713.
33 Duignan and Gann, *United States and Africa*, 240–46.

new was the extent to which religious belief was effectively harnessed. Combining earlier legends with the virtually universal belief in the power of traditional spiritualists, Mulele utilized indigenous myths with unprecedented success, convincing the local population that by taking doses of his witchdoctor's special *dawa* (medicine), his *jeunesse* (bands of young rebels) were impervious to bullets.[34]

Within a secular society, such beliefs would have solicited little more than a bemused smile. In the spiritually-infused Congolese context, however, belief in the power of traditional spiritualists was arguably *the* decisive factor in the rebellion's startling early success.[35] Over the next two years, thanks to the dawa legend, relatively well-equipped government soldiers were regularly routed by bands of Simba youth—sometimes needing little more than palm leaves or the fetishes of a local spiritualist.[36] Even the initial evidence of rebel self-discipline can be attributed largely to their indigenous supernaturalist worldview. As one missionary noted at the time, unlike the government soldiers "the Simbas can't steal. Otherwise they're no longer protected by the witchdoctor's dawa ... So they put a gun on the table or poke a rifle butt in your stomach and say, 'I'd like that.' Afterwards they say, 'Thank you Bwana, for having given me this.'"[37]

For their part, some earlier US policymakers had attempted to utilize religion as a weapon in the Cold War.[38] Indeed, although Kennedy publicly disavowed its use as a Cold War weapon, there is some evidence that these earlier efforts did allow a few US diplomats to see the extent to which religion was shaping the Congolese story.[39] Richard Sanger, for instance, spent considerable time in reports to Washington describing the use by pro-communist Congolese of traditional religious mysticism to achieve

---

34 Duignan and Gann, *United States and Africa*, 246. The belief appears to have its origins in a legend that the Belgian attempt to execute the founder of Kimbanguism had failed when the bullets meant for him turned to water before reaching their target; transcript of Alfred Larson of Unevangelized Fields Mission speaking at a church conference in Pennsylvania, March 1965, BGC/T295 R; Unnamed St. Andrews Presbyterian College staff member to Secretary of State Rusk, 20 June 1964, NARA/RG59/250/7/21/2/Box 3243.

35 Mulele's use of mystical supernaturalism did come back to haunt him on occasions. In particular, one diplomatic cable in March of 1964 noted that when Mulele's promise that any anti-government fighters killed would rise from the dead after three days failed to materialize, some village leaders began to turn against him. Leopoldville to Secretary of State, 4 March 1964, NARA/RG59/250/7/3-7/1964-66/Box 2713.

36 Reed, *111 Days in Stanleyville*, 11.

37 Bayly, *Congo Crisis*, 24.

38 Inboden, *Religion and American*; Preston, *Sword of the Spirit*, 411–81; Rotter "Christians, Muslims, and Hindus," 593–613; and Herzog, *Spiritual-Industrial Complex*.

39 "Remarks at the 10th Annual Presidential Prayer Breakfast," 1 March 1962, *Public Papers: Kennedy*, 175.

their revolutionary aims.[40] And in at least one case, the CIA effectively harnessed Congolese superstition by hiring a local "witchdoctor" to curse the new Soviet embassy in Leopoldville. "Jacques had him dance in front of the embassy for hours chanting the curse," the CIA station chief recalled in his memoirs. "We had no idea what it was all about, but we knew that most Congolese were extremely superstitious ... The cost, anyway, was minimal and we felt it was money well spent."[41]

Yet, by and large, the spiritual worldview of the Congolese was such a substantial departure from that of the American policymakers that most diplomats appear to have been initially incapable of perceiving the extent to which religious belief shaped the Simba rebellion. In this, at least, the secular elites of both East and West had more in common with each other than they did with the spiritually minded Congolese they sought to influence. Whether it was Che Guevara's difficulty in suppressing his laughter at the beliefs of his Congolese comrades or Ambassador Gullion's reference to the "ridiculous mysticism" of the Congolese, both East and West were equally dismissive.[42] As a result, it was perhaps inevitable that American attempts to utilize religion as a Cold War weapon would be characterized by displays of policy-debilitating ignorance. One telling example of this was George Ball's staggeringly ignorant assertion in an important 1963 memo on the use of religion in the Cold War that, "many of the citizens of the newly independent countries, particularly in Africa ... are not religious-minded."[43]

Unlike their policymaking compatriots, American missionaries understood Congolese spirituality and took its potential to shape the rebellion seriously. Shortly after leaving the Congo, a veteran Presbyterian missionary of eighteen years wrote to Secretary of State Rusk to offer his services. Convinced of the potency of the Congolese spiritual worldview, the missionary made a number of suggestions, including sending the Congolese army bullets "painted with a very bright yellow color with the instruction that this is to counteract the medicine made by the rebels."[44]

---

40 Richard Sanger to Hugh Cumming, "Secret" Memorandum 22 August 1960, NARA/RG59/250/63/10/Box 8.
41 Devlin, *Chief of Station, Congo*, 194–95.
42 Gullion to Sec. of State, 31 January 1964, NARA/RG59/250/7/37/1964-66/Box 2713; Guevara, *African Dream*, 14.
43 Department of State to All American Diplomatic and Consular Posts, "Soviet Government Restrictions on Religious Worship" 19 March 1963, NARA/RG84/350/c/59/7/Box 36.
44 Unnamed St. Andrews Presbyterian College staff member to Secretary of State Rusk, 20 June 1964, NARA/RG59/250/7/21/2/Box 3243.

Just over two weeks later, ranking members of the US military's Special Warfare Directorate met with the assistant director of the United States Information Agency (USIA) for Africa, the Africa division's chief of research, and several others to discuss the "Special Psychological Problems in the Congo." Not surprisingly, the participants began by acknowledging the fact that US diplomats and military representatives in parts of the country did not take the potential influence of Congolese traditional religion "very seriously."

Nevertheless, based in part on the suggestions of American missionary Sam Vinton and the "consensus of U.S. opinion [that is, missionary opinion] in Bukavu," the USIA official stated that "the subject of magic in the Congo is a legitimate point for discussion and concern," noting also that "Ambassador Godley share[s] this concern."[45] In this way, spiritually-minded missionaries helped to bridge the divide between their secular-minded policymaking compatriots and the spiritually-infused Congolese.

American Missionaries and the Simba Rebellion in Full Flower

After heavy fighting between rebels and government forces in the Spring of 1964, American diplomats believed that Mulele's "well-organized rural Maoist-style insurgency" had been largely contained.[46] This proved to be wrong. Throughout early 1964 weapons, guerrilla warfare manuals, and communist propaganda were quietly shuttled into the Congo by rebels based in the friendly neighboring regimes.[47] As a result, when the United Nations officially withdrew from the Congo on 30 June 1964, the embers of the Kwilu rebellion soon began to produce flash fires in many parts of the country which quickly, if chaotically, coalesced into the fully-fledged Simba Rebellion.

Within weeks, reports reached the US embassy of major rebel advances in the provinces of North Katanga and Kivu (eastern Congo) and significant activity in many other parts of northern Congo. By the third week of July, Kindu, the capital of Kivu, was largely in rebel hands, and the capture of Stanleyville, the important capital of Haut-Congo province just to the north (and the tribal home of the martyred Patrice Lumumba), appeared to be imminent.[48] Over the next year, the Simbas succeeded, if only briefly,

---

45 Confidential memorandum "Meeting Concerning Special Psychological Problems in the Congo," 7 July 1964, NARA/RG59/150/34/01-07/Box 24.
46 Hoyt, *Captive in the Congo*, 14.
47 Missionaries located near the Sudan and Uganda borders often witnessed the arrival of weapons and supplies. Carl and Gladys Becker, interview with the author, 9 July 2009.
48 Hoyt, *Captive in the Congo*, 30–38.

in establishing a "People's Republic" that included roughly half of the Congo, was recognized by the communist bloc and several non-aligned nations, and threatened the West's tenuous hold on the key African nation. Once again evangelical missionaries were set to play a critical role in the evolving Cold War drama.

Throughout the Simba rebellion, much of the intelligence that informed US diplomats in Congo originated from American missionaries based in the rural locales where the rebellion was unfolding. While the continuing flow of information between American missionaries and diplomats rightly implies a larger continuity in the relationship between the two, it unfortunately also serves to obfuscate the growing uneasiness many missionaries felt about the interaction they had with their government. To be sure, the vast majority of American evangelical missionaries had always viewed explicitly political activity with a degree of suspicion. This was particularly true among the more fundamentalist missionaries whose alienation from the mainstream of American cultural life simply reinforced their theological and historical allegiance to the principle of separation of church and state.[49]

Nevertheless, for many missionaries the extraordinary circumstances of the Congo justified at least a blurring of the line between church and state. As one conservative Presbyterian noted in a letter to Secretary of State Rusk, while his offer of assistance, "would not meet with the approval of other missionaries, preserving the Congo as an independent nation, not under the auspices of [the] Communist world ... is important, first of all, to make the land free that missionaries may continue their work."[50]

It is also important to recognize that a significant amount of the intelligence that originated from American missionaries during the Simba rebellion was not meant for government eyes. The existence in State Department records of a considerable number of missionary letters to their regional supervisors seems to indicate that these letters may have been pilfered by intelligence agents. Another possibility is that the missionaries' superiors, some of whom had developed a close relationship with the State Department, had themselves passed the letters to representatives of the US government. Whatever their path to the State Department may have been, these letters contained unguarded and detailed political analysis from missionary observers whose mastery of the local languages and close relationships with the people of rural Congo had provided them

---

49 Marsden, *Fundamentalism and American Culture*, 208; Noll, *Scandal of the Evangelical*, 168.
50 Unnamed St. Andrews Presbyterian College staff member to Secretary of State Rusk, 20 June 1964, NARA/RG59/250/7/21/2/Box 3243.

with insights that almost certainly would have escaped even seasoned intelligence agents.[51]

Just as unintentional, but equally important, was the information that passed casually between American missionaries and diplomats in social settings. As we have already seen, unlike their counterparts in Europe and parts of Asia, American diplomatic posts in Africa during the 1960s remained small and relatively isolated communities whose primary social contact was with either the sparsely populated international diplomatic community or the missionaries who made up the bulk of the American expatriate community. Despite its Cold War significance, the Congo was no exception. Whether it was at the American school, embassy social gatherings, or church services, the two communities interacted freely, and relationships sometimes developed that engendered a "very unusual" level of openness between the two groups.[52]

The radio network that had been so valuable to the missionary community during the uprisings of 1960 and 1961 was an additional channel through which intelligence passed informally between the American missionary and diplomatic communities. By 1964, virtually every Protestant mission station in the vast country, no matter how small, was equipped with a powerful radio system. The resulting radio network kept missionaries connected to a regional radio hub, which in turn kept the national network informed in the event of any important developments.[53]

By 1964, the system was functioning with clockwork efficiency. Every day, at set times, each station would radio in an update. Typically, the updates were related to the logistical needs of the station, the arrival or departure of a missionary family, or simply banter between friends.[54] During periods of political tension, however, these updates included political information that was vital to the safety of the missionary community and the Congolese converts whom they served. Both because of its responsibility to protect its citizens living in the Congo, and because it had almost no intelligence operation in the rural areas, the US embassy regularly listened in on the

---

51 Letter Rev. Norman G. Riddle Airgram to American Baptist missionary regional representative Rev. Chester J. Jump from American Baptist missionary, 13 January 1964, NARA/RG 59/250/7/21/2/Box 3243, No. A-103, Enclosure 18 October 1964, NARA/RG59/250/7/3-7/1964-66/Box 2727; Airgram No. A-103, Enclosure 2, 28 October 1964, NARA/RG59/250/7/3-7/1964-66/Box 2727.

52 John and JoAnn Ellington, interview with the author, 29 June 2009; Hoyt, *Captive in the Congo*, 29.

53 "Congo News," 12 February 1964, BGC/CN136/8/8.

54 Betty Pontier, interview with the author, 9 July 2009; "Dear MAFer" February 1964, BGC/CN 136/8/8; "Congo News," 12 February 1964, BGC/CN136/8/8.

communication between mission stations.⁵⁵ That this was an open secret is clear from the fact that US diplomats would occasionally use the network to pass on safety announcements to the missionaries.⁵⁶

Confirming the testimony of both US missionaries and diplomats regarding the critical role of the radio network was the frantic preoccupation that the rebels had with finding and destroying missionary radios. Convinced that the missionaries were reporting Simba positions to American bombers, invariably the first thing that the rebels did when entering a mission station was to demand the radio. Complicating matters considerably was the fact that most of the rebels had never seen a radio transmitter and so had very little idea of what to look for.⁵⁷

While missionary letters, friendships between diplomats and missionaries, and the missionary radio network were informal and often unintentional channels through which information passed to US policymakers, other more direct and intentional channels continued to be vital. In some cases, missionaries, or their US-based superiors, volunteered important information. Letters to Congo desk officer Arthur Tienken and Secretary of State Rusk from representatives of the Baptist Mid-Mission and the American Baptist Foreign Mission Society during February 1964 spoke of a consistent flow of intelligence between the missionaries and the State Department.⁵⁸

A host of additional telegrams and diplomatic cables from Leopoldville to Washington throughout 1964 confirm that in spite of concerns that they might compromise their spiritual calling, many American missionaries were enthusiastic sources of critical intelligence regarding the movement and make-up of the rebel forces.⁵⁹ Again, this is not to imply that the missionaries were CIA "assets" in the shadowy sense of the term. Rather, having witnessed first-hand the "diabolical" destruction of a country they loved at the hands of what they believed to be "communist-

---

55 Admission by both the State Department and the CIA of their lack of quality intelligence—especially in the interior of the Congo see Hoyt, *Captive in the Congo*, xvii, and Devlin, *Chief of Station, Congo*, 28–33. For evidence that the US government listened in on the missionary radio network see Betty Pontier, interview with the author, 9 July 2009.
56 Betty Pontier interview with the author, 9 July 2009.
57 Dowdy, *Out of the Jaws*, 38–39, 73–74.
58 Dr. W. Drew Varney to Arthur T. Tienken, 11 February 1964, NARA/RG59/250/7/21/2/Box 3243; Allan Lewis to Secretary of State Dean Rusk, 19 February 1964; and Airgram No. A-103, Enclosure 2, 28 October 1964, NARA/RG59/250/7/3-7/1964-66/Box 2727.
59 Bujumbura to SecState, Leopoldville, Bukavu, 20 March 1964, NARA/RG59/250/7/3-7/1964-66/Box 2713; Dean to Department of State, 15 June 1964, NARA/RG59/250/7/21/2/Box 3243; Unnamed St. Andrews Presbyterian College faculty member to Secretary of State Rusk, 20 June 1964, NARA/RG 59/250/7/21/2/Box 3243.

inspired youth bands," and believing the US government to be an agent of goodness and order, some missionaries believed that a close relationship with their government was, in this context, compatible with their missionary calling.[60]

As was the case in 1960–1961, interviews with recently evacuated missionaries were another channel through which important information was gleaned. In the wake of the Kwilu uprising and the buildup to the Simba capture of Stanleyville in August 1964, a host of missionaries were debriefed by US diplomats. Among other things, these interviews revealed a significant level of early local—and even occasionally missionary—sympathy for the rebels, the type and number of weapons being used, the varying degrees of discipline present within rebel bands, and the largely chaotic and undisciplined response of the Congolese army to the uprising.[61]

Missionary pilots, critical to the sustainability of many remote missionary stations, were also indispensable to efforts by the American government both in evacuating isolated and endangered American missionaries and in understanding the dynamically evolving Congolese uprising. Although many missionary organizations owned and operated one or two small planes, the bulk of the missionary air traffic was handled by the Missionary Aviation Fellowship (MAF), an organization started by Christian pilots, many of whom had flown for the US military in World War II. Keen to avoid the appearance of significant new intervention in the Congo, the US government relied on these missionary pilots to handle most of the initial fact-finding flights and subsequent evacuations of American citizens during the Kwilu Simba uprisings.[62] For their part, the missionary pilots had one aim, getting their colleagues to safety. Yet, in the process of these high-risk evacuations, they were also necessarily gathering and disseminating the most comprehensive and up-to-the-minute intelligence regarding the rural insurrection.[63]

---

60 John and Erna Strash to "Dear Praying Friends," March 1964, BGC/CN136/8/58; and Unnamed St. Andrews Presbyterian College faculty member to Sec. of State Rusk, 20 June 1964, NARA/RG 59/250/7/21/2/Box 3243.

61 Among others, Confidential Telegram from Gullion to Secretary of State 30 January 1964, NARA/RG59/250/7/3-7/1964-66/Box 2713; MacArthur (Brussels) to Secretary of State, 5 February 1964, NARA/RG59/250/7/3-7/1964-66/Box 2713; Leopoldville to Secretary of State, 18 February 1964, NARA/RG 59/250/7/3-7/1964-66/Box 2713.

62 "Mukedi Evacuated," 19 January 1964, BGC/CN136/8/9; "Report of Mr. and Mrs. Auguste Eicher," February 1964, BGC/CN136/8/9; and "Three Day Diary," Fairley, 1 February 1964, BGC/CN136/8/9.

63 *Congo News*, 12 February 1964, BGC/CN136/8/8; and "Dear MAFers," February 1964, BGC/CN136/8/8.

In short, by the time the Kwilu uprising had exploded into the full-fledged "Simba" rebellion in July 1964, the US government was developing an increasingly rich understanding of both the political and cultural context of the movement as well as the movement's key actors and actions. Because the movement did not develop in the metropolitan center of Leopoldville but instead in the villages and jungles of rural Congo, the US government was unusually reliant on non-traditional sources of intelligence. Foremost among them were the American evangelicals whose isolated missions dotted the vast rural Congolese landscape.[64]

This is not to say that the missionaries were the only source of US intelligence, nor should it imply that the information they passed on was always accurate or helpful. Indeed, the US sought out information wherever it could be found and at times the intelligence provided by the missionaries was distorted by either their sympathy for the local people or by the lenses of emotional trauma through which they interpreted the events they had witnessed.[65] In addition, as the Simba rebellion grew in global significance, and as many missionaries were forced to flee their rural mission stations, US policymakers were increasingly forced to rely on their own sources for intelligence in the Congo. Nevertheless, there can be little question that the US picture of the evolving Simba rebellion was profoundly influenced by American evangelical missionaries.

American Missionaries and Congolese Elites During the Simba Rebellion

In the summer of 1964, as the Congo appeared to be imploding, events took a turn that very few could have foreseen. On 9 July, Congolese President Joseph Kasavubu, himself increasingly close to American Baptist missionaries, and a recent convert to Protestantism, dismissed the ineffectual Prime Minister

---

[64] "Excerpts from Letter" to Rev. Chester J. Jump, Jr. (A.B.F.M.S Regional Representative) from Rev. Norman G. Riddle (A.B.F.M.S. Missionary in the Congo at Vanga Station) 13 January 1964, NARA/RG59/250/7/21/2/Box 3243; Unnamed St. Andrews Presbyterian College faculty member to Secretary of State Rusk, 20 June 1964, NARA/RG59/250/7/21/2/Box 3243; Bujumbura to Secretary of State, Leopoldville, Bukavu, 20 March 1964, NARA/RG59/250/7/3-7/1964-66/Box 2713; Gullion to Secretary of State 30 January 1964, NARA/RG59/250/7/3-7/1964-66/Box 2713; MacArthur (Brussels) to Secretary of State, 5 February 1964, NARA/RG59/250/7/3-7/1964-66/Box 2713; "Three Day Diary" Fairley, 1 February 1964, BGC/CN136/8/9.

[65] A good example of missionaries being unable or unwilling to admit that some of their Congolese friends were not being entirely forthright with them is found in a letter from Rev. Chester J. Jump Jr. to his mission's regional representative in January of 1964 in which he writes that despite the government's claim that "our area is honeycombed with [rebel] sympathizers and caches of arms. Our best leaders say that this is impossible, that our pastors would certainly get wind of anything like this." NARA/RG59/250/7/21/2/Box 3243.

Cyrille Adoula and replaced him with the former president of the rebellious Katanga province: the American-educated, Methodist lay minister, Moise Tshombe.[66] The New Frontiersmen still heading up the State Department's African Affairs Department were beside themselves. Sam Adams, the young CIA analyst who had accurately predicted Tshombe's surprising return, reported that upon hearing the news the recently-appointed US Ambassador Godley went into a "catatonic fit."[67] This was no more extreme than the reaction of Mennen Williams, who had likened Tshombe to "the devil."[68] In retrospect, it seems clear that the State Department's disdain for the "anathema" Tshombe blinded them to the exile's public efforts to successfully reposition himself in the months prior to his appointment as an independent but still pro-Western Congolese nationalist.[69]

It is significant that in this repositioning effort Tshombe believed both Congolese and Western support would rest, at least in part, on his identification as a missionary-educated Christian leader. In one of several interviews given to the European media while in exile, and reprinted in the Congo, Tshombe attempted to bolster his religious credentials by stressing the harmful effects on the Congo of anti-missionary communist propaganda and the need for "Christian prayers, love and understanding" in the nation's rehabilitation.[70] Months later, at arguably the bleakest moment in the Simba rebellion, the new prime minister's message was the same. Summarizing his private meeting with Tshombe in Leopoldville, the visiting Assistant Secretary of State Williams stated:

> Let me say again, that throughout the entire conversation [which was almost five hours in length], Prime Minister Tshombe was exceedingly cordial and, in fact, he spent a great deal of his time trying to ingratiate himself. He went through his whole history of American missionary training, the fact that most of his colleagues had American training or associations, and indeed, he said, that the Belgians frequently reproached them as being too pro-American.[71]

---

66 Kasavubu's personal doctor was an African American Baptist missionary doctor named Buford Washington and his own close connections to the American Baptist missionaries in his home area were well known. Armistead Lee to CWG: Amb. McIlvaine, 17 December 1964, NARA/RG59/150/34/01-87/B-3; "Joseph Kasavubu," NARA/RG59/250/63/10/Box 4.
67 Adams, *War of Numbers*, 10–13.
68 Williams, *Africa for the Africans*, 87, 98.
69 Adams, *War of Numbers*, 10.
70 As summarized in a cable from the American Consul in Elizabethville to Washington, 25 February 1964, NARA/RG59/250/7/3-7/1964-66/Box 2713.
71 Secret Memorandum of Conversation, Prime Minister Tshombe and Governor Williams, 15 August 1964, NARA/RG 59/150/24/01-07/Box 25.

Tshombe's intentional, and apparently authentic, identification of himself with his American missionary training and Methodist faith was equally apparent in his public appearances while prime minister. Not only did he regularly attend the Methodist church in Leopoldville but he frequently delivered the sermon. In fact, even during the height of the Simba rebellion, he went out of his way to attend missionary social functions, where he sought, and received, enthusiastic support.[72] Tshombe's tenure as prime minister was cut short when President Kasavubu dismissed him in October of 1965. Yet during his eighteen months in power Tshombe made no secret of his affection for his American missionary mentors and the nation that they represented—despite (or perhaps because of) his awareness of the deep-seated animosity that existed towards him among top US policymakers. In doing so, he symbolized the influence that American missionaries had on US-Congo relations through their Congolese converts.

Simba Treatment of American Missionaries and Their Congolese Converts

Perhaps the most intriguing and confusing sub-plot in the increasingly radical Simba Rebellion was the treatment of American missionaries by the otherwise violently anti-Western rebels. Throughout the rebellion it was not uncommon for a group of Simbas to attack a group of missionaries in one instance only to turn around and treat others from the same organization with deference and respect moments later.[73] At both the elite and rank-and-file levels, this wildly fluctuating treatment reflected the conflicting loyalties and the contradictions of the Simba rebellion.

The same contradictions could at times be seen in the way that the Simbas treated those Congolese Christians who had been converted and trained by American missionaries. Generally speaking, the Simbas viewed their American-trained Protestant compatriots as counterrevolutionaries because, as one Simba commander near AIM's Napopo station argued, "You worked for the Americans. That makes you just like them ... you are our enemy."[74] Yet standing opposed to the regular threats of violence and death against Protestants were many examples of explicit sympathy and

---

72 Marshall and Thelma Southard, interview with the author, 8 July 2009.
73 Report from Yonama Angondia, Director of Medical Work, AIM Oicha, 10 October 1964, BGC/CN81/33/25; Dr. A. Barlovatz to Isa, 15 December 1964, NARA/RG59/150/34/01-07/Box 25.
74 Olsen, *African Heroes*, 58.

support for these Congolese converts, such as the requirement by some Simba officers that their soldiers attend the services at American-initiated mission churches.[75] Nevertheless, when the tide began to turn against the rebels, and the revolution became increasingly and erratically violent, the examples of anti-missionary and anti-Christian violence multiplied.

Western-trained pastors and teachers, along with the police and any remaining local representatives of the central government, became the most obvious targets of Simba brutality. As one Congolese pastor confirmed in a report to American missionaries, "When the rebels enter a place, they do not kill everyone. They pick out those who are not following what they say, or those who are wearing good clothes, or anyone who is working for, or friendly with the Central Government, or Church leaders and Christians."[76] This anti-missionary and anti-Western pogrom came to a climax in Stanleyville, where one missionary reported to another that "Hundreds have been executed and the pavement is red with blood in front of the [Lumumba] monument near your house. Libi, Jalasiga, Jalawori, and the Chief at Gote," the missionary continued, "have been eliminated."[77]

Initially the Simbas were less violent towards the missionaries themselves. Indeed, outside of the American missionary Irene Ferrel, who had been killed early in the rebellion by a wayward Simba arrow, until August 1964 American missionaries had been harassed and intimidated but had largely escaped physical attack.[78] In fact, in some Simba-friendly regions, those missionaries who remained were allowed to continue their work unhindered. This was certainly true for the missionaries in Stanleyville before the city fell to the Simbas in early August.

Unlike the vast majority of the international community who had fled Stanleyville in the days prior to the city's fall, the entire American missionary community resisted pressure from their government and instead elected to stay. This prompted the new and clearly irritated American consul, Michael Hoyt, to suggest the missionaries were simply ignorant. "Believing themselves to be outside the political struggle, devoted to humanitarian and spiritual ends," Hoyt wrote in his memoirs, "the missionaries could not imagine that they would be considered hostile

---

75 Olsen, 55.
76 Report from Yonama Angondia, Director of Medical Work, A.I.M. Oicha, BGC/CN81/33/25.
77 "Paul and Betty" to Potockis, 8 October 1964, NARA/RG59/250/7/3-7/1064-66/Box 2727. Additional descriptions of Simba brutality from eye-witness Charles Davis, interview with the author, 9 July 2009.
78 *World Vision Magazine*, "Missionary Slain."

by the rebels."[79] Of course, the missionaries were not quite as naive as Hoyt assumed. Thanks to the missionary radio network, they were keenly aware of the dangers they faced.

Instead, history and faith were the primary reasons these missionaries stayed. When their lives had been in danger during the post-independence violence of 1960–1961, many of the missionaries had chosen to evacuate temporarily. Although most had returned to their work within months of evacuating, many had felt a deep sense of shame for having put their own lives ahead of their Congolese Christian brothers and sisters.[80] As one missionary who chose to remain in Stanleyville stated, "the shopkeepers and the beer makers and the mechanics are not leaving … When trouble comes, should the missionary be the first to run?" The answer was clear. "We are going to stay."[81] Even as the Simbas descended on the city and the consul's wife urged her missionary friends to join her on the last evacuation planes out of the city, they responded that they had "invested too much spiritually and materially in the Congo to abandon it now."[82]

There is another sense in which Hoyt's judgment was inaccurate, for as we have seen, to a significant extent the rebel rank-and-file did not view the missionaries as hostile. As events during the initial occupation of Stanleyville were to demonstrate, even in the face of an unpredictable, racially infused and ideologically antagonistic movement, the goodwill that the missionaries had built up over generations meant that it was not unreasonable for them to hope for fair treatment. Indeed, even as the Simbas reacted to Tshombe's White mercenary-led counter-offensive with increasingly desperate anti-imperialist and anti-American rhetoric, there were regular instances of pro-missionary sentiment at all levels of the Simba hierarchy.

Despite his own reliance on traditional African spiritualists, the Simba leader "General" Olenga personified the distinction many of the rebels made between Americans in general and American missionaries. In one instance, after discovering that the missionary Chuck Davis had been imprisoned with the American consul and the four other remaining consular staff, Olenga visited the prison personally to free Davis. Speaking to consul Hoyt, Olenga stated, "I have no quarrel with missionaries" who had "a special status." Turning to Davis, Olenga continued apologetically,

---

79 Hoyt, *Captive in the Congo*, xvii.
80 Odom, *Dragon Operations*, 10.
81 Dowdy, *Out of the Jaws*, 27.
82 Hoyt, *Captive in the Congo*, 38.

"You are not supposed to be here ... missionaries are good people. They help the Congolese."[83]

By mid-to-late October 1964, however, this pro-missionary sympathy had finally given way to a visceral anti-Americanism. By this point, the Simbas had become convinced that the missionary radio network was responsible for betraying rebel movements to a small but effective CIA-backed air force being piloted by anti-communist Cuban-exiles.[84] The false belief that the missionaries were intentionally acting in concert with both the CIA and Tshombe's advancing White mercenary force appears to have led directly to the disturbing developments that followed.

First came Christopher Gbenye's October announcement on Radio Stanleyville that "the missionaries are like other Belgians and Americans. They are imperialists like their governments. Arrest them all."[85] Next was an intercepted request to Olenga from a Simba commander in Stanleyville asking for authority to "execute all Americans in rebel territory," prompting Secretary of State Rusk to send a frantic cable to Ambassador William Attwood in Kenya urging President Kenyatta's immediate and personal intervention "to stop [this] deed which would shock [the] conscience of [the] world and do irreparable harm [to] Africa."[86] By this point, all the Americans in Simba territory were missionaries (aside from the five US diplomats held in Stanleyville) and most, including a number of women and children, were already Simba hostages.

Yet even at this time, many missionaries continued to receive special treatment. For instance, when moved from house arrest to more formal confinement, several Simbas ensured that the American missionaries were moved to a modest hotel and provided with mattresses—even going so far as to fix the room's broken air-conditioning unit. Later, one of these Simbas returned alone to seek forgiveness and ask how he might become a Christian.[87] Even as the public anti-missionary rhetoric reached its zenith, Brooklyn-born missionary Al Larson was able to secure a private meeting with Gbenye in which the Simba leader promised to ensure that the Congolese teachers and staff at a local mission station would be paid.[88]

---

83 Hoyt, *Captive in the Congo*, 147; Dowdy, *Out of the Jaws*, 79. It is likely that Olenga's pro-missionary feeling originated from his wife who was a regular visitor at the Protestant bookstore in Stanleyville and had sought out a Christian tutor for her four children from the missionaries that worked there. Dowdy, *Out of the Jaws*, 97.

84 Dowdy, 38–39, 73–74.

85 Dowdy, 93.

86 Rusk to AmEmbassy Nairobi, 14 October 1964, NARA/RG59/150/34/01-07/Box 25.

87 Dowdy, *Out of the Jaws*, 112–14.

88 Marshall and Thelma Southard, interview with the author, 8 July 2009.

As it had been in the independence-era crisis, the stubborn resilience of pro-missionary sentiment was noted by American policymakers. In fact, as soon as some areas of formerly Simba-held territory were reclaimed by the central government in late October, the US embassy in Leopoldville pleaded for the State Department to reverse its ban on American missionaries returning to their mission stations. In addition to concerns that the lack of returning Americans would pose a public relations problem for the US, the embassy stressed the "crucial political importance" of reclaiming stability in these traumatized areas, and the central role that the American medical and educational missionaries could play in that process. Besides, the embassy concluded, "living in many isolated parts of Congo has always posed some risks, and this is [the] type of challenge [the] missionaries have accepted and even sought. We need these people."[89]

Dr. Paul Carlson and American Public and Political Opinion

In the end, it was the violent death of an American missionary that became the lasting symbol of the Simba Rebellion. On 21 October, a missionary named Paul Carlson joined the others being held hostage by the Simbas in Stanleyville. Carlson had first come to the Congo with his wife and children in 1961 after responding to an urgent plea for more doctors by the Christian Medical and Dental Society. For three-and-a-half years, the talented and energetic physician poured himself into his work at the Wasolo mission hospital—a station so remote that the Congolese called it "*le coin perdu*" (the forgotten corner).[90]

However, by 31 August 1964, Simba activity in the area had led the US embassy to seek the evacuation of all American missionaries nearby. Virtually all women and children departed, but some of the men, including Carlson, chose to remain in their largely abandoned missions. On 18 September, after finishing what turned out to be his last radio call with his wife Lois, the Simbas attacked the station, killing two Congolese and taking prisoner Carlson and three Catholic priests from a nearby mission. Then, after being held hostage at a Catholic mission in Buta for almost a month, Carlson was moved to Stanleyville. Five days later, Gbenye announced on Radio Stanleyville that a "Major Carlson," "a mercenary," would stand trial as a spy.[91]

---

89 AmEmbassy Leopoldville to SecState, 31 October 1964, NARA/RG 59/250/7/21/2/Box 3243.
90 Carlson, *Monganga Paul*, 73.
91 Carlson, 155–67.

Dr. Carlson's story was no longer unusual. By late October, American missionaries remaining throughout Simba-held territory were being routinely imprisoned or placed under house arrest.[92] What made Carlson's case especially significant was the amount of attention it attracted across the globe, especially in the United States. In a twist of fate, months prior to the full flowering of the Simba rebellion a medical student from Johns Hopkins had come to work with the Carlsons at Wasolo.

During this time the *Baltimore Sun* sent a photographer to take photos for an article on the student's decision to do missionary work in the Congo. While he was not the subject of the article, Carlson and his work were prominently featured.[93] By the time the article came out on 6 September, disturbing stories about the Simba rebellion had forced the Congo back into the minds of many Americans, and the article was quickly picked up by the newspapers in Carlson's hometown of Los Angeles. Then, when Carlson was captured, falsely accused of being a spy, and threatened with execution the story made headlines across the country.[94]

Suddenly other missionary-related stories that had until this point circulated primarily in evangelical publications began to garner wider attention.[95] The combined impression created by these stories was that of a superstitiously driven and violently anti-Western rebellion in which significant numbers of American missionaries remained in mortal danger. Not surprisingly, letters from the public began to pour in forcing Washington into action.[96]

Of course, US policymakers had not been oblivious to the evolution of events in the Congo. The US government had put too much of its international prestige on the line during the Katangan secession to ignore the Congo completely. Nevertheless, relative to Vietnam and the racially-infused upheaval at home, the Johnson administration had little time for Africa—a reality for which Secretary Rusk was unapologetic, bluntly stating

---

92 Deputy Director Looram to Mr. Edward Randall, Field Secretary, Indiana Baptist Convention, NARA/RG 59/150/34/01-07/Box 25.

93 Carlson, *Monganga Paul*, 166.

94 *Washington Daily News*, "US Missionary Doctor"; *Washington Star*, "A Matter of Humanity"; *Dallas Morning News*, "Congolese Rebels Quiet"; *Dallas Morning News*, "Execution Postponed in Congo"; *Los Angeles Times*, "Wife of Missionary Denies." It is instructive to note that in the month of November 1964 the *NY Times* included approximately twenty articles in which Carlson's story was featured.

95 Garrison, "Congo Rebels Kill"; Garrison, "Priests Report U.S. Cleric."

96 Deputy Director Office of Central African Affairs to Mr. Edward Randall, Indiana Baptist Convention, 5 November 1964, NARA/RG59/150/34/01-07/Box 25.

in his memoirs that "Africa was not high on my list of priorities."[97] Africa, as another administration figure put it, was "the last issue considered, the first aid budget cut."[98] Under Johnson the large numbers of official visits by African heads of state to Washington under Kennedy dropped precipitously, and Africanists like Williams saw their power decline or were replaced by traditional Eurocentric policymakers.[99]

In short, with an election around the corner, and an increasing number of more pressing concerns vying for their attention, the Johnson administration had come to view the Congo as little more than an irritant. The fact that American missionaries had raised the stakes by putting themselves in harm's way simply added to the frustration of a president who, by his own admission, had no intention of getting "tied in on the Congo and have another Korea or another Vietnam, just because of someone wandering around searching for Jesus Christ."[100]

But it was too late. The story of the young American missionary doctor had already gripped the public imagination. From the middle of November, virtually every American cable regarding the Congo crisis related in some way to the fate of the young evangelical doctor.[101] Increased attention to Congo only served to highlight the volatility and complexity of the situation. Trapped between a desire to protect American missionaries and innocent Congolese from the widespread and ritualistic killings being perpetuated by the Simbas on the one hand, and the need to consider the bitter antagonism felt by most African leaders toward Tshombe and his White mercenary forces on the other, American policymakers could not win. Eventually, after two weeks of frenetic negotiations in the context of "acute and growing danger," Ambassador Attwood in Nairobi and Ambassador Godley in Leopoldville separately cabled Washington that there was "no alternative" but to support a proposed Belgian military rescue mission.[102]

---

97   Dean Rusk, *As I Saw It*, 246. It is also instructive to note that in his presidential memoir, *Vantage Point*, Johnson devotes entire chapters to the Caribbean, India, and the Space Program, but there is not a single mention of the Congo Crisis.
98   Morris, *Uncertain Greatness*, 17.
99   Lyons, "Keeping Africa off," 250; Odom, *Dragon Operations*, 25. It should be noted that an informal Congo working group headed by Averell Harriman was in place as early as 8 August, Odom, *Dragon Operations*, 15.
100 Ball, *Past Has Another Pattern*, 324.
101 "Top Secret," AmEmbassy Leopoldville to Rusk, 20 November 1964, NARA/RG59/250/7/3- 7/1964-66/Box 2727; Godley to Washington, 22 November 1964, NARA/RG 59/250/7/3-7/1964-66/Box 2727; Attwood to White House, DOD, CIA, 23 November 1964, NARA/RG 59/250/7/3-7/964-66/Box 2727.
102 AmEmbassy Nairobi to State, 23 November 1964, NARA/RG 59/250/7/3-7/1964-66/Box 2727; "Top Secret," Embassy Leopoldville to SecState, 23 November 1964, NARA/RG 59/250/7/3-7/1964-66/Box 2727.

The die had been cast. At 5 a.m. on 24 November, the first of six hundred Belgian paratroopers, transported by ten US C-130s, landed near Stanleyville and within a matter of hours took control of the city. In the process, the Belgians freed almost eight hundred foreigners and saved the lives of five American diplomats and approximately twenty American missionaries whose lives had hung in the balance. Yet the operation was not an unblemished success. Among the approximately thirty-five foreigners who were killed in the chaos were two American missionaries: Phyllis Rine, a young single missionary woman who had acted as a babysitter for US consul Hoyt and his wife, was the first. The second was Dr. Paul Carlson who had been shot by rebels as he was attempting to scale a wall to safety.[103]

The reaction of the US media was telling. Outside of dissent from a few academic and African American journals, Carlson's death was viewed as a tragically heroic symbol of American altruism which was explicitly juxtaposed with irrational African brutality.[104] The *Washington Post* highlighted Carlson's virtue within a Congolese context "where not even the humane purposes of a medical missionary are respected."[105] In cover stories in the next issues of both *Time* and *Life* magazines, the narrative was much the same.[106] *Life* magazine's managing editor, George Hunt, called Carlson a "heroic man of God who lived for the African—only to be killed by his hand."[107] And *Time* stated that Carlson's death "did more than prove that Black African civilization ... is largely a pretense."[108]

Many Africans saw the events differently. Aware of the strong anti-Tshombe feelings among most non-Congolese Africans, and sensitive to African and communist criticism of American interventionism, US policymakers had predicted angry reactions to the Belgian rescue effort from some quarters. But the response still surprised them. The pro-Western Kenyan government was the first to issue an official condemnation of the rescue operation, expressing "deep regret that in spite of several appeals by PM Jomo Kenyatta ... American, Belgian and white mercenaries ... have attacked Stanleyville [resulting in the loss of many lives] including that of Dr. Carlson."[109]

---

103 "Summary of Events in the Congo on 24 November 1964, NARA/CIA files CSD/NPIC 346/64; Hoyt, *Captive in the Congo*, 19; Davis, interview with the author, 9 July 2009. A number of critically injured hostages died from their wounds in the days following Dragon Rouge.
104 One example of this dissent was Bustin's, "After Stanleyville What?" 5–10.
105 *Washington Post*, "Death in the Congo."
106 *Time*, "The Congo Massacre"; *Life*, "Congo Martyr."
107 *Stanford Magazine*, September 1991.
108 *Time*, "The Congo Massacre"; *Life*, "Congo Martyr."
109 AmEmbassy Nairobi to SecState, 24 November 1964, NARA/RG59/250/7/3-7/1964-66/ Box 2728.

Unfortunately for the United States, Kenya's relatively restrained statement was not a harbinger of things to come. In the days following, one African nation after another railed against "the imperialist attack on the Congolese people."[110] The Ghanaians in particular lambasted the willingness of White governments to kill Africans in order to free "white mercenary criminals" who had killed "in the name of Christian humanitarianism and American aid."[111] The leftist Algerian government of Ben Bella spoke for many African nations in asserting that the "brutality of [US and Belgian] actions reveals [the] contempt in which they hold peoples they have dominated and shamefully exploited." On the other side, the conspiracy-minded Algerian press went so far as to claim that the "pretext of white hostages" was simply an "alibi permitting Tshombe to be supported."[112]

These accusations, coming from many African, communist, and non-aligned nations at the UN, soon built to such a climax that the normally measured Adlai Stevenson responded with what must stand out as one of the most unguarded and emotionally charged speeches delivered by an American diplomat in UN history. "Never before," Stevenson railed, "have I heard such irrational, irresponsible, insulting and repugnant language in these chambers; and language used, if you please, to contemptuously impugn and slander a gallant and successful attempt to save human lives of many nationalities and colors."[113] Stevenson spoke for many disillusioned liberals who, upon seeing their earnest labor on behalf of African nationalism yield nothing but injury and insult, turned away in disgust.

This disillusionment had important practical consequences. After the fallout from the US-Belgian rescue mission private contributions to the secular Operation Crossroads Africa dropped so sharply that the organization was forced to significantly scale back its programs. Summarizing this liberal frustration, *The New Republic*'s editor Murray Kempton wrote, "Africa hollers rape against us and does not even know that we no longer even care, let alone lust, and our reaction is to say, well, that's that and who's got a job for Soapy Williams."[114]

---

110 Conakry to SecState, 25 November 1964, NARA/RG59/250/7/3-7/1964-66/Box 2728.
111 AmEmbassy Accra to Department of State, 25 November 1964, NARA/RG59/250/7/3-7/1964-66/Box 2728.
112 AmEmbassy Algiers to SecState, 25 November 1964, NARA/RG59/250/7/3-7/1964-66/Box 2728.
113 Attwood, *Reds and the Blacks*, 227.
114 Attwood, 227–28.

The response by the American evangelical community was quite different. No doubt the events in the Congo had left a bitter taste, and undoubtedly acted to confirm previous prejudices some held about Africa and Africans. Yet instead of turning away in disgust, general evangelical interest in the Congo grew significantly. Thanks to the dramatic stories that had peppered both secular and Christian media outlets in the wake of the Belgian-American rescue attempt, evangelical missionaries like Chuck Davis returned from the Congo as unexpected celebrities. Upon disembarking his flight at JFK airport, Davis, a young AIM missionary who had been imprisoned with the US Consul in Stanleyville and in whose company Paul Carlson had died, was approached by news executives requesting an interview. Expecting a quiet meeting with a few reporters, Davis and his fellow evacuees instead walked into a full news conference with over one hundred reporters from most of the largest papers in the country. Over the next year, Davis travelled 115,000 miles as a regular guest on television and radio shows, including Billy Graham's *Hour of Decision*. He also gave approximately three hundred addresses nationwide, including one to twenty-two thousand people at the World's Fair in New York City.[115]

While extraordinary in breadth, Davis's experience was not unique. Whether they wanted to be or not, across the United States, missionaries returning from the Congo were in constant demand to speak at major Christian conferences and give interviews to both the mainstream and Christian media. During the following year, a host of books were published by major American publishers specifically related to the missionary role in the Congo crisis. Harper and Row led the way with four bestselling accounts of the crisis, including a biography of Paul Carlson written by his widow. Major Christian publishers such as Zondervan and Revell, and evangelical Christian magazines such as *World Vision Magazine* and *Christianity Today*, were no less active, ensuring that the Congo remained firmly lodged in the minds of many American evangelicals.[116]

Missionary accounts of the Congo crisis were often full of scenes of horrific violence and death—and in this sense, at least, they closely paralleled the coverage coming out of the mainstream media. Speaking at an American church conference in March 1965, missionary Al Larson,

---

115 Chuck and Muriel Davis, interview with the author, 9 July 2009.
116 Carlson, *Monganga Paul*; Hayes, *Captive of the Simbas*; Dowdy, *Out of the Jaws*; Anderson, *There was a Man*; Reed, *111 Days in Stanleyville*; Bayly, *Congo Crisis*; *World Vision Magazine*, "Carlson of Congo"; *World Vision Magazine*, "In the Congo."

who, himself, had led a daring rescue of twenty missionaries during the 24 November raid, spared no detail as he described the scenes in Stanleyville prior to the rescue.[117] The Congolese opponents of the Simbas

> were brought up before the Lumumba monument in the center of the city ... The lucky ones were shot. One had his hand cut off and stuffed into his own mouth [while] he died. Others had limbs cut off and [were] left to die in the sun. One had his liver taken out and could watch someone else eating it. Congolese killing Congolese, day after day. Some were our friends. We had known them for years.[118]

Yet beyond their common emphasis on the violence of the Congo crisis, secular and missionary accounts differed, most notably in their treatment of the Congolese. Where the Congolese were largely demonized by the mainstream press, missionary reports stressed the bonds of faith and humanity that they shared with the Congolese Christians, and balanced disturbing stories of Simba violence with stories of Congolese virtue and heroism. In these accounts, sympathetic Congolese regularly risked their lives in standing up for their faith or in protecting their missionary friends as they fled to safety.[119] *World Vision Magazine*, after recounting the martyrdom of the American-trained Congolese Pastor Yona, summed up the sentiment of much of the evangelical media: "The world knew everything about the death of the white missionary, Dr. Paul Carlson; it knew nothing about the death of an African national, Pastor Yona. Yet, in the reckoning of God they marched side by side in the unsegregated company of the martyrs."[120]

The second significant difference between the evangelical and mainstream responses to the Simba crisis was the level of ongoing commitment found within the American evangelical community. Indicative of this commitment was the modest growth in the number of American missionaries active in the Congo from just over one thousand in 1962 to almost twelve hundred in 1970.[121] There are a number of reasons for the resilience of the American missionary effort. The first was historical. Unlike the recent and largely cosmetic involvement of their secular

---

117 "Atlantan's key role."
118 Transcript of Al Larson address to a church conference in Lancaster, Pennsylvania, March 1965, BGC/T295 R.
119 Charles Davis, interview on the Barry Farber radio program on WOR, New York City, December, 1965, BGC; "Crisis Days in the Congo"; "Congo Legacy"; Olsen, *African Heroes*.
120 "Unsegregated Martyrs," *World Vision Magazine*, November 1965.
121 *Mission Handbook*, 5th ed.; *Mission Handbook*, 9th ed.

equivalents in the Peace Corps and Operation Crossroads Africa, over the previous three quarters of a century evangelicals had developed deep relational, spiritual, and cultural ties to the Congolese people.[122]

There was also a powerful emotional component to the continuing interest of evangelicals in the Congo. Far from weakening their bonds, the martyrdom of Carlson and seven other American missionaries only strengthened the emotional and spiritual bonds American Christians felt towards their Congolese counterparts.[123] This was symbolized in the decision by Carlson's widow to have her husband buried next to their Congolese church in Ubangi. "I know he would have chosen to stay with you," Carlson told the American and Congolese Christians gathered for the funeral.[124] With much the same sentiment Joseph Bayly concluded his bestselling account of the Simba rebellion stating, "The life that surges through the body [of Christ] is not Congolese life, or American life; it is the life of Christ. Each part of the body exists for the Head, and for every other part."[125]

Mobutu's Rise and the Decline of American Missionary Influence

The end of the Simba rebellion ushered in a new—but in some ways equally checkered—chapter in Congolese history. The rise to power of the quasi-Catholic, military strongman, Joseph Mobutu through a bloodless coup in late 1965 coincided with a noticeable decline in the influence of American evangelical missionaries on elite-level US-Congolese relations. There were several reasons for this decline. To begin with, by and large, missionaries could no longer boast of close ties to the inner circle of the new Congolese political elite. Like many of those surrounding him, Mobutu was a nominal Catholic whose worldview was dominated by the same traditional spiritualism that had animated the Simba rebellion.[126] As a result, Mobutu had none of the relational and ideological ties with American evangelicals that Tshombe, Sendwe, Kasavubu, and others before him had enjoyed.

In addition, by the late 1960s the US policymaking elite had grown less reliant on their missionary compatriots for cultural knowledge

---

122 McAlister, "What Is Your Heart?"
123 The list of American missionaries killed during the Simba rebellion includes: Mary Baker and William Scholten (Unevangelized Fields Mission); Irene Ferrel (Baptist Mid-Mission); William McChesney (Worldwide Evangelism Crusade); Burleigh Law (Central Congo Methodist Mission); James Tucker (Assemblies of God); and Dr. Paul Carlson (Evangelical Covenant Church of America). Bayly, *Congo Crisis*, 9–11.
124 Dowdy, *Out of the Jaws*, 233.
125 Bayly, *Congo Crisis*, 219.
126 Wrong, *In the Footsteps*, 72.

and political and social connections. Despite continuing close social relationships between some American missionaries and diplomats in the capital up through the 1970s, the State Department and CIA had reached a place where they believed they could go it alone.[127] Yet in a way, this sense of self-reliance was irrelevant. As we have seen, by 1975, long-standing concerns by missionary groups about the compromising roles missionaries had been asked to play in Cold War intrigues had encouraged evangelical Senator Mark Hatfield (OR) and others to introduce legislation criminalizing CIA approaches to missionaries abroad.

Together with the Church Committee's critical report of CIA ethics during the 1950s and 60s, the push by Hatfield and the evangelical Interdenominational Foreign Missions Association (IFMA) and the Evangelical Foreign Missions Association (EFMA) to protect the principle of separation of church and state ensured that, in the future, the relationship between American missionaries and their government's representatives abroad would be largely restricted by law to apolitical social and consular interaction.[128]

Finally, even if CIA policy had remained as it had been during the 1960s, evangelical missionaries had experienced first-hand the negative consequences that perceived complicity with their government could have on their work.[129] This renewed sensitivity to the moral ambiguity of geopolitical intrigue fit in very well with their historically apolitical intentions, and acted to confirm the separation by mutual consent that was already developing between the US government and their missionaries in the Congo and elsewhere.

Dr. William Close—The Exceptional Exception to the Rule

The one colorful exception to the decline of American missionary influence on elite US-Congolese relations during Mobutu's early years was the intriguing role played by the father of Hollywood actress Glenn Close. Theologically,

---

127 John and Joanne Ellington, interview with the author, 29 June 2009.
128 Mark Hatfield to William Colby, 26 August 1975, BGC/CN165/208/3; Colby to Hatfield, 13 September 1975, BGC/CN165/208/3; Hatfield to President Ford, 19 September 1975, BGC/CN165/208/3; Philip W. Buchen, Counsel to the President, 5 November 1975, BGC/CN165/208/3; "Report on the Involvement of CIA with Missionaries, EFMA," 1976, BGC/CN165/208/3; "Open Letter from W. Stanley Mooneyham (President of World Vision) to President Ford, *World Vision Magazine*, March 1976; Hatfield to Friends, 16 June 1976, BGC/CN165/208/3.
129 Charles Bennett (President of Missionary Aviation Fellowship) to Editor of *National Courier*, 2 October 1975, BGC/CN165/208/3; Wade T. Coggins (Executive Director, EFMA) to Joseph Bayly, *Eternity Magazine*, 12 April 1976, BGC/CN165/208/3.

Dr. William Close's status as a missionary with Moral Re-Armament (MRA) placed him well outside of the traditional definition of "evangelical."[130] Founded in 1921 in Oxford, England by an American Lutheran minister named Frank Buchman, MRA had already gone through a series of incarnations by the time Bill Close was introduced to it in the 1950s.[131]

While its roots in the "Cross of Christ" remained unmistakably Christian, its central emphasis on the individual's mystical experience of God's direct and unmediated "guidance" weakened its theological consistency, allowing MRA to cooperate with any and all faiths interested in the movement's idealistic and pan-religious aim of a "fear-free, hate-free, greed-free world."[132] Nevertheless, with its strong emphasis on forgiveness, anti-communism, and the "four absolutes" of honesty, purity, unselfishness, and love, MRA retained an evangelical ethos. As Close later recounted, MRA in the 1950s and 1960s could be summarized as "the Sermon on the Mount versus the Antichrist of communism."[133]

MRA's stress on the transformative conversion experience also betrayed its evangelical lineage. "The challenge was heady wine at the beginning," Close recounted years later. "Buchman's philosophy encouraged me to be honest about my sins and immediately jump into a world arena ... I felt God's charge to carry a message of personal change ... We committed our lives to God and MRA." Putting aside a prestigious medical residency in New York, and accepting the displeasure of friends and family, Close began touring the world with MRA teams in the mid-1950s, acting in plays and sharing Buchman's theologically flexible religious vision to audiences high and low.[134]

Close's travels eventually brought him and an MRA team to the Congo six weeks before independence. As subsequent events were to prove, the notion that in a number of weeks a few foreigners, armed only with their talents, a message of peaceful anticommunism, and new audio-visual technology might overcome hundreds of years of tribal and

---

130 As stated earlier, I have taken as my working definition of "evangelical" David Bebbington's widely accepted characterization as found in Bebbington, *Evangelicalism in Modern Britain*.
131 Boobbyer, "Moral Re-Armament in Africa," 213–15. Inboden, *Religion and American*, 192. Inboden's description of MRAs "direct and unmediated" guidance is important, because unlike the orthodox Christian view that experiences of apparent divine guidance should be tested against the teachings of the Bible and Church tradition, MRA made the individual's subjective experience paramount.
132 Boobbyer, "Moral Re-Armament in Africa," 216; Inboden, *Religion and American*, 192.
133 Close, *Beyond the Storm*, 41.
134 Close, 41–42.

racial antagonism was hopelessly idealistic. And yet, MRA did experience some success. During the first year of Congolese independence, it made close connections with large numbers of the nascent Congolese elite, which included private showings of their films to Lumumba (along with seventeen of his ministers), Kasavubu, Albert Kalonji, Tshombe, and Mobutu.[135] Mobutu even gave the introduction to a MRA film produced for the Congo.[136] Lacking quality programming for the national radio station, Lumumba's leftist minister of information, Aniset Kashamura, invited MRA to present regular radio programs—which they did twice a day for several months—before hostility to MRA's anti-communist message within the Lumumba government led to the program being taken off the air.[137]

Thanks to MRA's evangelical missionary ethos, zealous anti-communism, and its intentionally cultivated connections to the international diplomatic elite, Close almost immediately found himself at the nexus between American missionaries and the American and Congolese policymaking elites. Of course, neither Close nor his American evangelical missionary cohorts would have placed the maverick MRA man within the strictly evangelical camp. As his good friend, the veteran Presbyterian missionary David Miller, acknowledged, "Bill would be incensed if I said he was a 'born-again' Christian, because he could turn the air blue with his language, and frequently did."[138] And yet, there is no question that Close felt himself very much a part of the American missionary project. Throughout his time in Leopoldville/Kinshasa, he surrounded himself with missionary friends and colleagues. This is not surprising considering that even if MRA's theology was unorthodox, Close remained committed to following the example of Christ who "healed the sick, fed the hungry, and gave a prostitute new hope."[139]

Disturbed by the suffering he saw around him in the wake of the post-independence chaos, Close volunteered to help the overwhelmed *Hospital des Congolais* in Leopoldville.[140] This choice was to have important consequences. A couple of months after beginning his work at the hospital, an exhausted and frustrated Close happened to notice the car of the

---

135 Boobbyer, "Moral Re-Armament in Africa," 227–29.
136 Close, *Beyond the Storm*, 122.
137 Boobbyer, "Moral Re-Armament in Africa," 227–29.
138 David Miller, interview with the author, 30 June 2009.
139 Youmans, *When Bull Elephants Fight*; David Miller, interview with the author, 30 June 2009; John and JoAnn Ellington, interview with the author, 29 June 2009; Close, *Beyond the Storm*, 170.
140 Close, *Beyond the Storm*, 63–66.

Congolese army's chief of staff driving through Leopoldville and flagged it down.

Introducing himself to Colonel Mobutu as an American doctor volunteering at the hospital, Close then brazenly demanded that the army end the carnage that was filling his operating room. However naive and impudent the young doctor's comments may have been, two weeks later Mobutu's senior bodyguard appeared in the hospital to request that Close come to the colonel's residence immediately to tend to his great aunt. This successful medical intervention was quickly followed by other similar requests including one to circumcise Mobutu's newborn son just days later. Within months, Close was Mobutu's de facto personal physician.[141]

Close's work in the hospital also brought him into even closer contact with the US diplomatic elite than he had already had through MRA. Soon after Congo's independence several potentially life-saving medical interventions by the young American doctor on family members of US diplomats endeared him to that community. Close's affability and his infectious confidence allowed him to move freely within the highest ranks of the diplomatic community. As early as January 1961, Bill and his wife Tine were hosting MRA dinner parties for US Ambassador Edmund Gullion, CIA station chief Larry Devlin, and other US officials.[142] By the mid-1960s, this intimacy had grown substantially as hinted at by, among other things, Glenn Close's 1965 placement as an intern with the CIA-front organization WIGMO, the Cuban-piloted air force that played a critical role in crushing the Simba rebellion.[143]

Bill Close's unique role as the trusted physician for both US and Congolese policymakers meant that he was a natural choice for back-channel diplomacy. The first example came in December 1961, when Ambassador Gullion asked Close to help mediate crisis talks between Tshombe and the Adoula government. The US ambassador had been informed that Tshombe had developed a trust and affinity for the American doctor. Knowing that Tshombe would be surrounded by enemies, Gullion hoped that a friendly face might produce an atmosphere more conducive to profitable negotiations.

Initially Gullion's use of Close appears to have paid dividends as a relaxed Tshombe proved to be more flexible than had been anticipated. However, the fragile agreement that resulted from the talks was soon

---

141 Close, *Beyond the Storm*, 102–3.
142 Devlin, *Chief of Station, Congo*, 105; Close, 122.
143 Close, 181–86.

discarded by both sides.[144] This initial diplomatic role was followed by others in the early 1960s, prompting the CIA Station Chief to remark in his memoirs that "many of us in the diplomatic community owe the Close family a great deal."[145] But the role Close played in US-Congolese relations prior to 1965 paled in comparison to what lay ahead. In late November 1965, Mobutu seized power; and when he did, the importance of the MRA doctor to US-Congolese relations expanded exponentially.

The night before the 25 November coup, the American missionary doctor was given an all-too-worldly mission. "[A]t Mobutu's suggestion," Close later wrote, "I met with my former patient Tshombe in a darkened section of the Gombe suburb where he was more or less in hiding." Despite the fact that no records survive regarding the details of this conversation, it seems likely that Close discussed the possibility of a Mobutu coup with the recently ousted Tshombe and sought his support. For as Close was to relate, "I was not surprised by Mobutu's takeover." Neither, it appears, was Tshombe whose strong statement of support for the previous night's coup appeared in the next morning's paper. "That evening," Close related in his memoirs, "I congratulated him [Mobutu] by phone. I was to see him again in the morning."[146]

Over the next decade, Close was a constant part of the Mobutu entourage, meeting with him at least once on most days and travelling with the dictator on all diplomatic and personal trips outside of the country. Even on Close family holidays, the American doctor carried with him two radios, "one connected to the presidency and the other to the office."[147] The nature and extent of this relationship meant that, for better or worse, Close was with Mobutu during some of the most transformative moments of his early years in power. In May 1966, for instance, the evening before Mobutu chose to hang four politicians accused of plotting his overthrow, it was Close who Mobutu wanted at his side. As Close recounted,

> I was with Mobutu in his bedroom, the only room in the house he could call private. He was staring out the window, wrestling with the awful choice between life or death. He mentioned that the pope and other leaders had urged clemency ... Mobutu could have commuted the death sentence of the four plotters in prison. He didn't ... Over the next weeks, I read with dismay, and some shame, press reports from Europe and the United

---

144 Close, 136.
145 Devlin, *Chief of Station, Congo*, 105.
146 Close, *Beyond the Storm*, 177–78.
147 Close, 187.

States condemning Mobutu's cruelty. Acquaintances, both in and out of MRA, wondered what the hell I was doing with a man like Mobutu.[148]

When the dictator's venerated mother died, it was again Close who was with Mobutu at his suffering mother's bedside. "I remember when you and I sat with your mother, Mama Yemo, during her last moments," Close recalled to Mobutu many years later. "She kept saying to you, '*Il faut aimer ton people*—You must love your people.' You said, 'Yes, I know.' But she kept repeating ... The president stretched out his hand to stop me, and tears rolled down his cheeks."[149]

On 30 June 1969 (Congolese Independence Day), Mobutu awarded Close the Order of the Leopard, the nation's highest honor.[150] However, evidence of the American doctor's importance in US-Congolese relations had long been apparent. As his fellow missionaries acknowledged, if someone wanted something done in Congo, you went through Close. Indeed, it was not uncommon for those needing Mobutu's ear to go to evangelical missionaries in rural areas, who would then contact Close, who in turn would speak to the Congolese president.[151] For example, when threatened with a Mobutu "tax" they were unable to pay, diamond executives in Kasai approached the local Presbyterian missionary, David Miller, to ask if he might contact Close on their behalf. After discovering that Close was with Mobutu's entourage in Switzerland, Miller spoke to Close on the telephone, who spoke to Mobutu, and the situation was resolved.[152]

Close fulfilled a similar function with US and Congolese policymakers. Building on the role he had played in backchannel diplomacy in the pre-Mobutu era, Close often acted as an informal intermediary between the US government and his powerful patron. Three representative examples illustrate the influential role Dr. Close played in this important Cold War relationship. First, in his role as the head of FOMECA, Mobutu's national health-care initiative, Close was the principal link between official US medical aid and the Congo. His successful recruitment of American missionary doctors to run the nation's premier hospitals, and the role of

---

148 Close, *Beyond the Storm*, 192–95.
149 Close, 4.
150 Close, 237–38.
151 John and JoAnn Ellington, interview with the author, 29 June 2009; David Miller, interview with the author, 30 June 2009; Youmans, *When Bull Elephants Fight*, 200.
152 David Miller, interview with the author, 30 June 2009.

these former missionaries in recruiting the Congo's first wave of Peace Corps volunteers, were critical to the important official humanitarian link between the two nations.[153]

Second, Close's ongoing relationship with the US embassy meant that Mobutu often used him to seek out special favors or to help facilitate diplomatic initiatives. For instance, when Mobutu became obsessed with the idea of being the first African head of state to host the Apollo 11 astronauts, he did not approach the embassy directly but instead called Close in the middle of the night, who woke up the ambassador to successfully promote Mobutu's request.[154] Finally, the symbolic capstone of Close's diplomatic role came in the dictator's official state visit to the US in August 1970. During this successful trip in which Nixon showered praise on Mobutu as the leader of a "strong, vigorous, and stable" African nation, Close was a constant at the dictator's side—occasionally translating for him at private luncheons, accompanying him to most official functions (including the state dinner at the White House) and joining the dictator's family on a private trip to Disneyland.[155]

However, by the mid-1970s the relationship between Close and Mobutu began to deteriorate quickly. Mobutu's increasingly radical policies of nationalization in the context of widespread corruption and an economy spiraling out of control, apparently led to a decreasing tolerance by the dictator for Close's brazen private critiques. By 1976, after fourteen years as Mobutu's personal physician and trusted advisor, Close no longer felt welcome and returned to the United States, thus ending a remarkable, if unorthodox, chapter in the missionary influence on US-Congolese relations.

Conclusion

In many ways, Howard Brinton, Paul Carlson, and William Close are ideal symbols of the changing relationship between the American missionaries and US and Congolese policymakers in the 1960s and early 1970s. The three men had some important things in common. All were in the Congo thanks to a belief in God's calling on their lives. All developed significant relationships with the Congolese that resulted from their spiritual and humanitarian actions. And, while each would have placed God ahead of

---

153 Youmans, *When Bull Elephants Fight*, 209, 245, 272.
154 Close, *Beyond the Storm*, 251.
155 "Nixon, Greeting Mobutu"; Close, *Beyond the Storm*, 245.

country, all were also zealously anti-communistic and patriotic Americans. Nevertheless, although their time in the Congo overlapped, in many ways the evangelicals (Brinton and Carlson) and the MRA (Close) represent two qualitatively distinct periods in the missionary influence on US-Congolese relations.

Brinton and Carlson stand as archetypes of the numerically dominant and theologically orthodox evangelical missionary. Brinton's potency as a missionary-diplomat and Carlson's role as an American Cold War martyr were both unintended bi-products of their evangelical spiritual and humanitarian aims. Their interest in both Congolese and Cold War politics was always secondary to their religious values and their personal relationships with the Congolese. Brinton, Carlson, and the evangelical missionaries, ended up playing a critical role in the Congolese Cold War drama, but they did so as accidental diplomats—stagehands drafted into the play, not actors who had tried out for their roles.

As a result, when the spiritual and relational connection that the evangelicals enjoyed with Tshombe and other missionary-influenced Congolese elites diminished, the evangelical influence naturally declined. For similar reasons, the same natural decline can be seen in the evangelical missionary influence on US policymakers. Therefore, much like the pattern we observed in Ethiopia, by the late 1960s, thanks to the presence of a larger and more knowledgeable American diplomatic corps, the evangelical missionaries quietly returned to their spiritual work among the grassroots Congolese and their more natural place on the margins of Cold War politics.

For his part, Close acts as a symbolic bridge between the missionary-infused US-Congolese relationship prior to Mobutu and the more conventional and secular relationship that existed after 1965. Unlike most of the evangelical missionary community, which never felt completely at home in the limelight of international diplomatic intrigue, the unorthodox MRA reveled in it. Throughout its history the MRA had been intentionally focused on influencing the political elite. Indeed, when combined with its theological flexibility, the zealously anti-communist MRA's very worldly emphasis on garnering political power, made Close a perfect fit for the changing relationship between the religiously ambiguous Mobutu regime and the increasingly secular US policymaking community, as well as an appropriate symbol of the decline of American evangelical missionary influence on elite US-Congolese relations.

PART 3

Influence of American Evangelical Missionaries on US-Kenyan Cold War

CHAPTER 5

Constructing a Pro-Western Kenya, 1895–1963

"I think I need hardly say," began the guest of honor, "that it is a real and great pleasure to me to be here today, and to take my part at the laying of the cornerstone of the building, which I believe will be associated with real and permanent good to the people of East Africa ... an amount of good which we cannot at present foretell."[1] The date was 4 August 1909, and the cornerstone being laid was for the central building of the Africa Inland Mission's (AIM) new station at Kijabe, in the British colony of Kenya.[2] The guest at this isolated missionary outpost was the former American President Theodore Roosevelt.

The question of whether history has validated Roosevelt's optimism is at least partially dependent on how one defines "good." Yet from the vantage point of Cold War era US policymakers, the former president could not have been more prophetic. Indeed, even before Kenyan independence, this explicitly apolitical but American-dominated mission station was already the most important and effective beacon of US influence in East Africa. Yet the influence of American evangelical missionaries on Kenya's Cold War political orientation was always much larger than that of a single mission, let alone the AIM station at Kijabe. By tracing their story through the nation's highly contested transformation from a sparsely populated, pre-industrial collection of traditional people groups in 1895, through seventy years of British colonial rule, and up to independence in 1963, this chapter will explore the influence that American missionaries had on the cultural and political foundations of Kenya's ultimately, and unambiguously, pro-West Cold War orientation.

The Early Years of the American Missionary Enterprise in Kenya, 1895–1930

The first Western missionary to arrive in what was to become known as Kenya was Ludwig Krapf, a German missionary explorer sent by the British Church Mission Society (CMS). Losing his wife to a tropical disease

---
1 Banks, "Mr. Roosevelt at Kijabe," 8.
2 Technically Kenya was, at that point, still considered part of the larger British East Africa Protectorate. I have used Kenya throughout the chapter to avoid unnecessary confusion.

soon after his arrival in 1844, Krapf nevertheless remained in East Africa until 1853, when he returned to Europe because of failing health. Krapf was followed by a trickle of other CMS missionaries, as well as representatives of the British United Methodist Free Churches (1862), the short-lived Scottish Industrial Mission (1891) and the Church of Scotland Mission (1891).[3] For all of its sacrifice and earnestness, this initial phase of missionary activity along the Kenyan coast failed to make a significant cultural imprint among the local Muslim and religiously indigenous communities. In fact, by 1900, almost sixty years after Krapf had arrived, there were still only approximately twenty-three hundred African Christians in Kenya (or roughly 0.2 percent of the total population).[4]

Initially, the story of the first American missionaries in Kenya was equally bleak. In December 1895, Peter Cameron Scott, the charismatic founder and first missionary of AIM, arrived with a group of seven American missionaries. By 1901, when the next contingent of AIM missionaries arrived, only one of the original party remained—three had left with serious health problems and three others, including Scott, had died in Africa.[5]

Learning lessons from those who had preceded them, and thanks to the progress of the Uganda railroad ("the Lunatic Express"), the next wave of American missionaries pressed further inland. As they did, they set up stations at higher elevations where malaria and other tropical diseases were less prevalent, and also where Islam had yet to make significant headway. This second wave of American missionaries included not only AIM but also the Gospel Missionary Society (1898), the Friends Industrial Mission (1902), the Seventh Day Adventists (1902), the American Church of God (1905), and a number of short-lived "independent" missions.[6] For a host of reasons, including a worldview more receptive to the Christian message and an increasing number of healthy missionaries, the response inland to this next wave of missionary activity was, in David Barrett's words, "instantaneous and immense," with the numbers of new converts "doubling or even tripling for the first ten years after 1900."[7]

---

[3] Hildebrandt, *History of the Church*, 122–28, 183–87.

[4] Barrett, *World Christian Encyclopedia*, 426.

[5] "Short History of AIM," 9. The only remaining copy of this apparently unpublished history is located at the headquarters of the Africa Inland Mission in Pearl River, NY; Tignor, *Colonial Transformation of Kenya*, 117.

[6] Barrett, *World Christian Encyclopedia*, 427.

[7] Barrett, 427.

Similar to the pattern in Ethiopia and the Congo, the Anglo-American Protestant missionary effort in Kenya included evangelism and a multitude of humanitarian efforts including significant initiatives in education, health care, agricultural development, and land and resource management training. Because they placed such an emphasis on peoples' ability to read the Bible for themselves, from the very beginning schools were central to the Protestant missionary effort in Kenya. By 1906, the British CMS had supplemented their initial literacy efforts by starting their first school for the sons of chiefs in western Kenya.[8] The same year at the largely American AIM station at Kijabe, the mission began its first permanent school which initially catered for both Kenyan children and the children of the missionaries based at the station.[9] Within five years the conservative mission could boast of nine more African schools; and by 1915, that number had grown to thirty-seven schools with a student enrollment exceeding two thousand.[10]

Health care was also intimately connected to the Anglo-American missionary enterprise in Kenya. Like the East African Scottish Mission, which built its first hospital in Kenya in 1908, American mission groups like AIM and the Friends African Mission (FAM) stressed health care from the very beginning. This emphasis that meant many early stations included at least a clinic of some form, and several could boast of small hospitals.[11] Nevertheless, despite these energetic efforts, in the first two decades of the twentieth century the missionary imprint on the cultures and peoples of Kenya as a whole, while multi-faceted and growing steadily, was relatively negligible. As late as 1921, for instance, AIM's enrollment of twenty-seven hundred students remained a tiny fraction of the total potential student population in its sphere of influence, and the number of Christians in Kenya remained well under 10 percent of the total population.[12]

---

8 Hildebrandt, *History of the Church*, 186.
9 "Our Roots," the unpublished story of the Downing family written by the eldest daughter of AIM missionary Lee Downing, Billy Graham Center Archives (BGC)/CN 81.
10 Sandgren, *Christianity and the Kikuyu*, 23; Morad, *Founding Principles*, 301.
11 Provincial Medical Officer to The Director of Medical Services, "Kaimosi Hospital—FAM," 28 August 1962, Kenya National Archives, Nairobi (KNA)/BY/60/6; Hildebrandt, *History of the Church*, 229. Note that F.A.M. was initially called the Friends Industrial Mission.
12 Morad, *Founding Principles*, 301. The statistical estimates are based on numbers available in Barrett, *World Christian Encyclopedia*, 426.

Early American Missionaries and the Politicization of Kenya

However slight their numerical influence might have been, by the early 1920s there were increasing instances of significant American missionary influence on the politics of the British colony. One remarkable illustration of this influence is the story of American missionary John Stauffacher and the Maasai leader Mulungit Ole Sempele.[13] Like many pioneer missionaries, John Stauffacher was a strong personality and a person of unusual courage and spiritual convictions. For Stauffacher, the combination of Christian zeal and commitment to the Maasai often put him at odds with both his apolitical missionary colleagues and the colonial administration. The first example of this came early. In 1902 the British government had made the decision to set aside large portions of Kenya's Rift Valley and mountain highlands to White settlement, excluding many Africans from sparsely populated lands that had, nevertheless, been theirs from time immemorial. Stauffacher's response was unambiguous.

Writing in 1903 to his fiancée back in America, the young AIM missionary delivered an unparalleled broadside against the colonial treatment of the Maasai. Drawing comparisons to the plight of native Americans in the United States, Stauffacher condemned British officials who were, "intolerably cruel with the natives. They are driving the Maasai from their favorite pasture grounds, which have always been theirs, to a barren little strip of country on which their large numbers of sheep and cattle cannot possibly live, simply that a few wealthy snobbish English Lords may buy up the land for their own selfish interests." But Stauffacher was not finished. "[S]hould there be a general uprising and all the English people killed," he continued, "they would even then get much less than they deserve."[14] While Stauffacher's subsequent actions and pronouncements indicate that this diatribe was the private venting of a passionate, but ultimately non-violent person, it does, nevertheless, foreshadow the important role he was to play in the politicization of the Maasai in the coming years.

One of the first to convert to Christianity under Stauffacher's ministry was a Maasai leader named Mulungit Ole Sempele. Over the next few years, Stauffacher and his wife Florence educated and mentored Sempele

---

13 Broadly defined as any opposition to the colonial government, there were, of course examples of "politicization" of the African population from the very first moments of European colonial contact in Kenya. But with regards to opposition based upon the foundation of a modern and Western political justification, the Mulungit story is certainly among the first—if not the first—in Kenya.

14 Stauffacher to Florence Minch, 15 July 1904, BGC/CN 281/2/1. Reference to Stauffacher's comparing the Maasai and native American plights is found in King, "Kenya Maasai," 121, 123.

and a small group of new Christians, culminating in the missionary couple taking Sempele with them to the United States in 1911.[15] Having sold a large number of his own cattle to pay for his passage to the United States, Sempele then stayed on for an additional three years, becoming the first African Kenyan to study in America and perhaps the first to study outside of Africa.[16] Thanks to his experience with racism in the American south, when Sempele returned from his studies at two Black colleges, the spirit of self-determination that Stauffacher had encouraged had morphed into a potent and often bitter form of modern political nationalism.[17]

Ironically, the first to feel the effects of this heightened politicization was not the colonial government or the White settlers, but Stauffacher himself, as Sempele increasingly challenged the authority of his mentor.[18] At one point the district commissioner grew so concerned about the political ramifications of this evolving religious coup d'état, that he urged all missionaries to leave the area. Instead, the Stauffachers disregarded the colonial officer's warning and stayed among the Maasai, turning their attention to translating the Bible into Ki-Maasai, the local language in which they were now fluent. And when Sempele eventually led many Maasai Christians out of the mission in order to start their own independent church, the deeply wounded and disapproving Stauffacher nevertheless "humbly joined them for worship."[19]

Stauffacher's willingness to identify himself with the Maasai, by learning their language, living amongst them, and reluctantly accepting their rejection of his authority, appears to have had a lasting influence on the Maasai. As Kennedy King has noted, "Stauffacher is remembered today ... for identifying himself strongly with the Maasai cause." Indeed, he continues, "it seems clear that a major factor in the politicization of a few of the Maasai was Stauffacher himself."[20] In the long run, just as significant was the fact that Stauffacher's commitment to the Maasai allowed the mission church to eventually take root. It appears that even

---

15 Waller, "They Do the Dictating," 92; King, "Kenya Maasai," 121.
16 King, "Kenya Maasai," 123.
17 Anderson, *We Felt Like Grasshoppers*, 48–51; King, "Kenya Maasai," 124.
18 Harper, *Western Educated Elites*, quoted in Horne, manuscript version of *Mau Mau in Harlem?*, 428.
19 Anderson, *We Felt Like Grasshoppers*, 48–51. Another account by Waller, demonstrates the extent to which Stauffacher's stubbornness and misinterpretation of the Maasai church rebellion meant that while he did attend the service, it was somewhat reluctantly, as seen by his unwillingness to accept the right of the Maasai church elders to serve communion. Waller, "They Do the Dictating," 100–6.
20 King, "Kenya Maasai," 121.

Sempele's relationship with AIM underwent a spiritual and political softening that foreshadowed the stories of many African Christians in the years ahead. As one AIM physician related in her memoirs, in one meeting with AIM converts in the 1930s Sempele "was so moved that in the evening he told the elders he wished to make a confession." After citing a host of indiscretions, he stated, "Today, my brothers in Christ, I call you to witness that I bring these evil things from this dark heart and ask the Saviour to forgive me."[21]

Early American Missions and Education

The story of Sempele touches on another recurring theme in the history of decolonization and missions—the sometimes-bitter debate over the level of education offered by American evangelical missions in particular. As we have seen, because reading the Bible for oneself was so foundational to evangelical Protestantism, schools and missionary work often went hand in hand. Conservative American missions like AIM were, therefore, on the vanguard of providing education to Africans in Kenya. "The Church grew out of the school room" one AIM missionary observed, "in fact, this is where it was born."[22] And the facts bear this out. As a 1924 AIM report noted, "fully ninety-five percent of our church members have passed thru [sic] our schools."[23]

Yet, the commitment of AIM and most of the other American evangelical missions to education was not absolute. Influenced profoundly by the modernist controversy, American evangelical missions were often suspicious of advanced education, seeing it instead as a worldly means to a spiritual end. As one African critic complained in a letter to his AIM missionary mentor, "I have heard you many times telling me ... that you came to win souls for God, and not to prepare people for worldly pleasure."[24]

Finances were also a concern. Unlike the British missions that were arms of large and wealthy mainline denominations, the American missionaries in Kenya were largely non-denominational organizations funded by individual churches or supporters on, what they called, a "faith basis." The result was that the American evangelical missions lagged well behind their British and mainline equivalents when it came to the funding

---

21 Blakeslee, *Beyond the Kikuyu Curtain*, 206–7.
22 Gration, *Relationship of the African*, 156.
23 Gration, 158.
24 Amolo to Skoda, 17 October 1945, KNA/PC/KSM/1/10/42/AIM.

required to start and maintain a strong school. Finally, the American commitment to the separation of church and state also had ramifications on the quality of the education provided by many evangelical missions. As AIM's Field Director Ralph Davis noted in 1936, the mission's refusal to accept government funds meant that other missions were able to provide far more than AIM by way of quality teachers, facilities, and resources.[25]

The consequence of these factors for most of the American missions was a relatively large, but underfunded and academically weak, educational program that, when compared to the British missions, was often found wanting. Many African Christians, who like Sempele saw the political and economic significance of a strong education, either agitated for improvements or left for better schools.[26] The colonial government was just as critical. Despite continuing to see the American missions as vital to the colony's education efforts, they often singled out those missions for criticism. After visiting one AIM school in the 1930s, a government inspector wrote, "it was far from satisfactory," but noted that he had seen "an even worse school under the same mission." Common to most complaints was the lack of quality teachers in the American evangelical schools. "I am afraid there will be little improvement" the inspector concluded, "until they [AIM] can train and employ better teachers."[27]

The American Gospel Missionary Society and Harry Thuku

Perhaps the first example of modern-style politicization of an African in Kenya, Sempele was by no means the most important early product of American missionary influence. That distinction is held by Harry Thuku. Acknowledged as the most important pioneer of African nationalism in Kenya, Thuku was responsible for initiating and leading the influential East Africa Association (EAA).[28]

The political mobilization that Thuku initiated also led to Kenya's first violent political rally during which anywhere from twenty-one to fifty-six Kenyans were killed protesting Thuku's arrest and imprisonment by the colonial government.[29] This protest, more than any other single event, was

---

25 Gration, *Relationship to the African*, 164.
26 Maseno, et al. to The District Commissioner, Kisumu, "Kandolo Sector School. AIM Mission, Ogada," 15 February 1935, KNA/PC/KSM/1/10/42/AIM.
27 Inspector of Schools, Nyanza to Rev. Skoda, 18 August 1936 and Inspector of Schools, Nyanza to Provincial Commissioner, Kisumu, 18 August 1936. KNA/PC/KSM/1/10/42/AIM.
28 Thuku, *Harry Thuku: An Autobiography*, 20. The initial name for the EAA was the Young Kikuyu Association, but it changed its name to reflect greater inclusivity in 1922.
29 Anderson, *Histories of the Hanged*, 16–17.

responsible for the politicization of Kenyatta and the generation who were to lead the struggle for independence in Kenya over the next forty years.[30] Scholars have gone to great effort to explain the development of the EAA and its later effects. However, outside of the passing and vague reference to his missionary education, little attention has been given to the early formation of Harry Thuku's politics.[31] This is unfortunate, as the story is illuminating.

Despite the predominance of the English Anglicans (Church Mission Society) and the Scottish Presbyterians (Church of Scotland Mission) in the Kikuyu areas of Kenya, Thuku was associated with neither. Instead, it was a small and obscure American group, the Gospel Missionary Society (GMS) that shaped the future pioneer of nationalism. Unlike the larger missions which could boast relatively large reservoirs of financial and bureaucratic support, the GMS was the product of a single, small and independent evangelical church in New Britain, Connecticut. Inspired by the revivals of D. L. Moody and Ira Sankey, the People's Church of Christ (PCC) began in 1888 with a tiny congregation of thirty-three and grew to approximately four hundred before a church split in 1916 brought the membership back under two hundred. What it lacked in numbers, the PCC made up for in missionary zeal. At its peak in 1912, the small church alone funded and supported an astonishing seventeen full-time missionaries in Kenya.[32]

A small mission station at Kambui acted as the hub of GMS activity in Kenya, and it is here in 1902 where the young Harry Thuku first encountered "European[s]"—in the form of Rev. and Mrs. Knapp, an American couple with the GMS.[33] Despite the initial reluctance of many Kikuyu parents, Thuku and a small group of children joined the rudimentary school that had been established by the Knapps. Over the years, Thuku's relationship with the Knapps deepened to the extent that for four years Thuku became a part of the American family's household, even acting as the regular child-minder for the Knapps only child, Elma.[34] While Thuku left the GMS station in his late teen years to go to Nairobi in search of employment, the influence of the American missionaries remained with him. Even after

---

30 Branch, *Defeating Mau Mau*, 180.
31 In some indication of the shallow work that has been done by otherwise excellent scholars on Thuku's early political formation, David Anderson refers to Thuku as having been raised a Methodist and Gerald Horne refers to Thuku as having been "weaned at the African Inland Mission." Thuku, of course, was neither, although Horne is closer to the truth as the GMS and AIM worked together quite closely prior to World War II. Horne, *Mau Mau in Harlem?*, 58; Anderson, *Histories of the Hanged*, 15.
32 Wamagatta, "Roots of the Presbyterian Church," 387–91.
33 Thuku, *Harry Thuku: An Autobiography*, 3.
34 Thuku, 8.

ten years of government detention following his arrest in 1922, when the nationalist movement he inspired sought his support for a more militantly anti-European agenda, Thuku demonstrated an abiding loyalty to his American missionary mentors and their message. "I will remain GMS," he vowed. "Where I started, there I will finish."[35]

But what exactly did that influence look like? Ironically, like many of the fundamentalist or conservative evangelical American missions, the GMS was explicitly apolitical. As Thuku himself noted, "I did not get any political education from the missionaries for they did not discuss political matters."[36] Nevertheless, whether explicitly political or not, it was soon clear that the principles and practices communicated and modelled by the Knapps were foundational to the budding political activism of Thuku and several other important GMS converts.

The most politically potent Christian conviction taught and modelled by the GMS missionaries was the notion of humanity's ultimate equality before God. This foundational principle led to two important outcomes. First, unlike the White settlers and some other missions, the GMS did not accept land grants from the colonial government without having first sought the approval of the local elders. Considering the sacred value of land in Kikuyu and other indigenous cultures, the GMS assumption that the land was African land immediately placed the American mission on the side of the local African community.[37] Second, this egalitarianism also meant that the GMS were noticeably proactive in supporting African leadership at the very first opportunity. Their method of leadership development is instructive. Unlike other missions whose otherwise similar aims were accomplished through the prism of a formal and hierarchical educational process, the GMS developed leaders principally through mentorship—often bringing converts like Thuku to live with their families for long periods as they sought to model Christian living and leadership.[38]

The results were telling. In a region dominated by the large and wealthy British missions, it was the converts of the GMS who led the way in the initial fight for African self-determination. Of the three leaders imprisoned and deported by the colonial government for their

---

35 Thuku, 52.

36 Thuku, 8. It is important to note that this quote does conclude with the words, "with us" which could be construed to imply a racial divide. However, GMS was consistently apolitical and the Knapps in particular appear to have had no qualms in discussing any and all matters with their Kenyan friends and converts.

37 Thuku, *Harry Thuku: An Autobiography*, 3.

38 Anderson, *We Felt like Grasshoppers*, 41.

leadership of the EAA, two were products of the tiny American mission.[39] In addition, many EAA documents from the time, including two of the most significant, demonstrate the influence of the missionaries. The most famous of these was the momentous telegram sent in July 1921 to the British prime minister protesting the "Hut and Poll" tax and compulsory labor practices. Contrasting missionaries with the European settlers and the colonial government, the Thuku-edited telegram explicitly named the missionaries as the Africans' "best friend" in the struggle for justice.[40]

Less well-known, but perhaps equally significant, is the EAA's "Prayer for Our Leader Harry Thuku and his Associates." In this explicitly Christian prayer, the GMS emphasis on equality and God's active participation in the world is balanced with the Christian duty to honor those in authority—the bedrock of American evangelicalism's apolitical outlook. However, in Thuku's hands, this typically conservative political principle was given a radically anti-colonial application. For in the EAA prayer, it is Africans who are assumed to be the God-ordained leaders to whom honor is rightfully given.

Beginning with an appeal to Kenyans to "pray that [the EAA leaders] may not come to any harm, since they have been chosen by the Almighty to be our leaders," the prayer concludes with the conviction that God is intervening to promote equality and justice. "God has not gone away on a journey, and he is not going on one now. It is to Him we should pray for he is our master ... [for] before God there is no difference between whites and blacks; we are all human beings—equal in the sight of God."[41] In 1923, partially in response to a political feud between the White settlers, former railway workers of Indian origin, and missionaries, and partly in response to the Thuku-led African politicization, the British colonial secretary penned the Devonshire Declaration, which while often ignored in practice, stated that if the interests of the Kenyan constituencies were in conflict, those of the majority African population should be treated as paramount.[42]

---

39 Thuku, *Harry Thuku: An Autobiography*, 30.
40 "Resolutions of the East," 10 July 1921, Oldham Papers, Edinburgh House, London, reprinted in Thuku, *Harry Thuku: An Autobiography*, 83. Some sources claim that the first draft was written by the conservative Kikuyu Association before being taken, edited, and sent by Thuku, but this is uncertain. John Lonsdale and Marshall S. Clough are among those scholars who believe this was the case. Nevertheless, regardless of its origins, Thuku and the EAA, by sending it in their name, were also taking responsibility for its content. Clough, *Fighting Two Sides*, 52–58.
41 "Prayer for Our Leader," translated from the Kikuyu, Coryndon Papers, Rhodes House, Oxford, reprinted in Thuku, *Harry Thuku: An Autobiography*, 85.
42 Kenneth, et al. "Kenya Colony"; The Devonshire Declaration, also known as the "White Paper."

Not all American missionaries were supportive of the way Thuku applied biblical principles to the colonial context. Perhaps fearing that too close an association with these apparently anti-colonial subversives would jeopardize their work in the colony, several AIM missionaries openly denounced Thuku and the EAA.[43] Writing in AIM's periodical *Inland Africa*, Reverend McKentrick, for instance, described Thuku as a "bitter ... self-willed, and rebellious lad."[44] There were even some voices of concern among the GMS community.[45] Nevertheless, as Thuku's detention wore on it became clear to both Thuku and his associates that, while the GMS sought to encourage the colonial government's aims of promoting development, religious liberty, and law and order, the small American mission remained supportive of Thuku and the ultimate aims of the EAA. During Thuku's detention, for instance, Mrs. Knapp "would put a map of Kenya up in her class, and pointing at the dot on it which was Marsabit (where Thuku was imprisoned), she would ask the class, 'Do you know what fearless man is staying in that place?'"[46]

For his part, Rev. Knapp facilitated the travel of Christian friends to visit Thuku while he was in detention; and Dr. Henderson, another GMS mentor, gave evidence in favor of Thuku's movement before a colonial commission on native rights.[47] Like the case of the Stauffachers amongst the Maasai, the strong and positive impression left by the willingness of the GMS to display solidarity with their converts in the face of strong pressure from the settlers, the colonial administration, and even many other missionaries, was to prove significant in the years to come.

Early American Missionaries and the Politics of Culture: Bible Translation

The Stauffacher-Mulungit and Knapp-Thuku examples place American missionaries at the very earliest and most significant moments of Kenya's modern political mobilization. In these important examples, American missionaries spurred the push for self-determination by teaching and living out the biblical precepts of human equality and social justice. The same missionaries also played an important, if unintentional, role in Kenya's

---

43 Blakeslee, *Beyond the Kikuyu Curtain*, 160; Thuku, *Harry Thuku: An Autobiography*, 30, 32; "Thuku Movement in East Africa," 1–2.
44 "Thuku Movement in East Africa," 1–2.
45 Thuku, *Harry Thuku: An Autobiography*, 12.
46 Thuku, 9.
47 District Commissioner's Office, Kiambu to District Commissioner, Marsabit, 16 May 1929, KNA/DC/MBT/7/7/1; and Thuku, *Harry Thuku: An Autobiography*, 8.

political evolution by introducing a conception of political authority that Thuku and other Africans applied to their context in unexpected and radical ways. Significantly, the American missionary influence during this period also extended beyond manifestations of concrete politics and into the politics of culture.

At the heart of the Protestant conception of Christianity is the conviction that, as God's Word, the Bible is the unrivalled authority in the Christian life, trumping both the church and Christian tradition.[48] As sixteenth century Europe discovered, the democratic logic of this concept was politically revolutionary. But this conviction (*sola scriptura*) also assumed the vernacularization of the Scriptures—that is, the translation of the Bible into the common languages. Generally speaking, the more radically Protestant a missionary was, the more weight they placed on biblical translation. It is not surprising then, that American missionaries who came to Kenya during this period, as the purest embodiment of this ideal within, arguably, the most culturally Protestant nation in the world, considered the "translation, production, and distribution" of the Bible "in the language of the common people" their "supreme task."[49]

They were true to their word. From the very beginning, almost every American missionary organization was involved in the work of biblical translation. Among the Maasai, AIM's John Stauffacher and his small team of converts had managed to translate one of the Gospels into Ki-Maasai as early as 1905, before completing the entire New Testament in 1922.[50] AIM also led efforts among many other groups resulting in translations of the New Testament into, among others, Kipsigis, KiKamba (1920), and Nandi (1931).[51] The American-dominated mission could also boast of having completed the first translation of the entire Bible into a vernacular language, completing the Nandi Bible in 1939.[52]

---

48 Where Catholic and Orthodox Christians would place the authority of the church and church tradition as co-equals with the Bible, and some Quakers and other more mystical Protestants may privilege the more subjective experience of the Holy Spirit, the Protestant distinctive is that while each of these sources of authority are valid, their legitimacy is to be measured by whether their message is in line with the teachings of Scripture, as interpreted by the individual believer within the context of the Christian community, being led by the Holy Spirit.

49 "'Unreached Field' in Missions," 9.

50 Barrett, *Kenya Churches Handbook*, 23–24.

51 Honer, *Missy Fundi, Kenya Girl*, 321; Barrett, *Kenya Churches Handbook*, 24; Bryson, *Light in the Darkness*, 90.

52 Bryson, *Light in the Darkness*, 8. It is important to note that, while AIM was dominated by American missionaries and had a clearly American organizational culture, it also included some evangelicals from both Britain and Australia. A case in point is Stuart Bryson who was British.

Other American mission groups were no less involved. Efforts by the Friends African Mission produced a translation of the New Testament in Luragoli in 1927 and the complete Bible in 1951.[53] The Seventh Day Adventists were likewise successful in translating the Gospel of Matthew into Gisii in 1929.[54] Even the tiny Gospel Missionary Society played a prominent role as the mission's John Henderson was responsible, along with Rev. Leakey of the Anglican CMS, for the first Kikuyu translation of the New Testament (1926) and then of the entire Bible (1951).[55]

The missionaries expected both the process and the product of Bible translation to be transformative for the people who would now be able to read God's Word in their own languages. And they were right. The intimate experience of hearing God speak directly into their cultural context allowed the roots of Christian faith to sink deep into the worldview of many Kenyans. As one missionary later concluded in reference to his mission's use of the mother tongue, "Because [the Bible college] was taught in the vernacular, the faith [went] deeper into the belief systems of those early pastors."[56]

But the process of Bible translation, itself, carried with it some important messages. As the timeline of successful translation projects indicates, the missionaries involved in this work spent years, and in some cases decades, learning not only the languages but the cultures of the peoples they were working amongst. And for what? Because there was no worldly reward waiting for the missionary, the message reasonably received was that the missionaries cared not only about the people, but that the language and culture of the people were valued by Christians and the Christian God. The response of the Kenyans was often enthusiastic. For instance, when the first Nandi New Testaments arrived, the Brysons recalled, "people came in from all quarters to secure their precious books ... for the first time all over the church Nandi hands turned the pages and Nandi eyes followed the Scriptures in their own language."[57]

Bearing in mind its considerable religious effects, the work of Bible translation also had a number of important political consequences. The first such consequence was the encouragement of indigenous pride and ethnic nationalism. As one scholar has argued, "A vernacular Bible standardized

---

53 Angell, "Quaker Women in Kenya," 115.
54 Barrett, *Kenya Churches Handbook*, 24.
55 Irele and Jeyifo, *Oxford Encyclopedia of African*, 49–50.
56 Dick Gehman, interview with the author, 10 July 2009.
57 Bryson, *Light in the Darkness*, 95.

... a common language, imagined a holy people with a common destiny, and created a more conscious community among those who read it."[58] With this in mind, it is not surprising that some Nandi refer to AIM's Stuart Bryson as the "father of the Nandi."[59]

The second important political consequence of biblical translation was the power it gave the literate to challenge the traditional order. As Derek Peterson has shown, prior to the appearance of the New Testament in 1926, power and status in Kikuyu society had been rooted in the concept of *Ugi*—that is, wisdom demonstrated through property. In the New Testament, however, Kikuyu converts (referred to as "readers") found both a critique of *Ugi* and the exaltation of a concept of wisdom rooted instead in knowledge, or *Menya*. Applying this biblical critique, the young and often poor Kikuyu "readers" successfully undermined the traditional power structure and eventually rose to positions of prominence within the colonial order. Of course, this indigenous use of the vernacular Scriptures could, and indeed did, cut both ways. As we shall see, in the lead up to Mau Mau a later generation of disillusioned youth would attack the power of the now successful "readers" with an indigenous biblical critique of their own. "God," one young radical declared, "had to be brought to our side."[60]

Early American Missionaries and the Politics of Culture: Female Circumcision

Intimately related to the political importance of the translation process was the significant role played by American missionaries in the next watershed moment in Kenya's political history, the controversy over female circumcision. Unlike earlier controversies, in which the missionaries largely sided with the Africans against the settlers and colonial government, in this acrimonious debate most of the American missionaries—much to the consternation of the colonial government—lined up in opposition to the majority of African public opinion.[61]

As early as the first decade of the twentieth century, a number of British and American missionaries had expressed concern over female circumcision, believing the practice to be unhealthy and immoral.[62] Thanks

---

58 Peterson, "Rhetoric of the Word," 166. A similar claim is made by Hasting and by Sanneh, *Encountering the West*.
59 Lunn, "Foreword," 8.
60 Peterson, "Rhetoric of the Word"; Kaggia, *Roots of Freedom*, 57.
61 Gration, *Relationship of the African*, 145.
62 Rosberg and Nottingham, *Myth of "Mau Mau,"* 112.

to the activism of its well-known doctors, Elwood Davis and Virginia Blakeslee, since at least 1914 the self-proclaimed apolitical American AIM had been among the leaders in lobbying for the abolition of the practice. Dr. Davis in particular argued that, in addition to its harmful physical effects, female circumcision was "a sacrifice to the goddess of fertility and is the very life of native heathen practices."[63] By 1918, missionary opinion had largely coalesced against the practice as seen in the petition from the Alliance of Protestant Missions (which included both British and American missions, mainline and evangelical) that suggested "absolutely forbidding the circumcision of girls."[64] In 1921, AIM led the way in formally banning the practice among its members.[65]

For some time, the response of many of the mission's African converts to the anti-circumcision mandate was to ignore it. As one AIM missionary reported in May 1927, "the day after Mr. Downing left the station, several daughters of our very best Christian elders were circumcised."[66] Interpreting the converts' actions as instances of either religious infidelity or defiance against church leadership, AIM and several other missions, chose to make the issue a test of Christian commitment, going so far as to threaten excommunication to those who continued in the practice.[67]

This decision turned out to have profound political consequences. Aware of the increasing alienation felt by many African Christians, and desirous of expanding its appeal, the EAA's more militant successor, the Kikuyu Central Association (KCA), successfully turned the debate over female circumcision into the most politically potent issue of the day. Indeed, outside of land reform, between the Thuku riots in 1922 and the Mau Mau Emergency in the 1950s, no other issue was more central to Kenya's political history.[68]

Initially, most Kenyan Christians did not believe that female circumcision was incompatible with their faith and, therefore, sought a middle way. As a character in Ngugi's renowned novel *The River Between* declared, "I want to be a real girl, a real woman, knowing all the ways of the hills and ridges ... Father and mother are circumcised. Are they

---

63 Gration, *Relationship of the African*, 153.
64 Gration, 136.
65 Gration, 137.
66 Gration, 140.
67 Gration, 140.
68 Elkins, *Britain's Gulag*, 21; Tignor, *Colonial Transformation of Kenya*, 235–47; and Gration, *Relationship of the African*, 141–42.

not Christians?"⁶⁹ As a result, one AIM missionary noted, "It seems impossible for some of our native Christians to see the harm in allowing this ceremony."⁷⁰

While there was virtually universal agreement among the missionary community that the practice was physically harmful, there remained a considerable amount of uncertainty as to whether female circumcision should be a litmus test for faith in the Kenyan context. It appears, for instance, that the American GMS refused to break ties with African Christians who held onto the practice, continuing to preach and interact with the independent churches that had left missionary supervision after the Thuku riots.⁷¹ As late as 1927, even some AIM missionaries expressed ambivalence. In a letter to the mission's American Home Secretary, AIM's Hulda Stumpf quoted an article in the *International Review of Missions* approvingly to the effect that, "To thrust upon African Christians rules of conduct that have not grown out of their own convictions is more likely to breed hypocrites, than to unravel perplexities. Each case needs not the mechanical application of an infallible formula, but the brotherly counsel of someone [sic] familiar with local thought and custom ... they need to be taught why one custom is to be avoided, another utilized and a third purified."⁷²

But this less rigid perspective did not become official mission policy. The result was that even many devout Christians felt forced to choose between their faith and their culture. One Kikuyu paramount chief, speaking in 1921, had predicted the divisive potential of the issue. "You white men came among us," he exclaimed, "and we, seeing that you were good men, welcomed you with both hands. We readily do all that you tell us to do," he continued, "you tell us to lie down, we lie down; you tell us to stand up, we do so. You impose taxes on us, and we obey without a murmur; when your taxes become more than we can pay, we will come as supplicants and tell you so. But in this matter of our girls we cannot see eye to eye with you and we cannot agree to obey you if you attempt to coerce us."⁷³

By 1928, the intransigence of both the missions and the KCA had led to widespread unrest. At the AIM's mission station at Kijabe, students at

---

69 Ngugi, *River Between*, 29–30. Ngugi is more widely known today by his Kikuyu name, Ngugi wa Thiong'o.
70 Gration, *Relationship of the African*, 140.
71 Gration, 144.
72 Gration, 147.
73 McIntosh, *Scottish Mission in Kenya*, 410.

both of the high schools began secret meetings culminating in a series of temporary hunger strikes.[74] Soon a trickle of Kenyan Christians leaving the missions to establish their own churches and schools turned into a flood. Particularly outspoken in their opposition to female circumcision, the American-dominated AIM was hit hard. By the end of 1929, between 80 and 90 percent of AIM congregants had left the mission to join the independent church movement.[75]

On New Year's Day 1930, tensions finally erupted into violence with the murder of AIM's veteran missionary Hulda Stumpf.[76] The circumstances and the nature of her murder left little doubt in the minds of contemporaries that it was directly related to the circumcision controversy. Despite her private ambivalence regarding AIM's stand, Stumpf had publicly condemned the practice and, to the disgust of traditionalists, actively sought to empower the minority of local Kikuyu women who had sided with the mission. Just days before the murder, it was Stumpf who had dutifully taken down the names of those mission-loyalists who had braved increasingly vitriolic threats to join the missionaries in Sunday worship at Kijabe.[77] While the widespread rumors of her forced circumcision were inaccurate, the brutal and apparently sexual nature of the killing meant that the incident would forever be steeped in symbolism.[78]

In a colony where cultural issues were at the heart of the movement for self-determination, the murder acted as a political watershed. For the most militant anti-colonialists, it appears to have solidified the conviction that a culturally pure and politically radical self-determination was worth killing for. For those devout Christians who had already publicly aligned themselves with the missions, the murder likewise meant that they were now committed. Notwithstanding the role played by the European settlers as agents provocateurs, it was the political ancestors of this religious and cultural dispute that, a generation later, produced the civil war that we now refer to as the Mau Mau uprising.

---

74 Blakeslee, *Beyond the Kikuyu Curtain*, 187–88. These two high schools were the mission's boys and girls high schools located just below the mission station at Kijabe—not the school they created for the children of their own missionary children, the Rift Valley Academy.
75 "Letter of Lee Downing," 15; Gration, *Relationship of the African*, 144.
76 Anderson, *Histories of the Hanged*, 20. It should be noted that Anderson places the murder on 3 January, where the first physician to examine the body did so on 1 January 1930. See Blakeslee, *Beyond the Kikuyu Curtain*, 191.
77 Bill Barnett, interview with the author, 30 June 1998; "Doc" Propst, interview with Rich Dilworth, 9 August 1997; *Inland Africa*, "Editorials," 8; Anderson, *Histories of the Hanged*, 20.
78 *Inland Africa*, "Editorials," 8.

But for the missions themselves, and for the majority of Kenyans who—whatever their sympathies—were not yet committed to either of the extremes, the death of the American missionary was the catalyst for reflection and re-evaluation. Indeed, despite all the attention given by scholars to the principal antagonists in the Mau Mau crisis, it was the verdict rendered by this, as of yet, uncommitted middling majority that would determine whether the political culture of an independent Kenya would be radical and anti-European, or moderate and pro-West. Based on the massive exodus of Kenyans from mission churches in the late 1920s, it appeared the smart money was on the former.

Education, Health Care, and Conversions: The American Missionary Advance, 1930–1963

As we have already seen, prior to the Stumpf murder, the growth of the churches associated with both the British and the American Protestant missions had been built largely on the back of their educational efforts. In spite of the circumcision controversy, for many young Africans the appeal of a missionary education remained strong. This was true even for those associated with the American missions. Between 1939 and 1952, AIM's educational program grew from having around ten thousand students being taught by approximately 280 African teachers (only 10 percent of whom were qualified to teach) to having roughly eighty-five thousand students under the tutelage of almost one thousand increasingly equipped teachers.[79]

Other American mission groups such as the Church of God, the Friends African Mission, and the Seventh Day Adventists also had education programs stretching back to the early years of the twentieth century.[80] And by the late 1940s, newcomers like the Southern Baptists and the Indiana-based World Gospel Mission (WGM) were also making significant headway. By the late 1950s, for instance, WGM was responsible for fifty-four primary and intermediate schools, 163 teachers, and a student enrolment of 6,644.[81] Especially significant was the impressive record of

---

79 Schuit, "Our Threefold Teaching"; Gration, *Relationship of the African*, 170.
80 District Officer, Bungoma to The Provincial Commissioner, Kisumu, "Senior Secondary School, North of Nzoia River," 26 July 1954, KNA/PC/NZA/3/6/58/Friends; Nyachae, *Walking through the Corridors*, 14, 43. The Church of God had an even smaller scale mission but continued to have a representative sitting on the influential Christian Council of Kenya's (CCK) Advisory Committee on African Education (ACAE) throughout the 1940s, as well as being responsible for schools at Mwihila and Bunyore. CCK, ACAE, Report, 8 February 1949, KNA/MSS/61/668c; CCK, ACAE meeting minutes for 14 December 1950, KNA/MSS/61/668c.
81 Trachsel, *Kindled Fires in Africa*, 40.

the mission's lone high school which, by 1952, could boast of having the highest percentage of Form II passes in the entire colony.[82] While they may have lagged behind the efforts of their British Protestant and Catholic peers, through their vast educational efforts American missionaries were nevertheless having a major influence on those who would one day be Kenya's governing classes.[83]

American missions were also influential in the important area of health care. While other missions had started a series of dispensary networks earlier, it was the Friends mission that in 1917 built the first American missionary hospital in Kenya.[84] By the mid-1950s, most of the major American missions could boast of at least one flagship hospital supporting an increasing network of simple dispensaries.[85] The Friends hospital at Kaimosi, for instance, had grown into being a regional center with 136 beds, including separate surgical, maternity, and tuberculosis wards.[86] For its part, by the mid-1950s AIM could rely on a missionary medical team of thirteen to oversee an increasingly large and well-trained Kenyan staff, at work at ten different sites, and serving approximately 150,000 patients a year.[87] All told, by the 1950s, each year several hundred thousand Kenyans were receiving quality medical care thanks to the work of American missionaries.

At least as significant as the numbers in terms of its long-term cultural influence was the growing conviction among many Africans that the powers of the missionary doctor exceeded those of the traditional spiritual healer. After being successfully treated for ulcerated lesions at one of AIM's roving open-air clinics, one elderly Kikuyu man's response indicates the extent to which contact with the missionaries' Western medicine had opened the door to a sweeping transformation of the traditional worldview.

---

82 World Gospel Mission, "Education in WGM and AGC," undated annual report (late 1950s), World Gospel Mission Archives (WGMA), Marion, Indiana.

83 According to WGM records, when they began their work in Kenya in 1932, 92 percent of all education work in the colony was in the hands of the missions. Instead of taking more responsibility for education, the colonial government in the remaining years before independence simply funded the already well-established missionary educational system. Fish and Fish, *Call to Battle*.

84 Provincial Medical Officer to the Director of Medical Services, 28 August 1962, KNA/BY/60/6.

85 Those American missions with at least one major hospital by the 1950s were AIM, WGM, and FAM. It is likely that other missions also had hospitals.

86 Provincial Medical Officer to the Director of Medical Services, 28 August 1962, KNA/BY/60/6.

87 *Inland Africa*, "Kenya and Medical Advance," 2–3; Africa Inland Mission Memorandum from the Kenya Field, 18 August 1956, BGC/81/34/4.

As the missionary nurse present reported to supporters in the United States, "Then Mutua, the aged one, walked directly home, told his wife what he had done," which included converting to Christianity, "and ordered her to the local Indian shop to buy a pair of trousers for him—no longer was he a heathen man in a blanket."[88]

Considering the strong appeal of the education and health care provided by the missionaries, it is easy to dismiss the increasing rates of conversion to Christianity during this period as simply the means through which aspiring Kenyans could achieve modernity's more worldly benefits.[89] However, this sort of reductionism does not adequately explain the astonishing pace of Christian expansion, or the depth of commitment displayed by Kenyan converts. While clearly true at times, the reductionist thesis also fails to take seriously the significant personal cost paid by many converts to evangelical Christianity during the colonial period. As one scholar noted, it was not unusual for early converts to be disowned. "My body is not your body!" went a typical parental curse. "My blood is not your blood! My flesh is not your flesh! You are not mine. You are dead!"[90]

The threat of being disowned by your family and tribe was complemented by the radical behavioral demands placed on many new converts by the pietistic missionaries. As one early American evangelical baptism of two young Kenyans makes clear, simply tacking on a few new rituals to an otherwise unchanged life was not enough:

> Each of these had for two years or more given evidence of the change of heart and life wrought by the power of God. They were asked six questions, separately, before all the people assembled. 1st Whether they accepted and would obey all the words of God as written in His word. 2nd If they refused to accept the affairs of the (evil) spirits. 3rd If they refused all the evil customs of their tribe. 4th If they refused to drink native beer and use tobacco. 5th If they would agree not to marry more than one wife. 6th If they would refuse to accept the *ithitu* (native charm). All of these were answered satisfactorily.[91]

---

88 *Inland Africa*, "Kenya and Medical Advance," 2–3. This is an instructive example as the step into modernism for this Kikuyu was not, at least initially, synonymous with a progressive view of gender equality.

89 Donham, *Marxist Modern*, 83. Donham, applying this reasoning to a similar evangelical Christian expansion in Ethiopia during the Cold War argued that the principal appeal of evangelical Christianity for most Ethiopians was its "ability to offer an entrance to modernity."

90 Clough, *Fighting Two Sides*, 26.

91 *Hearing and Doing*, "Witch Doctor Saved," 10.

In choosing to publicly repudiate important elements of traditional culture, these converts risked, and often experienced, the permanent pain of social and economic ostracism. Without dismissing the attraction that Western modernity held for many Kenyans, in the end, as Philip Jenkins argues, "We can suggest all sorts of reasons why Africans ... adopted Christianity, whether political, social, or cultural; but one all-too-obvious explanation is that individuals came to believe the message offered, and found this the best means of explaining the world around them."[92]

While precise statistics are not available regarding the growth of Christianity in Kenya between 1930 and 1964, we do know that by 1948 the Christian population had grown significantly to approximately 1.6 million people (30 percent of the total population). We also know that between 1948 and 1970, the pace of Christianity in Kenya grew at an unparalleled rate, leading to an estimated 7.2 million Christians by 1970 (or 63 percent of the total population). However, because these figures include Catholics and Christians from the mainline Protestant denominations not associated with the work of the American missionaries, they do not necessarily give us a reliable indication of the strength of the American-influenced evangelical population.

One way to get a reasonable estimate of that relative strength is to consider the number of schools sponsored by the various Christian denominations during the same period. These figures indicate that in 1971 the government was responsible for 1,478 schools, the Catholic Church was responsible for 1,876 schools, the mainline Protestants associated with the British missionary effort were responsible for roughly 1,240, and the evangelical Protestants associated with the American missionary effort were responsible for approximately 1,370. Assuming that the strong links between schools and religious affiliation seen in earlier eras hold, it is reasonable to conclude that by the 1950s the particularly zealous brand of evangelicalism introduced and encouraged by the American missionaries made up approximately 20 percent of the country's rapidly growing Christian population.[93]

---

92 Jenkins, *Next Christendom*, 52.
93 The calculations in this section are based on the statistics available in Barrett, et al., "Kenya," and table two in the *Kenyan Churches Handbook*, 1973. It must be remembered that this is based on the educated population, but the schools usually existed within a large sphere of religious influence also dominated by the group responsible for the schools. It should also be noted that in the late 1960s the Kenyan government officially took responsibility for all schools in Kenya. However, they encouraged the churches who had previously maintained the schools to be in charge of the religious education taking place in those schools. The figures above represent, therefore, the numbers of schools that each group had maintained prior

The Growth of the Independent Church and School Movement

At this point, it is worth recalling that in 1930 the missions had suffered a near-fatal setback, temporarily losing as much as 90 percent of their congregants to the independent churches established by the more radical successors to Thuku's EAA. The circumcision controversy and its political and religious fallout forced many missionaries into a period of critical self-reflection.[94] Whatever their personal distaste of the practice, did they believe that a rejection of female circumcision was central to the evangelical salvation message? In the end, most of the evangelical missions decided that, while the practice should be discouraged, it should not be seen as a litmus test for authentic Christian faith. Thanks in part to this period of critical self-reflection, the missionary effort recovered, and indeed grew substantially, to the point that by the late 1940s the mission churches had regained a prominent place in the cultural and political life of the colony.

Yet while this impressive missionary resurgence was taking place, a competing narrative was developing. Having broken away from the missions during the late 1920s, the indigenous independent church and school movement continued to develop during the 1930s free from the theological and cultural constraints of the Western missionaries. Thanks to the newly available vernacular translations of the New Testament, the indigenization of Christianity grew especially amongst the alienated grassroots of the Kikuyu, Embu, and Meru peoples where the messages of the Bible were applied in ways that were both increasingly political, and peculiar to Kikuyu traditional culture. Bildad Kaggia was one personification of this religious dynamic. "I felt charged by God to liberate Kenya, just as Moses was commanded to liberate the Israelites from Egyptian bondage," the Pentecostal prophet and future Mau Mau leader recalled. "I studied the Old Testament again and was moved by how Moses' army, consisting of humble slaves, who knew nothing of warfare, could be victorious."[95] In the missionary message, Kaggia and others had discovered the impetus for radical political action.

---

to the late 1960s. Finally, and significantly, it should also be noted that the figure of 1,478 "government" schools likely refers to the schools started and/or maintained by the African Independent Churches (AICs) that resulted from the female circumcision controversy and other similar cultural disputes with the mission churches. During Mau Mau most of these schools were shut down and then opened under the auspices of the government.

94 Sandgren, *Christianity and the Kikuyu*, 94–95. It should be noted that Sandgren sees AIM's response as a cynical capitulation and ultimately ineffective. While he is correct that many of those leaving the church never came back, the ultimate resurgence of the mission churches overall, and of the AIM in particular, between 1930 and independence suggests otherwise.

95 Kaggia, *Roots of Freedom*, 55.

Lacking substantial economic and organizational resources but armed with this powerful religious critique and a festering anti-colonial anger, the independent church and school movement represented a real threat to the religious and political colonial order. That threat grew substantially thanks to the leadership of several former "mission boys." Perhaps most significant was the role played by the Koinange family led by Chief Koinange wa Mbiyu. As one of the four loyalist chiefs who had, with government backing, initiated the Kikuyu Association in 1920, Koinange seemed destined for a prominent place in the colonial hierarchy.

In 1934, however, a colonial Land Commission report that Koinange had publicly supported was published. Angered and humiliated by the report, which appeared to legitimize the loss of large parts of previously Kikuyu lands to the settlers, Koinange and his family became increasingly antagonistic towards the colonial government, redirecting their considerable political prestige to the independent church and school movement.[96] After receiving his Master's degree in the United States, a second member of the Koinange family, Peter (Mbiyu) Koinange, returned in 1938 to lead the independent school movement's flagship teacher's college—an important move that provided this greenhouse of African nationalism with a level of organization and political prominence that it had been lacking.[97] By the 1940s, the independent school movement was widely recognized as the most important source of radical anti-colonial politics in Kenya.[98]

Complementing the thriving independent church and school movement was the return to Kenya of Jomo Kenyatta. Viewed by the biblically-infused Kikuyu grassroots as the African "Moses" returning to lead the new "Israel" out from oppression, Kenyatta's return in 1946 unleashed a generation of pent up anti-colonial and anti-mission hostility.[99] Within a year rumors of sacred oaths being administered by anti-colonial radicals began circulating throughout central Kenya.[100] And by 1952, missionaries and the colonial government believed that a substantial percentage of the tribes of central Kenya had taken the most basic of an increasingly

---

96 Anderson, *Histories of the Hanged*, 15, 20–22.
97 Blakeslee, *Beyond the Kikuyu Curtain*, 214; Blundell to unnamed recipient, 21 April 1955, KNA/MSS/66/170.
98 "Mau Mau," An English Press Production, 1953, WGMA.
99 Lonsdale, "Jomo Kenyatta, God," 53; Okot, *Historical Dictionary of Kenya*, xii; Ngugi, *Weep Not, Child*, 49–50, 88–89.
100 Blakeslee, *Beyond the Kikuyu Curtain*, 239–40.

disturbing series of oaths.[101] Nevertheless, until October of 1952, Mau Mau remained largely shrouded in mystery, with only scattered indications of the movement's violent potential. On 7 October 1952, this changed with the dramatic and highly symbolic assassination of American missionary product, Senior Chief Waruhiu. Mau Mau had arrived.

American Missionaries, Chief Waruhiu, and the War over Kenya's Political Soul

Waruhiu's murder, the first high profile Mau Mau killing, was Kenya's crossing of the Rubicon. Within hours of Waruhiu's death, the newly arrived and clearly shaken colonial governor cabled London and urgently requested permission to declare a state of emergency.[102] Two days later, the guest list at the senior chief's funeral was a who's who of the colony's religious and political establishment, including the colony's governor and the future face of the independence struggle, Jomo Kenyatta. Finally, two weeks later, as the Mau Mau composed songs celebrating the murder, a state of emergency was declared and approximately 180 alleged Mau Mau leaders, including Bildad Kaggia and Jomo Kenyatta, were detained.[103]

While these murders drew the world's attention, it was Chief Waruhiu's assassination that had the greatest significance within the colony. Much more than the death of a powerful political figure, Waruhiu's murder was a universally recognized manifestation of the cultural war over the future nation's soul. Once again, the roots of the story can be traced directly to the tiny American GMS. In 1902, a destitute woman who had recently lost her husband and three children to famine and disease, sought refuge at the GMS station at Kambui. Seeing that she had no land and no way to provide for her remaining children, the Knapps welcomed her with open arms.

The effect of this Christian charity proved to be transformative for the widow and two of her remaining sons.[104] Almost immediately Toro, the eldest, began a mentorship with the GMS's Dr. Henderson, ultimately going on to run his own dispensary as the mission's first African medical assistant. Largely overshadowed by his older brother until the latter's death in 1913, young Waruhiu was also being profoundly shaped by his contact with GMS. Converted to Christianity one year after his arrival in Kambui, Waruhiu had enrolled in the mission's make-shift school,

---

101 Carothers, *Psychology of Mau Mau*; Rolands, District Officer, Meru, Report of 7 May 1953, BCG 81/34/4.
102 Branch, *Defeating Mau Mau*, 48; Elkins, *Britain's Gulag*, 34–35.
103 Elkins, *Britain's Gulag*, 34–35.
104 Samuel Waruhiu, interview with the author, 13 October 2009.

excelling to the point that Mrs. Knapp set aside special time to mentor her hard-working protege.

Between 1906, when he left Kambui to help another GMS couple set up a new station, and 1913, when he returned to Kambui as the mission's first African head teacher, Waruhiu got married in a Christian wedding officiated by yet another GMS missionary and gained a reputation as the mission's most zealous lay-evangelist.[105] In short, the future senior chief's formative years, including his conversion, his education, his marriage and his first professional position, all took place under the close mentorship of missionaries from this small American mission.

Two additional interactions with missionaries played a central role in Waruhiu's political formation. The first was a successful 1915 surgery performed on Waruhiu's elephantiasis-plagued leg by the Scottish missionary Dr. John Arthur; the second was the forgiveness he received from GMS missionaries and the growing local church after admitting to an adulterous affair in 1918. While the surgery solidified his conviction that Western ideas and practices were often superior to those available in traditional Kikuyu culture, the experience of forgiveness from a community deeply disappointed by his affair intensified his allegiance to the evangelical Christian faith introduced to him by his American mentors.[106]

By 1920, Waruhiu's reputation as a loyal, hardworking, and effective Christian leader had attracted the attention of the colonial government.[107] Together with Kikuyu chiefs Koinange, Karanja, and Njonjo, Waruhiu had been instrumental in establishing the Kikuyu Association, which was to act as the loyalist foil to the EAA of the GMS's Harry Thuku. By 1922, Waruhiu had effectively positioned himself as the government's successor to the incompetent local chief Waweru.

While the two products of the American GMS were later to become strong allies in support of a moderate, pro-Western and multi-racial nationalism, the greatest threat to Waruhiu's 1922 quest to become chief was Thuku and his allies in the independent church and school movement.[108]

---

105 Wamagatta, "African Collaborators," 295–314; Samuel Waruhiu, interview with the author, 13 October 2009.

106 Wamagatta, 303–5;

107 "'Chiefs' Character Book, 1922–1952," KNA/DC/KBU/11/1.

108 Thuku, *Harry Thuku: An Autobiography*, 28–29. It should also be noted at this point that thanks to the church split of the PCC and the still struggling US economy at the time, when Rev. and Mrs. Knapp both died in Kenya in the early 1940s, the work of the GMS was passed onto the CSM. It is therefore worth noting that even as the Scottish Presbyterian influence grew in Kiambu, the American imprint left by the Knapps and GMS was to linger for many years to come.

In the end, the government's choice to impose Waruhiu as chief over the objections of some of the traditional Kikuyu leaders, when combined with his obviously increasing wealth, his unapologetic deference to the missionaries, and his out-spoken pro-government positions in the years leading up to the emergency, eventually made the Christian Waruhiu a hero to the European and moderate Kenyan communities and the object of unrivalled hatred among the alienated and militant grassroots nationalists who populated Mau Mau.

Waruhiu's assassination produced an extreme response by the colonial government and an equally extreme counter-response from the Mau Mau. Within a few months the emergency had engulfed all of central Kenya and was making inroads across the country. In terms of both its scope and its intensity, Mau Mau dwarfed the female circumcision controversy. But the two periods had a great deal in common. Indeed, in many ways Mau Mau was simply the rehashing of the same set of issues. What was different was the heightened intensity and sophistication of the new generation of militants. In 1930, the clash between the mission churches and the defenders of African traditionalism had yielded a clear victor. The mission churches had been devastated and the trajectory of the colony seemed to be consistent with the formation of a fundamentally radical and anti-Western political culture. But in the intervening generation both the mission-church community and their independent church rivals had grown in strength and influence. The next few years would determine which of these contrasting, and missionary-influenced, visions would win the battle for Kenya's political soul.

American Missionaries and the Crucible of Mau Mau

In the 1940s and early 1950s, the indicators were not promising for the mission church community. The KCA-backed independent church and school movement was strong and influential and some vulnerabilities within the mission church community seen in the 1930s remained unresolved. In part because they had struggled to keep pace with the ever-increasing demands for improved education, AIM were among the first to see the extent to which dissatisfaction had also infected portions of the mission-church. Sitting down to breakfast one morning near the end of 1947, Dr. Virginia Blakeslee received a letter signed by the leading teachers and elders of her district. "You missionaries have done good work," the local leaders began. "We are grateful for what you have done, but now we ask you to leave Githumu district. We wish to carry on."

Recounting the letter in her memoirs, Blakeslee recalled her "shock to see the signatures of men with whom we had labored in the gospel for many years, yet so strong was the spirit of nationalism abroad in their land that few Agikuyu were unaffected by it."[109] Perhaps of even greater concern to the American-dominated mission was the fact that the same sentiment appeared to be spreading beyond central Kenya and into the staunchly loyal Kamba around Machakos, home of the mission's leading Bible college.[110] When added to the abundant evidence of militant discontent among the nationalists outside of mission influence, these events within the African mission-church community had the American missionaries preparing for the worst.

What happened next took almost everyone by surprise. Instead of being decimated as they had been by the female circumcision controversy, the visceral anti-mission anger of Mau Mau seemed to strengthen the American mission-churches. Among the Kalenjin peoples, where AIM and WGM in particular were predominant, this is not surprising; for the tribes that made up that community were geographically and culturally distant from the Kikuyu locus of Mau Mau sentiment.[111] However, among the Kamba, who were ethnic and political cousins to the Kikuyu, the strength of the mission-church was unexpected. Referring to the products of the mission's training schools among the Kamba, an AIM representative wrote that the mission-Christians had "stood practically one hundred per cent loyal to Christ our Lord and to the Government during the Emergency."[112]

Even more unexpected was the response of the Kikuyu mission-Christians. Multiple missionary accounts suggest that church attendance at mission-churches increased by as much as 300 percent during the Emergency. At the AIM church at Kijabe, for instance, regular church attendance grew from six hundred prior to the Emergency to over seventeen hundred by late 1953.[113] Despite many Christians being killed by Mau Mau insurgents in the central highlands, the same phenomenon was apparent

---

109 Blakeslee, *Beyond the Kikuyu Curtain*, 229.
110 World Gospel Mission, "African Missionaries Facing."
111 Barnett, "Political Situation in Kenya," 9; Atkins, "Dawn in Kenya," WGM, *CTP*, September 1953, WGMA.
112 African Inland Mission, Memorandum from the Kenya Field, 18 August 1956, BGC/81/34/4. Veteran AIM missionary Lillian Davis specifically noted the colonial government's decision to provide virtually unlimited radio time to AIM was a direct result of the moderate political influence that AIM had had among the Kamba prior to and during Mau Mau. Lillian Davis, interview with the author, 10 July 2009.
113 Atkins, "Dawn in Kenya," WGM, *CTP*, September 1953, WGMA.

in the GMS-influenced areas in Kiambu, where Harry Thuku observed that "very few of the Gathirimu people took any part [in Mau Mau]. So our area became known amongst the loyal Kikuyu as a safe area."[114]

Thuku's own response to Mau Mau serves as a potent symbol of the deep-seated allegiance to mission-Christianity that had developed between 1930 and the Emergency among many Kenyan Christians. "I opposed Mau Mau quite openly," the pioneer of Kenyan nationalism recalled in his memoirs. "I did not care what they did to me."[115] In a letter written at the height of the Emergency, Thuku explained why. "The evils of [the] devil have for three years tried to shake the good work done by the churches. But I am glad to say that Christians of all denominations stood firm in their faith in Christ. Many have been murdered coldly by terrorists, others tortured, and their property maliciously destroyed; but they have never denied their faith in Christ."[116]

In the end, to an extent that even the female circumcision controversy could not match, the violence of the Mau Mau uprising forced Kenyans to take sides. But the choice was not, as most have assumed, between African nationalism and loyalty to the colonial system. Virtually all African Kenyans were opposed to the idea of a perpetual colonial state. Instead, the choice was between two competing visions of nationalism—the radical anti-colonialism of the independent churches and the moderately pro-government politics of the mission-churches. Thanks to the breadth of their humanitarian efforts, their empowering emphasis on the authority of Scripture, and the transformational nature of the evangelical conversion experience, American evangelical missionaries and their numerous Kenyan converts played a central role in this violent debate.

At this point, two significant caveats are in order. First, it is important to remember that while the majority of the products of AIM, GMS, WGM, and the other American evangelical missions became active members of the anti-Mau Mau group, there were important exceptions to the rule. One of the most important was Paul Ngei. The son of AIM convert and Kamba paramount chief Masaku, Ngei was raised in the AIM church and school system until leaving for Alliance High School in the late 1930s. However, while he continued to maintain contact with AIM missionaries into the early independence period, Ngei appears to have never accepted the

---

114 Thuku, *Harry Thuku: An Autobiography*, 70.
115 Thuku, 69.
116 Thuku, 100.

American version of Christianity, or its deference to political authority.[117] Indeed, Ngei's inclination for radical anti-Western politics made him a focal point for the limited Kamba involvement in Mau Mau, a role that led to his detention with Kenyatta from 1952 to 1961.[118]

The second important caveat is that while the Kenyan products of the American missionary effort played a vital role in the anti-Mau Mau movement, they did not make up the entirety of that movement. Another group of Christians, those influenced by the East African Revival, played an equally significant role in defeating Mau Mau and placing Kenya on a moderate and pro-Western political trajectory. As a largely African indigenous movement that affected mostly the mainline British denominations, the East African Revival nevertheless had important roots in American evangelicalism.

A Cambridge-educated evangelical Anglican missionary, Dr. Joseph Church, was the only non-African found at the hub of the East African Revival. Yet as the person responsible for introducing and encouraging the theological underpinnings of the movement, Church's influence looms particularly large in the history of the movement. Although British, the three main characteristics of the movement (the "born again" conversion experience, a commitment to holy living, and equality before God) all derive their most immediate roots from the transatlantic evangelical exchange, and in particular, the American partner in that exchange. The "self-conscious model" for Church's understanding of both "full surrender" conversion and Christian holiness, for instance, was the nineteenth century American revivalist, Charles Finney, whose *Revival of Religion* acted almost as a second Bible for Joseph Church and the African revivalists who crisscrossed the region during the 1930s, 1940s, and 1950s.[119]

The influence on the East African Revival of Church's early and frequent interaction with Moral Re-Armament's American founder, Frank Buchman, was equally apparent in the movement's distinctive stress on equality before God. As one future Kenyan diplomat influenced by the movement stated, what the East African Revival did was to "break a number of barriers, and [emphasize] what was the essence of Christianity ... that

---

117 Art Davis, interview with the author, 28 November 2009.
118 Branch, *Defeating Mau Mau*, 6, 54. Ngei's anti-Western tendencies were also on full display in the early post-independence years, when Ngei teamed up with Odinga and others to press for a pro-Soviet stance in the Cold War.
119 Noll, *New Shape of World*, 183.

we are all children of God ... we are all saved by Christ."[120] Significantly, this theological principle had the effect of inverting the relative importance of the adherent's tribal identity and increasing their allegiance to other Christians, including the missionaries. "The Revival Fellowship," stated one scholar, "saw itself as a new clan."[121]

This rapidly growing movement hit its zenith in the years surrounding the Mau Mau Emergency and acted as a powerful complement to the moderate politics of the equally evangelical American mission converts. Like many converts of AIM and GMS, those influenced by the East African Revival often refused to take the oaths, and as a result became Mau Mau targets in a civil war where the middle ground had largely disappeared. The mother of future Ambassador and Permanent Secretary for Foreign Affairs Joseph Muchemi was one of many products of the movement who were killed for putting faith ahead of ethnicity. As Muchemi remembered, "a lot of people were killed, including my mother, [but] as a result of that persecution, Christianity became stronger."[122]

American Missionaries, African Evangelicals, and Moderate Pro-Government Politics

Even before the Emergency, the colonial government had recognized the moderating influence that the American evangelical missions in particular seemed to have on their converts. Accurate or not, one practical implication of this stereotype was the often-disproportionate presence of the Kamba and Kalenjin in the colonial police force. In one district of the Rift Valley, for instance, of the ninety-two members of the police force employed at the end of 1950, over 60 percent (fifty-six) hailed from the two AIM-dominated Kamba and Kalinjin communities, whereas the numerically larger Kikuyu and Luo communities had a combined representation of three, with the remaining ten tribes accounting for the remaining thirty-three policemen.[123]

During the Emergency, this impression was solidified as the evangelical churches, including the British mission-churches influenced by the East African Revival, consistently lined up against the Mau Mau uprising. At one AI-sponsored conference at Kijabe in early 1954, for instance, the attendees issued a spontaneous statement of support for the colonial government

---

120 Bethwell Kiplagat, interview with the author, 19 April 2010.
121 Park, *Spirituality of Kenyan Pastors*; Bethwell Kiplagat, interview with the author, 19 April 2010.
122 High Commissioner Joseph Muchemi, interview with the author, 10 June 2009.
123 "Handing Over Notes—Masai Division," (1950), KNA/PC/NGO/1/18/7/Police Reports.

that concluded unambiguously, "We the Christians of the Africa Inland Church declare that we will be faithful and obedient to our Sovereign, Her Majesty Queen Elizabeth II."[124] Statements like these led Michael Blundell, one of the leaders of the British settlers, to note approvingly at the height of the uprising, that those standing against Mau Mau were, "fortified by their deep precepts of Christianity and *this* has given them the will to resist."[125]

Convinced that hopes for a moderate and pro-West independent Kenya would rise or fall largely with the cultural and political fortunes of the mission-church converts, the colonial government sought to harness and bolster its influence by providing protection and political support to the missions and their churches wherever possible. The government also went to some lengths to quietly provide moral support for the loyalists, accepting invitations to preside over mission-church conferences, speaking out publicly in favor of the role of the Bible in society, and even criticizing the often-hypocritical religion of the White settler community.[126]

By far the Government's most controversial use of missionaries and their mission-church leaders was as evangelists in the infamous Mau Mau detention camps. Astonishingly, many of the American missionaries and their converts appeared to have been genuinely oblivious to the risks posed to their Christian message by such clear collusion with the often-brutal detention program. Instead, they chose to see the government invitation in one-dimensionally spiritual terms, as simply God's way of opening the door to the preaching of the gospel to hardened sinners.[127]

Not surprisingly, many detainees who had been part of the Kikuyu independent churches and schools movement responded to the message with anger and cynicism. "They used to preach and preach," recalled one former detainee. "We just sat there and listened to them and couldn't believe our ears. Hah, the hypocrisy of it all only made us more determined

---

124 "An Address of Appreciation and Loyalty," Africa Inland Church Leaders Conference, 26 April—3 May 1954, KNA/GH/27/1. AIM Field Director, in passing on this statement to Gov. Blundell, vouched for the integrity of the statement, stating, "I assure you that both the Tea Party and the Address were quite spontaneous on the part of the African leaders." K. L. Downing to the Governor of Kenya, 24 July 1954, KNA/GH/27/1.

125 3 April 1953 the *East African Standard*, as quoted in World Gospel Mission, *CTP*, September 1953, WGMA (italics in the original).

126 P. Lehrer to Sir Evelyn Baring, 5 December 1955, KNA/GH/27/2; L. F. G. Pritchard to Rev. P. Lehrer, 15 December 1955, KNA/GH/27/2; Governor Baring's Broadcast commemorating the "Kenya Bible Week" campaign, July 1953, KNA/GH/27/1; Carothers, *Psychology of Mau Mau*, 27, challenges the colonial government officials and settlers in this government sponsored report on Mau Mau, "Let us face the fact that this gift [Christianity] cannot be given by the missionaries unless we others aid them by living Christian lives."

127 "Mau Mau Evangelism," written by an unnamed AIM missionary who took part in detention camp evangelism, BGC/81/34/4.

not to give in."¹²⁸ Others reacted by completely rejecting everything related to Christianity, returning instead to a pure form of Kikuyu traditional religion.¹²⁹ Yet, there was a sizable minority who appeared to experience a genuine evangelical-style conversion and, according to another former detainee, became "real Christian fanatics."¹³⁰ As one AIM missionary reported in 1956 regarding the Mackinnon Road detention camp, "a great change has certainly come over hundreds of detainees in this Camp; an almost unbelievable transformation. Never in sixteen years of missionary service in East Africa, have I seen so much evidence that the gospel 'is the power of God unto salvation to everyone that believeth,' as during the last six months."¹³¹

No one embodied the complex internal struggle over Kenya's cultural and political soul more completely than the nation's founding father and first president, Jomo Kenyatta. The grandson and apprentice of a prominent Kikuyu witchdoctor, Kenyatta was nevertheless among the first generation of Kenyans to receive their education in the mission schools.¹³² Despite growing up near the GMS station that produced Thuku and Waruhiu, Kenyatta enrolled at the CSM school at Thogoto. It was here that Kenyatta was successfully treated for a potentially serious illness by the mission's Dr. John Arthur, learned to read and write, and completed a two-year catechism class, culminating in his baptism in 1912 and a vow to abandon his tribal life.¹³³

However, his commitment to mission Christianity appears to have waned when he joined his peers on the increasingly well-worn path to Nairobi in the search for profitable employment. It was here that Kenyatta came into contact with the ideas of American missionary prodigal, Thuku, and his short-lived EAA. Eager to carry on the imprisoned Thuku's fight, Kenyatta rose quickly in the newly formed KCA, and in 1929 represented the group in his first trip to London. Although Kenyatta returned briefly to Kenya in 1930, the formative next fifteen years of his life were spent primarily in England.¹³⁴

---

128 Elkins, *Britain's Gulag*, 172.
129 Elkins, 175.
130 Elkins, 186.
131 "Mau Mau Evangelism," written by an unnamed AIM missionary who took part in detention camp evangelism, BGC/81/34/4.
132 Kenyatta, *Facing Mount Kenya*, xx.
133 Aseka, *Jomo Kenyatta: A Biography*, 8–9.
134 Lonsdale, "Jomo Kenyatta, God," 32; Irele and Jeyifo, *Oxford Encyclopedia of African*, 31–32.

It is of supreme importance that the colony Kenyatta left in 1930 was deeply embroiled in the missionary-provoked controversy over female circumcision. Indeed, for the next fifteen years, Kenyatta continued to fight this cultural battle within the context of European anti-colonial politics, eventually producing his celebrated defense of Kikuyu traditional culture, *Facing Mount Kenya*. A sophisticated articulation of the anti-missionary critique evolving in Kenya at the time, *Facing Mount Kenya* also provided strong evidence of the extent to which mission-Christianity was shaping the evolution of even militant politics in Kenya. For instance, while Kenyatta spoke out strongly against some facets of the missionary movement, he often used the Kikuyu translation of the Bible as his starting point. Regarding the traditional practice of polygamy he wrote, "In the holy book the African failed to find evidence to convince him ... On the contrary, he found that many of the respected characters in the Book of God, *Ibuku ria Ngai* (as the Bible is translated in Gikuyu), are those who have practiced polygamy."[135]

Kenyatta's evolving thought attracted the attention and approval of the British left, and during the 1930s he accepted an offer to study for a year in Moscow, where Ralph Bunche incorrectly reported that Kenyatta felt he was "treated royally" and "given all sorts of special privileges."[136] Armed with a sophisticated critique of Western colonialism, Kenyatta returned to Kenya in 1946 to a hero's welcome. Within a year he was made the president of the Kenya African Union (KAU) and assumed the role of leader of the African movement for self-determination. But in at least two important ways, the Kenya he returned to was not the one he had left all those years ago. First, the cultural-political schism that had erupted between the mission-Christians and the independent churches and other traditionalists in the late 1920s had grown deeper and more militant. Second, beaten up and left for dead in 1930, the mission-churches had recovered and were now a formidable political force.

The transformation of Kenyatta's political message from his arrival back in Kenya in 1946 to the run-up to the national elections in 1963 is a fascinating window into the future president's adaptation to the rising influence of pro-Western political moderation in his country. Initially Kenyatta's political message mirrored his writings so closely that the first year-and-a-half after his return might be described as an extended book tour.

---

135 Kenyatta, *Facing Mount Kenya*, 271.
136 Horne, *Mau Mau in Harlem?*, 126. As will be pointed out later, the belief that Kenyatta harbored an affection for Soviet communism was largely inaccurate. Andrew, *Defence of the Realm*, 455–56.

Reporting in January 1948, one colonial official summarized the message of Kenyatta's speeches as a plea for Kikuyu nationalism and a call to "get back to the old religion, [because] Christianity is like the weevils that spoil the corn, and we [the Kikuyu] are the corn."[137]

However, as Kenyatta interacted with regional leaders who had come to prominence during his self-imposed exile, his tone became more moderate and his references to Christianity more flattering. Kenyatta's increasingly moderate message was especially apparent during his visit to the AIM stronghold of Eldama Ravine during the immediate build-up to the Mau Mau uprising where he spoke out strongly against the movement.[138] Nevertheless, Kenyatta's reputation for ardent African nationalism, his close ties to the militant independent school movement, and his former links to Moscow and European leftists, all made him a target of suspicion within the colonial government. As a result, in 1952, along with five others including the Pentecostal prophet Bildad Kaggia and the AIM product Paul Ngei, Kenyatta was found guilty of Mau Mau involvement and detained indefinitely.[139]

Unjustly accused and then detained for nine years with five bitterly anti-colonial co-defendants was a recipe for political radicalization. Yet for Kenyatta imprisonment produced the opposite. Indeed, his moderate turn appears to have been the root of a bitter division that developed between Kenyatta and his more radical fellow prisoners, Bildad Kaggia and Paul Ngei. Also indicative of Kenyatta's conservative political trajectory were the influential visits to Kenyatta in detention of mission-church Christians like the AIM product, Daniel arap Moi, and East African Revival product Bishop Obadiah Kariuki (a Kenyatta relative through marriage). After praying with Kenyatta, both men returned from their visits claiming Kenyatta's desire was not for revenge, but for racial reconciliation, Christian forgiveness, and political moderation.[140]

---

137 "Weithaga, 30 January 1948," KNA/MSS/129/35.
138 Morton, *Moi: The Making*, 68.
139 Another indication of the colonial government's increasing trust in the American missionary effort is its choice to ask AIM missionary Ken Downing to act as the Kikuyu to English interpreter during Kenyatta's trial. Evidence that the AIM missionaries were not entirely politically naive is found in the fact that Downing turned down the request, not wanting to be seen as the "mouthpiece for the government." Jonathan and Dottie Hildebrandt, interview with the author, 10 July 2009.
140 Clough, *Mau Mau Memoirs*, 49; American Consul General to Department of State, 6 December 1959, NARA RG84/2844/7; Boobbyer, "Moral Re-Armament in Africa," 226. It should be said that Bishop Kariuki prayed with Kenyatta, and that both men spoke out about Kenyatta's moderate message, but while it is likely, there is no proof that Moi and Kenyatta prayed together.

As we saw in the Congo, the quasi-evangelical Moral Re-Armament also appears to have been influential during Kenyatta's detention. In the early days of the Emergency, MRA had used its political connections to gain access to a number of the detention centers, including the important Athi River camp where Kenyatta's son Peter was being held. Within the spiritually vibrant but racially charged context of Mau Mau-era Kenya, MRA's vision of changing the world through divinely guided introspection, humble confession and equality before God had significant traction.

In one remarkable scene, the commandant at the camp, an MRA adherent, lined up the detainees and publicly apologized to them for his attitude of superiority and the poor treatment they had received. According to one scholar, the response was extraordinary. "Some men broke ranks and rushed up to him with enthusiasm." One Mau Mau detainee recalled, "when I heard this white man apologize for his superiority towards us Africans ... I lost my hatred and decided to fight with clean hands and a pure heart." Over time, approximately five hundred detainees at the camp renounced Mau Mau at least in part thanks to MRA's message of racial reconciliation at Athi River.[141]

Among this group was Peter Kenyatta, who was so taken with the MRA message that he was given permission to visit his father in detention, where he sought—and apparently received—his father's blessing to join the camp's screening team.[142] Kenyatta's contact with MRA did not end there. Later in his detention, he watched the MRA play, *The Forgotten Factor*, and its film, *Freedom*, which he suggested should be translated into Swahili to reach a larger audience.[143]

Other indications that MRA's message resonated with Kenyatta include a later visit by his daughter to MRA headquarters in Europe, a full-page MRA advertisement on the eve of Kenyan independence calling Kenyatta a "prophet voice" of unity and forgiveness, and a condolence letter from several members of Kenyatta's first cabinet to the widow of MRA's second leader in 1965.[144] Christian enough to connect him to the mission-Christianity of his youth, but sufficiently vague to allow for the less orthodox versions of the traditional African theism of his middle-age, MRA seems to have been an ideal vessel through which the future leader

---

141 Boobbyer, "Moral Re-Armament in Africa," 222–25.
142 Elkins, *Britain's Gulag*, 201.
143 Boobbyer, "Moral Re-Armament in Africa," 226–27. In the lead-up to the nation's first free elections in 1961, over one million Kenyans were to view *Freedom*.
144 Horne, *Mau Mau in Harlem?*, 294; Boobbyer, "Moral Re-Armament in Africa," 226–27.

could reconcile the militant anti-colonial nationalism of his past to the pro-Western moderation of Kenya's future.

Whether it was a result of his own childhood conversion, the pragmatic need to adapt to the growing political strength of the politically moderate mission-church products, his family's relationship with MRA, or some combination of these and other factors, when Kenyatta was released from detention, he came out preaching peace and reconciliation. Standing in stark contrast to the acidic bitterness of Lumumba's independence speech in the Congo is one scene that could have come directly out of a MRA play or an East African Revival testimonial. "If I have done a mistake to you in the past," Kenyatta told a nervous gathering of White settlers shortly before independence, "it is for you to forgive me. If you have done a mistake to me, it is for me to forgive you. The Africans cannot say the Europeans have done all the wrong and the Europeans cannot say the Africans have done all the wrong. The good thing is to be able to forget and forgive one another."[145]

Conclusion

Between 1895 and the colony's independence in 1963, the American missionary community had grown substantially in both size and significance. Ironically, the explicitly apolitical American missionaries had played a central and disproportionate part in the shaping of the future nation's political culture. Thanks to the willingness of some early American missionaries to live out the radically egalitarian logic of American evangelicalism, American missionaries like the Stauffachers and the Knapps were responsible for mentoring pioneers of modern-style African nationalism in Kenya like Mulungit ole Sempele and Harry Thuku. It is significant that in both cases, this brand of missionary-influenced nationalism was ultimately both moderate and pro-West.

But the radical religious conversion demanded by many of these missionaries also provoked a militant and anti-colonial response. Thanks to its ethnocentric cultural baggage, the demands placed on American mission-church converts in particular helped trigger the influential independent church and school movement and their radicalized Mau Mau descendants. Indeed, perhaps the two most significant political murders in pre-independence Kenya—the killing of American missionary Hulda Stumpf at Kijabe in early 1930, and the assassination of GMS product Chief Waruhiu—can both be directly attributed to the uncompromising cultural demands that American missionaries placed on their converts.

---

145 Attwood, *Reds and the Blacks*, 166.

Finally, when combined with the popular goodwill created by seventy years of missionary humanitarianism, the American evangelical political theology of submission to governing authority inspired in many mission-church converts a remarkably enduring deference to the colonial government—a phenomenon also found amongst many of those touched by the East African Revival. More than any other factor, it was this influential and grassroots support for the government that defeated Mau Mau. Yet, whether the short-term defeat of Mau Mau signaled a lasting victory for moderate pro-Western politics in Kenya remained a matter of considerable debate. Indeed, in the final lead-up to independence, many British and American policymakers remained anxious regarding the future nation's political stability and Cold War orientation.

CHAPTER 6

"A Broad Popular Consensus," 1963–1991

Despite his apparent conversion to pro-Western politics, Kenyatta remained at the center of American anxiety over Kenya.[1] Prior to his detention, Kenyatta's lengthy study trips to the Soviet Union, association with the British left, and conviction as the leader of the Mau Mau movement all suggested that his moderate post-detention rhetoric might not be genuine.[2] But more recent events also aroused anxiety. The sudden arrival in 1960 of Czech-produced badges bearing Kenyatta's image raised fears that the famous nationalist was willingly being used by the communists as a Lumumba-like symbol of anti-colonialism.[3] These concerns were amplified when US diplomats were given intelligence that strongly suggested communist funds were being channeled to Kenyatta through Odinga.[4] As one US policymaker pessimistically concluded, Kenyatta remained "an uncertain element in Kenya politics ... we may well see a far less desirable kind of government come to power after independence."[5]

Events immediately after Kenya's independence in 1963 did little to ease these anxieties. Internally, the intense domestic struggle over which group could legitimately claim the mantle of Kenya's "freedom fighters" intuitively favored populists like Kaggia, Ngei, and Odinga whose actions or rhetoric were closely linked to the violent radicalism of Mau Mau.[6] In addition, the fact that the media was controlled by Odinga's radical ally

---

1 Amcongen, Nairobi to Department of State, 6 November 1959, NARA/RG84/2844/7; "Memorandum of Conversation, Political Situation in Kenya and East Africa," 18 April 1961, NARA/RG59/1552/5.
2 John Lonsdale is among several prominent scholars who have concluded that, had he been given a fair trial, Kenyatta would not have been convicted. Nevertheless, for many, the conviction acted to confirm Kenyatta's radical credentials.
3 Amcongen, Nairobi to Department of State, 16 December 1960, NARA/RG84/2844/7.
4 Amcongen, Nairobi to Department of State, 18 July 1960, NARA/RG84/2844/9; Undated (likely 1965), "Kenya, Oginga Odinga," NARA/RG59/5235/37.
5 Elbert G. Mathews to Governor Williams, 7 November 1962, NARA/RG59/3110/1.
6 The extent to which Kenyatta felt the need to continually defend his nationalist credentials against the leftist populism of Oginga Odinga and others can be seen as late as his Kenyatta Day speech in 1975 in which he turns the tables on the leftist, accusing them of being "collaborators of the imperialists" and obliquely referring to Odinga as one who does "not know what the inside of a colonial jail looked like." KNA/OP/KA/4/20.

Oneko heightened Congo-inspired concerns that government-sponsored radical rhetoric might undermine the stability of the young nation and make it vulnerable to communist influence.[7]

External events also threatened the position of the pro-West moderates. Less than a year after Kenyan independence, the Belgian-American rescue mission in the Congo had stoked anti-colonial fervor in Africa to an unprecedented level. Making matters worse, Kenyatta's central role in the failed negotiations between the Stanleyville regime and the United States had left him vulnerable to charges of neo-colonialism and feeling betrayed and humiliated by the United States.[8] In short, when combined with Kenyatta's own ideologically ambiguous past, the domestic and diplomatic context of Kenya in the early years of independence gave US policymakers good reason to be fearful.

Yet the fact that Kenyatta was willing to risk political capital by intervening in the Stanleyville crisis, and that the radical populists like Kaggia and Ngei felt alienated by his domestic policies, should have been cause for optimism among Western observers. Indeed, while Kenyatta remained wary of attacks from the left throughout his presidency and, therefore, maintained a moderate and officially "non-aligned" Cold War posture, it soon became apparent that Kenya was staking out a relatively unambiguous pro-Western path. The first clear indication was Kenyatta's choice of cabinet ministers. While political necessity required that some left-leaning politicians such as Odinga and Oneko be included, the independent republic's first cabinet was dominated by moderate mission-church products. At least seven of the twenty cabinet posts were filled by products of American mission schools, three others had completed either their university or graduate training in America, and the majority of the rest could boast of similarly strong links to British missionaries.[9]

---

7 Attwood, *Reds and the Blacks*, 239; Daniel Branch quotes US embassy sources as saying that the state-run radio and television stations were, thanks to Oneko, "largely in USSR or Czech hands," Branch, *Kenya: Between Hope*, 42.

8 Kenyatta, *Suffering Without Bitterness*, foreword.

9 The list of the first cabinet used comes from Makau Mutua, "Remembering Jomo's Cabinet", *Nation*, October 23, 2022. From this list I tracked each minister's educational history. Those ministers coming from at least an early American missionary education include: Otiende (Friends); Mwendwa (AIM); Ngei (AIM); Sagini (SDA); Moi (AIM); Mwanyumba (AIM); Ayodo (SDA). Those who did their university or graduate training in the US included: Sagini, Ayodo, and Ngei (University of Hawaii); but also products of the British Protestant Missions, Mungai (MD, Stanford), Kiano (Antioch College and Stanford), and Koinange (Columbia). It is notable that this list does not even include the cabinet minister who had had the most direct—and positive—interaction with US policymakers, Tom Mboya.

Of course, as the fervently anti-colonial politics of Odinga (CMS), Oneko (CMS) and Ngei (AIM-CMS) demonstrate, not all mission-church products became political moderates.[10] Nevertheless, the educational histories of Kenyatta's cabinet gave US Ambassador Attwood and other American policymakers reason to hope that the politics of Kenya's governing elites would reflect the influence of their American teachers—many of whom were strongly anti-communist evangelical missionaries. As subsequent events demonstrated, their optimism was justified.[11]

The Kenyan cabinet's latent pro-West sympathies were quickly awakened by the events of 1964–1965. In January 1964, just weeks after Kenyan independence, army mutinies broke out in Kenya, Uganda, and Tanzania; and an explicitly communist revolution erupted on the island of Zanzibar. Together these incidents served notice of the extent to which moderate politics, and the lives of the moderate politicians, in independent East Africa remained vulnerable. Although the army mutiny in Kenya was put down relatively easily with the help of British troops, the trauma of these early weeks was to leave a lasting impression on Kenyatta and his first cabinet.[12]

For radicals in the cabinet, these events had a very different effect than they had had on the moderate majority. Odinga appears to have been emboldened, for he soon departed on official tours of communist China and the USSR. These tours secured considerable foreign aid, including a $15 million grant from China for an important irrigation project and Soviet promises to build a large hospital in Odinga's home area, as well as a political training institute in Nairobi. Soon after Odinga's return, a series of mysterious shipments also began to arrive from Eastern Europe which Odinga's allies allowed to by-pass the normal checks at customs. According to Western intelligence sources, at least some of the shipments included arms and other contraband. When combined with the hundreds of thousands of dollars Odinga had allegedly accepted from the Soviet Union and his consistently anti-Western rhetoric, these developments appeared to confirm his revolutionary ambitions.[13] As a result, US diplomats in Nairobi, no doubt influenced by recent events in the Congo, concluded in 1965 that political prospects in Kenya remained "uncertain and perhaps revolutionary."[14]

---

10 Odinga, *Not Yet Uhuru*, 30–60.
11 Attwood, *Reds and the Blacks*, 161. Attwood claimed with satisfaction that five ministers had received their higher education in the US. The actual number was at least six.
12 Branch, *Kenya: Between Hope*, 37; Attwood, *Reds and the Blacks*, 156.
13 Attwood, 238–44; Branch, 38–43.
14 "Secret Comments by Country Team Nairobi on National Policy Paper on Kenya," 1965, NARA/RG59/5235/37.

This threat from the left had the effect of pushing Kenyatta and many in his cabinet closer to the West. Perhaps the first indication that Kenyatta would no longer tolerate Odinga's revolutionary politics came in November 1964. Using the dissolution of KADU into KANU as his pretense, Kenyatta expanded and shuffled his cabinet which allowed him to strip the Vice President (Odinga) and his allies of several key portfolios including immigration and internal security. In a clear statement of political intent, these two responsibilities were now entrusted to the newly promoted minister of home affairs—the American mission-educated Daniel arap Moi.[15]

If Kenyatta hoped that the new minister would help him restrain Odinga and his associates, Moi immediately exceeded expectations. In early 1965, Moi led the opposition to Odinga's attempt to handpick the replacement for his murdered ally Pio Pinto. At a time in which public sympathy could have easily sided with the leftists allied to the murdered Pinto, Moi nevertheless played a critical role in parliament's decisive 71–34 vote against Odinga and in favor of the pro-Kenyatta candidate.[16] Just days later, without any prior warning, Moi expelled six communist diplomats and correspondents (including the first and second secretaries of the Soviet embassy). As the obviously pleased US ambassador recalled, "all six happened to be intelligence agents with records of close association with Odinga."[17]

Then, less than two months later, Moi approved a series of raids on the homes and offices of Odinga's allies which, according to Israeli intelligence sources, included the recovery of a stockpile of weapons consisting of five hundred sub-machine guns, large amounts of ammunition, and a host of other small arms.[18] On the back of these raids came accusations that Odinga had secretly met with Tanzanian revolutionaries. When Odinga and the Tanzanians both forcefully rejected the claims, Moi then proceeded to make public the "exact time, place and license numbers" involved.[19]

Moi's zealous efforts were clearly inspired by his loyalty to Kenyatta. However, they also betrayed an underlying commitment to a zealous and missionary-inspired anti-communism, as well as a conservative political

---

15 Branch, *Kenya: Between Hope*, 44.
16 Hornsby, *Kenya: A History*, 147–50; Attwood, *Reds and the Blacks*, 244–45; Morton, *Moi: The Making*, 123.
17 Attwood, *Reds and the Blacks*, 266.
18 Hornsby, *Kenya: A History*, 150, Branch, 48.
19 Attwood, *Reds and the Blacks*, 268.

philosophy that saw stability and order as the necessary foundation for prosperity, peace, and freedom. One example of Moi's pro-US sentiment in particular was his politically risky efforts to rebuild the US-Kenya relationship soon after the fallout from the Stanleyville rescue. After returning from America to mobs of Kenyans protesting US intervention in the Congo, Ambassador Attwood received a request from Moi to come by his office. As Attwood recalled the conversation, "He came right to the point. 'I wanted to tell you personally,' Moi said, 'that you have many friends—America has many friends—both in and out of the government. The demonstrators mean nothing. I hope you understand that.'"[20]

As Attwood was to discover, Moi was not bluffing. Despite regular outbursts of anti-Americanism in Kisumu and Nairobi, pro-American sentiment ran deep in early post-colonial Kenya.[21] In fact, just hours after his discussion with Moi, Attwood met with some of the approximately fourteen hundred American missionaries working in the country whose reports of widespread pro-American sentiment produced in the diplomat an optimistic prognosis for US-Kenyan relations.[22]

Confirming the reports of the missionary community was a 1965 public opinion poll in which 50 percent of Kenyans responded that of all the world's nations, America had "done the most to help their country." Also encouraging for Western observers was the fact that Britain, despite being the colonial power of record, ranked second with an additional 42 percent of the vote, leaving only 8 percent to be divided up by the rest of the world. As the official US representative, Attwood was understandably quick to praise the efforts of his government in producing this pro-American sentiment.[23] Privately, however, much greater stock was placed on the continuing role of the missionary community, which analysts in Nairobi argued "have in the past exerted great influence on Kenya's evolution [and] are likely to continue to do so."[24]

Other important indicators of pro-American sentiment in Kenya also pointed to the central role that American missionaries had played. Perhaps most significant was the relationship the young Kenyan government had with the missionary community. As we have seen, many members of the

---

20 Attwood, *Reds and the Blacks*, 234.
21 "Secret, Comments by Country Team Nairobi on National Policy Paper on Kenya," 1965, NARA/RG59/5235/37.
22 Attwood, *Reds and the Blacks*, 234.
23 Attwood, *Reds and the Blacks*, 288–89.
24 "Secret, Comments by Country Team Nairobi on National Policy Paper on Kenya," 1965, NARA/RG59/5235/37.

government had been educated or influenced by American missionaries and actively encouraged missionary participation in building the new Kenya. For instance, in a visit to an American missionary hospital soon after independence, Kenyatta's Stanford-educated minister of health, called the missionary effort "magnificent" and a "valuable contribution to our country."[25] Later, speaking at the graduation ceremony of AIM's boarding school for missionary children, Kenyatta's minister of education encouraged the graduates to return to build on the work of their parents. "You students who were born and trained here," the Honorable Jeremiah Nyagah stated, "are the ones that we would like to see come back and help us, for we know the value of second-generation missionaries."[26]

With apparently widespread rural support for his pro-Western policies (outside of Odinga's Nyanza province, at least) and a group of able and pro-West ministers willing to do his legwork, Kenyatta was free to position himself above the ideological battle, while simultaneously tightening the screws on the left-leaning Odinga. Moi's public criticisms of Odinga in late 1965 and early 1966, therefore, were almost expected. Of course, personal and ideological antagonism also played a part. It was no secret that Moi had no time for Odinga's leftist flirtations; and for his part, Odinga made little effort to conceal his scorn for the "influence by the missions" on Moi and his inability to "make independent judgement[s]."[27] Yet clearly more was at work than a personality conflict. Public criticism of a sitting vice president by a senior minister was either political suicide or had been sanctioned from the very top.[28]

At KANU's national conference in Limuru in March 1966, Kenyatta removed any remaining doubts. In a thinly veiled attack on Odinga, Kenyatta warned that "the Government would not tolerate one man or group of people bent on corrupting the masses with foreign ideologies or engaged in subversive activities." During the party elections that followed, Odinga's allies were routed. Seeing the political writing on the wall, Odinga resigned as vice president shortly after the conference's close and started his own party—the leftist Kenya People's Party.[29] Attempting to retain KANU's image as a genuinely national party in which diverse opinions

---

25 *East Africa Standard*, "Missionaries Praised for Health."
26 The Honourable Jeremiah Nyagah speaking at the Rift Valley Academy commencement ceremony, 25 July 1967, handwritten notes of the address are available in the archives of the Rift Valley Academy, Kijabe, Kenya.
27 Odinga, *Not Yet Uhuru*, 143; Attwood, *Reds and the Blacks*, 234.
28 Morton, *Moi: The Making*, 124.
29 Branch, *Kenya: Between Hope*, 58.

and peoples could peacefully co-exist, Kenyatta initially appointed Pio Pinto's close friend and Odinga sympathizer, Joseph Murumbi, as vice president. However, apparently unable to reconcile his promotion with the murder of his fellow Goan, Murumbi resigned from political life at the end of 1966.

American Missionaries, Moi's Promotion, and US-Kenyan Relations, 1967–1978

Kenyatta's decision to replace Vice President Murumbi with Moi was the clearest sign yet that Kenya had thrown its lot in with the West. It also demonstrated the continuing influence that missionaries and the missionary network were having on Kenya's political trajectory. The strong support for Moi by Kenyatta confidant, Attorney General Charles Njonjo is a case in point. Njonjo and Moi shared a common pro-Western political philosophy, but the bond went deeper than politics.[30] While Njonjo was a product of Canon Leakey and the British CMS, and Moi a product of the largely American AIM, both were staunch Christians whose political ideals were firmly rooted in theological convictions. This religious bond also included an important family connection. Njonjo's wife, Margaret, was the daughter of the AIM missionaries who had baptized the young Moi and who were among the several evangelical missionaries who mentored Moi into young adulthood and beyond.[31]

While Margaret Njonjo's parents hailed from Northern Ireland, the majority of the AIM missionaries who played a prominent role in Moi's spiritual, educational, and political development were American. Moi's initial contact with AIM came in 1934, when he left his village as a ten-year-old to attend the AIM school fifty miles away in Kabartanjo. It was here that Moi was converted to evangelical Christianity by AIM missionaries and where he was baptized two years later. As his missionary education progressed, Moi became increasingly close to the Barnett family whose twin sons acted like his older brothers, and whose mother had been among Moi's favorite missionary teachers.[32]

In 1940, after six years living and studying under AIM missionaries, Moi successfully passed the colonial government's education exam and was admitted into the government's teacher training program at Kapsabet.

---

30 Margaret Njonjo, interview with the author, 13 November 2009.
31 Daniel arap Moi, interview with the author, 16 August 2011. Moi and Njonjo are each godfathers to one of the other's children, Margaret Njonjo, interview with the author, 3 December 2009.
32 Morton, *Moi: The Making*, 47–58.

Yet even here, his ties to his missionary mentors remained strong. Indeed, most school holidays found Moi returning not to his own home but to the Barnetts, or to the leading family of AIM converts in the area, the Bomets. After becoming one of the first government-certified African school teachers in the region, Moi married the Bomet's daughter Helena. Not surprisingly, the 1950 wedding was officiated by Moi's long-time friend, Paul Barnett. Two years later, the couple's first child was dedicated by Paul's twin brother and fellow AIM missionary, Erik Barnett.[33]

Moi's close connection to AIM continued into his early political career. In 1955, in the midst of the Mau Mau crisis, Moi was asked to run for a seat on the Legislative Council, the premier governing body in the colony. Despite AIM's general aversion to worldly politics, the blessing of one AIM missionary was critical to Moi's transition into government. Having been born and raised in Kenya as a child of missionaries, the Kalenjin-speaking Earl Andersen was a natural bridge between the Western and African worlds that Moi was now navigating.

Although by this point the widely respected Moi had been promoted to Headmaster at the government school in Kapsabet, before he could run for office, he still needed the written recommendation from the area's inspector. Andersen, who happened to be both a missionary with AIM and a government school's inspector, not only wrote the recommendation but forcefully encouraged the still reluctant Moi to pursue politics, arguing that Kenya needed Christians in leadership. Moi went on to decisively defeat the rival candidate and, later in 1955, became the Rift Valley's first representative on the Legislative Council. From this point, until his death in 1985, AIM's Earl Andersen was to be among Moi's closest confidants as he negotiated the minefields of colonial and post-colonial politics in Kenya.[34]

In short, from the moment the young Moi joined the AIM school at Kabartanjo up through his entry into politics, AIM missionaries had been among his closest friends and mentors, playing a central role in every significant milestone in the new vice president's life, including his conversion and baptism, his education, his marriage, the dedication of his children, and finally, his entry into politics.

The result of Moi's intimate relationship with the missionaries of AIM was not simply a lifelong loyalty to the missionaries and the missionary enterprise, but a worldview that, while distinctly Kalenjin, reflected the values and political sympathies of the American-evangelical brand

---

33 Morton, *Moi: The Making*, 62–67.
34 Ray and Jill Davis, interview with the author, 27 November 2009; Dilly Andersen, interview with the author, 28 November 2009; Howard Andersen, personal correspondence with the author, 10 September 2009; Morton, *Moi: The Making*, 63–75.

of Christianity under which he was raised. Considering Moi's already well-established track record of pro-West sympathies, it was reasonable to predict that his promotion to the position of vice president would precipitate a further strengthening of US-Kenyan relations. And it did. The next year, the highest ranking American official ever to visit the country, Vice President Hubert Humphrey, arrived in Nairobi.[35] The year after that, Moi made an official visit to the United States where—over initial objections—he held meetings with, among others, Secretary of State William Rogers, National Security Advisor Henry Kissinger, and President Richard Nixon.[36]

For a vice president of an African country to receive this sort of attention was unprecedented. But the State Department had a number of reasons for pushing the visit. First, it was now widely known that Kenyatta had suffered a stroke in 1968 and, while his health had improved, he was not expected to live much longer. Second, since independence, Kenya had become increasingly important to both American investors and to the stability of East and Central Africa. And third, the two countries were on the cusp of what, for America, was an unprecedented level of diplomatic cooperation in that region. Calling Kenya's "conservative government ... very friendly towards the United States," Secretary Rogers singled out Moi in particular as one with whom the American embassy in Nairobi enjoyed "excellent" relations. "A Presidential call" Rogers urged Nixon, "would have a powerful impact on the man we expect to be Kenya's next President."[37]

Despite the United States' bumbling of the logistics and protocol surrounding Moi's visit, the results were even more positive than Rogers had hoped. Moi arrived home to a rapturous response. On the front page of the *Daily Nation*, over a picture of Nixon and Moi shaking hands, ran the headline, "Nixon Pays Tribute to Kenya." Other dailies were equally exuberant citing the "growing cordiality" between the countries and Moi's reception by America's most powerful men as the "most prominent sign of [the] growing attunement [sic] of American attitudes to the aspirations of Africans."[38] As one US diplomat remarked, "reactions of ministers [which]

---

35 Nixon to Kenyatta, 29 April 1969, Nixon Presidential Library (NPL)/WHCF/Country Files/47/Kenya 1969–70.

36 NSC staffer Roger Morris argued that an appointment with Moi was not worth the President's time and Kissinger agreed, arguing to Nixon that Moi was not the only likely, or desired, presidential successor to Kenyatta. Morris to Kissinger, 21 April 1969; and Kissinger to Nixon, 23 April 1969, NPL/NSC/Country File/738/Kenya.

37 Rogers to Nixon, "Memorandum for the President," 15 April 1969, NPL/NSC/Country File/738/Kenya.

38 Kissinger to Morris, 13 May 1969, NPL/NSC/Country File/738/Kenya.

ranges from enthusiastic to ecstatic" were indicative of the fact that US-Kenyan relations had reached "a high point."[39]

This close relationship between Kenya and the United States that Moi had helped to forge continued largely uninterrupted during the remainder of the Kenyatta presidency. Nevertheless, both Moi and Kenya maintained a significant degree of political independence. Indeed, while Kenya's UN voting record was consistently more US-friendly than that of its East African neighbors, it remained more in line with other non-aligned nations than with pro-US nations like Britain and Israel.[40] Even Kenya's zealous anti-communism should not be seen principally as an attempt to curry favor with the Americans and the British, but instead as an authentic expression of its collective political values, which (thanks in part to the evangelical missionary movement) happened to largely coincide with America's own core values. According to Moi, Kenya's Cold War alignment with the United States was "not because of the Western world" per se; but was rather a reflection of the deep religious antipathy Kenyans held towards communism. The communists "did not believe in God," asserted Moi; communism "was contrary to our way of life."[41]

In 1976, Kenya's missionary and spiritually inspired alignment with US interests took a curious turn. This turn had less to do with how the two nations related directly to each other and more to do with how they related to Israel. On 4 July 1976, America's bicentennial celebration as fate would have it, Israeli commandos staged a startling rescue operation at Uganda's Entebbe airport, freeing 102 of the 106 hostages being held by members of the Popular Front for the Liberation of Palestine. Israelis, Americans, and some Europeans responded ecstatically. Innocent people had been saved, and the specter of terrorism that had been hanging over the world since the Munich Olympics had been dealt a firm blow. Yet for many in the Arab world, as well as for the Ugandan government, the Entebbe raid was humiliating. Uganda's Muslim dictator, Idi Amin, was furious, particularly with the Kenyan government whose logistical cooperation with the Israelis had played a significant role in the raid's success.[42]

---

39 AmEmbassy Nairobi to SecState, 15 May 1969, NPL/NSC/Country File/738/Kenya.
40 Kenya's vote, over strenuous US lobbying, to admit the People's Republic of China to the UN is just one notable example of Kenya's political independence. SecState to AmEmbassy Nairobi, 21 October 1971, NPL/NSC/Country/738/Kenya.
41 Daniel arap Moi, interview with the author, 16 August 2011.
42 Ben-Porat, Haber, and Schiff, *Entebbe Rescue*, 261–62, 309, 333–34. Amin had the lone remaining Israeli (who was in the hospital) executed as retribution, he executed the four people manning the control tower at Entebbe, and reportedly had three thousand people whose villages straddled the Uganda-Kenya border arbitrarily executed. Dunstan, *Entebbe*, 58.

The fallout from Kenya's support for Israel was not long in coming. In the United Nations, the raid and its backers were lambasted by none other than the UN Secretary General Kurt Waldheim who called the raid "a serious violation of the sovereignty of a State Member of the United Nations."[43] Just months later, a plane returning from Kampala carrying the Kenyan cabinet minister Bruce Mackenzie was blown up by a bomb allegedly planted by Ugandan agents.[44] Then, three years later, thirteen people were killed when Kenya's iconic and Jewish-owned Norfolk Hotel was destroyed by a terrorist bomb.[45] However, considering the context, the fallout could have been even worse.

Since the Yom Kippur War (1973) anti-Semitic feeling had been running high. Globally, OPEC had begun to use its economic muscle to punish nations, including the United States, who provided support to Israel during the conflict. In Africa, pressure from OPEC and the Muslim-dominated nations of North Africa led almost every African nation to break diplomatic relations with Israel. While Kenya's reluctant choice to follow suit was a largely cosmetic effort to stay in line with the official position of the OAU, in many of Kenya's neighbors anti-Israeli anger was real enough. Sudan and Somalia had large Muslim majorities and very close ties to the Middle East. Tanzania to Kenya's south and Ethiopia to its north also had large Muslim minorities that were increasingly strident in their demands for anti-Israeli positions. Finally, Kenya itself included important pockets of Muslims who, despite their relatively small numbers, had consistently acted as one of the greatest threats to the nation's internal security. By almost any geopolitical measure then, the potential costs of supporting Israel in the Entebbe raid far outweighed the benefits.[46] So why did Kenya do it?

In a meeting with an Israeli envoy soon after his release in 1961, Kenyatta provided the first hint. "We Kikuyu," the future president stated, "are the Jews of Africa."[47] Despite his own ambiguous relationship to

---

43 UN Press Release, SG/SM/2343 (8 July 1976) at 2, para. 9.
44 Dunstan, *Entebbe*, 58.
45 UPI/*NYTimes*, "Around the World."
46 Nadelmann, "Israel and Black Africa," 188–216.
47 Naim, "Perspectives: Jomo Kenyatta." *Jewish Political Studies Review*, 17:3-4. It is notable that based on his meetings with Naim, a future Israeli Ambassador to Kenya, Kenyatta asked Israel to train the former Mau Mau leader Waruhiu Itote as a potential future leader of the Kenyan Armed forces. Israel accommodated Kenyatta's request and established a close military and intelligence link with Kenyatta and Moi, thereby demonstrating that Kenya did have some geopolitical interests served by their relationship with Israel.

orthodox Christianity, Kenyatta, like most Kenyans whose education had been steeped in the biblical teachings of the missionaries, had come to identify his own story with that of the story of Israel. Significantly, this was equally true for the products of both the mission churches and the independent churches, albeit for slightly different reasons. For the syncretistic independent churches, the Jewish narrative had merged seamlessly with their own tribal myths. As Ngugi described it, in this re-imagining "black people were really the children of Israel. Moses was no other than Jomo himself."[48] Thanks to the translation of the Bible into the vernacular, this narrative gained even more rhetorical force. As one scholar has put it, "the God of Israel [became] the God of the Kikuyu and vice versa."[49] This phenomenon was not unique to the Kikuyu. The Kalenjin, for instance, believed themselves to be the descendants of the "wandering Jews" of ancient times.[50]

For mission-church congregants, this tribal identification with the biblical Jewish story was supplemented by the strongly pro-Israel sentiments within the evangelical missionary community, especially the Americans. In America, support for the state of Israel among conservative Protestants was already strong by 1948. However, by the early 1970s, this sentiment had become almost fanatical.[51] Pouring fuel on the fire in 1970, was Hal Lindsay's *The Late Great Planet Earth*—a sensationalistic, pro-Israel and anti-communist tale of Armageddon that quickly rose to the top of the *New York Times* bestseller list, where it stayed for the next decade, amassing sales of over thirty million copies. Pro-Israel sentiment among fundamentalist and evangelical Protestants had political consequences. For instance, in 1971, then Governor Ronald Reagan became the latest American political figure to publicly embrace this narrative, telling a Californian audience: "Ezekiel tells us that Gog, the nation that will lead all powers of darkness against Israel, will come out of the north ... it didn't make sense before the Russian Revolution ... Now it does."[52]

---

48 Ngugi wa Thiong'o, *Weep Not, Child*, 50.
49 Sanneh, *Encountering the West*, 156.
50 Morton, *Moi: The Making*, 23.
51 Perhaps the best example of the political significance of both the rising political muscle of the American evangelicals and their strong affinity for Israel, is the choice of the Nixon White House (likely with Israel's approval) to invite Billy Graham to the state dinner held in honor of Israeli Prime Minister, Golda Meir, and then to have him seated next to her during the dinner. Graham to Nixon, 5 March 1973, NPL/WHCF/Alpha Files/Billy Graham; Oren, *Power, Faith and Fantasy*, 523; Diamond, *Spiritual Warfare*, 15.
52 Gifford, *New Crusaders*, 13, 18.

For the products of the mission-church, the united effect of the indigenization of the Jewish story and the zealously pro-Israeli and anti-communist message of the missionaries was a potent combination. As future Permanent Secretary for Foreign Affairs Bethwell Kiplagat stated, Kenyatta's closest advisors during this period, men like "Njonjo and Moi ... had a very close sympathy with Israel" that was both "ideological" and "theological." For the American-trained vice president in particular, like the Jews of old, the modern state of Israel represented "the chosen people."[53] When combined with Israel's history of military and intelligence support for Kenyatta's moderate government, the powerful theological and cultural connection felt by many of Kenyatta's advisors helps explain Kenya's otherwise perplexing, and geopolitically risky choice to support the Entebbe raid. In the end, the choice appears to have been an easy one for the Kenyans. As one Israeli source noted, when Israel suggested that Kenya be rewarded for its support, the Kenyan government (likely Moi) replied that there would be "no charge." The cost of the aircraft fuel and medical services was simply "Kenya's contribution to the rescue."[54]

There is little question that during much of Kenyatta's regime it was Mzee himself who called the shots. However, outside of his own family members, perhaps the most powerful and influential Kenyan was Kenyatta's American-missionary-educated and ardently pro-West vice president. As minister of home affairs, it was Moi who had led the largely successful push to isolate the leftist Odinga. It was also Moi who went to great lengths to ensure that US-Kenyan relations remained close at a time when anti-Americanism was at its zenith in Africa. And, not surprisingly, it was Moi who presided over the increasingly numerous and public diplomatic exchanges between his government and the government of his missionary mentors. Yet as vice president, the extent to which Moi could determine Kenya's Cold War allegiances was always limited by the somewhat more ambiguous allegiances of the president. That was about to change.

---

53 Ambassador Bethwell Kiplagat, interview with the author, 29 April 2010.
54 Ben-Porat, Haber, and Schiff, *Entebbe Rescue*, 334. Kenya's strong pro-Israel stance grew even further under President Moi, as Kenya led the push for African rapprochement with Israel, and quietly but effectively supported Israel within the United Nations. Nadelmann, "Israel and Black Africa," 200–16; Ambassador Bethwell Kiplagat, interview with the author, 29 April 2010.

American Missionaries and US-Kenyan Relations in the Early Moi Years, 1978–1982

At 4 a.m. on 22 August 1978, the restless vice president was stirred by a faint ping on the chronically malfunctioning telephone in his rural Kabarak home. "The eyes of Kenyatta have closed," said the voice on the other end of the line. "Your Excellency, please keep your eyes open." Knowing of a plot by a cabal of Kikuyu insiders to seize power upon the president's death, Moi wasted no time in getting on the road to Nairobi. Indeed, just thirty minutes later, roadblocks set up by the conspirators to capture Moi were in place. But it was too late. Moi had already passed by safely on his way to Nairobi, where, with his hand placed on the Bible, he was duly sworn in as Kenya's second president. Had his unreliable phone failed, or had he been able to sleep better that night, Moi might not have lived to see the dawn. Reflecting the evangelical belief in divine intervention, Moi later told his biographer that that ping had "saved a president ... It was God's will that I got through."[55]

At least a year-and-a-half earlier, American policymakers were concerned enough about the stability of a post-Kenyatta Kenya that they quietly implemented a "political support program" to "strengthen elements likely to ensure stability" after the patriarch's passing. This included, among other things, at least two official working visits to the United States by Moi-led Kenyan delegations—one in early 1977 and one in early 1978, both of which included meetings with President Carter and his senior advisors.[56] Despite the legitimate fears of both Moi's domestic supporters and US policymakers that the pro-West vice president was vulnerable, the initial transition was smooth, producing in the words of one US policymaker, "a sense of elation" that Kenya was "on the threshold [of a] unique accomplishment in Africa: attainment of a peaceful transition of power within [a] constitutional framework."[57] Following free national elections, three months later Moi was inaugurated as Kenya's second president with several of his missionary mentors looking on proudly.[58]

---

55 "Significant Intelligence," 9 August 1978, Carter Presidential Library (CPL)/Recently Declassified Documents (RDD)/NLC-10-14-2-28-3; Morton, *Moi: The Making*, 162–64.
56 Vance to Carter, 28 February 1977, CPL/RDD/NLC-15-25-9-41-4; Henze to Brzezinski, 2 March 1977, CPL/NSA/Horn/3/3-77; Henze to Brzezinski, 16 March 1977, CPL/NSA/Horn/1/77; "Meeting with Kenyan Delegation," White House Statement, 2 March 1978, *Public Papers: Carter, 1978*; Carter to Kenyatta, March 1978, CPL/NSA/Horn/2/3-78.
57 Henze to Brzezinski, 29 August 1978, CPL/RDD, NLC-10-14-6-5-4.
58 Charles Njonjo, interview with the author, 16 August 2011.

Moi's post-Cold War reputation as a typical African strongman tends to obscure the fact that in the early years of his presidency he was seen by friends and foes alike as a genuine democratic reformer. Calling the first KANU election for years, Moi also presided over an improved human rights record and a 1979 election that one NSC staffer called "the only democratic election that has taken place in Africa in a long time."[59] As one of Kenyatta's political prisoners and self-proclaimed "people's watchdog," Martin Shikuku declared early in Moi's presidency, "I have no job. The job has been taken over by the president. I just follow."[60]

From the perspective of US policymakers, Moi's early domestic successes were trumped only by the even more explicitly pro-West foreign policy that developed under him. Outside of the close relationship that Moi had developed with the United States during his years as vice president and minister of home affairs, the first confirmation of his strong American affinity as president came in the 1979 debate over Uganda's post-Amin future. Ironically, in this case, although national interests were central for both nations, it was Kenya's pro-Western ideological purity that created problems for the more pragmatic US approach to the developing regional crisis.

Having come to power in 1971 through a military coup, by the mid-1970s the rule of the former Colonel Idi Amin had gone from erratic incompetence to a racially fueled barbarism that rivalled the Congo's Simba rebellion a decade earlier.[61] By February 1979, the rapidly deteriorating economic and humanitarian situation in Uganda had brought Amin's rule to the brink of collapse. Outside of their concern over the fate of the approximately 140 "hard core" American missionaries who had refused to evacuate, the primary US interest was seeing the end of Amin's regime and some semblance of stability return to the country.[62] American policymakers therefore welcomed the armed intervention of the Chinese-backed Tanzanian government, in spite of OAU opposition.

From Kenya's perspective, America's appeal to cooperate with the socialist Tanzanians was nothing short of mystifying. Since independence China had been Tanzania's largest external donor, supplying it with approximately four billion dollars in aid while actively promoting violent revolutions within Tanzania's pro-Western neighbors, Kenya and Zaire

---

59 Brzezinski to Vice President, 16 December 1978, CPL/RDD/NLC-6-69-7-16-6; Funk to Brzezinski, 2 April 1979, CPL/RDD/NLC-10-19-5-20-3.
60 Branch, *Kenya: Between Hope*, 141.
61 Shillington, *History of Africa*, 388, 418.
62 Vance to Carter, 2 February 1978, CPL/RDD/NLC-128-13-5-1-9.

(Congo).⁶³ Therefore, not only would a Tanzanian-backed Ugandan government mean that Kenya would be surrounded by ideologically-hostile neighbors, but that any Kenyan cooperation would likely create hostility toward Kenya amongst the Arab nations who were supporting the Muslim Amin—a fact that would almost certainly embolden Somalia's incessant demands for large pieces of Kenyan territory inhabited by ethnic Somalis.⁶⁴

In the end, it appears to have taken the personal intervention of President Carter to convince Moi to work quietly with the Tanzanians to support Amin's collapse. As the US ambassador who delivered Carter's message reported, Moi "sincerely wants to be helpful on this issue" but that his decision to block supplies from getting to Uganda and to begin a dialogue with Nyerere were "about as far as he feels he can go in accommodating our position."

Three points stand out regarding US-Kenya relations during the first regional crisis of Moi's presidency. The first was that Kenya was more concerned about the ideological composition of its neighbor than was the United States. Second was the obviously earnest desire by Moi to be helpful despite concerns over the potential negative consequences to Kenya's security interests—a fact repeated again and again by the US ambassador, who concluded one cable with the conviction that Moi's affinity for his American "friends" was "wholly genuine and very deeply felt." Third was the important role that the personal relationship between Carter and Moi had in shaping the outcome—a point we will return to shortly.⁶⁵ By May 1979, American policymakers were reporting that, from an American perspective, Kenya's condition domestically and diplomatically was "excellent" and that Kenya was cooperating in the stabilization of the post-Amin Uganda.⁶⁶

Just one month later, in June 1979, Moi arrived in London to begin his first official state visit as president. The choice to make Britain the location of his first state visit was rich in symbolism and evidence that, like his predecessor, Moi had come to view the colonial metropole not as a former oppressor but as a friend and ally. That the roots of his affection for Britain lay in his Christian faith and the influence of his missionary mentors was on display throughout the visit. Acting as first lady in the absence

---

63 Baregu, "Three Faces," 155.
64 AmEmbassy Nairobi to SecState, April 1979, CPL/RDD/NLC-16-20-3-6-3.
65 AmEmbassy Nairobi to SecState, April 1979, CPL/RDD/NLC-16-20-3-6-3.
66 Henze to Brzezinski, 2 May 1979, CPL/NSA/Horn/3/5-79.

of Mrs. Moi was the wife of the senior member of the Kenyan delegation, Attorney General Charles Njonjo. It was Margaret's AIM parents who had baptized Moi some forty years previously and who had played a critical role in the translation of the Bible into Moi's Kalenjin language group. The presence of Njonjo's Kenya-raised British wife effectively bridged the cultural gap between Moi and the British leaders. Thanks at least in part to this missionary bridge, British Secretary of State for Foreign Affairs Peter Carington, in particular, developed a close relationship with Moi that was to help lay the groundwork for a long and close diplomatic partnership with the UK.[67]

But there were other ways Moi's missionary-colored religion permeated the visit. At his insistence, a special Sunday service was arranged at which Tom Houston, the former pastor of Nairobi Baptist Church and the future president of World Vision, preached. This was followed by a trip to Bible House, the home of the British and Foreign Bible Society, where to his obvious pleasure, Moi was presented with a special copy of the Kalenjin Bible. Finally, near the end of the state visit, a special dinner was held at Lambeth Palace, the official home of the Archbishop of Canterbury. As Margaret Njonjo recalled, "on that occasion, it was raining, pouring with rain, and we had to get out of our vehicles to walk into the [dinner] and there was no cover. And [Moi]," Njonjo continued, "went to greet people in the pouring rain ... That was a huge boost to Kenya's image and his stature as a Christian leader."[68]

Just months later, Moi's faith again acted as a critical piece in Kenya's relationship with the United States. On 4 November 1979, radical supporters of Iran's Islamic revolution occupied the American embassy in Tehran. In the process, fifty-two Americans were taken hostage prompting an international diplomatic crisis. Moi's public response was curious for a head of state. Instead of diplomatic platitudes or calls for sanctions, he called for a national day of prayer in Kenya, and followed that up by writing to other heads of state to encourage them to do the same.[69] Whatever Moi's motives may have been, the effect on Carter appears to have been profound. Calling Moi a "friend and a brother" in a letter written a month after the hostage crisis began, Carter thanked the Kenyan

---

67 Margaret Njonjo, interview with the author, 3 December 2009. By this point Moi had separated from his wife, something both Moi and his missionary mentors were evidently embarrassed by.

68 Margaret Njonjo, interview with the author, 3 December 2009.

69 "Agenda, Meeting of December 18 with Mrs. Carter," CPL/WHCF /Subject Files/Co 80.

president in the most religiously intimate terms. "Words cannot express," Carter began, "the deep appreciation Rosalynn and I have for your concern and care that you have demonstrated for us during these days. Thank you for the spiritual leadership you have given throughout the world at this time to call the people of all nations to pray … We are very grateful," he continued, "for your personal expressions of love in Christ and the prayers of you and your countrymen … May the Lord's blessing be upon you."[70] In turn, when Moi made a private visit to the United States just two weeks later, the effect of Carter's letter was apparent. As one NSC staffer reported to Brzezinski, a team of State and Defense officials who had met with Moi during the visit had been given an "all we require" by President Moi.[71]

Had US-Kenya relations been unimportant, this deepening relationship between the two evangelical Christian leaders could easily be dismissed as an interesting but largely irrelevant footnote in the history of Cold War Africa. But circumstances made this relationship increasingly important to both nations. Kenya's destabilizing growth rate of nearly 4 percent made it one of the world's fastest growing nations. When combined with a dramatic collapse in the price of coffee and tea (Kenya's major exports) and the paucity of unused arable land, Kenya was entering a period of acute economic and political instability. In the short term at least, Kenya needed wealthy friends with open pockets.[72] Kenya's importance to the United States had also grown thanks to the region's geopolitical circumstances. Ethiopia's now clearly hard-lined pro-Moscow tilt and Somalia's untrustworthy diplomatic opportunism meant that, in Africa's strategic horn, only Sudan and Kenya were allies; and of the two, only Kenya was seen as a viable base for the US Navy's increasingly important presence in the area. These strategic concerns were about to increase exponentially. On Christmas Eve 1979, the Soviet Union invaded Afghanistan and America began to rally its friends.[73]

Moi was back in Washington two months later, but this time on an official state visit, the first ever for a Kenyan president.[74] US policymakers meeting with Moi privately prior to and during the state visit confirmed the presence of this ideological bond and seemed genuinely taken aback by

---

70 Carter to Moi, 4 December 1979, CPL/Plains Files/Presidential Personal Foreign Correspondence/2/Kenya.
71 Funk to Brzezinski, 21 December 1979, CPL/RDD/NLC-24-123-6-5-8.
72 Briefing Paper, 12 February 1980, CPL/NSA/Brzezinski/VIP/10/Kenya-Moi.
73 Funk to Brzezinski, 18 December 1979, CPL/RDD/NLC-17-55-4-21-6.
74 Louis Martine to Phil Wise and Fran Voorde, 30 January 1980, CPL/WHCO/Subject Files/CO80.

the depth of Moi's anti-communism, the pride he took in being associated with the US, and how "strikingly similar" Moi's analysis of recent Cold War developments were to their own.[75] Also conspicuous was just how closely Moi identified with his evangelical "brother" Carter and with the United States. The results were dramatic. Despite being well aware of the "considerable fire" Kenya would receive from both the Eastern bloc and many non-aligned nations, Moi confirmed that Kenya would not only allow the US Navy full access to the Mombasa port, they would also join the US boycott of the Moscow Olympics.[76]

Outside of the hallowed image of Jomo Kenyatta, there was nothing that Kenyans took more pride in than the success of their renowned athletes on the global stage. As a result, Moi's choice to remove Kenya from the world's greatest international athletic event for the purpose of symbolically supporting the West, in a dispute that had little direct impact on Kenya, carried with it considerable domestic political risks.[77] Moi conceded as much in his toast at the state dinner. Unlike other nations who were participating in the boycott, "with no prospects of securing medals," Moi noted, Kenya was making a significant "sacrifice because we were very hopeful that we were going to secure gold medals."[78]

From the US perspective, the state dinner was an unequivocal success and deepened the bond between the nations to the extent that the relationship would largely weather the challenges to it brought on by the end of the Cold War and the increasing authoritarianism of Moi's government in the late 1980s and early 1990s. The role of Moi's Christian faith and his American-mission-influenced worldview played a central role in the early stages of this diplomatic bond. As Carter acknowledged at the state dinner, "[Moi] and I have gotten to be good friends through our frequent communications with one another ... We share moral values. We share religious faith, and we share political values as well, not only on a personal basis but among the people of our two countries."[79]

---

75 David Aaron to the President, 5 February 1980, CPL/RDD/NLS-1-14-1-10-3; Warren Christopher to the President, 21 February 1980, CPL/RDD/NLC-128-15-2-15-5.

76 "Daily Report," Aron to Carter, 5 February 1980, CPL/RDD/NLC-1-14-1-10-3. Exchange of Remarks between the President and His Excellency President Daniel T. arap Moi, President of Kenya, February 18–22, 1980, CPL/Speechwriters/Chronological Files/64/Moi.

77 Henze to Ermath, 21 January 1980, CPL/NSA/Horn/4/1-80.

78 Exchange of Remarks between the President and His Excellency President Daniel T. arap Moi, President of Kenya, February 18–22, 1980, CPL/Speechwriters/Chronological Files/64/Moi.

79 Arrival Statements, 18 February 1980, CPL/Speechwriters/Chronological Files/64/Arrival Statement/Moi.

The momentum created by the Carter-Moi relationship continued into the Reagan administration. Within months of becoming president, Reagan's State Department began pushing for an official working visit for Moi who had just assumed the chairmanship of the Organization of African Unity (OAU). Recognizing, as Paul Bremer argued, America's "need" for "Kenya's and arap Moi's continuing support," a two-day visit was duly scheduled for September 1981.[80] Once again, personal faith and religiously based ideology played a central role.

Perhaps less substantial and more sentimental than the faith of his predecessor, there is little question that Reagan viewed the Cold War in fundamentally religious terms.[81] The attempt on his life just months earlier had also heightened Reagan's religious sensibilities. As he confided in his journal shortly after the shooting, "Whatever happens now I owe my life to God, and will try to serve him in every way I can!"[82] The president's renewed religiosity and the Americans' keen awareness of the importance of Moi's faith resulted in an unusually high profile for religion during the visit. As Reagan stressed in his remarks at the official lunch, the "natural bond" enjoyed by the two nations went beyond realpolitik. It was based on a "commonality of belief and value." "We are," Reagan continued, "importantly, both God fearing people ... And while others may dismiss this as irrelevant, you and I, President Moi, know just how important it is."[83]

Less blatant, but perhaps just as significant, was the American-missionary-flavored composition of Moi's top foreign policy team. Of the four Kenyans who met together with Reagan privately during the visit, at least three had close educational and religious ties to American missionaries. In addition to Moi, whose American missionary history was already well-known, both Foreign Minister Robert Ouko and Permanent Secretary in the Office of the President Simeon Nyachae could boast strong American missionary pedigrees.

---

80 Richard Allen to Michael Deaver, 6 July 1981, Reagan Presidential Library (RPL)/WHORM Files/Subject File/ CO-080/040000-299999; Bremer to Allen, 10 June 1981, RPL/WHORM Files/Subject File/ CO-080/040000-299999.

81 Preston, *Sword of the Spirit*, 579–600.

82 Entry for 30 March 1981, *Reagan Diaries Unabridged: Vol. 1*.

83 It is unclear whether the last, most personal phrase, in this quote was actually said at the Luncheon. Multiple drafts of the speech exist in Reagan archives. In the two last edits, one includes the phrase, and one has the phrase penciled out. Either way, the speech is an example of Reagan and his speechwriters explicitly reaching out to Moi based on his strong Christian convictions and his emotional connections to America through his missionary mentors. "Luncheon for Moi," version of 24 September 1981, RPL/WHORM/ Subject File/CO-080/Kenya/0-39999.

Nyachae, for instance, had been baptized and educated by American Seventh-Day Adventist (SDA) missionaries in his home area of Kisii. He was also the young civil servant who had helped organize Moi's efforts to bring world leaders together in prayer during the Iran hostage crisis.[84] While Nyachae's view of God did not always stay within the narrow confines of SDA theology, the influence of the mission—especially through the faith and ethics of his deeply devout mother—was unmistakable throughout his political career.[85] Through daily Bible reading, prayer, abstinence from alcohol, punctuality, and hard work, Nyachae stressed in his memoirs, "My mother had an indelible influence in my life." "She never forgot to remind us," Nyachae continued, "that nothing happened to us without God's involvement. It is because of her influence that we pray daily in my household. I pray before I go to sleep or when I am about to make a decision on a major issue. I have maintained this since my childhood."[86]

The influence of American missionaries on Foreign Minister Ouko was even more direct. Robert Ouko had received his early education at the AIM school at Ogada and had been mentored as a boy by the American missionaries Rev. and Mrs. Skoda, whose eldest son had been close childhood friends with the future foreign minister.[87] As an up and coming civil servant, Ouko and his evangelical wife Christabel had developed a strong relationship with the Southern Baptist Hampton family; and when Ouko had moved to Arusha, Tanzania as Kenya's Minister for East African Affairs, his family had forged an even closer relationship with Robert and Jean Ward, American evangelical Lutheran missionaries working there.

Indeed, this relationship was so close that the Wards became godparents to Ouko's daughter Lillian. And when the Wards were forced to leave Tanzania under duress, it was Robert who stayed up with them through the night as they packed and then drove them across Tanzania and Kenya to the Ouko's family home in Kora, where the Wards were guests until the Kenyan government granted them visas to continue their work in Kenya.[88] While the Christian faith that Ouko claimed throughout his life was not always lived out with the same puritanical zeal found in his president, his political and ideological sympathies appear to have closely reflected those

---

84 Nyachae to Douglas Coe, 23 December 1980, BGC/CN459/236.
85 Grace Nyachae, interview with the author, 24 May 2010.
86 Nyachae, *Walking through the Corridors*, 29–32; Leonard, *African Successes*, 269, 222.
87 Skoda, *Ogada: An African Passage*, 8, 26.
88 Robert and Jean Ward, interview with the author, 17 December 2009.

of his American missionary teachers, mentors, and friends. As future US Ambassador Smith Hempstone noted, it was not without reason that Ouko, "was regarded as pro-West ... with many friends in the West."[89]

The fact that Moi had chosen to surround himself with others who had been influenced by American missionaries is significant and, considering his own background and missionary-inspired worldview, certainly makes sense. It is especially unsurprising when we consider the extent to which American missionaries continued to interact with Moi during his early years as president. Interactions at multiple public events such as his regular church attendance, participation in international Christian conferences, and other missionary or church related ceremonies ensured that, symbolically at least, Moi would not lose touch with the American missionary community.[90] However, it was the volume of private meetings that missionaries enjoyed with the Kenyan president that demonstrated most clearly the degree to which that community maintained its influence on Moi. Among the veteran American missionaries active in the early 1980s, almost all had at least met the president, with many having shared meals with him at either his Kabarak home or at State House.[91] As Charles Njonjo noted, Moi "had time for them, even at State House. He would make time to see them."[92] Indeed, on more than one occasion, he delayed cabinet meetings or kept foreign diplomats waiting in order to spend a few more minutes with his American mentors and friends.[93]

Yet while it seems clear that Moi continued to have a great deal of affection for the American missionary community, and that his own Cold War allegiances fundamentally aligned with those of his missionary friends, it appears that most of these relationships were largely apolitical.

---

89 Hempstone, *Rogue Ambassador*, 65

90 Roy and Judy Entwistle, interview with the author, 11 July 2009; Dick and Flo Gehman, interview with the author, 10 July 2009; Moi Speech, 75th Anniversary of AIM work in Kenya, 12 July 1981, BGC/CN81/34/18; Chuck and Bobbi Kinzer, interview with the author, 11 July 2009; Art Davis, interview with the author, 28 November 2009; Ray and Jill Davis, interview with the author, 27 November 2009. It should be noted that among other ongoing interactions with the American missionaries, Moi also sent two of his sons to AIM's school for missionary children, the Rift Valley Academy. Mike and Janet Atkins, interview with the author, 1 October 2009; Tim Cook, interview with the author, 1 October 2009; Phil Dow, "School in the Clouds", 252; AIC Kijabe Medical Centre Report, 1979, BGC/CN81/34.

91 Roy and Judy Entwistle, interview with the author, 11 July 2009; Chuck and Bobbi Kinzer, interview with the author, 11 July 2009; Art Davis, interview with the author, 28 November 2009; Ray and Jill Davis, interview with the author, 27 November 2009.

92 Charles Njonjo, interview with the author, 16 August 2011.

93 Mary Honer, interview with the author, 16 February 2010; Chuck and Bobbi Kinzer, interview with the author, 11 July 2009.

There were, however, exceptions to this rule. Perhaps the most fascinating was his lifelong relationship with AIM's Earl Andersen. From Andersen's 1954 endorsement of Moi for a seat on the Legislative Council, throughout his time as vice-president, and then as he began his presidency, the Kalenjin-speaking missionary had been a "personal friend and confidant." Indeed, as Moi's years in politics grew and the circle of people he could trust decreased, Moi appears to have found in his AIM mentor the ideal advisor—a religious kindred spirit with a deep understanding of both the Kenyan and Western worldviews and a forty-year track record of loyalty.[94]

According to a number of well-placed sources, right up until Andersen was killed in a car accident in 1985, he had virtually unfettered access to Moi. Andersen visited Moi at his Kabarak home often and was "never turned away." "Even at odd times," Andersen's children remarked, he "would be welcomed."[95] But the relationship was far from a one-way street. In fact, more often, it was Moi who would call Andersen in for advice. While Andersen never divulged the content of the meetings, he did acknowledge that at times the meetings regarded, "matters of State."[96] Another Moi confidant, the Kenyan bishop of the African Inland Church confirmed as much stating, Moi consulted with missionaries regularly, and "not only on spiritual matters. He was also consulted on what the West was thinking about us."[97] Whatever the content of these meetings may have been, Andersen's strong, and generally pro-US, political opinions make it likely that during the first seven years of Moi's presidency Washington had a powerful advocate close to the Kenyan president.[98]

During the same period, American evangelicals also had a direct influence on Kenya's diplomatic affairs through the Fellowship. Previously

---

94 Howard Andersen, interview with the author, 10 September 2009.
95 Dilly Andersen, interview with the author, 28 November 2009; Ray and Jill Davis, interview with the author, 27 November 2009; Howard Andersen, interview with the author, 10 September 2009.
96 Dilly Andersen, interview with the author, 28 November 2009; Howard Andersen, interview with the author, 10 September 2009.
97 Bishop Silas Yego, interview with the author, 18 December 2009; in an interview by the author with Moi, when asked if he did seek out advice from his missionary friends, the former Kenyan president simply answered, "Yes, of course ... all the time." Daniel arap Moi, interview with the author, 16 August 2011.
98 Dilly Andersen, interview with the author, 28 November 2009. The continuing influence on Moi was assumed even as late as the early 1990s, when Smith Hempstone, clearly irritated by this possible influence, stated in his memoir, "Whether he was encouraged in [his authoritarian policies] by American fundamentalist missionaries, who were in Kenya in great numbers and tended to be pro-Moi, I do not know." Hempstone, *Rogue Ambassador*, 38.

known as International Christian Leadership (ICL), the Fellowship was the quietly influential organization responsible for hundreds of bipartisan prayer groups around Washington; and, as we saw in Ethiopia, an international network of increasing diplomatic significance.[99] Moi's own association with the Fellowship had begun prior to independence. In 1960, Eisenhower's right-hand man, Kansas Senator Frank Carlson, had invited Moi and another rising Kenyan leader to ICL's annual international meeting in the Netherlands.[100] Although he attended, Moi's contact with ICL was sporadic until 1979, when US Senators Sam Nunn and Roger Jepsen visited Kenya and met with Moi. This meeting was followed by an invitation to Moi to attend the annual National Prayer Breakfast in Washington. Because the National Prayer Breakfast came less than two weeks before his state visit, Moi did not attend. Instead, the Fellowship arranged for a special prayer breakfast at Blair House near the end of the state visit, which included a number of prominent American policymakers and during which Moi gave a well-received address. The group, wrote Fellowship leader Douglas Coe, "were very very pleased and encouraged" and "felt that the Holy Spirit really guided you in your comments."[101]

It was not long before Moi's reconnection with the Fellowship bore significant diplomatic fruit. Sometimes referred to as an "underground State Department," in 1981 this network was at the center of an unexpected rapprochement between Kenya and its volatile neighbor, Somalia.[102] Since independence, Somalia's ethnically based claims to significant portions of Ethiopian and Kenyan territory had made it the center of regional tensions. Indeed, from 1963–1967, Kenya had fought a guerrilla war against Somali-backed insurgents who had sought inclusion into a "Greater Somalia."

Popularly known as the Shifta War, the conflict had destabilized the young Kenya and left a legacy of deep mistrust toward Somalia within

---

99   Lindsay, *Faith in the Halls*, 36. Lindsay cites, "several hundred" such groups. However, his numbers are from the turn of the twenty-first century. Nevertheless, according to the Washington Post in 1981, there were "dozens" of Fellowship prayer groups within the Senate alone, and other weekly groups meeting virtually every day in both the Pentagon and the State Department. The Fellowship was equally active in the House of Representatives and other government bodies, making the claim of "hundreds" highly plausible. Suplee, "Power and the Glory," H1.

100 Frank Carlson to Patrick Renison, Governor of Kenya, 29 March 1960, BGC/CN459/236.

101 Coe to James Mageria, 22 December 1979, BGC/CN459/236; Coe to Moi, 22 December 1979, BGC/CN459/236; Coe to Moi, 8 January 1980, BGC/CN459/236; Coe to Moi, 5 March 1980, BGC/CN459/236; Coe to Ouko, 5 March 1980, BGC/CN459/236; Coe to Njonjo, 5 March 1980, BGC/CN459/236; Njonjo to Coe, 17 March 1980, BGC/CN459/236.

102 Lindsay, *Faith in the Halls*, 32–36.

the first generation of Kenya's political elite.[103] Somalia's well-earned reputation as a force of regional instability was confirmed in 1977, when it invaded Ethiopia. The Ogaden War provoked a Cold War-infused regional arms race during which the USSR provided upwards of one billion dollars in military aid and Cuba provided roughly fifteen thousand troops in support of their zealous new communist convert's attempt to resist Somalia's invasion. Despite the fact that Somalia had previously modelled its governance on scientific socialism, the USSR's decision to back the more ideologically pure Ethiopian regime threw Somalia at the mercy of the United States, who duly obliged by providing significant, albeit much more modest, amounts of aid to its former ideological enemy.[104]

While the war officially ended in March 1978, Somali-backed guerrilla warfare continued until at least 1981. Although Ethiopia's radical turn to the left was anathema to Moi and the Kenyans, Somalia's public support for the destabilizing concept of a "greater Somalia" and its history of aggression placed Kenya on the side of Ethiopia and at odds with Somalia—America's newest "friend" in the strategic horn of Africa. The continuing tensions between Kenya and Somalia, then, acted to undermine US efforts to isolate the radical Ethiopian regime and bring pro-Western stability to the region.[105] Somalia's unwillingness to publicly relinquish its demands for a greater Somalia meant that rapprochement between it and Kenya was virtually unthinkable in 1981. As Njonjo made clear to one US diplomat, Kenya's "principal concern militarily is Somalia. If [it] would renounce its claim on our territory and leave us in peace, we would scrap the whole arms build-up program."[106] Within Somalia, however, the concept of greater Somalia was the most potent unifying force in an otherwise dysfunctional nation-state deeply divided along clan lines. As a result, to Somali strongman Barre, continuing support for the principle was a non-negotiable. The ensuing stalemate did not bode well for either US interests or regional peace.[107]

Early in 1981, an American associated with the Fellowship visited Barre in Somalia and explained to him the Fellowship's desire to see world leaders seeking peace "in the spirit of Christ." Astonishingly, at

---

103 Vance to the President, 28 February 1977, CPL/RDD/NLC-15-25-9-41-4; Branch, *Kenya: Between Hope*, 29–33.
104 Westad, *Global Cold War*, 250–87.
105 "Somalia-Kenyan Reconciliation Effort," CPL/RDD/NLC-15-47-10-2-1.
106 Njonjo quoted in Funk to Brzezinski, 15 January 1979, CPL/RDD/NLC-10-17-6-22-2.
107 "Somalia-Kenya: Presidential Meeting," 8 September 1979, CPL/RDD/NLC-17-21-47-14-4.

the meeting's conclusion, the Muslim Barre told the American that, on that basis, he would be willing to meet with Moi. When the American returned to Washington, he passed on this information to members of the Fellowship's Pentagon prayer group. When Barre visited Washington late that May to discuss Somalia's military needs, one of the American generals involved in these meetings recalled the Fellowship representative's report and invited the Somali dictator to the Pentagon prayer breakfast the next morning. Barre's attendance led to a private suggestion by the chairman of the Joint Chiefs of Staff, General David Jones, that Barre meet with Moi.

Barre's apparent interest then led to the Under-Secretary of the Navy, another Pentagon prayer group member, making a US aircraft carrier available for a secret meeting between the two African leaders. This secret meeting, in turn, laid the groundwork for an unexpected joint communiqué at the end of the 1981 meeting of the OAU. On its surface, the communiqué between Kenya and Somalia was relatively modest, stating a mutual "commitment to continue to promote better understanding and collaboration" between the two countries. Nevertheless, this meeting initiated a dialogue that ultimately produced Kenya's first state visit to Somalia in 1984 and a Kenya-brokered Ethiopia-Somalia dialogue in the following year—both previously unthinkable. In short, the Fellowship's considerable diplomatic connections, and its long-term relationship with Moi, helped produce a religiously inspired diplomatic breakthrough that would have been difficult to otherwise predict.[108]

American Missionaries and US-Kenyan Relations, 1982–1991

On 1 August 1982, Kenyans woke to the music of Bob Marley and an announcement on government radio that "our country is fully and firmly under the control of the armed forces." Had things gone exactly according to plan, this might have been accurate. As it was, Nairobi was soon embroiled in a two-day gun battle between the majority of the armed forces who remained loyal to Moi and the largely Luo coup-plotters who had seized the radio station and a few other strategic installations in the early hours of the morning. In retrospect, it was a poorly planned attempt by a tribal minority who wrongly believed that popular opinion was against Moi, and it was put down with relative ease and minimal loss of life. However, the long-term effects of the attempted coup were considerable.[109]

---

108 Johnston and Sampson, *Religion, the Missing Dimension*, 321–23. The joint communiqué is quoted in Makinda, *Superpower Diplomacy*, 48.
109 Branch, *Kenya: Between Hope*, 154–58; Nyachae, *Walking through the Corridors*, 91–93.

According to future US Ambassador Smith Hempstone, "the person most profoundly and fatefully changed by the abortive 1982 coup was Moi himself."[110] Feeling he could no longer afford the level of trust he had placed in others, Moi tightened his circle of confidants and increasingly privileged ethnic ties at the expense of expertise and competence—something he had largely avoided in his early years as president.[111] The most obvious example of this was his decision to have his powerful Kikuyu confidant— the staunchly pro-West minister of constitutional affairs, Charles Njonjo— investigated for alleged connections to the coup attempt. The subsequent inquiry was largely inconclusive, but it had the effect of removing Njonjo from government and dramatically weakening the power and influence of Njonjo and the Kikuyu elites on Moi's administration.[112] In their place came an increasingly dubious assortment of ethnic allies or those who had, like Moi's permanent secretary of internal security, Hezekiah Oyugi, demonstrated extraordinary personal loyalty to the president during the coup attempt.[113]

Until 1985, this growing ethnic insularity was at least partly balanced by Moi's continued reliance on the advice of AIM missionary Earl Andersen and other remnants of the older generation of missionaries who had mentored the Kenyan president over the years. In fact, in the weeks prior to their deaths, the Andersens had, for ten days, been Moi's guests at his Lake Baringo home. However, on 29 September 1985, the vehicle in which Andersen and his wife were travelling was struck by a truck. Esther Andersen was killed immediately, and shortly thereafter Earl succumbed to his injuries. At the funeral, a deeply moved Moi placed a wreath on the grave as "a representative of the family."[114]

While the influence of American missionaries on Moi's day-to-day decision-making almost certainly declined with Andersen's death, their impact on Kenya as a whole showed no sign of diminishing. Thanks to the Kenyan government's pro-missionary sentiment and the significant amount of religious freedom present in the country, post-colonial Kenya

---

110 Hempstone, *Rogue Ambassador*, 37.
111 Margaret Njonjo, interview with the author, 13 November 2009; Bishop Silas Yego, interview with the author, 18 December 2009.
112 Morton, *Moi: The Making*, 195–204; Charles Njonjo, interview with the author, 16 August 2011; Margaret Njonjo, interview with the author, 13 November 2009.
113 Morton, *Moi: The Making*, 190.
114 Honer, *Missy Fundi, Kenya Girl*, 367–68; Dilly Andersen, interview with the author, 28 November 2009; Howard Andersen, interview with the author, 10 September 2009.

had experienced an explosion of missionary activity.[115] During the 1970s and 1980s, American missions were particularly influential in the health care and development sectors. At the end of the Cold War, over 30 percent of Kenya's hospitals continued to be run by missions—with most being evangelical American.[116] The growth in the evangelical population in Kenya during this period is even more significant. Between 1970 and 1990, the evangelical population in Kenya quadrupled from 2.75 million to 11 million. Even when the nation's rapid population growth is factored in, Protestant evangelicalism grew during this period from roughly 24 to 47 percent of the total population.[117] While these statistics can obscure the important indigenization of Christianity in Africa, they do suggest the significant influence American evangelical missions continued to have during the last two decades of the Cold War—leading one scholar to conclude that, "far from being irrelevant, US evangelical missions [were] at the heart of some of the most important changes occurring in the political economy of the country since independence."[118]

Whether it was a desire to tap into the political potential of this growing religious movement, a result of his own religious convictions, or some combination of the two, Moi often justified his domestic program in distinctly evangelical Christian terms. This tendency was especially conspicuous in his 1986 book, *Kenya African Nationalism*, which laid out the principles behind his *Nyayo* governing philosophy.[119] Beginning by thanking his "teachers and Christian missionaries" who gave him his education and "the Christian faith which has permanently reshaped my life," Moi goes on to make explicit the influence of that faith on his political philosophy.[120] "Nyayoism ... the cornerstone in the building of a nation" Moi argued, is "fired by the eternal

---

115 Hearn, "'Invisible' NGO," 41. The ratio of US Protestant missionaries to the population in 1992 was roughly: (Brazil—1:69K); (Philippines—1:32K); (Mexico—1:51K); (Japan—1:76K); and (Kenya—1:18K). In short, of the top five nations in terms of US Protestant missionary numbers, Kenya almost doubled its nearest competitor in terms of missionary density.
116 Hearn, "'Invisible' NGO," 47–56.
117 Barrett, Kurion, and Johnson, *World Christian Encyclopedia*, 426. These numbers combine "Evangelicals" with "Charismatic/Pentecostal" which is fairly standard practice.
118 Hearn, "'Invisible' NGO," 156.
119 Moi, *Kenya African Nationalism*. It is important to note that much of the book promotes policies that, relative to the African political context, most Western observers would continue to consider "liberal" or "progressive" including Moi's stress on education, the rights of women, the need for indigenous African leadership to answer African problems, and the value of individualism, hard work, and integrity in political leadership. It is primarily in his defence of curtailing academic freedom, and his support for a one-party state, that we see the seeds of authoritarianism.
120 Moi, *Kenya African Nationalism*, xvi.

concepts of a living Christian faith" and "singularly embeds the kernel of the principles of Christian life into the national philosophy," principles he explicitly applied to himself stating that, "depending upon its management and application, and depending upon the moral rectitude and positive response of those being led, leadership can procreate glory or disaster. After all," Moi concluded, "even Satan is a leader, but a leader to the eternal disaster of consuming hell."[121]

Unfortunately, the decidedly mixed nature of the remaining sixteen years of his presidency, which included increasing authoritarianism and decreasing political and intellectual freedom, were largely an indictment of Moi's inability to live up to these Christian principles domestically. As a result, even some of the once unswervingly loyal evangelical community in Kenya began to distance themselves from their Christian president. While the missionary community either continued to support Moi or kept their opinions to themselves, evangelical Kenyans, especially those outside of the president's Kalenjin community, were increasingly vocal in their opposition. In the ethnically dominated Kenyan political landscape it was assumed that non-Kalenjin evangelicals from mainline denominations would be critical. However, by the mid-1980s, even some within the constellation of American-influenced groups, such as Mutava Musyimi, the influential pastor of Nairobi Baptist Church, had become outspoken in their critique of the Moi government and the president himself.[122]

In terms of diplomacy, however, Moi's record was more consistent with his stated Christian ideals. During the final years of the Cold War, Moi's government was at the forefront of multiple regional peace efforts including Kenya's rapprochement with Somalia, attempts at improving the relationship between Ethiopia and Somalia in the aftermath of the Ogaden War, efforts to stabilize the post-Amin Uganda, the re-opening of the Kenya-Tanzania border, and the successful efforts to initiate mediation in civil wars in Sudan and Mozambique.[123]

Despite his largely successful peace-making efforts (efforts which were consistently in-line with US interests in the region) and his consistent and zealous pro-Western anti-communism, by the late 1980s Moi's increasingly checkered domestic record had begun to damage his relationship with

---

121 Moi, 24, 36, 31, 79.
122 Dan, "Kenyan Intellectuals," 22–38.
123 Fields to Cherono, "Peace Talks for Ethiopia, Sudan, and Mozambique," 29 November 1989, World Vision Archives (WVA)/Admin Files/Kenya; Bethwell Kiplagat, interview with the author, 29 April 2010; Cohen, *Intervening in Africa*, 12; Smith, "Kenyan ambassador for peace."

the United States. While relations remained officially strong, as seen by the effusive praise Reagan gave Kenya both publicly and privately during Moi's second official working visit in 1987, cracks were beginning to appear.[124] Indeed, even Reagan's strong praise had been made over objections from prominent policymakers.[125] Making matters worse, in the days surrounding his departure, the sentiments behind these objections were publicly and embarrassingly aired in a *Washington Post* article criticizing Moi's human rights record.[126]

Growing concerns aside, with the Cold War's end still apparently in the distant future, Washington was not willing to cast off a loyal supporter. Even as late as 1989, when Smith Hempstone arrived in Nairobi as the new US ambassador to Kenya, official American sentiment remained essentially pro-Moi.[127] However, the fall of the Berlin Wall that same year and the subsequent reappraisal of US interests in the post-Cold War world, exposed the extent to which US support for Moi had begun to crumble. Over the next decade, the US increasingly drew a distinction between its support for Kenya and its support for Moi, leaving the famous product of American missions feeling, in the words of one confident, "betrayed."[128] Despite this sense of betrayal, Moi's lifelong affection for the United States (as well as important pragmatic considerations) meant that while the US grew increasingly critical, Moi and his government remained generally steadfast in their pro-US sympathies. The result was that when Moi stepped aside in 2002 upon the election of Mwai Kibaki as president, US relations with the new government were cordial—if not as intimate as they had been during the Cold War zenith of Moi's presidency.

---

124 In addition to Reagan's glowing public comments, the US president confided in his journal on the day of the departure statements, "Kenya thanks to him [Moi] is the best organized country in Africa and the most free enterprise one. Our meetings were very good and he's overjoyed." 12 March 1987, *Reagan Diaries Unabridged: Vol. 2*.

125 Reagan Presidential Remarks, Departure Statement for President Moi of Kenya, 12 March 1987, RPL/WHORM Files/Subject Files/CO 080/483257; Memorandum, Herman J. Cohen to Grant S. Green, 9 March 1987, RPL/WHORM Files/Subject Files/CO080/483257.

126 Harden, "Police Torture Is Charged." The article, submitted on the day of the departure statements, was not actually published until the day after the departure statements; although Moi may still have been in the country when the article was published.

127 Hempstone, *Rogue Ambassador*, 39.

128 Bethwell Kiplagat, interview with the author, 29 April 2010.

"A Broad Popular Consensus," 1963–1991

Conclusion

It is important to remember that there was nothing inevitable about Kenya's pro-West Cold War path. The majority of the region's nations (even those like Tanzania and Uganda who had otherwise similar colonial and cultural histories) had nowhere near the same level of consistent enthusiasm for the United States. Only Ethiopia and the Congo/Zaire might be held up as potential rivals. Yet, as we have seen when Ethiopia's pro-American Emperor was overthrown in 1974–1975, the new Ethiopian regime quickly and dramatically turned their backs on the United States—demonstrating the extent to which that relationship had been rooted in the person of Haile Selassie. Even the relatively consistent relationship between the US and Mobutu's Congo cannot be held up as one of a natural political affinity, but rather as a pragmatic association in which American policymakers, in the pursuit of regional stability, willingly propped up the ideologically ambiguous Congolese dictator.

The previous two chapters have argued that the uniquely consistent and strong relations between Kenya and the United States during the Cold War can be traced, at least in part, to the unparalleled influence of American evangelical missionaries. What made Kenya unique among the nations of East and Central Africa during the Cold War was not the presence of American missionaries, or even the significant role they played in US relations with their host country. It was the extent to which American-style evangelicalism had influenced the cultural and religious values of the nation.

Unlike the examples of Selassie in Ethiopia and to a lesser extent even Tshombe in the Congo, Moi was not so much an exception but a symptom of a grassroots and missionary-inspired pro-West sentiment, a point made by National Security Advisor Zbigniew Brzezinski in 1980 when he noted that Moi's pro-West convictions were, "backed by a broad popular consensus."[129] This is not to say that Cold War Kenya was universally pro-American. It certainly was not. It is only to say that during this period, to a degree unique in the region, the products of the evangelical missionary effort made up a politically viable critical mass—and it was this critical mass that allowed pro-American political figures like Moi to cultivate a relationship with the United States that would have been untenable and unsustainable in the other nations of the region.

---

129 Daily Report, Brzezinski to Carter, 22 April 1980, Jimmy Carter Presidential Library (JCPL), Recently Declassified Document Database (RDD), NLC-1-15-2-5-7.

Conclusion

Do not store up for yourselves treasures on earth, where moths and rust destroy, and where thieves break in and steal. But store up for yourselves treasures in heaven ... For where your treasure is, there your heart will be also ... [instead] seek first the kingdom of God and his righteousness, and all these things will be added to you.
Matthew 6:19–21, 33 (ESV)

The period between 1945 and 1991 was one of dynamic and sometimes radical change. Nowhere was this more evident than in sub-Saharan Africa where, within a couple generations, the vast majority of the continent moved from pre-literate to literate cultures, from pre-modernity to technological modernity, and from colonial domination to political self-determination. Within one remarkable three-year period, for instance, from 1960 to 1962, no fewer than twenty-seven former colonies became independent nations. The vertigo created by this unprecedented pace of change created a uniquely fungible historical moment as many Africans sought to formulate a new intellectual and religious framework capable of meeting the demands of their rapidly changing lives. In the ideological struggle that ensued, the outcome was anybody's guess.

While largely ignored during the first decade of the Cold War, by the mid-1950s Africa's uncertain ideological trajectory, and economic and political vulnerability, had attracted the attention of both superpowers, producing anxiety among the Americans and hope within among the Soviets. Despite America's extraordinary economic might and political prestige, Western vulnerability in the African Cold War was clear to everyone. The dominant narrative of Western colonialism which included racial prejudice, cultural arrogance, and economic exploitation had the United States and its Western European allies on the defensive from the onset.

Soviet-style communism, by contrast, could reasonably present itself as a racially blind and egalitarian ideology that offered a proven path to the rapid modernization that many Africans sought. In this African moment, the Russian and their allies saw an opportunity to break the Cold War stalemate and grabbed it with both hands. As early as November of 1955, American officials were expressing concern over a new Soviet strategy seeking to exploit this vulnerability that combined anti-colonial propaganda with generous economic aid packages, and that was "global in scope," "well-planned ... vigorous, selective, and opportunistic."[1]

---

1 Memorandum of Discussion at NSC Meeting, 15 November 1955, FRUS, 1955–57, McMahon, "How the Periphery Became," 29.

It is within the larger contexts of decolonization and the Cold War that the stories of Vera Hillis and the rest of our missionary subjects unfolded. Vera first left the American Midwest for the Belgian Congo in 1946, as a twenty-seven-year-old, single, missionary nurse. For the next thirty years, she worked in rural Congo with the African Inland Mission. Vera had, at best, sporadic contact with American diplomats and Congolese elites, and she was never at the center of any political intrigues. Instead, living on the shoe-string budget of a "faith-basis" missionary, Vera worked long hours at the mission's leprosy colony and clinics where she cared for the sick, taught hygiene and basic modern medicine, and shared the Christian message with the local Congolese people. Had she not worked with the legendary missionary doctor, Carl Becker, she would almost certainly be forgotten today.[2]

Like Vera, the vast majority of American evangelical missionaries who served on the African mission field during this time did so quietly and without any intention of aiding their nation's geopolitical objectives. To be sure they were generally loyal and patriotic Americans, but their aims were driven, first and foremost, by their religious faith and their calling to preach and live out the Christian message among cultures and peoples who had not yet heard it. The historical record bears this out. Although there were important exceptions, most of the American missionaries of this period did not serve near the political or cultural epicenters. Instead, they were often to be found on the periphery, in the forgotten corners of rural Africa, or among the economically or politically marginal.

And yet, in each of the countries we have looked at, despite their explicitly religious and humanitarian aims, these missionaries inadvertently played a central role in their nation's Cold War triumph in the region. As we have seen, and in direct conflict with the anti-colonial narrative of Western exploitation, in the fields of education and medicine American missionaries were responsible for providing schooling and health care for millions of Ethiopians, Congolese, and Kenyans. While ties to colonialism and the racist or paternalistic attitudes of some missionaries at times also provoked anti-Western and anti-American reactions, in each of our case studies the evidence demonstrates that American missionary humanitarian efforts were often critical in encouraging generally pro-American sympathies at both the grassroots and elite levels.[3]

Just as important was the type of health care and education the missionaries offered. Consciously or subconsciously, the missionaries

---
2 Vera Hillis, interview with the author, 9 July 2009; Peterson, *Another Hand on Mine*, 136.
3 AmEmbassy Leopoldville to SecState, 31 October 1964, NARA/RG 59/250/7/21/2/Box 3243.

Conclusion

encouraged in many Africans a strong affinity for a distinctly American-flavored version of modernity. In the field of education, for instance, the implications of this were most clearly—and ironically—seen in Ethiopia where the egalitarian-minded and critical-thinking products of the American missionary schools played a decisive part in both the rise and fall of Ethiopia's communist revolution. As Donald Donham noted, a significant appeal of American missions to Ethiopians was their ability to "offer entrance into modernity," reality confirmed when the communist revolution "appropriated virtually all of the institutions that the SIM and other evangelical missions had created."[4]

Similarly, in all three countries, the democratic structures and practices established by American missionaries in the churches they planted were also of critical importance. This was especially true in Ethiopia and the Congo where modern democracy had not been encouraged by the colonial or imperial governments. Regular elections, term limits, and authoritative constitutions, were all standard practice among American missionary organizations and the indigenous churches that they had established. When added to their ethnically empowering work of translating the Bible into the vernacular, this missionary-inspired democratic example helped fan the flames of African nationalism.

In a few cases, such as Kenya's Mau Mau war, the Katangan secession, and Ethiopia's communist revolution, this quest for self-determination did not play out in ways that were in line with either the wishes of the missionaries or in the interests of the United States government.[5] Yet, thanks to their biblically-inspired deference to authority and their explicitly apolitical worldview, American evangelical missionaries generally encouraged a moderate form of pro-Western democracy. This was evident to different degrees in all three case studies but was most clearly seen in Kenya where the American-missionary product Daniel arap Moi and the Evangelical Churches of Kenya (ECK) plotted an unapologetically pro-Western course during the last two decades of the Cold War.[6]

---

4 Donham, *Marxist Modern*, 83.
5 As one African nationalist put it, "When Europeans took our country we fought them with our spears, but they defeated us because they had better weapons ... But lo! ... The Bible is now doing what we could not do with our spears." Lonsdale, "Missionary Christianity," 195.
6 It is interesting to note that even while evangelicals in Kenya were largely united in their enthusiastic support for the West in the Cold War, and supported democracy, by the late 1980s they had become divided politically with the American missionary-influenced Evangelical Churches of Kenya (ECK) taking an "apolitical" stance that gave de facto support to the Moi regime, and the East African Revival influenced National Council of Churches of Kenya (NCCK) leading the call for multiparty democracy and political reform. Karanja, "Evangelical Attitudes toward Democracy," 67–93.

However, perhaps the most important way that American missionaries influenced US relations with East and Central Africa at the grassroots level was also the most obvious—through religious conversions. While many African evangelicals were not converted directly by American missionaries, virtually all could trace their spiritual lineage to Western missionaries, of whom the majority were American. If the number of converts had been minimal, this religiously inspired affinity could be overlooked; but the numbers were anything but small. In Ethiopia, for instance, despite initially struggling to take hold, the evangelical message gained considerable traction, with the number of converts growing from just over one thousand in 1927 to between five and six million at the end of the Cold War.[7]

In Kenya the numbers were even more astonishing, with the number of evangelical Christians growing from perhaps no more than two thousand in 1900 to almost eleven million at the end of the Cold War.[8] Evangelical Christianity in all three countries took on characteristics of the cultures into which it had been grafted, but in almost every case it also retained many of the foundational beliefs and practices taught by the missionaries who had first introduced the faith—creating a generally identifiable transnational evangelical community.

The potency of this bond was considerable, forming what Lauren Berlant has called an "intimate public"; that is, a transnational attachment rooted in shared foundational beliefs. This bond was to have Cold War consequences.[9] In all three countries this religiously-rooted transnational bond produced a strong and resilient pro-American sentiment within large portions of the populations of those countries—most dramatically during the Simba Rebellion in the Congo, but most substantially in Kenya during the 1970s and 1980s. In each case this was noted by American diplomats, such as when National Security Advisor Zbigniew Brzezinski noted that Moi's religiously inspired pro-West convictions were, "backed by a broad popular consensus."[10]

This spiritually rooted affective bond also had consequences on the other side of the Atlantic. Because of the missionary effort, many evangelicals in the United States also came to feel a deep loyalty and affection for their

---

[7] Eshete, *Evangelical Movement in Ethiopia*, 274, 310.
[8] Barrett, Kurion, and Johnson, *World Christian Encyclopedia*, 426.
[9] McAlister, "What is Your Heart," 879.
[10] Daily Report, Brzezinski to Carter, 22 April 1980, Jimmy Carter Presidential Library (JCPL), Recently Declassified Document Database (RDD), NLC-1-15-2-5-7.

brothers and sisters in Africa. Through the decentralized and sprawling American evangelical network, millions of American Christians imbibed what Melani McAlister has called an "enchanted internationalism"—an enchantment that sometimes produced political engagement.[11] Once again, we saw this in each of the three case studies, but perhaps nowhere more clearly than in the evangelical support for the Katanga lobby during 1961–1962, and in the affinity felt by African American evangelicals for Ethiopia during the reign of Haile Selassie.[12] At times, such as the international attention produced by the martyrdom of American doctors Hockman (Ethiopia) and Carlson (Congo), missionaries were also instrumental in creating an affective bond between an African nation and the US public as a whole. Generally speaking, however, stories of missionary sacrifice, the dynamic African church, and American humanitarianism were limited to the evangelical population and produced in this community a powerful, if romanticized, vision of Africa.

This missionary-inspired vision prompted a sustained financial, spiritual, and practical engagement in these nations by the increasingly influential American evangelical population. Missionary-inspired news of religious persecution against Ethiopian evangelicals by the communist regime, for instance, was instrumental in producing increased pressure on the Derg during the 1980s. As we have already noted, the same dynamic was at work—to even more dramatic effect—during the US-backed UN military action against Tshombe's Katanga during the early 1960s. In both cases, American missionaries speaking out of loyalty to their African evangelical friends forced American policymakers to confront issues they would otherwise have willingly ignored. In addition, this on-going engagement often meant that African leaders linked to American missionaries were seen by large numbers of Americans in unrealistically positive terms. For instance, in the important cases of Haile Selassie in Ethiopia, Moise Tshombe in the Congo, and Daniel arap Moi in Kenya, it was often American missionaries who were responsible for encouraging the strong support that these African leaders initially received from large portions of the American public.

While less common, there were also a number of direct and formal avenues through which American missionary influence flowed. For instance,

---

11 McAlister, *Kingdom of God*, 9. The influence of this "enchanted internationalism" on global affairs is also found in Lauren Turek's excellent study of American evangelical influence on American human rights policy during the last quarter of the twentieth century. See Turek, *To Bring the Good News to All Nations*.

12 In this case, racial solidarity was also a significant factor.

American missionaries occasionally played an important role as backchannel diplomats at key points during the Cold War in Africa. The cases of Howard Brinton and William Close in the Congo are noteworthy here. Thanks to his close and life-long friendships with Katangan president Moise Tshombe, Congolese vice president Jason Sendwe, and other key Congolese political elites, Howard Brinton was at the center of attempts by US and Congolese leaders to achieve a peaceful and lasting solution to the Katangan crisis. Brinton's failure to bring the multiple parties together does not diminish the fact that, in one of the greatest diplomatic crises in Cold War Africa, it was an American missionary that was looked to as the most promising link between the diplomatic elites of the contending parties.

At other times, especially during crisis periods, American missionaries, wittingly and unwittingly, provided critical intelligence to American policymakers. During the independence-era chaos in the Congo, and perhaps to an even greater degree during the Simba rebellion that followed, American missionaries also provided the US government with detailed information that was critical to their understanding of the immensely complex political and cultural dynamics at work in this vital Cold War arena. Missionary perspectives also played a central role in creating a positive and long-lasting view among American policymakers of Haile Selassie as a fundamentally progressive and pro-American monarch—an only partially accurate view which, as we saw, nevertheless influenced US policy towards Ethiopia for at least twenty years.

While not, strictly speaking, missionary organizations, American-based groups like the Fellowship ICL, the Billy Graham Evangelistic Association, and even the quasi-evangelical, MRA, also played a vital role in US relations with East and Central Africa by bridging the divide between the American missionary community and the religious and political elites in Washington. Billy Graham's Africa tour in 1960, and his subsequent meetings with Eisenhower, Nixon and other prominent political, military, and diplomatic figures is a case in point. At a time when Africa was on the cusp of a radical political transformation, Billy Graham's missionary-inspired and missionary-informed tour played an important role in boosting the profile of Africa among both the American public at large and its political elites.[13] In a much quieter way, there were multiple instances in which the Fellowship (ICL) played an equally significant role in backchannel diplomacy such as the surprising rapprochement between Kenya and Somalia in the early 1980s.

---

13 Graham, *Just As I Am*, 338–49.

Finally, American evangelical missionaries in each country played an important role in the relationship between the US and their host country through the intimate relationships they often enjoyed with the political leaders of those countries. We have already been reminded that, in the case of Howard Brinton in the Congo, these long-standing personal relationships could form the foundation of important diplomatic bridges between leaders and nations. However, these religiously infused relationships also appear to have been vital in producing in some of these leaders a deep and diplomatically significant affection for the United States. In the case of Haile Selassie, we saw the role that Della Hanson and other American missionaries played in helping to form in the monarch an affinity for the United States that disturbed his advisors and flew in the face of strong anti-American currents in Ethiopian culture. The same dynamic was working with at least equal effect in the case of Kenyan president Daniel arap Moi, where from an early age, and up to at least his early years as president, missionaries like Earl Andersen and Paul Barnett were among the Kenyan leader's most trusted mentors and intimate confidants.

In the end, what can we conclude? While they rarely aspired to political or diplomatic influence, in Ethiopia, the Congo, and Kenya, American evangelical missionaries nevertheless played a critical role in their nation's ultimate Cold War triumph. Their political and diplomatic influence was largely accidental—an unintentional bi-product of their religious and humanitarian aims. They came to Africa to save souls and to give a practical demonstration of God's love, but they also ended up influencing the trajectory of the Cold War.

Acknowledgments

This book is the culmination of many years of work in multiple locations. As a result, it is not possible to create an inclusive list of all those whose significant influence can be found in these pages. Instead, I am going to limit myself to just a few key people.

Andrew Preston, my PhD supervisor at Cambridge, has been consistently and enthusiastically supportive of this project. Beyond the insights I gained from our regular meetings at Clare, it was his own ground-breaking work on the influence of religion on US foreign relations that opened the door for studies like mine. I am also grateful for the enthusiastic support of the talented team at William Carey Publishers in particular Melissa Hicks, Vivian Doub, Brad Vaughn, and Mike Riester.

Several other historians have also played a key role in the creation of this book. While sometimes coming to different conclusions, Melani McAlister has played a particularly important role, giving countless hours to provide valued feedback as this book moved from a PhD dissertation to its current form. While less involved in my work, others have been highly influential either through their own work or through timely engagement with mine. For very different reasons, the following historians have had a significant influence on this book: David Hollinger, William Inboden, Walter Russell Mead, Mark Noll, David Landes, Leo Ribuffo, Axel Shafer, Bruce Laurie, Andrew Walls, Tony Badger, Andrew Rotter, Lamin Sanneh, and TVSB.

My wife Catherine, to whom this book is dedicated, deserves special mention. There is absolutely no way that I would have been able to complete the PhD upon which this book rests without some significant sacrifices on her part. For those sacrifices, and for her faithful support of me and this project, I am deeply grateful. Our two daughters, Emma and Sophie also played an inspirational role—but in very different ways (Emma and Sophie, you know what I mean). Finally, I need to say thank you to my parents (Stewart and Elaine Dow), my in-laws (David and Patricia Maidment) and to my incredible colleagues at Black Forest Academy and Rosslyn Academy. For all those listed above and for countless others not listed, thank you. I am grateful.

Bibliography

Primary Sources

Archives:

Africa Inland Mission Papers, Pearl River, New York (now housed at the Billy Graham Archive and Research Center).

Billy Graham Archive and Research Center, Wheaton College, Wheaton, Illinois.
- World Congress on Evangelism (CN—14).
- Walter F. Bennet and Company (CN—54).
- African Inland Mission (CN—81).
- Evangelical Foreign Missions Association (CN—165).
- The Robert William and Winifred Thompson Hockman Papers (CN—200).
- Papers of Ruth Margaret Mellis (CN—363).
- Billy Graham Evangelistic Association Press Reports (CN—360).
- The Fellowship Foundation (CN—459).

Jimmy Carter Presidential Library and Museum, National Archives, Atlanta, Georgia.
- National Security Advisor Files, Horn of Africa.
- National Security Advisor Files, Brzezinski.
- Plains File, Presidential Memoir Papers, Foreign Correspondence.
- RAC Project Documents (Recently Declassified Documents).
- Speechwriter's Files, Chronological.
- White House Central Files, Country Files.
- White House Press Office.

Kenya National Archives, Nairobi, Kenya.

National Archives II, College Park, Maryland.
- Department of State (RG—59).
- Foreign Service Posts of the Department of State (RG—84).
- War Department, General and Special Staff (RG—165).
- Central Intelligence Agency (RG—263).

Presbyterian Historical Society, The National Archives of the PC (USA), Philadelphia, Pennsylvania.

Richard Nixon Presidential Library and Museum, National Archives, Yorba Linda, California.
- National Security Council, Country Files.
- National Security Council, Presidential Correspondence Files.
- Pre-Presidential Papers.
- White House Central Files, Country Files.
- White House Central Files, Religious Matters.
- White House Central Files, Alpha Files.

Rift Valley Academy Archives, Rift Valley Academy, Kijabe Kenya.

Ronald Reagan Presidential Library and Museum, National Archives, Simi Valley, California.
- Executive Secretariat, National Security Council Files.
- White House Office of Records Management, Subject Files.

SIM Archives, Sudan Interior Mission, Fort Mill, South Carolina.
- SIM East Africa Collection.
- SIM General Collection.
- SIM 1 Collection.

General Commission on Archives and History, United Methodist Church, Drew University, Madison, New Jersey.

World Gospel Mission Archives, Marion, Indiana.

World Vision International Archives, Monrovia, California.

Oral Interviews:

Addis Ababa, Ethiopia, 14 December 2007:
- Dr. Paulus Dubale, assistant professor at Addis Ababa University and researcher in the capacity building program of the six-million-member, Kale Haywet Church.
- Dr. Tesfaye Yacob, general secretary of the Kale Haywet Church.
- Dr. Nigatu Chuffo, former university president, and professor of engineering, and current head of capacity building for the Kale Haywet Church.

Addis Ababa, Ethiopia, 17 December 2007:
- Shiferaw Wolde Michael, former Ethiopian minister of justice and current board chairman of the six-million-member, Kale Haywet Church.
- Ato Mamo Gebremeskel, retired general manager of the Ethiopian Petroleum Corporation and former board chairman of the Kale Haywet Church.

Addis Ababa, Ethiopia, 18 December 2007:
- Rev. Alemu Shetta, general secretary of Evangelical Churches Fellowship of Ethiopia and former professor of theology.
- Ato Kursie Shefano, deputy director of the Kale Haywet Church.

London, England, 10 June 2009:
- His Excellency, the Kenya high commissioner to the United Kingdom, Mr. Joe Muchemi.

Montreat, NC, 29 June 2009:
- John and JoAnn Ellington, Presbyterian missionaries to Congo (1965–1983).

Montreat, NC, 30 June 2009:
- David Miller, Presbyterian missionary to Congo (1954–1994).

Bibliography

Penny Farms, FL, 8 July 2009:
- Marshall and Thelma Southard, former Unevangelized Fields Mission missionaries to Congo (1954–1974).

Minneola, FL, 9 July 2009:
- Betty Pontier, former Africa Inland Mission missionary to Congo (1955–1975).
- Carl and Gladys Becker, former Africa Inland Mission missionaries to Congo (Carl from 1929–1974).
- Vera Hillis, former Africa Inland Mission missionary to Congo (1946–1976).
- Chuck and Muriel Davis, former Africa Inland Mission missionaries to Congo (1964–1978).

Minneola, FL, 10 July 2009:
- Lillian Davis, former Africa Inland Mission missionary to Kenya (1954–1977).
- Mary Modricker, former Africa Inland Mission missionary to Ethiopia (1971–1976).
- Dick and Flo Gehman, former Africa Inland Mission missionaries to Kenya (1965–2002).
- Jonathan and Dottie Hildebrandt, former Africa Inland Mission missionaries to Kenya (1968–2003).

Minneola, FL, 11 July 2009:
- Chuck and Bobbi Kinzer, former Africa Inland Mission missionaries to Kenya (1964–1992).
- Roy and Judy Entwistle, former Africa Inland Mission missionaries to Kenya (1962–1998).

Gigiri, Kenya, 9 September 2009:
- Dan Ward, Lutheran missionary kid (Tanzania) and Christian Blind Mission missionary to Kenya (1978–2009).

Kijabe, Kenya, 1 October 2009:
- Tim Cook, AIM missionary child and Africa Inland Mission missionary (superintendent of Rift Valley Academy).
- Mike and Janet Adkins, AIM missionary children and Africa Inland Mission missionaries.
- Dr. Richard Bransford, Africa Inland Mission doctor in East Africa from 1976 to 2010.

Nairobi, Kenya, 13 October 2009:
- Samuel Waruhiu, prominent Nairobi attorney and son of loyalist Chief Waruhiu killed by Mau Mau.

Gigiri, Kenya, 13 November 2009:
- Margaret Njonjo, daughter of Africa Inland Mission missionaries and wife of Charles Njonjo, Kenya's first attorney general and later member of parliament and minister of constitutional affairs.

Kijabe, Kenya, 27 November 2009:
- Ray and Jill Davis, AIM missionary child (Ray) and Africa Inland Mission missionaries in Kenya (1971 to present).

Kijabe, Kenya, 28 November 2009:
- Art Davis, AIM missionary child and Africa Inland Mission missionary (1972 to present).
- Dilly Anderson, AIM missionary child and Africa Inland Mission missionary (1963 to present).

Gigiri, Kenya, 3 December 2009:
- Margaret Njonjo (see description of 13 November interview).

Gigiri, Kenya, 17 December 2009:
- Reverend Robert and Mrs. Ward, Evangelical Lutheran Church of America missionaries in East Africa from 1954 to 1992.

Nairobi, Kenya, 18 December 2009:
- Bishop Silas Yego, bishop of the Africa Inland Church, the church created by the Africa Inland Mission and the denomination of President Moi.

Nairobi, Kenya, 29 April 2010:
- Ambassador Bethwell Kiplagat, former Kenya ambassador and permanent secretary of foreign affairs.

Nairobi, Kenya, 24 May 2010:
- Grace Nyachae, wife of Simeon Nyachae, former long-serving member of parliament and cabinet member.

Nairobi, Kenya, 16 August 2011:
- President Daniel arap Moi, former president of the Republic of Kenya (1978–2002).
- Honorable Charles Njonjo, Kenya's first attorney general and later member of parliament and minister of constitutional affairs.

Personal Correspondence (Letters/emails to the author from most recent):

Anderson, Howard. Child of AIM missionaries and Africa Inland Mission missionary to Kenya (1930s to 1990s), 10 Sept. 2009.

Anonymous (for reasons of personal safety), Southern Baptist Convention missionary, 5 and 7 Apr. 2008.

Bedsole, Jerry. Southern Baptist Convention missionary to Ethiopia, (1970–1994), 5 Apr. 2008.

Brogden. Assemblies of God missionary, 7 Mar. 2008.

Erickson, Ed and Sue. Baptist General Conference missionaries to Ethiopia, 2007.

Honer, Mary. AIM missionary child, daughter of Earl Anderson, 16 and 17 Feb. 2010.

Keefer, Jim and Aurelia. Veteran SIM missionaries to Ethiopia, 13 Dec. 2007.

Kurtz, Harold. Veteran Presbyterian missionary to Ethiopia, 25 Sept. 2007.

Lindholm, Ray and Lauralee. Veteran Southern Baptist missionaries to Ethiopia, 10 Nov. 2007.

Petree, Richard (Ambassador). Former US political officer to Ethiopia, 25 Apr. 2008.

Smith, Kevin. Assemblies of God missionary, 7 Mar. 2008.

Memoirs, Official US Government Publications, and First-Hand Reports:

Adams, Sam. *War of Numbers: An Intelligence Memoir*. South Royale, VT: Steerforth, 1994.

Attwood, William. *The Reds and the Blacks: A Personal Adventure*. New York: Harper & Row, 1967.

Ball, George. *The Past Has Another Pattern*. New York: W. W. Norton & Co., 1982.

Bascom, Kay. *Hidden Triumph in Ethiopia*. Pasadena: William Carey Library, 2001.

Blakeslee, Virginia. *Beyond the Kikuyu Curtain*. Chicago: Moody Press, 1956.

Bliss, Howard. "The Modern Missionary." *Atlantic*. May 1920.

Blyden, Edward. "Ethiopia Stretching Out Her Hands unto God; or Africa's Service to the World" (May 1880). In *Readings in African Political Thought*, edited by Gideon-Cyrus M. Mutiso and S. W. Rohio. Nairobi: Heinemann, 1975.

Bolton, Francis. "A View of Africa." *Annals of the American Academy of Political and Social Science*, 306 (July 1956): 121–27.

Bolton, Francis. "Report of the Special Study Mission to Africa, South and East of the Sahara." Washington, DC: US Government Printers, 1956.

Braschler, Peter. *Change: My Thirty-Five Years in Africa*. Wheaton, IL: Crossway, 1979.

Bryson, Stuart. *Light in the Darkness: The Story of the Nandi Bible*. Eastbourne: Perry Jackman, 1959.

Cannata, Sam, and Ginny Cannata (with Jack R. Taylor). *Truth on Trial*. Nashville, TN: Broadman Press, 1978.

Carlson, Lois. *Monganga Paul: The Ministry and Martyrdom of Paul Carlson, M.D.* New York: Harper & Row, 1966.

Carothers, J. C. *The Psychology of Mau Mau*. Nairobi: The Government Printers, 1954.

Close, William T. *Beyond the Storm: Treating the Powerless and the Powerful in Mobutu's Congo/Zaire*. Marbleton, WY: Meadowlark Springs Productions, 2007.

Cohen, Herman J. *Intervening in Africa: Superpower Peacemaking in a Troubled Continent*. Hampshire, UK: Palgrave Macmillan, 2000.

Collins, Jodie. *Code Word: Catherine*. Wheaton, IL: Tyndale House, 1984.

Cumbers, John. *Count It All Joy: Testimonies from A Persecuted Church*. Kearney, NE: Morris Publications, 1995.

Cumbers, John. *Living with the Red Terror: Missionary Experiences in Communist Ethiopia*. Charlotte, NC: Morris Publications, 1996.

Davis, Raymond J. *Fire on the Mountains*. Grand Rapids: Zondervan, 1966.

Devlin, Larry. *Chief of Station, Congo*. New York: Public Affairs, 2007.

Dortzbach, Karl, and Debbie Dortzbach. *Kidnapped*. New York: Harper & Row, 1975.

Eisenhower, Dwight D. *Waging Peace, 1956–1961: The White House Years*. New York: Doubleday and Co., 1965.

Fish, Gerald, and Burnette Fish. *The Call to Battle*. Marion, IN: World Gospel Mission, 1982.

Foreign Relations of the United States, Africa, 1964–1968. Washington, DC: United States Government Printing Office, 1999.

Forsberg, Malcolm, and Enid Forsberg. *In Famine He Shall Redeem Thee*. Cedar Grove, NJ: Sudan Interior Mission, 1975.

Friederichsen, Kathleen Hockman. *Dr. Bob Hockman: A Surgeon of the Cross*. Grand Rapids, MI: Kessinger Publications, 1937.

Graham, Billy. *Just As I Am: The Autobiography of Billy Graham*. London: Harper One, 1997.

Guevara, Ernesto. *The African Dream: The Diaries of the Revolutionary War in the Congo*. New York: Grove Press, 1999.

Hanson, Herbert, and Della Hanson. *For God and the Emperor*. California: Unknown Press, 1958.

Hayes, Margaret. *Captive of the Simbas*. New York: Harper & Row, 1966.

Hege, Nathan B. *Beyond Our Prayers: An Amazing Half Century of Church Growth in Ethiopia, 1948–1998*. Scottsdale, PA: Herald Press, 1998.

Hempstone, Smith. *Rogue Ambassador: An African Memoir*. Sewanee, TN: University of the South Press, 1997.

Hoare, Mike. *Congo Mercenary*. London: St. Edmundsbury Press, 1967.

Honer, Mary. *Missy Fundi, Kenya Girl*. New York: iUniverse, 2003.

Hoyt, Michael P. E. *Captive in the Congo: A Consul's Return to the Heart of Darkness*. Annapolis, MD: Naval Institute Press, 2000.

Johnson, Lynden Baines. *The Vantage Point: Perspectives of the Presidency 1963–1969*. London: Holt, Reinhart, & Winston, 1972.

Kaggia, Bildad. *Roots of Freedom, 1921–1963: The Autobiography of Bildad Kaggia*. Nairobi: East Africa Publishing House, 1975.

Kenyatta, Jomo. *Facing Mount Kenya*. London: Secker & Warburg, 1953.

Kenyatta, Jomo. *Suffering without Bitterness: The Founding of the Kenya Nation*. Nairobi: East Africa House Publications, 1968.

Kenyatta, Jomo. "Views on Non-Alignment." Kenya News Agency Handout, No. 368 (1 June 1965). In *Readings in African Political Thought*, edited by Gideon-Cyrus M. Mutiso and S. W. Rohio. Nairobi: Heinemann, 1975.

Korn, David A. *Ethiopia, the United States and the Soviet Union*. London: Croom Helm, 1986.

Lambie, Thomas. *A Doctor without a Country*. New York: Fleming H. Revell, 1937.

Lumumba, Patrice. *My Country*. London: Praeger, 1962.

"Manifesto of the Belgian-Congolese Elite" (1956). In *Readings in African Political Thought*, edited by Gideon-Cyrus M. Mutiso and S. W. Rohio. Nairobi: Heinemann, 1975.

Mboya, Tom. *Freedom and After*. London: Unknown Press, 1963.

McClure, Don, and Marian Fairman, eds. *Red-Headed, Rash and Religious*. Indiana, PA: Board of Christian Education of the Presbyterian Church of North America, 1954.

McGhee, George. *Envoy to the Middle World: Adventures in Diplomacy*. New York: Harper & Row, 1983.

McGhee, George. *On the Frontline in the Cold War: An Ambassador Reports*. Westport, CT: Praeger, 1997.

Moi, Daniel T. arap. *Kenya African Nationalism: Nyayo Philosophy and Principles*. London: Macmillan, 1986.

Mutiso, Gideon-Cyrus M., and S. W. Rohio, eds. *Readings in African Political Thought*. Nairobi: Heinemann, 1975.

Nixon, Richard. *In the Arena: A Memoir of Victory, Defeat, and Renewal*. New York: Simon & Schuster, 1990.

Nyachae, Simeon. *Walking through the Corridors of Service*. Nairobi: Unknown Press, 2010.

O'Brien, Conor Cruise. *To Katanga and Back: A UN Case Study*. New York: Simon & Schuster, 1962.

Odinga, Oginga. *Not Yet Uhuru*. New York: Hill & Wang, 1967.

Partee, Charles. *Adventure in Africa: The Story of Don McClure*. Grand Rapids: Zondervan, 1990.

The Public Papers of the Presidents: Harry S. Truman, 1949. Washington, DC: US Government Printing Office, 1964.

The Public Papers of the Presidents: John F. Kennedy, 1961. Washington, DC: US Government Printing Office, 1962.

The Public Papers of the Presidents: Richard Nixon, 1969. Washington, DC: US Government Printing Office, 1971.

The Public Papers of the Presidents: Ronald Reagan, 1983, Book II. Washington, DC: US Government Printing Office, 1999.

The Public Papers of the Presidents: Ronald Reagan, 1984, Book I. Washington, DC: US Government Printing Office, 1986.

Reagan, Ronald. "Evil Empire Speech." http://www.voicesofdemocracy.umd.edu/Reagan-evil-empire-speech-text. Accessed last, 20 April 2012.

Reagan, Ronald. *The Reagan Diaries Unabridged, Volumes 1 & 2*. New York: Harper, 2009.

Report to Congress on Voting Practices in the United Nations. Washington, DC: US Government Printing Office, 1983, 1985, 1988.

Rusk, Dean. *As I Saw It: A Secretary of State's Memoirs*. London: I. B. Taurus & Co., 1991.

Selassie, Haile. "Appeal to the League of Nations." June 1936, Library of Congress text accessed at: https://www.loc.gov/item/2021667904.

Skoda, C. P. *Ogada: An African Passage*. Bloomington, IN: Authorhouse, 2008.

Spencer, John. *Ethiopia at Bay: A Personal Account*. Algonac, MI: Reference Publications, 1984.

Thiong'o, Ngugi Wa. *The River Between*. London: Heinemann, 2007.

Thiong'o, Ngugi Wa. *Weep Not, Child*. London: Heinemann, 1988.

Thuku, Harry. *Harry Thuku: An Autobiography*. Nairobi: Oxford University Press, 1970.

UNESCO, "Education: From COVID-19 School Closures to Recovery." http://en.unesco.org/covid19/educationresponse. Accessed 16 April 2020.

United Nations Press Release. 8 July 1976.

The United States Congressional Record—Senate.

The United States Department of Commerce, "Current Population Reports: Income of nonfarm families and individuals." Washington, DC: US Government Printing Office, 1946.

The United States Department of Commerce, "Current Population Reports: Money Income of Households and Persons in the United States." Washington, DC: US Government Printing Office, 1987.

Williams, G. Mennen. *Africa for the Africans*. Grand Rapids: Eerdmans, 1969.

Willmott, Helen M. *The Doors Were Opened*. London: Hazel Watson & Viney, 1961.

Youmans, Roger L. *When Bull Elephants Fight: An American Surgeon's Chronicle of Congo*. Tarentum, PA: Word Association, 2006.

Newspapers, Periodicals, and Organizational Publications:

Africa Now
- "Famine Relief Complicated By Disease, Rain." *Africa Now*. January-February, 1974.
- "Crisis Builds." *Africa Now*. July-August, 1977.
- "Ethiopia: SIM sends food aid to famine area." *Africa Now*. August-October, 1980.
- "Church, mission thriving in Ethiopia." *Africa Now*. November-December, 1980.
- "Ethiopia: Land of the Lion." *Africa Now*. July-August, 1981.
- "SIM provides more famine relief in Ethiopia." *Africa Now*. September-October, 1981.
- "Ethiopia: Famine conditions build, SIM sends aid." *Africa Now*. January-February, 1983.
- "Ethiopia: Famine conditions worsen; SIM increases aid." *Africa Now*. July-August, 1983.

Africa Today
- "After Stanleyville What?" *Africa Today*. December 1964.

America
- "Eyes of Africa." *America*. December 17, 1960.

Amnesty International
- "Ethiopian Political Imprisonment and Torture." *Amnesty International*. June, 1986.
- "Ethiopia Political Imprisonment and Torture." *Amnesty International*. July, 1986.

Asbury Alumnus
- "Brinton Committed to Work in Congo." *Asbury Alumnus*. April 1962.

Associated Press
- "[Emperor Haile Selassie's] Grandchildren to Hear Billy." *Associated Press*. March 8, 1960.

Atlantic
- "The Modern Missionary." *Atlantic*. May 1920.

Atlanta Journal-Constitution
- "Atlantan's key role in 1964 Congo rescue mission holds place in hearts." *Atlanta Journal-Constitution*. November 21, 2014.

The Chicago Defender
- "Hail Haile Selassie." *Chicago Defender*. June 1954.

Christianity Today
- "Safari's End." *Christianity Today*. March 28, 1960.
- "Graham Crusade." *Christianity Today*. July 4, 1960.
- "Thirty Years Later: Haile Selassie in Berlin." *Christianity Today*. October 28, 1966.
- "A Call for Evangelical Unity." *Christianity Today*. November 11, 1966.
- "Famine in Africa: It's Worse." *Christianity Today*. April 12, 1974.
- "Breakfast with the President." *Christianity Today*. February 14, 1975.
- "Haile Selassie." *Christianity Today*. September 12, 1975.
- "The Campaign to Root Out 'Alien' Religion in Ethiopia." *Christianity Today*. September 7, 1979.
- "The Forgotten Final Resting Place of William Borden." *Christianity Today*. February 24, 2017 (online edition).

The Dallas Morning News
- "Congolese Rebels Quiet on Fate of American Doctor." *Dallas Morning News*. November 17, 1964.
- "Execution Postponed in Congo." *Dallas Morning News*. November 19, 1964.

The East African Standard
- "Missionaries praised for health work." *East African Standard*. September 28, 1964.

The Ethiopian Herald
- "Honorary Degree Is Conferred..." *The Ethiopian Herald*. August 8, 1949.
- "New York Times' Features Prayer Breakfast." *The Ethiopian Herald*. February 5, 1971.

The Guardian
- "The day the bribe went sour." *The Guardian*. April 27, 1974.

Hearing and Doing
- "Mr. Roosevelt at Kijabe." *Hearing and Doing*. September 1909.
- "A Witch Doctor Saved." *Hearing and Doing*. April 1910.

Inland Africa
- "The Thuku Movement in East Africa." *Inland Africa*. June 1927.
- "Editorials." *Inland Africa*. February 1930.

Bibliography

- "Letter of Lee Downing." *Inland Africa*. Vol. 15, Issue 3, 1931.
- "An 'Unreached Field' in Missions." *Inland Africa*. November-December 1946.
- "Our Threefold Teaching Responsibility." *Inland Africa*. July-August 1952.
- "The Political Situation in Kenya." *Inland Africa*. March-April 1953.
- "Kenya and Medical Advance." *Inland Africa*. May-June 1957.
- "Congo Legacy." *Inland Africa*. July-August 1965.

Life Magazine
- "Haile Selassie's housekeeper—She is a Seventh-Day Adventist from Minnesota." *Life*. June 7, 1943.
- "Congo Martyr." *Life*. December 4, 1964.

The Los Angeles Times
- "Wife of Missionary Denies He Ever Spied." *Los Angeles Times*. November 18, 1964.
- "Showing Faith in Discretion." *Los Angeles Times*. September 27, 2002.

New York Herald Tribune
- "Missionary Tells First-hand Story of Ethiopian War." *New York Herald Tribune*. November 18, 1935.
- "Dr. Hockman's Death by Bomb Stirs Ethiopia." *New York Herald Tribune*. December 14, 1935.
- "Haile Selassie Back In A Palace, Glad Ethiopia & U.S. Are Free." *New York Herald Tribune*. May 2, 1941.

New York Times
- "Missionaries to Stay in Ethiopia." *New York Times*. July 7, 1935.
- "American Missions To Stay In Ethiopia." *New York Times*. October 11, 1935.
- "Death of Hockman Blow to Red Cross." *New York Times*. December 15, 1935.
- "Ethiopian Emperor Lands Here Amid Noisy Welcome." *New York Times*. May 26, 1954.
- "Text of Haile Selassie's Address to U.S. Congress." *New York Times*. May 28, 1954.
- "Selassie at Ball Park Gets Diplomats Upset." *New York Times*. June 1, 1954.
- "Visiting Emperor Hailed in Parade." *New York Times*. June 2, 1954.
- "25,000 Hear Graham…" *New York Times*. March 10, 1960.
- "Congo Rebels Kill 'Intellectuals', as Enemies of the Revolution." *New York Times*. October 4, 1964.

- "Priests Report U.S. Cleric Died After Beating by Congo Rebels." *New York Times*. October 24, 1964.
- "Nixon, Greeting Mobutu, Lauds the Congo." *New York Times*. August 5, 1970.
- "Prayer Breakfasts Introduced in Ethiopia." *New York Times*. January 17, 1971.
- "Nurse Kept Faith During Captivity." *New York Times*. July 3, 1974.
- "Kin of Selassie, Torn by Fears, Resettle in U.S." *New York Times*. September 26, 1977.
- "Around the World; Kenya Hunts for Suspect in Fatal Hotel Bombing." *New York Times*. January 2, 1981.

The Pentecostal Evangel
- "Crisis Days in the Congo." *The Pentecostal Evangel*. February 14, 1965.

Pittsburgh Sun-Telegraph
- "Dr. Hockman, First U.S. Casualty." *Pittsburgh Sun-Telegraph*. December 14, 1935.

Revelation
- "In the Emperor's Palace." *Revelation*. August 1946.

Sudan Witness
- "Greater Love." *Sudan Witness*. October 1941.
- "Visit to Anglo-Egyptian Sudan and Ethiopia." *Sudan Witness*. October 1943.
- "The Testimony of His Imperial Majesty Haile Selassie." *Sudan Witness*. 1946.
- "The King Came." *Sudan Witness*. 1952.

Time
- "The Administration: An Abuse of Power." *Time*. December 28, 1962.
- "Death in the Congo." *Time*. December 4, 1964.

The Times
- "The Bombing of Daggah Bur." December 19, 1935.

Toronto Star
- "Ethiopians Get 15 Days to Quit Christian Faith." *Toronto Star*. March 11, 1979.

United Evangelical Action
- "The Church in Ethiopia." *United Evangelical Action*. December 15, 1948.
- "Graham Confers with President." *United Evangelical Action*. May 1960.

The Washington Daily News
- "US Missionary Doctor: Congo Rebels to Kill American as a 'Spy.'" *Washington Daily News*. November 17, 1964.

The Washington Post
- "Death in the Congo." *Washington Post*. November 25, 1964.
- "Ethiopia: The Final Days of a Nearly Bloodless Coup." *Washington Post*. September 8, 1974.
- "Seized Missionary Freed by Ethiopia." *Washington Post*. April 22, 1977.
- "Police Torture Is Charged in Kenya." *Washington Post*. March 13, 1987.

The Washington Star
- "A Matter of Humanity." *Washington Star*. 17 November 1964.
- "Great-Grandchildren of an Emperor Flee." *Washington Star*. September 26, 1977.

World Vision Magazine
- "Facts of a Field: Congo Republic." *World Vision Magazine*. September 1960.
- "Missionary Slain." *World Vision Magazine*. March 1964.
- "Carlson of Congo." *World Vision Magazine*. February 1965.
- "Unsegregated Martyrs." *World Vision Magazine*. November 1965.
- "In the Congo: Aftermath of Terror." *World Vision Magazine*. June 1966.
- "An Open Letter to President Ford." *World Vision Magazine*. March 1976.
- "Open Letter from W. Stanley Mooneyham (President of World Vision) to President Ford." *World Vision Magazine*. March 1976.

Secondary Sources

Abrams, Elliot, ed. *The Influence of Faith: Religious Groups and U.S. Foreign Policy*. Lanham, MD: Rowan & Littlefield, 2001.

Ajami, Fouad. "The Summoning." *The Clash of Civilizations? The Debate*, edited by Samuel Huntington. New York: Foreign Affairs, 1996.

Ampiah, Kweku, and Sanusha Naidu, eds. *Crouching Tiger, Hidden Dragon: Africa and China*. South Africa: University of KwaZula-Natal Press, 2008.

Amstutz, Mark R., and Andrew S. Natsios. "Faith-Based NGO's and U.S. Foreign Policy." In *The Influence of Faith: Religious Groups and U.S. Foreign Policy*, edited by Elliott Abrams. Lanham, MD: Rowan & Littlefield, 2001.

Anderson, C. P. *There Was a Man: His Name–Paul Carlson*. New York: Covenant Press, 1965.

Anderson, David. *History of the Hanged*. London: W. W. Norton, 2005.

Anderson, Dick. *We Felt Like Grasshoppers: The Story of the Africa Inland Mission*. Nottingham, UK: Inter-Varsity Press, 1994.

Andrew, Christopher. *Defend the Realm: The Authorized History of MI5*. London: Knopf, 2009.

Aseka, Erik K. *Jomo Kenyatta: A Biography*. Nairobi: East African Educational Publishers, 1992.

Askins, Steve. "Mission to Renamo: The Militarization of the Religious Right." *Issue* 18, no. 2 (Summer 1990): 29–38.

Baffour, Agyeman-Duah. *The United States and Ethiopia: Military Assistance and the Quest for Security, 1953–1993*. New York: University Press of America, 1994.

Baissa, Lemmu. "United States Military Assistance to Ethiopia, 1953–1974: A Reappraisal of a Difficult Patron Client Relationship." *Northeast African Studies* 11, no. 3 (1989): 51–70.

Bakke, Johnny. "Models of Leadership in Ethiopia: The Missionary Contribution." In *The Missionary Factor in Ethiopia*, edited by Getatchew Haile, Aasulv Lande, and Samuel Rubenson. Berlin: Peter Lang, 1998.

Balmer, Randall. *God in the White House: A History*. New York: Harper One, 2008.

Balsvik, Randi Ronning. *Haile Selassie's Students*. East Lansing, MI: Michigan State University Press, 1985.

Barrett, David B., George T. Kurian, and Todd M. Johnson, eds. *World Christian Encyclopedia: A Comparative Survey of Churches and Religions in the Modern World*, Vol. 1, 2nd ed. Oxford: Oxford University Press, 2001.

Barrett, David B. *Kenya Churches Handbook*. Nairobi: Evangel Publishing House, 1973.

Bartley, Robert L. "The Case for Optimism." *Foreign Affairs* (September/October 1993): 15.

Bayly, Christopher. *The Birth of the Modern World, 1780–1914: Global Connections and Comparisons*. Oxford: Wiley Blackwell, 2003.

Bayly, Joseph T. *The Congo Crisis: Charles and Muriel Davis Relive an Era of Missions during Weeks of Imprisonment in Stanleyville, Africa*. Grand Rapids, MI: Zondervan, 1966.

Bays, Daniel H., and Grant Wacker, eds. *The Foreign Missionary Enterprise at Home*. Tuscaloosa: University of Alabama Press, 2003.

Beaver, Pierce. "Missionary Motivation through Three Centuries." In *Reinterpretation in American Church History*, edited by Jerald Brauer. Chicago: University of Chicago Press, 1968.

Bebbington, David. *Evangelicalism in Modern Britain: A History from the 1730s to the 1980s*. London: Routledge, 1989.

Bekoe, Dorina A., ed. *East Africa and the Horn: Confronting Challenges to Good Governance*. London: Lynne Rienner Publishers, 2006.

Bibliography

Belmonte, Laura A. "Review of William C. Inboden's *Religion and American Foreign Policy, 1945–1960: The Soul of Containment.*" From "A Roundtable Discussion of William C. Inboden's *Religion and American Foreign Policy, 1945–1960: The Soul of Containment,*" *Passport* (April 2009).

Ben Porat, Yeshayahu, Eitan Haber, and Zeev Schiff. *Entebbe Rescue*. New York: Delacorte Press, 1977.

Boobbyer, Philip. "Moral Re-Armament in Africa in the Era of Decolonization." In *Missions, Nationalism, and the End of Empire*, edited by Brian Stanley. Grand Rapids, MI: Eerdmans, 2003.

Borstelmann, Thomas. *Apartheid's Reluctant Uncle: The United States and South Africa in the Early Cold War*. Oxford: Oxford University Press, 1983.

Borstelmann, Thomas. *The 1970s: A New Global History from Civil Rights to Economic Inequality*. Princeton: Princeton University Press, 2011.

Bouscaren, Anthony. *Tshombe*. New York: Twin Circle Publishing, 1967.

Branch, Daniel. *Defeating Mau Mau, Creating Kenya*. Cambridge: Cambridge University Press, 2009.

Branch, Daniel. *Kenya: Between Hope and Despair, 1963–2011*. London: Yale University Press, 2011.

Brauer, Jerald, ed. *Reinterpretation in American Church History*. Chicago: University of Chicago Press, 1968.

Breslaver, George B., ed. *Soviet Policy in Africa: From the Old Thinking to the New Thinking*. Berkeley: University of California Press, 1992.

Brouwer, Steve, Paul Gifford, and Susan D. Rose. *Exporting the American Gospel: Global Christian Fundamentalism*. New York: Routledge, 1996.

Brown, Nathan. *The Rule of Law in the Arab World: Courts in Egypt and the Gulf*. Cambridge: Cambridge University Press, 1997.

Callahan, Alan Dwight. *The Talking Book: African Americans and the Bible*. New Haven: Yale University Press, 2006.

Carpenter, Joel, and William Shenk, eds. *Earthen Vessels: American Evangelicals and Foreign Missions 1880–1980*. Grand Rapids, MI: Eerdmans, 1990.

Carr, E. H. *What Is History?* London: Vintage, 1964.

Casper, Jayson. "The Forgotten Final Resting Place of William Borden." *Christianity Today*, February 2017.

Chapman, George. *Edgar Bryson: Missionary to Kenya*. Lurgan, UK: Unknown Press, 1971.

Clapham, Christopher. "The Ethiopian Coup d'Etat of December 1960." *The Journal of Modern African Studies* 6, no. 4 (December 1968): 495–507.

Clapham, Christopher. *Transformation and Continuity in Revolutionary Ethiopia*. Cambridge: Cambridge University Press, 1990.

Clough, Marshall. *Fighting Two Sides: Kenyan Chiefs and Politicians, 1918–1940*. Niwot, CO: University Press of Colorado, 1990.

Clough, Marshall. *Mau Mau Memoirs: History, Memory, Politics*. Boulder, CO: Lynne Rienner Publishers, 1998.

Cohen, Herman. *Intervening in Africa: Superpower Peacemaking in a Troubled Continent*. New York: Palgrave Macmillan, 2000.

Cohen, Warren, and Nancy Bernkopf Tucker, eds. *Lyndon Johnson Confronts the World: American Foreign Policy, 1963–1968*. Cambridge: Cambridge University Press, 1994.

Costigliona, Frank, and Thomas G. Paterson. "Defining and Doing the History of United States Foreign Relations: A Primer." In *Explaining the History of American Foreign Relations*, edited by Michael Hogan and Thomas Paterson. Cambridge: Cambridge University Press, 2004.

Cotterell, Peter. *Born at Midnight*. Chicago: Moody Press, 1973.

Crawford, John. "Protestant Missions in Congo, 1960–65." *International Review of Missions* (1965, date blurred).

Crummey, Donald. "The Politics of Modernization: Protestant and Catholic Missionaries in Modern Ethiopia." In *The Missionary Factor in Ethiopia*, edited by Getatchew Haile, Aasulv Lande, and Samuel Rubenson. Berlin: Peter Lang, 1998.

Daniels, David D. https://www.christiancentury.org/blog-post/guest-post/martin-luthers-fascination-ethiopian-christianity, 31 October 2017.

Den Dulk, Kevin. "Evangelical Elites and Faith-Based Foreign Affairs." *The Review of Faith and International Affairs* 4, no. 1 (Spring 2006): 21-29.

DeRoche, Andy. *Black, White, and Chrome: The United States and Zimbabwe, 1953 to 1998*. Trenton, NJ: African World Publishers, 2001.

Diamond, Sara. *Spiritual Warfare: The Politics of the Christian Right*. London: Southend Press, 1989.

Donham, Donald. *Marxist Modern: An Ethnographic History of the Ethiopian Revolution*. Berkeley: University of California Press, 1999.

Dow, Philip. "Romance in a Marriage of Convenience: The Missionary Factor in Early Cold War US-Ethiopian Relations, 1941–1960." *Diplomatic History* 35, no. 5 (Nov. 2011): 859–95.

Dow, Philip E. *"School in the Clouds": The Rift Valley Academy Story*. Pasadena, CA: William Carey Library, 2003.

Dowdy, Homer E. *Out of the Jaws of the Lion*. New York: Harper & Row, 1965.

Duignan, Peter, and L. H. Gann. *The United States and Africa: A History*. Cambridge: Cambridge University Press, 1984.

Dunch, Ryan. "Beyond Cultural Imperialism: Cultural Theory, Christian Missions, and Global Modernity." *History and Theory* 41, no. 3 (October 2002): 301–25.

Dunstan, Simon. *Entebbe*. New York: Rosen Young Adult, 2011.

Eide, Oyvind. *Revolution and Religion in Ethiopia*. Uppsala, Norway: Uppsala Universitet, 1996.

Elkins, Caroline. *Britain's Gulag: The Brutal End of Empire in Kenya*. London: Bodley Head, 2005.

Eshete, Tibebe. *The Evangelical Movement in Ethiopia: Resistance and Resilience*. Waco, TX: Baylor University Press, 2009.

Fairbank, John. "Assignment for the '70s." *American Historical Review* 74, no. 3 (Oxford Academic, New York, February 1969): 861–79.

Fairbank, John, ed. *The Missionary Enterprise in China and America*. Cambridge, MA: Harvard University Press, 1974.

Fairbanks, Michael. "Changing the Mind of a Nation: Elements in a Process for Creating Prosperity." In *Culture Matters: How Values Shape Human Progress*, edited by Lawrence E. Harrison and Samuel P. Huntington. New York: Basic Books, 2000.

Farr, Thomas F. *World of Faith and Freedom: Why International Religious Liberty Is Vital to American National Security*. Oxford: Oxford University Press, 2008.

Fish, Gerald, and Burnette Fish. *The Call to Battle*. Marion, IN: World Gospel Mission, 1982.

Foglesong, David. *The American Mission and the "Evil Empire."* Cambridge: Cambridge University Press, 2007.

Freston, Paul. *Evangelicals and Politics in Asia, Africa and Latin America*. Cambridge: Cambridge University Press, 2001.

Frey, Sylvia, and Betty Wood. *Come Shouting to Zion: African American Protestantism in the American South and British Caribbean to 1830*. Chapel Hill: University of North Carolina Press, 1998.

Fukui, Katsuyoshi, and John Markakis, eds. *Ethnicity & Conflict in the Horn of Africa*. London: James Currey, 1994.

Fukuyama, Francis. "Social Capital." In *Culture Matters: How Values Shape Human Progress*, edited by Lawrence E. Harrison and Samuel P. Huntington. New York: Basic Books, 2000.

Gaddis, John Lewis. *We Now Know: Rethinking Cold War History*. Oxford: Oxford University Press, 1997.

Gardner, Lloyd C. "The Cold War Crusade." From "A Roundtable Discussion of William C. Inboden's *Religion and American Foreign Policy, 1945–1960: The Soul of Containment*," *Passport* (April 2009).

Geva, Nehemia, and D. Christopher Hanson. "Cultural Similarities, Foreign Policy Actions, and Regime Perception: An Experimental Study of International Cues and Democratic Peace." *Political Psychology* 20, no. 4 (December 1999).

Gibbs, David. *The Political Economy of Third World Intervention: Mines, Money, and U.S. Policy in the Congo Crisis*. Chicago: University of Chicago Press, 1991.

Gibbs, Nancy, and Michael Duffy. *The Preacher and the Presidents*. New York: Center Street, 2007.

Gienow-Hecht, Jessica C. E. "Cultural Transfer." In *Explaining the History of American Foreign Relations*, 2nd ed., edited by Michael J. Hogan and Thomas G. Paterson. Cambridge: Cambridge University Press, 2004.

Gifford, Paul. *The New Crusaders: Christianity and the New Right in Southern Africa*, rev. ed. London: Pluto Press, 1991.

Gleijeses, Piero. *Conflicting Missions: Havana, Washington, and Africa, 1959–1976*. Chapel Hill: University of North Carolina Press, 2002.

Grabill, Joseph. "The 'Invisible' Missionary: A Study in American Foreign Relations." *Journal of church and state* 14, no. 1 (Winter 1972): 903–5.

Grabill, Joseph. *Protestant Diplomacy and the Near East: Missionary Influence on American Policy, 1810–1927*. Minneapolis: University of Minnesota Press, 1971.

Gration, John Alexander. "The Relationship of the African Inland Mission and Its National Church in Kenya Between 1895 and 1971." PhD diss., New York University, 1974.

Griffith, Robert. "The Cultural Turn in Cold War Studies." *Reviews in American History* (March 2001): 150–57.

Haile, Getatchew, Aasulv Lande, and Samuel Rubenson, eds. *The Missionary Factor in Ethiopia*. Berlin: Peter Lang, 1998.

Hanely, Mark. "Revolution at Home and Abroad: Radical Implications of the Protestant Call to Missions, 1825–1870." In *The Foreign Missionary Enterprise at Home*, edited by Daniel Bays and Grant Wacker. Tuscaloosa: University of Alabama Press, 2003.

Hansen, Holger Bernt, and Michael Twaddle, eds. *Christian Missionaries and the State in the Third World*. London: James Currey, 2002.

Harper, Jim C. *Western Educated Elites, 1900–1963: The African-American Factor*. New York: Routledge, 2006.

Harris, Joseph E. *African-American Reactions to War in Ethiopia, 1936–1941*. Baton Rouge: Louisiana State University Press, 1994.

Harrison, Lawrence, and Samuel P. Huntington, eds. *Culture Matters: How Values Shape Human Progress*. New York: Basic Books, 2000.

Bibliography

Hastings, Adrian. *Construction of Nationhood*. Cambridge: Cambridge University Press, 1997.

Hastings, Adrian. *A History of African Christianity, 1950–1975*. Cambridge: Cambridge University Press, 1979.

Hearn, Julie. "The 'Invisible' NGO: US Evangelical Missions in Kenya." *Journal of Religion in Africa* 32, no. 1 (February 2002): 32–60.

Herberg, Will. *Protestant, Catholic, Jew: An Essay in American Religious Sociology*. New York: Doubleday, 1955.

Herzog, Jonathan. *The Spiritual-Industrial Complex*. Oxford: Oxford University Press, 2011.

Hildebrandt, Jonathan. *History of the Church in Africa: A Survey*, 4th Edition. Achimota, Ghana: African Christian Press, 1997.

Hill, Patricia. "Religion as a Category of Diplomatic History." *Diplomatic History* 24, no. 4 (Fall 2000): 633–40.

Hochschild, Adam. *King Leopold's Ghost: A Story of Greed, Terror, and Heroism in Colonial Africa*. New York: Houghton Mifflin, 1999.

Hogan, Michael, and Thomas G. Paterson, eds. *Explaining the History of American Foreign Relations*, 2nd ed. Cambridge: Cambridge University Press, 2004.

Hogan, Michael, ed. *America in the World: The Historiography of American Foreign Relations Since 1941*. Cambridge: Cambridge University Press, 1995.

Hogan, Michael, ed. *Paths to Power: The Historiography of American Foreign Relations to 1941*. Cambridge: Cambridge University Press, 2000.

Hollinger, David. *Protestants Abroad: How Missionaries Tried to Change the World but Changed America*. Princeton: Princeton University Press, 2017.

Horne, Gerald. *Mau Mau in Harlem? The US and the Liberation of Kenya* (Pre-published manuscript version), 2009.

Hornsby, Charles. *Kenya: A History Since Independence*. London: I. B. Taurus, 2012.

Hunt, Michael. *Ideology and U.S. Foreign Policy*. New Haven: Yale University Press, 1987.

Huntington, Samuel. "The Clash of Civilizations." In *The Clash of Civilizations? The Debate, Foreign Affairs*, edited by Samuel Huntington. New York: Foreign Affairs, 1996.

Huntington, Samuel. "Cultures Count." In *Culture Matters: How Values Shape Human Progress*, edited by Lawrence Harrison and Samuel P. Huntington. New York: Basic Books, 2000.

Huntington, Samuel. "If Not Civilizations, What?" In *The Clash of Civilizations? The Debate*, edited by Samuel Huntington. New York: Foreign Affairs, 1996.

Huntington, Samuel. "Religious Persecution and Religious Relevance in Today's World." In *The Influence of Faith: Religious Groups and U.S. Foreign Policy*, edited by Elliott Abrams. Lanham, MD: Rowman & Littlefield, 2001.

Huntington, Samuel. *Who Are We? America's Great Debate*. Great Britain: Free Press, 2004.

Hutchison, William. *Errand to the World: American Protestant Thought and Foreign Missions*. Chicago: University of Chicago Press, 1987.

Immerman, Richard. "Psychology." In *Explaining the History of American Foreign Relations*, 2nd ed., edited by Michael Hogan and Thomas Paterson. Cambridge: Cambridge University Press, 2004.

Inboden, William. *Religion and American Foreign Policy, 1945–1960: The Soul of Containment*. Cambridge: Cambridge University Press, 2008.

Inboden, William. "A Roundtable Discussion of William C. Inboden's *Religion and American Foreign Policy, 1945–1960: The Soul of Containment*. Author's Response." *Passport* (April 2009).

Inglehart, Ronald. "Culture and Democracy." In *Culture Matters: How Values Shape Human Progress*, edited by Lawrence Harrison and Samuel P. Huntington. New York: Basic Books, 2000.

Irele, Abiola, and Biodun Jeyifo, eds. *The Oxford Encyclopedia of African Thought*. New York: Oxford University Press, 2010.

Iriye, Akira. "Culture and International History." In *Explaining the History of American Foreign Relations*, 2nd ed., edited by Michael Hogan and Thomas Paterson. Cambridge: Cambridge University Press, 2004.

Iriye, Akira. "The Internationalization of History." *American Historical Review* 94, no. 1 (1989): 1–10.

Iriye, Akira, and Pierre-Yves Saunier. *The Palgrave Dictionary of Transnational History*. New York: Palgrave Macmillan, 2009.

Iyob, Ruth, and Edmund J. Keller. "US Policy in the Horn: Grappling with a Difficult Legacy." In *East Africa and the Horn: Confronting Challenges to Good Governance*, edited by Dorina Bekoe. London: Lynne Rienner, 2006.

Jackson, Donna. *Jimmy Carter and the Horn of Africa*. Jefferson, NC: McFarland, 2007.

Jacobs, Seth. "'Our System Demands the Supreme Being': The U.S. Religious Revival and the 'Diem Experiment.'" *Diplomatic History* 25 (Fall 2001): 589–624.

Jacobs, Seth. "Review of William C. Inboden's *Religion and American Foreign Policy, 1945–1960: The Soul of Containment*." In "A Roundtable Discussion of William C. Inboden's *Religion and American Foreign Policy, 1945–1960: The Soul of Containment*." *Passport* (April 2009).

Jenkins, Philip. *The Next Christendom: The Coming of Global Christianity*, rev. ed. Oxford: Oxford University Press, 2007.

Johnston, Douglas, ed. *Faith-Based Diplomacy, Trumping Realpolitik*. Oxford: Oxford University Press, 2003.

Johnston, Douglas, and Cynthia Sampson. *Religion: The Missing Dimension of Statecraft*. Oxford: Oxford University Press, 1994.

Kalb, Madeleine. *The Congo Cables: The Cold War in Africa—From Eisenhower to Kennedy*. New York: Macmillan, 1982.

Kaplan, Robert. *The Arabists: The Romance of an American Elite*. New York: Free Press, 1993.

Karanja, John. "Evangelical Attitudes toward Democracy in Kenya." In *Evangelical Christianity and Democracy in Africa*, edited by Terence Ranger. Oxford: Oxford University Press, 2008.

King, Kennedy. "The Kenya Maasai and the Protest Phenomenon." *Journal of African History* 12, no. 1 (1971).

Kirby, Dianne, ed. *Religion and the Cold War*. Hampshire, UK: Palgrave Macmillan, 2003.

Kisse, Edward. "The Politics of Famine in US Relations with Ethiopia, 1950–1970." *The International Journal of African Historical Studies* 33 (2000).

Kuklick, Bruce. *Churchmen and Philosophers: From Jonathan Edwards to John Dewey*. New Haven: Yale University Press, 1985.

Lakoff, George, and Mark Johnson. *Metaphors We Live By*. Chicago: University of Chicago Press, 2003.

Landes, David. "Culture Makes Almost All the Difference." In *Culture Matters: How Values Shape Human Progress*, edited by Lawrence Harrison and Samuel P. Huntington. New York: Basic Books, 2000.

Latourette, Kenneth Scott. "By Way of Inclusive Retrospect." In *Perspectives on the World Christian Movement*, edited by Ralph Winter and Steve Hawthorne. Pasadena, CA: William Carey Library, 1981.

Leffler, Melvyn. *The Preponderance of Power*. Stanford: Stanford University Press, 1992.

Leffler, Melvyn. *The Specter of Communism: The United States and the Origins of the Cold War, 1917–1953*. New York: Hill & Wang, 1994.

Leonard, David. *African Successes: Four Public Managers of Kenyan Rural Development*. Berkeley: University of California Press, 1991.

Lessing, Pieter. *Africa's Red Harvest: An Account of Communism in Africa*. New York: John Day, 1962.

Levine, Donald Nathan. *Wax and Gold: Tradition and Innovation in Ethiopian Culture*. Chicago: University of Chicago Press, 1965.

Lewis, C. S. *Mere Christianity*. New York: Macmillan Publishing Company, 1960.

Linsday, D. Michael. *Faith in the Halls of Power: How Evangelicals Joined the American Elite*. Oxford: Oxford University Press, 2007.

Lockot, Hans Wilhelm. *The Mission: The Life, Reign and Character of Haile Selassie I*. London: Front Line Distribution, 1989.

Lonsdale, John. "Jomo Kenyatta, God & the Modern World." In *African Modernities*, edited by Jan-Georg Deutsch, Peter Probst, and Heinke Schmidt. Oxford: Heinemann, 2002.

Lonsdale, John. "Missionary Christianity and Settler Colonialism in Eastern Africa." In *Christian Missions and the State in the Third World*, edited by Holger Bernt Hanson and Michael Twaddle. Oxford: Oxford University Press, 2002.

Lyons, Terrence. "Keeping Africa off the Agenda." In *Lyndon Johnson Confronts the World: American Foreign Policy, 1963–1968*, edited by Warren Cohen and Nancy Bernkopf. Cambridge: Cambridge University Press, 1994.

Mahoney, Richard. *JFK: Ordeal in Africa*. Oxford: Oxford University Press, 1983.

Makinda, Samuel. *Superpower Diplomacy in the Horn of Africa*. Beckenham, UK: Palgrave Macmillan, 1987.

Marcus, Harold. "American Security and Ethiopia, 1948–1953." In *The Proceedings of the Seventh International Conference of Ethiopian Studies*, edited by Sven Rubenson. Berlings, Sweden: University of Lund, 1984.

Marcus, Harold. *Ethiopia, Great Britain, and the United States, 1941–1974*. Berkeley: University of California Press, 1983.

Marcus, Harold G. "1960, the Year the Sky Began Falling on Haile Selassie." *Northeast African Studies New Series* 6, no. 3 (1999): 11–26.

Marsden, George. *Fundamentalism and American Culture: The Shaping of Twentieth Century Evangelicalism, 1870–1925*. Oxford: Oxford University Press, 1982.

Marty, Martin. *Modern American Religion, Vol. 3: Under God, Indivisible—1941–1960*. Chicago: University of Chicago Press, 1996.

Marty, Martin. ed. *Modern American Protestantism and Its World*, Vol. 13 Missions and Ecumenical Expressions. Berlin: K. G. Saur Verlag, 1993.

McAlister, Melani. *The Kingdom of God Has No Borders: A Global History of American Evangelicalism*. Oxford: Oxford University Press, 2018.

McAlister, Melani. "What Is Your Heart For?: Affect and Internationalism in the Evangelical Public Sphere." *American Literary History* 20, no. 4 (2008): 870–95.

McClure, Don. Missionary Summary Video. https://www.youtube.com/watch?v=s2F60sCMrSo. Accessed 1 December 2018.

McIntosh, Brian. "The Scottish Mission in Kenya, 1891–1923." PhD diss., University of Edinburgh, 1969.

McLoughlin, William. *Revivals, Awakenings and Reform: An Essay of Religious and Social Change in America, 1607–1977*. Chicago: University of Chicago Press, 1980.

McMahon, Robert. "How the Periphery Became the Center." In *Foreign Policy at the Periphery: The Shifting Margins of US International Relations since World War II*, edited by Bevan Sewell and Maria Ryan. Lexington, KY: University of Kentucky Press, 2017.

McVety, Amanda. "Pursuing Progress: Point Four in Ethiopia." *Diplomatic History* 32 (June 2008): 371–403.

McVety, Amanda Kay. "The 1903 Skinner Mission: Images of Ethiopia in the Progressive Era." *Journal of the Gilded Age and the Progressive Era* 10, no. 2 (April 2011): 187–212.

Mead, Walter Russell. "God's Country?" *Foreign Affairs* (September/October 2006).

Mead, Walter Russell. *Special Providence: American Foreign Policy and How It Changed the World*. New York: Routledge, 2002.

Monsma, Stephen. "Faith-Based NGO's and the Government Embrace." In *The Influence of Faith: Religious Groups and U.S. Foreign Policy*, edited by Elliott Abrams. Lanham, MD: Rowman & Littlefield, 2001.

Morad, Stephen. "The Founding Principles of the Africa Inland Mission and Their Interaction with the African Context in Kenya from 1895–1939: The Study of a Faith Mission." PhD diss., University of Edinburgh, 1997.

Morris, Roger. *Uncertain Greatness: Henry Kissinger and American Foreign Policy*. New York: Harper, 1977.

Morton, Andrew. *Moi: The Making of an African Statesman*. London: Michael O'Mara Books, 1998.

Munro-Hay, S. C. *Aksum: An African Civilization of Late Antiquity*. Edinburgh: Edinburgh University Press, 1991.

Nadelmann, E. A. "Israel and Black Africa: A Rapprochement?" *The Journal of Modern African Studies* 19, no. 2 (June 1981): 183–219.

Naim, Asher. "Perspectives: Jomo Kenyatta and Israel." *Jewish Political Studies Review* 17, no. 3–4 (Fall 2005): 75–80.

Nathaniel, Ras. *50th Anniversary of His Imperial Majesty Emperor Haile Selassie's First Visit to the United States (1954–2004)*. Victoria, Canada: Unknown Publisher, 2000.

"New US envoy says no let-up in fight against corruption," 27 May 2011. https://nation.africa/kenya/news/new-us-envoy-says-no-let-up-in-fight-against-corruption--770324.

Nichols, J. Bruce. *The Uneasy Alliance: Religion, Refugee Work, and U.S. Foreign Policy*. Oxford: Oxford University Press, 1988.

Noer, Thomas. *Cold War and Black Liberation: The United States and White Rule in Africa, 1948–1968*. Columbia, MS: University of Missouri Press, 1985.

Noer, Thomas. *Soapy: A Biography of G. Mennen Williams*. Ann Arbor: University of Michigan Press, 2005.

Noll, Mark. *One Nation under God: Faith and Political Action in America*. New York: HarperCollins, 1988.

Noll, Mark. *The New Shape of World Christianity*. Downers Grove, IL: IVP Academic, 2009.

Noll, Mark. *The Scandal of the Evangelical Mind*. Grand Rapids, MI: Eerdmans, 1994.

Novick, Peter. *That Noble Dream: The "Objectivity" Question and the American Historical Profession*. Cambridge: Cambridge University Press, 1988.

Nugent, Paul. *Africa Since Independence*. New York: Palgrave MacMillan, 2004.

Odom, Major Thomas P. *Dragon Operations: Hostage Rescue in the Congo, 1964–65, Leavenworth Paper No. 14*. Leavenworth, KS: Unknown publisher, 1988.

Ogot, Bethwell, ed. *Historical Dictionary of Kenya*. London: Scarecrow, 1981.

Olsen, Hal. *African Heroes of the Congo Rebellion*. Kijabe, Kenya: Africa Inland Mission, 1969.

Oren, Michael B. *Power, Faith, and Fantasy: American in the Middle East, 1776 to the Present*. New York: W. W. Norton & Co., 2007.

Park, Sung Kyu. "Spirituality of Kenyan Pastors: A Practical Theological Study of Kikuyu PCEA Pastors in Nairobi," PhD diss., Pretoria, 2008.

Patterson, James. *Grand Expectations: The United States, 1945–1974*. New York: Oxford University Press, 1996.

Peterson, Derek. "The Rhetoric of the Word: Bible Translation and the Mau Mau in Colonial Central Kenya." In *Missions, Nationalism, and the End of Empire*, edited by Brian Stanley. Grand Rapids: Eerdmans, 2003.

Peterson, William. *Another Hand on Mine: The Story of Dr. Carl K. Becker of Africa Inland Mission*. New York: Masthof Press, 1967.

Pew Research Center. "Global Christianity: A Report on the Size and Distribution of the World's Christian Population." http://www.pewforum.org/GlobalChristianity-exec.aspx. Accessed last 21 Apr. 2012.

Pierard, Richard. "Pax Americana and the Evangelical Missionary." In *Earthen Vessels: American Evangelicals and Foreign Missions 1880–1980*, edited by Joel Carpenter and William Shenk. Grand Rapids, MI: Eerdmans, 1990.

Pierard, Richard. "From Evangelical Exclusivism to Ecumenical Openness: Billy Graham and Sociopolitical Issues." In *Modern American Protestantism and Its World*, edited by Martin E. Marty. Berlin: K. G. Saur Verlag, 1993.

Pierson, Paul. "The Rise of Christian Mission and Relief Agencies." In *The Influence of Faith: Religious Groups and U.S. Foreign Policy*, edited by Elliott Abrams. Lanham, MD: Rowman & Littlefield, 2001.

Porter, Michael. "Attitudes, Values, Beliefs and the Microeconomics of Prosperity." In *Culture Matters: How Values Shape Human Progress*, edited by Lawrence Harrison and Samuel P. Huntington. New York: Basic Books, 2000.

Preston, Andrew. "Bridging the Gap between the Sacred and the Secular in the History of American Foreign Relations." *Diplomatic History* 30, no. 5 (November 2006): 783–812.

Preston, Andrew. "The Politics of Realism and Religion: Christian Responses to Bush's New World Order." *Diplomatic History* 34, no. 1 (January 2010): 95–118.

Preston, Andrew. *Sword of the Spirit, Shield of Faith: Religion in American War and Diplomacy*. New York: Knopf, 2012.

Ranger, Terence, ed. *Evangelical Christianity and Democracy in Africa*. Oxford: Oxford University Press, 2008.

Reed, David. *111 Days in Stanleyville*. New York: Harper & Row, 1966.

Remnek, Richard. "Translating 'New Thinking' into Practice: The Case of Ethiopia." In *Soviet Policy in Africa: From the Old Thinking to the New Thinking*, edited by George Breslaver. Berkeley: University of California Press, 1992.

Ribuffo, Leo. "Religion in the History of U.S. Foreign Policy." In *The Influence of Faith: Religious Groups and U.S. Foreign Policy*, edited by Elliot Abrams. Lanham, MD: Rowman & Littlefield, 2001.

Robert, Dana. "'The Crisis of Missions': Premillennial Mission Theory and the Origins of Independent Evangelical Missions." In *Earthen Vessels: American Evangelicals and Foreign Missions 1880–1980*, edited by Joel Carpenter and William Shenk. Grand Rapids, MI: Eerdmans, 1990.

Robert, Dana. "The Influence of American Missionary Women on the World Back Home." *Religion and American Culture: A Journal of Interpretation* 12, no. 1 (2002).

Robert, Dana. "From Missions to Mission to Beyond Missions: The Historiography of American Protestant Foreign Missions Since World War II." In *New Directions in American Religious History*, edited by Harry Stout and D. G. Hart. Oxford: Oxford University Press, 1997.

Roelker, Jack. *Mathu of Kenya: A Political Study*. Stanford: Stanford University Press, 1976.

Rosberg, Carl, and John Nottingham. *The Myth of "Mau Mau" Nationalism in Kenya*. Nairobi: Praeger, 1966.

Rose, Susan, and Steve Brouwer. "The Export of Fundamentalist Americanism: U.S. Evangelical Education in Guatemala." *Latin American Perspectives* 17, no. 4 (Autumn, 1990): 42–56.

Rotter, Andrew. "Christians, Muslims, and Hindus: Religion and U.S.-South Asian Relations, 1947–1954." *Diplomatic History* 24, no. 4 (Fall 2000): 357–80.

Rubenson, Sven. "The Missionary Factor in Ethiopia: Consequences of a Colonial Context." In *The Missionary Factor in Ethiopia*, edited by Getatchew Haile, Aasulv Lande, and Samuel Rubenson. Berlin: Peter Lang, 1998.

Rubenson, Sven, ed. *The Proceedings of the Seventh International Conference of Ethiopian Studies*. Berlings, Sweden: Unknown Press, 1984.

Said, Edward. *Orientalism*. New York: Vintage, 1979.

Sandgren, David. *Christianity and the Kikuyu, Religious Divisions and Social Conflict*. New York: Peter Lang, 1989.

Sanneh, Lamin. *Abolitionists Abroad*. Cambridge: Harvard University Press, 2000.

Sanneh, Lamin. *Encountering the West: Christianity and the Global Cultural Process*. New York: Orbis, 1993.

Sanneh, Lamin. *Translating the Message: The Missionary Impact on Culture*. New York: Orbis, 1998.

Sanneh, Lamin. *Whose Religion Is Christianity?: The Gospel Beyond the West*. Grand Rapids, MI: Eerdmans, 2004.

Schäfer, Axel. *Countercultural Conservatives: American Evangelicalism from the Postwar Revival to the New Christian Right*. Madison: University of Wisconsin Press, 2011.

Schlesinger, Arthur Jr. "The Missionary Enterprise and Theories of Imperialism." In *The Missionary Enterprise in China and America*, edited by John Fairbank. Cambridge, MA: Harvard University Press, 1974.

Schraeder, Peter. *United States Foreign Policy Toward Africa: Incrementalism, Crisis, and Change*. Cambridge: Cambridge University Press, 1994.

Schwartz, David. *The Moral Minority: The Evangelical Left in an Age of Conservativism*. Philadelphia: University of Pennsylvania Press, 2014.

Sharlet, Jeff. *The Family: The Secret Fundamentalism at the Heart of American Power*. New York: Harper, 2008.

Shillington, Kevin. *History of Africa*. New York: Bloomsbury Academic, 1989.

Showalter, Nathan. *The End of a Crusade: The Student Volunteer Movement for Foreign Missions and the Great War*. London: Scarecrow Press, 1998.

Silk, Mark. *Spiritual Politics: Religion and America Since World War II*. New York: Touchstone, 1989.

Smith, Drew, ed. *Freedom's Distant Shores: American Protestants and Post-Colonial Alliances with Africa*. Waco, TX: Baylor University Press, 2006.

Smith, Michael. "Kenyan Ambassador for Peace: Bethuel Kiplagat Believes That Africa's Development Depends on Peace." *For a Change* (October-November 2000).

Snyder, Sarah. *Human Rights Activism and the End of the Cold War: A Transnational History of the Helsinki Network*. Cambridge: Cambridge University Press, 2011.

Sorenson, John. *Imagining Ethiopia: Struggles for History and Identity in the Horn of Africa*. New Brunswick, NJ: Rutgers University Press, 1993.

Spear, Thomas, and Isaria N. Kimambo, eds. *East African Expressions of Christianity*. Oxford: Oxford University Press, 1999.

Stanley, Brian, ed. *Missions, Nationalism, and the End of Empire*. Grand Rapids, MI: Eerdmans, 2003.

Stephanson, Anders. *Manifest Destiny: America's Expansion and the Empire of Right*. New York: Hill and Wang, 1995.

Stout, Harry, and D. G. Hart. *New Directions in American Religious History*. Oxford: Oxford University Press, 1997.

Sweet, Leonard I. "Nineteenth Century Evangelicalism." In *Encyclopaedia of the American Religious Experience*, Vol. 2, edited by Charles Lippy and Peter Williams. New York: Unknown Publisher, 1998.

Taylor, Mrs. Howard. *Borden of Yale '09*. Oxford: Benediction Classics, 2017.

Tignor, Robert. *The Colonial Transformation of Kenya*. Princeton: Princeton University Press, 1976.

Trachsel, Laura. *Kindled Fires in Africa*. Marion, IN: World Gospel Mission, 1961.

Tucker, Nancy Bernkopf. "Lyndon Johnson: A Final Reckoning." In *Lyndon Johnson Confronts the World: American Foreign Policy, 1963–1968*, edited by Warren Cohen and Nancy Bernkopf Tucker. Cambridge: Cambridge University Press, 1994.

Turner, Fredrick Jackson. "The Significance of the Frontier in American History." Address to the American Historical Association, 12 July 1893.

Turek, Lauren Francis. *The Bring the Good News to All Nations: Evangelical Influence on Human Rights and U.S. Foreign Relations*. Ithaca: Cornell University Press, 2018.

Twaddle, Michael. "Christian Missions & Third World States." In *Christian Missionaries and the State in the Third World*, edited by Holger Bernt Hansen and Michael Twaddle. London: James Currey, 2002.

Tyrrell, Ian. *Reforming the World: The Creation of America's Moral Empire*. Princeton: Princeton University Press, 2010.

Tyrrell, Ian. *Transnational Nation: United States History in Global Perspective since 1789*. New York: Palgrave Macmillan, 2007.

Vestal, Theodore. "Emperor Haile Selassie's First State Visit to the United States in 1954: The Oklahoma Interlude." *International Journal of Ethiopian Studies*, no. 1 (Summer/Fall 2003): 133–52.

Vestal, Theodore. *The Lion of Judah in the New World*. Santa Barbara, CA: Praeger, 2011.

Waller, Richard. "They Do the Dictating & We Must Submit." In *East African Expressions of Christianity*, edited by Thomas Spear and Isaria N. Kimambo. Oxford: Oxford University Press, 1999.

Walls, Andrew. *The Missionary Movement in Christian History*. New York: Orbis, 1996.

Wamagatta, Evanson. "African Collaborators and Their Quest for Power in Colonial Kenya: Senior Chief Waruhiu wa Kung'u's Rise from Obscurity to Prominence, 1890–1922." *International Journal of African Historical Studies* 41, no. 2 (2002): 295–319.

Wamagatta, Evanson. "The Roots of the Presbyterian Church of Kenya: The Merger of the Gospel Missionary Society and the Church of Scotland Mission Revisited." *Journal of Religious History* 31, no. 4 (Dec. 2007): 387–402.

Weeks, Albert. "Do Civilizations Hold?" In *The Clash of Civilizations? The Debate*, edited by Samuel Huntington. New York: Foreign Affairs, 1996.

Westad, Odd Arne. *The Global Cold War: Third World Interventions and the Making of Our Times*. Cambridge: Cambridge University Press, 2007.

White, George, Jr. *Holding the Line: Race, Racism, and American Foreign Policy toward Africa, 1953–1961*. Lanham, MD: Rowman & Littlefield, 2005.

Williams, William Appleman. *The Tragedy of American Diplomacy*. New York: Delta, 1971.

Winter, Ralph. *The 25 Unbelievable Years, 1945–1969*. Pasadena, CA: William Carey Library, 1970.

Woodberry, Robert. "The Missionary Roots of Liberal Democracy." *American Political Science Review* 106, no. 2 (May 2012): 244–74.

Wrong, Michela. *I Didn't Do It for You: How the World Used and Abused a Small African Nation*. New York: Harper Perennial, 2005.

Wrong, Michela. *In the Footsteps of Mr. Kurtz: Living on the Brink of Disaster in Mobutu's Congo*. New York: Harper Perennial, 2001.

Wrong, Michela. *It's Our Turn to Eat: The Story of a Kenyan Whistle-Blower.* New York: Harper Perennial, 2009.

Wuthnow, Robert. *The Restructuring of American Religion.* Princeton: Princeton University Press, 1998.

Young, Crawford. *Politics in the Congo: Decolonization and Independence.* Princeton: Princeton University Press, 1965.

Zietsma, David. "Shining Religion's Psychic Light on William C. Inboden's *Religion and American Foreign Policy, 1945–1960: The Soul of Containment.*" From "A Roundtable Discussion of William C. Inboden's *Religion and American Foreign Policy, 1945–1960: The Soul of Containment,*" Passport (April 2009).

Zimmerman, Andrew. *Alabama in Africa: Booker T. Washington, the German Empire, and the Globalization of the New South.* Princeton: Princeton University Press, 2012.

Zwede, Bahru. *A History of Modern Ethiopia: 1855–1991,* 2nd ed. Oxford: Oxford University Press, 2001.

Zwede, Bahru. *Pioneers of Change in Ethiopia: The Reformist Intellectuals of the Early Twentieth Century.* Oxford: Oxford University Press, 2002.

Index

A

Adair, Ross   45, 47
Addis Ababa   11
Africa Inland Mission (AIM)   84, 86–87, 90, 113, 127, 136, 149–52, 154–55, 159–60, 162–67, 174–76, 178, 180, 182, 184, 189, 192–94, 203, 207, 209, 213
African self-determination   10
American University of Beirut   xxii, xxiv
Amnesty International   66
Andersen, Earl   194, 209, 213, 225
Andom, Aman   50
Anuak   xix, 19
Arab-Israeli conflict of 1973   49
Assemblies of God   xxviii
Attwood, William   130, 133, 189, 191

B

Ball, George   119
Barnett family influence   193–94, 225
Barre, Mohamed Siad   211–12
Bebbington, David   xxvii
Becker, Carl   88–89, 93, 220
Belgium   xxxi, 73–80, 84–87, 90, 100, 104, 108, 113, 133–36, 188, 220
Berlin World Congress on Evangelism   24
Bible   v, xxi, xxiii, xxvii, 4, 20, 26, 31–32, 62–64, 83, 87–88, 90–91, 97, 151, 153–54, 159–61, 170, 175, 177, 179, 181, 198, 200, 203, 207, 221
Bible translation   90, 160–62, 181, 198, 203
Black America and Ethiopia   25

Blakeslee, Virginia   163, 174
Blundell, Michael   179
Bolton, Francis   32
Borden, William   xxi–xxv
Brinton, Howard   96, 99, 104–9, 145–46, 224–25
Brown v. Board of Education   29–30
Bryant, William Jennings   xxv
Bryson, Stuart   162
Brzezinski, Zbigniew   59, 217, 222
Buck, Pearl S.   xxiv–xxv

C

Carlson, Frank   33, 35, 44–45, 210
Carlson, Paul   34, 131–32, 134, 136–38, 145–46, 223
Carter, Jimmy   22, 59, 200, 202–6
Catholicism   xxviii, xxxi, xxxiii, 42, 77–78, 83, 111–12, 114–15, 131, 138, 167, 169
Chefoo School   8, 10
Chefoo School diaspora   10
Chief Koinange   171, 173
Chief Waruhiu   172–74, 180, 184
China   xxi–xxii, xxiv, 8, 10, 116–17, 189, 201
Chinese interventionism   xxi, 81, 116–17, 201
Christian and Missionary Alliance   83
Church Mission Society (CMS) - Anglican   150–51, 161, 189, 193
CIA   42, 57, 61–62, 73–76, 116, 119, 123, 126, 130, 139, 142–43
CIM   xxi–xxii
Close, William   82, 139, 140, 145, 224
Coe, Douglas   45, 46, 210

Cold War xix–xx, xxvi–xxxiv, 4, 12, 15, 23–25, 28, 30–31, 34–37, 54–55, 59, 62, 68–69, 73–78, 83, 85, 94, 100–1, 105–6, 109–10, 118–19, 121–22, 139, 144, 146, 149, 185, 188, 196, 199, 201, 204–6, 208, 211, 214–17, 219–25

Communism xxvii–xxviii, 19–20, 35, 94, 96, 116, 140–41, 190, 196, 205, 215, 219

Communist propaganda 81–82, 94, 117

Congo xx, xxxi–xxxiii, 73–95, 97–113, 116–17, 119–27, 129, 131–33, 136–40, 142, 144–45, 151, 183, 184, 188–89, 191, 201–2, 217, 220–25

Congregationalist xx

Cumbers, John 46, 57

D

Davis, Chuck 129, 136

Derg, the 50, 52, 54, 59–61, 65–66, 223

Desta, Prince Eskender 33, 46

Devlin, Larry 73, 142

Devonshire Declaration 158

Dodd, Thomas J. 98–9, 108

Donham, Donald 52–3, 221

E

East Africa Association (EAA) 155–56, 158–59, 163, 170, 173, 180

East African Revival 177–78, 182, 184–85

Egypt 3

Eisenhower, Dwight D. xxviii, 29, 33, 35–6, 44, 75, 90, 109, 210, 224

Endalkachew, Lij 46–47

Entebbe raid 196–197, 199

Equal Rights Amendment xxvi

Eritrea 15, 38, 49–50, 54, 58

Eritrean Liberation Front (ELF) 58

Ethiopia 3–4, 8

Ethiopian 5
  Crown Prince 34, 40, 42
  coup attempt of 1960 40–41
  famine of 1973–1974 47
  famine of 1984–1985 66
  Orthodox Church 40–1, 51, 63
  Red Cross 9
  Revolution 37, 49–50, 54, 59

Evangelical Foreign Missions Association (EFMA) 139

Evangelical Free Church xxvi

F

Fellowship, the 44–47, 68, 209–12, 224

female circumcision 162–65, 170, 174–76, 181

Ford, Gerald 45

fundamentalists xxv

G

Garvey, Marcus 26–7

Gbenye, Christopher 130–31

Gizenga, Antoine 79

Gospel Missionary Society (GMS) 156–59, 164, 172–73, 176, 178, 180, 184

Graham, Billy xxvii, xxx, 19, 21, 24, 32, 34–6, 43, 68, 136, 224

Great Depression xxv, xxix

Griggs, H. E. 85

Guevara, Che 119

Gullion, Edmund 108, 111, 117, 119, 142

H

Hall, William 46

Hansberry, Lorraine 28

Index

Hanson, Della 16–20, 31, 225
Hatfield, Mark 42, 45–6, 139
Hempstone, Smith 87, 208, 213, 216
higher criticism xxiii
Hillis, Vera 220
Hocking Report xxiv–xxv, xxix
Hockman, Robert 8–10
Hoffacker, Lewis 98, 107–8
Hollinger, David xxiv–xxv
Hoyt, Michael 128–29, 134
Humphrey, Hubert 45, 195

I

Interdenominational Foreign Missions Association (IFMA) 139
International Christian Leadership (ICL) 32–36, 44, 210, 224
Islam xxi, xxix, 5, 6, 19, 20, 150, 197
Israel 171, 196–99
Italian occupation of Ethiopia 3, 7, 10–11

J

Jenkins, Philip xxix, 169
Jones, E. Stanley xxiv

K

Kaggia, Bildad 170, 172, 182, 187–188
Kasai Province 81, 101, 144
Kasavubu 81–82, 92, 116, 125, 127, 138, 141
Katanga 77, 81, 85, 94, 96–99, 101, 105–9, 111, 120, 126, 223
Kennedy, John F. xxviii, 46, 53, 111, 118, 133, 153

Kenya xx, xxxi–xxxiv, 58, 87, 130, 135, 149, 150–52, 154–56, 159–60, 162–63, 166–67, 169–72, 174–75, 177, 179–81, 183–85, 187–89, 191–97, 199–207, 209–17, 221–25, 232, 243
Kenya Africa National Union (KANU) 190, 192, 201
Kenyatta, Jomo 130, 134, 156, 171–72, 177, 180–84, 187–90, 192–93, 195–201, 205, 250
Kikuyu Central Association (KCA) 163–64, 174, 180
Kikwit 80, 102, 111–12
Kimbanguism 79
King Leopold 74, 77, 83
King Solomon 5
Knapp, Rev. and Mrs. 156, 159, 173
Korn, David 56
Krapf, Ludwig 149–50

L

Lambie, Thomas 7, 22
Larson, Al 130, 136
Laubach, Frank xxii
Lausche, Frank 45
League of Nations 10
Lend-Lease program 3
Leopoldville 76, 84, 100–102, 112, 119, 123, 125–27, 131, 133, 141
Luce, Henry 10, 43
Lumumba, Patrice 76, 79, 81–2, 91, 93–4, 101, 103, 116, 120, 128, 137, 141, 184, 187

M

Machen, J. Gresham xxii
Madame Andree Blouin 82
Mainline denominations xxii–xxvi, xxix–xxx, xxxiii–xxxiv, 154, 163, 169, 177, 215
Martin Luther 5

Marxism   xxxiii, 37, 54, 56, 60–61, 64, 67–69
Mau Mau   162–63, 165–66, 170, 172, 174–79, 182–85, 187, 194, 221
McClure, Don   xviv–xx, 19, 22, 46
McGhee, George   98, 111
McGloughlin, William   xxvi
Mekane Yesus Church (MYC)   50
Mekonnen, Endelkachew   33
Melady, Thomas   34
Mengistu (Lieutenant Colonel)   40, 59, 61, 68
Mennonites   xxxiv, 24, 63, 102
Methodist   xx, xxxiii, 83, 85, 89, 96, 97, 99, 104, 106, 108, 126–127, 150
missionaries and American intelligence   12–13, 122, 190
Missionary Aviation Fellowship (MAF)   124
missionary educational efforts   xix, xxiii, xxvi, 6, 8–9, 14, 16, 24, 29, 39, 41, 52, 57, 62–63, 82, 87–90, 93, 98, 104, 113–14, 131, 133, 142–44, 151, 154–55, 157, 165–67, 169, 175, 179–80, 188–89, 193, 206, 220–21
missionary evangelism efforts   xx, xxvii, 5, 52, 53, 56, 61, 65, 78, 122, 127–28, 140, 150, 154, 157, 159–60, 162–63, 168–69, 173, 176–80, 184–85, 187, 194, 221–22
missionary health care efforts   14, 24, 113, 151, 167–68, 214, 220
Mobutu, Joseph   138–39, 141–46, 217
Moi, Daniel arap   182, 190–96, 199–217, 221–23, 225
Moody, D. L.   xxi–xxii, 156
Moral Re-Armament (MRA)   140–44, 146, 177, 183–84, 224
Mulele, Pierre   116, 118, 120
Mutual Defense Assistance Agreement of 1953   28

N

National Prayer Breakfast   32, 44–47, 210
Nazism   xxv
Neway, Germane   40
Ngugi, wa Thiong'o   163, 198
Nixon, Richard M.   32, 34–36, 46, 98, 145, 195, 224
Njonjo, Charles   193, 203, 208, 213
Nyachae, Simeon   206–7
Nyayoism   214

O

Odinga, Oginga   187–90, 192–93, 199
Oicha   89
Olenga, (General)   129–30
Ole Sempele, Mulungit   152–55, 184
Orthodox Christianity   53, 55
Ouko, Robert   206–8

P

Parti Solidare Africaine (PSA)   79, 102
Peace Corps   39, 84, 138, 145
Peking Union Medical College Hospital   xxiii
Point Four Agreement   3
Point Four Program   15
Presbyterian   xx, xxviii, xxxiii, 6, 8, 14, 19, 21, 28, 74, 83–84, 86–89, 93, 100, 119, 121, 141, 144, 156
Presbyterian Hospital   9
Presbyterian Muskingum College   8
President Eisenhower   3
Protestantism   xx, xxii–xxiv, xxvi, 62, 79, 125, 154, 245

Q

Quakers   xxxiv, 150–51

Index

R

Reagan, Ronald xxviii, 198, 206, 216
Red Terror 59–60
Reischauer, A. K. xxiv
Rockefeller, John D. xxiv
Roosevelt, Franklin D. 3, 12, 15, 36
Roosevelt, Theodore 149
Rusk, Dean 108, 119, 121, 123, 130, 132

S

Sanger, Richard 79, 102, 118
Scopes Trial xxiii
Selassie, Haile xix, 3–4, 6–8, 10–21, 23–25, 27–33, 35–38, 40–41, 43–46, 49–53, 55, 65, 68, 217, 223–25, 236, 250
Sendwe, Jason 98, 106, 138, 224
Seventh Day Adventists 6, 16, 21, 89, 96, 150, 161, 166
Sheppard, William 74
Simba rebellion xxxii, 111–12, 114–21, 123–33, 137–38, 142, 201, 222, 224
Simonson, Joseph 33–34
Somalia xix, 38, 49, 54, 59, 197, 202, 204, 210–12, 215, 224
Southard, Addison 12
Southern Baptists xxvi, 58, 207
Soviet Union xxxiii, 38, 53–56, 66, 68, 116–17, 187, 189, 204, 211, 219
Spencer, John 40
Stanleyville 120, 124, 128–31, 134, 136–37, 188, 191
Stauffacher, John 152–53, 159–60
Stevenson, Adlai 98, 111, 135
Struelens, Michel 97
Student Volunteer Movement (SVM) xxi

Stumpf, Hulda 164–66, 184
Sudan Interior Mission (SIM) 6–7, 21, 23–24, 46–48, 50–52, 57, 59, 61–62, 64, 66–67, 221

T

Thuku, Harry x, 155–60, 163–64, 170, 173, 176, 180, 184
Tigray 54, 67
Truman, Harry xxviii
Tshombe, Moise 97–99, 101, 105–8, 111, 126–27, 129–30, 133–35, 138, 141–43, 146, 217, 223–24

U

United Presbyterian mission board 8
US-Ethiopian Mutual Defense Agreement 22

V

Vance, Cyrus 59

W

Wall Street Crash of 1929 xxv
Westad, Odd Arne 37, 53, 68
Western expatriates 6
White House 3
Williams, G. Mennen 98–99, 108, 111, 126, 133, 135
World Gospel Mission (WGM) 166, 175–76
World War I xx, xxii–xxiii, xxv
World War II xxv, xxxiv, 75, 78

Y

Yale xxi
Yonsei University xxiii

visit us at missionbooks.org

To the Ends of the Earth: And What Happened on the Way There

Malcom Hunter

An expert on nomadic peoples, Malcolm Hunter shares stories from a lifetime of working in some of the world's most remote, colorful, and neglected communities. In the early 1960s Malcolm and his wife, Jean, arrived in Ethiopia with only their professional skills—medicine and engineering—and a desire to show God's love to those in need. Over the next forty years God led them across Africa, to a dozen people groups who hadn't heard the gospel. This book is full of astonishing true accounts of Jesus preparing the world's least reached peoples to encounter Him.

Hidden Triumph in Ethopia

Kay Bascom

When Kay Bascom and her doctor husband landed at a hospital in southern Ethiopia, they found themselves face-to-face with first-generation believers in their first love for the Lord Jesus Christ. Witnessing the Marxist Revolution and the subsequent persecution of the Christian church, Kay was burdened to make known the incredible account of "hidden triumphs in Ethiopia" to the outside world. After interviewing over one hundred people, she chose Negussie's true-life story as representative of that era's triumph.

Women and Leadership (Revised Edition): The Baptist Convention of South Africa

Nelson Hayashida

This book exposes the gap between carefully crafted statements affirming women and the reality of reluctant submission to women in leadership. The questions raised, the voices heard, and the potential corrective measures are a vital contribution to an important conversation within the church community. While this book is mainly focused on the Baptist church in South Africa, it presents many possibilities for stimulating debates and policy and experiential changes in other faith communities.

www.ingramcontent.com/pod-product-compliance
Lightning Source LLC
Chambersburg PA
CBHW052133070526
44585CB00017B/1802